# Dirty Blvd.

## The Life and Music of
## LOU REED

### AIDAN LEVY

CHICAGO
REVIEW
PRESS

An A Cappella Book

Copyright © 2016 by Aidan Levy
All rights reserved
Published by Chicago Review Press Incorporated
814 North Franklin Street
Chicago, Illinois 60610
ISBN 978-1-61373-736-1

**The Library of Congress has cataloged the hardcover edition as follows:**
Levy, Aidan, 1986–
    Dirty Blvd. : the life and music of Lou Reed / Aidan Levy.
        pages cm
    Includes bibliographical references and index.
    Discography: page    .
    ISBN 978-1-61373-106-2
  1.  Reed, Lou. 2.  Rock musicians—United States—Biography.  I. Title.
    ML420.R299L48 2015
    782.42166092—dc23
    [B]
                        2015018528

Cover design: Marc Whitaker/MTWdesign.net
Cover photo: Lex Van Rossen/MAI/Redferns/Getty Images
Interior design: Nord Compo
Printed in the United States of America
5  4  3  2  1

To my parents,
Pattie and Harlan, and my sister, Allegra

When the soul of a man is born in this country there are nets flung at it to hold it back from flight. You talk to me of nationality, language, religion. I shall try to fly by those nets.

—James Joyce

This is the way that night passes by, this
Is the overnight endless trip to the famous unfathomable
abyss.

—Delmore Schwartz

# CONTENTS

# ACKNOWLEDGMENTS

**Ellen Willis said it best:** "Here's a man I think is such a genius that once when I was face to face with him in a hotel room I couldn't say a word (what I wanted to say was 'Your music changed my life,' which would have been most uncool)." It was March 19, 2013, and there was Lou Reed himself, on the bimah at the Downtown Seder, and I was starstruck. If I told him how he had changed my life, I can only imagine what he would have said. Plans for this book were already in the works, and if I had known it was my last chance to see him—my rabbi—I might have told him how many times listening to *The Blue Mask* on evening commutes home made me understand something about myself that I thought I knew intellectually but couldn't quite grasp emotionally. And how many times it helped me get back on the train the next day. Then again, some things are better left unsaid. Yet Lou was one of the great risk-takers. So here is this book.

Lou Reed seemed to know exactly what to say; the way he turned a phrase could be immensely gratifying or beyond devastating, could make a week or ruin a year, and I wasn't surprised to discover how many people remembered things he had said—verbatim. This project was enriched immeasurably by the help of the numerous interviewees who shared their remembrances, insights, and intimate details. I am indebted to Shelley Albin, Aram Bajakian, Angel Balestier, Rick Bell, Randy Brecker, Ray Colcord, Tony Conrad, Marty Fogel, Nick Forster, Danny Frankel, Sean Fullan, Gail Garcia, Elliot Garfinkel, James Gorney, Chuck Hammer, Phil Harris, Barbara Hodes, Allan Hyman, Steve Katz, Reba Katz, Bettye Kronstad, Vinny Laporta, Jan Machacek, George Manney, Dr. Irwin Mendelsohn, Richard Mishkin, Martha Morrison, Steve Nelson, Judy November, Wendy Oxenhorn, Terry Philips, Sylvia Ramos, Jim Riswold, Jeff Ross, Arthur Scheer, Jonathan Shebar, Richard Sigal, Karl Stoecker, Lydia Sugarman, Alan Walters, Merrill Weiner, Doug Wieselman,

Barbara Wilkinson, and Victoria Williams for their candid, moving, and frequently hilarious accounts that enlivened this story. A biography of Lou Reed would be nothing without some classic Lou Reed anecdotes—those piercing moments of infamy, ecstasy, and debauchery that created the legend, at once so deeply human yet beyond belief.

Even when he wasn't speaking or singing, or speak-singing, Lou could chew the scenery like few others, and he had a way of evoking an atmosphere just by being in the room. This book attempts to capture that scene-stealing quality with a selection of photographs and memorabilia generously provided by David Arnoff, Martin Benjamin, Gene Ching, Richard Conde, Melanie Einzig, Chuck Hammer, George Manney, Steve Rossini, Richard Sigal, Alan Walters, Barbara Wilkinson, the William J. Clinton Library, the Montreal Jazz Festival, and the Syracuse University Archives. It is impossible to fully encapsulate Lou in any one image, article, or monograph, but the photographs represented here illuminate his poetic spirit, if only for a frame.

Surviving as a writer in New York is no easy feat, and I am exceedingly grateful to my extended family in film production that has facilitated my efforts along the way, especially to Steve Lawler, Dana Hook, Pepe and Joey Bird, and Rob Ackerman. I am also grateful to Richard Eder at Brown University for inspiring me to pursue arts journalism, and for the encouragement and guidance of Steve Molton at Long Island University as I began this process. Thanks for the incisive remarks and flexibility of my professors and colleagues at Columbia University during the course of this journey.

I began as a journalist, and as deadlines come and go, I always remain a journalist in spirit. I would like to express my appreciation to the editors I have worked with over the past decade—Stacey Anderson, Phil Freeman, Evan Haga, Rob Harvilla, Maura Johnston, Nick Lucchesi, Nick Murray, Andy Newman, and Brittany Spanos—and to Stephen Buono and Matt Merewitz for being early supporters of this project. I don't get to say it enough, but a good editor makes all the difference, and these are some of the best.

Apropos of that, I am immensely thankful for the continuing support of my editor at Chicago Review Press, Yuval Taylor, for his depth of thought and constructive comments that have shaped this book, as has the commitment of Devon Freeny and the entire staff there. Many thanks to my literary agent, Russell Galen, for his persistence and vision, and for believing in me over the years. None of this would have been possible if it were not for the love and support of my family, Patricia, Harlan, and Allegra, and my friends and relatives, whose thoughts have been enormously helpful throughout this process. Special thanks go to my two cats, who sat patiently for untold hours listening to the Velvet Underground as they watched me write what eventually became this book. Finally, thanks to my caring, infinitely patient partner, Kaitlin Mondello, for including Lou Reed in our lives and discussions for the past two years. I could not have done this without you.

# PROLOGUE

**Somewhere in the suburbs,** a listless teenager turned the key in the ignition of his parents' car and shifted into gear. It was Wednesday night before Thanksgiving, and there was nothing to do but drive to the McDonald's parking lot where people from school sometimes got together, hoping for anything to happen that would pass the time. When he pulled up, he saw that no one was there. McDonald's wasn't even open; all was dark but a flickering neon light at the liquor store next door. It was the most boring night of the year in the most boring town on Earth. All he had was the glow of the radio and the eerie desolation of a strip mall past 9 PM.

When the bass came in quietly, with its mellow glide underneath a laid-back guitar strumming two repeating chords and the insouciant shuffle of a hi-hat, he hardly noticed. Then he heard that voice, a gravelly, nasal baritone, half-singing, half just telling it like it is for all us misfits, the truth and nothing but, even if it didn't happen:

> *Holly came from Miami, FLA*
> *Hitchhiked her way across the USA*

There, sitting in that parking lot, he heard the raw sound of a world he knew he would one day escape to if it was the last thing he did—a world free of SAT tests, trigonometry, and disapproving looks. He didn't know it yet, but his life had just been saved by rock 'n' roll.

Years earlier, another teenager sat in a Ford Fairlane idling in neutral, thinking about unrequited love and the meaning of the blues as the Long Island Rail Road coasted by on its lonely eastward journey. Alan Freed was playing a new tune by Dion and the Belmonts:

*I wonder why I love you like I do*
*Is it because I think you love me too*

It was the sound of freedom, of someone who understood the alienation and heartache, who had heard what he heard and more, a mainline to the soul. At that moment, his life too was saved by rock 'n' roll, and he would never be the same again. He was a boy who grew up on the edge, in that liminal sphere we call suburbia, where, like the man said, you can see all kinds of things you can't see from the center. Then he journeyed into the darkness, and from that hell began the long journey home to where it all began, out there on the edge.

# PART I

## DOO-WOP WASTE LAND

That night, Lou was flanked in adjacent halls by Pierre Boulez conducting the New York Philharmonic's performance of Mozart's Horn Concerto No. 2 and the Metropolitan Opera's production of Puccini's *La Bohème*, but at Alice Tully, there was no feigning bohemianism. Ignoring the de facto dress code, Lou showed up in his black leather jacket and jeans, menacing black mascara and nail polish, and an unruly plume of curls—the fiercest Jew-fro in history—with his teenage Yonkers backing band, the Tots, and turned the amplifier to eleven as he limned a murky portrait of street life for the unwashed masses that had gathered to hear their Bacchanalian rock god eviscerate their senses.

It took some social lubrication to overcome the jitters of a two-year hiatus—more than a little. He was thirty years old and had just gotten married two weeks prior, but no institution, musical or matrimonial, could restrain the irrepressible force that was Lou Reed. On this night, set free by Scotch, the only thing that could restrain him was his leather. As the band launched into "White Light/White Heat," the message was clear. Respectability be damned. This was rock 'n' roll.

Lou had resurfaced after leaving the Velvets at Max's Kansas City on a balmy summer night in 1970 and moving home to Long Island with his parents, taking a menial forty-dollar-a-week job working for his father. It would take him a lifetime to truly learn to collaborate, but with the help of Mick Ronson and his biggest fan, David Bowie, the newly transformed Phantom of Rock—RCA's honorific—had released *Transformer*, a descent into a sadomasochistic underworld that would soon slip under the ears and over the heads of the censors, who just didn't know what "giving head" really meant. When "Walk on the Wild Side" hit, it was like a bomb going off as the seamy underbelly of Andy Warhol's Factory exploded into cars and basements across America, where adolescents full of pent-up political frustration and raging hormones found the voice of rebellion that put a vicious spin on the meaning of flower power.

That December, the *New York Times* did not mince words about Lou: "The public has never discovered him, and, unfortunately, *Transformer* will not help his cause." Ellen Willis, who rhapsodized about the Velvet Underground, trashed the album in the *New Yorker*, calling it "terrible—lame, pseudo-decadent lyrics, lame, pseudo-something-or-other singing, and a just plain lame band." The imperious Dean of American Rock Critics, Robert Christgau, gave it a B– in his vaunted *Village Voice* Consumer Guide. But

Lou was unfazed by the media machine; his indomitable metal machine ate journalists for breakfast.

Leading up to the release of *Transformer*, RCA took out ads in the *Village Voice* featuring a graffiti artist painting Lou's name on a subway car. The New York City Department of Parks and Recreation promptly put out a cease and desist for this flagrant "act of vandalism." The ad never appeared again, but Lou had already begun making his indelible black mark on the sanitized veneer of the rigid establishment. His graffiti vandalized virgin ears, and once it was heard, it could never be unheard; the damage was irreversible. The avant-garde cognoscenti already revered Lou as the amoral gutter poet of the Velvet Underground—Rimbaud with a guitar, the scowl that launched a thousand bands—but now he was coming out as, among other things, a bona fide rock star, much to his chagrin. Fifteen minutes of fame would have been enough for Lou; all that mattered to him was the music.

Lincoln Center was the Normandy invasion of Lou's carefully orchestrated comeback. As part of the city's transgressive avant-garde intellectual demimonde, Lou had been to the opera, but this was a far ride uptown from the boho-chic grittiness of Max's Kansas City; the Tots had never even set foot on the hallowed ground of New York's cultural mecca. That hadn't stopped Lou's manager, Fred Heller, from calling the programming director at Alice Tully Hall to arrange for his triumphant return to New York.

The venue had only been christened three years prior, under the supervision of CorningWare heiress and philanthropist Alice Tully, who had donated millions for an intimate chamber hall that would serve as a home to the Juilliard School. Brutalist architect Pietro Belluschi designed an angular, modern building with a jagged edge that jutted out into Broadway, a beacon of high culture at the epicenter of the asphalt jungle. Lou Reed's musical training started and stopped at his first lesson; Juilliard material he was not, but he would certainly give audiences a more intimate experience than they asked for and a whole new meaning to brutalism as he brought the cacophony of the street inside.

When Heller called the Lincoln Center brass, charming his way in with well-rehearsed pleasantries, to his surprise, they were receptive to the idea. Little did they know, they had just arranged for spectators to pay six dollars a ticket to witness the deflowering of Alice Tully Hall.

To stoke the flames of defiance, Lou recruited Garland Jeffreys as his opening act. A half–Puerto Rican, half–African American singer-songwriter those who feel deeply to clamp down on emotion before it ruins the garden party. "Rock & Roll" was an assault on the mechanized order, a clarion call that embraced the sweat, grit, and guts of raw human experience, blemishes and all. There was nothing perfect about it—not Lou's voice, not the shambolic shifts in rhythm of the drums, not the offbeat accents of the guitar or the percussive hit of the bass. Lou knew that perfection was a myth, and that all that mattered was this high-voltage poetry, within it fecundity, death, bloom, and decay, the secrets of desire and its unholy consummation. The audience began to clap in rhythm as the band unraveled into a resounding crescendo, dissonance and lyricism merging into an overpowering shout, the sound of raw emotion. Then rhythm dropped out altogether as the noise rose to a peak before the final cymbal crash. "Good to see y'all. Good night," Lou said. "It's nice to be back in New York." As applause rang out, Lou stared into the crowd with a bemused look and wondered if the audience's lives had also been saved. Evidently, yes; they wanted an encore.

Lou came out from the wings and turned up the distortion with a plaintive cry on the guitar as a drumroll got the pheromones stirring. "This is the sad, sad story of Sister Ray," he said. The song was the closing track on *White Light/White Heat*, an eighteen-minute pressure cooker hung around the sordid story of a transgender heroin dealer, Sister Ray. Ray and her band of marauding drag queens have a drug-fueled orgy with some sailors during Fleet Week, searching for functional veins and the American Dream gone awry before the police intervene. Lou wasn't singing so much as hollering in his inimitable guttural growl, exuding the savage wit and nihilism of the French New Wave as he narrated a Godard-esque orgiastic murder.

Yet in 1973, cold-blooded murder would not be the most verboten transgression in this profane litany of shock and awe—fellatio would. For Lincoln Center, Lou made a slight adjustment to the lyrics from the record, which only used the female pronoun; now, he removed all doubt as to the brand of sexual and gender indeterminacy suggested by the song, confounding the rigid classification the IRS relied on when law-abiding citizens checked off *male* or *female* on their annual 1040 check-up.

And so Lincoln Center was violated: acoustically, normatively, and spiritually. It was the ultimate taboo.

The band unleashed a raging sound and fury, pushing blues pentatonics to the brink, dueling guitars battling to the death as the bass and drums shunted onward into oblivion. The crowd erupted. Lou went blank. His newlywed wife, Bettye, came onstage and shoved a bouquet of roses into his hands. This was Lincoln Center, and though Lou was far from standing on ceremony—more like trampling on it—they didn't want to flout ovation rituals altogether. So there he stood, holding his guitar in one hand, a bouquet of roses in the other. Despite himself, he had done it.

Backstage, Lou saw a familiar face, a man he had not seen in good spirits since he unceremoniously fired him in 1968: Andy Warhol. Warhol was a lifelong Ruthenian Catholic—his name shortened from Warhola—and the beatific impresario apparently couldn't hold a grudge. Though Warhol was only thirteen years older, he knew Lou viewed him as an artistic father figure, and he couldn't miss the birth of his Factory-made rock star as a solo artist. So when Andy approached Lou and Bettye, the reunion was a long time coming. He took out his infamous Polaroid—a tool used to document countless timeless moments in the history of New York's avant-garde pantheon—and snapped a picture of the two newlyweds. Andy handed it to him; if the record tanked, Lou could always sell the photo.

For Lou's triumphant return, the label spared no expense; at the after-party, the bohemian Max's Kansas City crowd crammed into the posh Sherry-Netherland on Fifth Avenue, amounting to a punk incursion into upper-crust society. Lou and Bettye spent the night at the Plaza across the street on the label's dime; even though they had a studio across town on the east side, the occasion called for a more celebratory atmosphere than their shag carpeting would allow. For one night only, the sultan of sulk was on top of the world.

It was as though he had always been there, perched atop a black onyx throne, the demonic ruler of an edgy underworld of glitter and smut with no taboos or conventions, a malevolent smirk on his face. But before his name became a byword for the excesses of rock, he had toiled in the salt mines of much humbler beginnings; before he was Lou, he was Lewis, an accountant's son growing up in Freeport, New York, where he felt far from free, and the ebb and flow of the tides in his waterfront community served as a constant reminder that he was marooned in the suburbs. Back then, he was only thirty miles from Lincoln Center, but a world apart; it would take more than the Long Island Expressway to get there. To distill that potent

They were Jews first and foremost, but reaping the full benefits of upward mobility in a free-enterprise economy that extended beyond the boundaries of the ersatz shtetl they had re-created in Borough Park meant cutting down on the pumpernickel and assimilating into white-bread American society. A name like Sidney Rabinowitz—polysyllabic, phlegmatic, and unmistakably Jewish—was not neutral enough. The name that suited his ambitions sounded much more like Reed.

Not far away, Lou's maternal grandparents were living a similar story of immigrant striving in a brick row house in the Brownsville section of Brooklyn. Rebecca had immigrated from Poland in 1906 and married another Polish Jew, Louis Futterman, who had arrived three years earlier and was ten years older. Louis worked as a skirt manufacturer in a Jewish-run garment factory in Brownsville owned by Hyman Feingold until his death. After the passing of her husband, Rebecca presided over the household and her children—Leon, an accountant slightly younger than Sidney; Ralph, who had not even had his bar mitzvah yet; and Toby, a beautiful court stenographer—as well as Irving Turner, a forty-year-old lodger who offset their living expenses. Leon, who went by his more innocuous middle name instead of his first name, Abraham, had a twin brother, Samuel, who had already moved out of the house.

After high school, Toby had joined the workforce to help support her family. She quickly got hired as a court stenographer by United Lawyers Service, possessing the combination of good looks, an even-tempered demeanor, and a keen intellect that the company valued. Between nursing, teaching, and secretarial work—the standard career trajectory for women of her generation working under the glass ceiling—employment in the legal system came with enough of a learning curve to provide a challenge and access to a wide pool of her peers.

Six months after her eighteenth birthday, she was nominated by the firm for the annual Stenographers' Ball, a beauty pageant for young women whose typing skills were only rivaled by their beauty. In 1939 Jewish girls generally were not included in beauty pageants; black girls were strictly banned from Miss America, and though the anti-Semitism was never an institutional policy, it wasn't until 1945 that the first and only Jewish Miss America was crowned. The Stenographers' Ball was about as close as they could get. Much to her surprise, Toby won.

"Miss Toby Futterman of 139 Dumont Ave., a pert brunette, will be crowned Queen of Stenographers," read the article in the *Brooklyn Eagle*, next to her headshot, eyes upturned and beaming, her hair pulled back, a classic beauty reminiscent of film stars Barbara Stanwyck and Ava Gardner. It was the "fourth annual gathering of the pothook girls," a pun on the "pothook" shorthand character used in court as opposed to an implement used in the kitchen.

The ball also introduced her to the "Steno Strut," a new dance routine based on the quotidian life of stenographers and secretaries, radically different from "the Ostrich," a group dance her son would one day create as an assault on the staid pageantry of his parents' generation. At the ceremony on Saturday, February 11, 1939, held at the prestigious Manhattan Center on Thirty-Fourth Street next to Penn Station, she was crowned queen, an honor that vaulted her into instant fame beyond her insular neighborhood in Brownsville. It also made her the hottest catch in Brooklyn.

Yet Toby's strutting days were short-lived. Soon, Sidney and Toby were engaged. They got married, and when Toby was twenty, they were expecting their first child. Sidney had his last name legally changed to Reed, and the couple began to imagine a future for themselves that built on their parents' sacrifices. As second-generation immigrants, they planned to assimilate into middle-class society; Toby would raise the children, and when the time was right, provided Sidney had the financial means, they would participate in the wave of eastward migration into the suburbs to enjoy a better quality of life away from the endless bustle of Brooklyn. But before they had the down payment on a house, they moved into a cramped apartment by Kings Highway, a major thoroughfare in South Brooklyn and a hub of commercial activity that was equidistant from their parents.

On March 2, 1942, the night of a total lunar eclipse, Lewis Allan Reed came screaming into the world at Beth-El Hospital in Brownsville, only five blocks from where Toby grew up. In keeping with Jewish tradition, they named him Lewis in honor of his late grandfather. Yet Jewish tradition was increasingly out of step with the broader culture. Three months earlier, Japan had attacked Pearl Harbor, and President Roosevelt responded to the great collective trauma by declaring war the next day, plunging the United States into World War II. Two weeks after Lou was born, across the Atlantic, the covert Operation Reinhard officially began the Holocaust as Hitler's henchmen opened the first extermination camp at Belzec, silently killing thousands of Polish Jews in its gas chambers. It was the height of the swing era, and Glenn Miller's "Moonlight Cocktail" was the number-one hit; in best egg cream, a tasty palliative to the harsh experience of PS 192. Fox's U-bet chocolate syrup was a kosher product manufactured by H. Fox & Company, a local business based not far from his apartment in Brownsville, and the unofficial standard-bearer for the quintessential Brooklyn beverage. Sitting at a banquette and savoring the cool, frothy effervescence of a chocolate egg cream was a rite of passage.

During his early childhood, as far as Lou was concerned, Brooklyn's cultural advantage ended at comestibles, with Totonno's Pizzeria and Al and Shirley's ice cream parlor. Though the swinging rhythm of Benny Goodman, Artie Shaw, and Count Basie was not far away, it never permeated the Reed household. In nearby Bedford-Stuyvesant, a predominantly black neighborhood, Charles Mingus, Miles Davis, and a young John Coltrane were fomenting the anarchic aesthetic of post-bop at jazz haunts such as Sonia's Ballroom, the Arlington Inn, and Turbo Village, but it would be a long time before Lou was exposed to the intoxicating tonalities of jazz. Along Kings Highway, Lou's only joys were simple: egg creams and his beloved Brooklyn Dodgers.

The Dodgers played at Ebbets Field in Flatbush, the adjacent neighborhood, and were the pride of Brooklyn. Lou had grown up avidly following their peaks and valleys on radio broadcasts. In 1947 they made history when manager Branch Rickey broke the color barrier and signed Jackie Robinson, the biggest star of the Negro leagues. Though the radio left something to be desired musically—Lou would have to wait until 1954 for Alan Freed to bring his *Moondog* radio show to New York—the tag team of Robinson at first base and Pee Wee Reese at shortstop made for thrilling listening.

With his unflappable mien and stoic athleticism, Robinson hot-footed it past even the swiftest infielders, flying by nets both politically and physically, and led the Dodgers to a pennant victory his rookie season, the harbinger of the ineluctable demise of Jim Crow each time he crossed home plate. In 1948 Roy Campanella, another Negro leagues star, got signed as catcher; Robinson would not be the token representative of integration. The Dodgers did not win in 1948, but the following season, Lou had the excitement of seeing another minority player who literally came out of left field: a twenty-five-year-old Jewish outfielder named Cal Abrams.

Abrams, who was soon nicknamed Abie, was a dyed-in-the-wool Brooklyn boy who grew up in the Madison section of Sheepshead Bay, a graduate of the mostly Jewish James Madison High School. Instead of college, Abie eschewed the yoke of his prescribed lot in life and turned pro immediately. Though there had only been a handful of Jews in the major leagues, Abie came prepared to confront the inevitable anti-Semitism. He was six feet tall, muscular, and had a weathered earnestness that seemed to spring from the mean streets of Flatbush. He would never be an All-Star, but to the Jews slaving away along Kings Highway, he represented what freedom could be in postwar America. He only had twenty-four at-bats his rookie season, but his mere presence, even on the bench, signified a cultural victory. To Lou, he was a hometown hero—they even had the same birthday.

On April 19, 1949, Lou listened intently as Abrams debuted at number 32, a number worn a decade earlier by the Jewish Dodgers outfielder Goody Rosen and later worn by Sandy Koufax. A month after Abie started, the Dodgers enhanced the trailblazing diversity of their integrated roster, signing the brash young African American pitcher Don Newcombe. They would win the pennant that season.

Lou relished every time he went to Ebbets Field with his father. Unlike many boys growing up in Brooklyn, he knew early on that he wouldn't be a major league ballplayer, but he idolized Abie and the Brooklyn Bums, and vowed to one day make his mark. To Lou, the Dodgers were everything—not only did the team irrevocably change what it meant to be "All-American," they represented a microcosm of life as it was truly lived in Brooklyn, a beacon of hope that one day he could rise above his humble beginnings and dodge the overbearing mitt of the establishment; that he, too, could fly by nets.

The 1950 season consigned Abie to a less admirable page in Dodgers history. In the final game of the regular season, the Dodgers squared off against the Philadelphia Phillies for the National League pennant. With the score tied at 1–1 in the bottom of the ninth and two outs for the Dodgers, Abrams was on second base when Duke Snider hit a line drive. Abrams dashed to third and got waved on by the third-base coach; he was tagged out at home plate. The Dodgers went on to lose the game, ending the season. Lou was devastated.

In 1951, though, Abie batted .280, hitting his first home run early in the season. In a sport where hitting the ball three out of ten times is a nearly impossible feat, this was an admirable showing. It was the type of fearless risk-taking that Lou would later embody in the recording studio; in baseball, everything can change in an instant. In the playoff for the National League pennant that would decide whether the Giants or the Dodgers went on to face the rival Yankees in the World Series, the Dodgers saw defeat snatched from the jaws of victory when Bobby Thomson hit the Shot Heard 'Round the World, a three-run homer that brought the game to a devastating close.

It was one of Lou's last memories of the Dodgers as a Brooklyn resident; the Reeds soon left for the greener climes of Long Island. Several years later, in 1958, the Dodgers would move to Los Angeles; in 1960, the last vestige of Lou's early childhood vanished when Ebbets Field was demolished and replaced by a housing project.

"I couldn't have been unhappier in the eight years I spent growing up in Brooklyn, but I say that not having realized what it would then be like being on Long Island, which was infinitely worse," Lou later recalled in the 1995 film *Blue in the Face.* "There was probably a childhood trauma that I had, other than the Dodgers leaving Brooklyn, which, if you think about it, is a reason why some of us are imbued with a cynicism that we never recovered from. Obviously, you're not a Mets fan, and you can't possibly be a Yankees fan, so baseball is eliminated from your life, because of being born in Brooklyn."

In the postwar boom, Lou's father got hired as the treasurer of Cellu-Craft, a plastics manufacturer on Long Island, finally securing a position that would allow the family to leave Brooklyn. Regarding the move, Lou was torn between the intense desire to escape the drudgery and danger of his Brooklyn childhood and a fear of the unknown in a dubiously comfortable environment where Brownsville rules no longer applied. The suburbs presented new challenges and a growing push to conform to the conventions of the middle-class ideal his parents were striving for, a perspective he in no way shared.

Lou's new life in Freeport, though a jarring adjustment from Brooklyn, proved a fertile incubator for the angst that fueled his later work; Lou's violent reaction to the experience of growing up in the suburbs would eventually be his ticket out. In Freeport, he faced a slew of more insidious slings and arrows—bar mitzvah lessons, soda shop gossip, and Republican neighbors—but coming in at a fever pitch on 1010 WINS, he also found the transformative power of rock 'n' roll.

# 3

Freeport in 1952 was the terminus of the American Dream. Situated on the south shore of Long Island in Nassau County, it offered urban strivers a peaceful redoubt along Baldwin Bay with a burgeoning real estate market amenable to family expansion and a school system ready to impart the lessons of American exceptionalism to their privileged progeny. Bordered by the never-setting Sunrise Highway and the Long Island Rail Road, access to the city by land and sea ensured a thriving economy that would easily reward a fledgling tax accountant. Other than basketball courts and the allure of the Sound, though, Freeport was lacking in diversions that would pass the time for the younger generation. Lou would have to create his own sound.

Sandwiched between Baldwin in the east and Merrick in the west, Freeport was the largest village in Nassau County, with a population exceeding twenty thousand and growing. Compared to the melting pot of Brooklyn, Freeport was much less ethnically diverse—with fewer Jews—and more financially elite, where the briny air was shared by the likes of bandleaders Guy Lombardo and Archie Bleyer, and Dodgers manager Branch Rickey. Radio personality Gabriel Heatter also lived in Freeport, and once tried to sell his house to Lena Horne, though the community backlash at having a black neighbor queered the deal; Freeport began its integration process with the Jews.

For $10,000, the Reeds moved into 35 Oakfield Avenue, a three-bedroom ranch house with a two-car garage and a modest yard, abutting a golf course in the northwest subsection of Freeport that as a result of the postwar baby boom had experienced a sudden influx of Brooklyn Jews. Unlike the harsh brick of Lou's youth, the house on Oakfield possessed that unmistakable quintessence of suburban life that divides it from the city: vinyl siding. Lou finally had the privacy of his own room, a lawn that needed mowing, and a den ideally suited for afternoon listening sessions.

The fastidious residents of Freeport's bedroom community presented a sobering suburban heaven that smeared nonconformists into the whitewashed majority; the convenience store didn't sell punks. Compared to Brownsville, this windblown suburban idyll had none of the distractions or dangers Lou had grown to treat with a love-hate disdain; in Brooklyn, at least things happened. He had little interest in the Nautical Mile, a marshy stretch of waterfront where old baymen went oystering and wizened commercial fishermen traversed the brackish waters before emptying into one of the numerous dive bars dotting the canals. In fact, he had little interest in much of anything when he and his family arrived.

As a third-grader, Lou spent his time in dread of his new redbrick prison, Caroline G. Atkinson Elementary School on Seaman Avenue, and the conservative synagogue around the block on North Main Street, Congregation B'nai Israel, where he was sentenced to Hebrew school three times a week until his bar mitzvah. To make it bearable, Lou developed a bone-dry wit and performed uncanny impressions of his teachers.

In 1954, with the arrival of the disc jockey Alan Freed, Lou found his escape from the humdrum rhythm of school days in the suburbs. Freed had hosted the first rock 'n' roll concert in Cleveland in 1952, dubbed the Moondog Coronation Ball and syndicated nationally—a racially integrated concert featuring the Hucklebuckers, Rockin' Highlanders, and the Dominoes. Yet it would be two years before Moondog arrived in New York. On September 8, 1954, Freed had his debut broadcast of the *Moondog* show on 1010 WINS. Soon, Lou was introduced to Bill Haley and His Comets and "Shake, Rattle and Roll," entranced by the honking disruption to his tedious routine. There wasn't much to see, but with "The Wind" by Nolan Strong and the Diablos blowing into Lou's basement, he had finally found the outlet for his frustration and an antidote for encroaching ennui, a form of self-expression that captured his emotions—rock 'n' roll.

Earlier that summer, Elvis Presley had recorded his debut single at Sun Studio in Memphis, "That's All Right," often considered the first rock 'n' roll record. Produced by Sam Philips and backed by bassist Bill Black and guitarist Scotty Moore, the rollicking single covered a tune by Arthur "Big Boy" Crudup, exuding an insouciant swagger and raw desire that appropriated the deep feeling of the blues but sublimated the white guilt rooted in the suffering of the disenfranchised black experience. Destined to be the King, Elvis became the public face of rock 'n' roll, a bewitching hybrid of country and blues that brought a guileless lust into the cultural lexicon. Elvis was the king of sex and rock 'n' roll, but drugs were an undertone; Lou would make drug use overt. Lou's appropriation of the blues tradition would come from behind closed doors, stemming from the existential stasis of suburban ennui and sexual repression. Stuck in the suburbs, amplifiers became a relief valve; drugs represented a way to escape without ever leaving.

As the Brooklyn-born new kid in Freeport, Lou was slow to make friends, but found an ally in Allan Hyman, the son of a prominent Jewish lawyer who lived around the block. Lou and Allan began listening to music, walking to school together, and playing basketball.

As an urban transplant, Lou's macho self-image and Brooklyn bravura didn't square with his new environs. "He moved to the Island in the heart of suburbia in third grade, and grew up in a family where his father was an accountant and his mother was a typical suburban housewife, so for him to say that he grew up in the mean streets of the city was kind of funny, because it was so far from the truth," Hyman says. He counteracted this cognitive dissonance with deep sarcasm and acts of defiance. "He was definitely a guy that was rebellious from the time that he was very young. And his rebellious side is something that comes out in his music. I always thought that he would do something shocking whenever we were together, and I really admired that about him," Hyman recalls. Beneath the hardened veneer, though, Lou had a well-guarded sensitive side. "He had a hamster that he absolutely loved. He was always either holding it or having it nearby."

In Brooklyn, Lou had fostered a healthy disrespect for authority that he carried to his new hometown; his parents attempted to curb his rebellious behavior with bar mitzvah lessons. Congregation B'nai Israel was established in 1915, a small temple that expanded with the Jewish exodus from Brooklyn soon after Lou arrived. It was a conservative synagogue that allowed recent arrivals in Freeport to compromise their Orthodox background and maintain their traditions while assimilating into the broader community. The temple was a sparsely decorated white building with interior wood paneling and concrete steps under its imposing Doric columns where stultified Hebrew school students would congregate after sneaking out of interminable services. A ramshackle colonial next door housed the Hebrew school.

Rabbi Reuben Katz held court; educated at Brooklyn College and the Jewish Theological Seminary, he had little patience for the type of impiety Lou increasingly grew to embody. As if a draconian foil to Alan Freed and his salacious predations on America's impressionable youth, Rabbi Katz delivered weekly sermons from the bimah that implored students to eschew the dark cloud of temptation and seek refuge in God. In 1954 Katz's didactic sermon on fidelity and conservative family values, "The Jew Looks at Marriage," was selected for publication in *Best Jewish Sermons of 5714*. Accordingly, Lou developed a negative view of marriage and its attendant hypocrisy. Three times a week for two hours, Lou sacrificed his Tuesdays, Thursdays, and Sundays for mandatory lessons of the Torah interpreted by the old crones of the Hebrew school, its true meaning obfuscated by a language he couldn't understand.

"All the kids would sneak out and hang out on the steps and then go back in. These services would go on for hours, whether it was bar mitzvahs or High Holidays," recalls John Shebar, a fellow Hebrew school classmate who attended Lou's bar mitzvah. "The education was oppressive. The rabbi was self-righteous. The guy who read the Torah on Saturday was always drunk."

Rabbi Katz's strident approach was softened by Harry Altman, the young and affable cantor, who had traded a prospect to join the Brooklyn Dodgers farm system for a higher calling; as Sandy Koufax later discovered, it was nearly impossible to turn pro and keep the Sabbath. Altman was Lou's last music teacher who didn't rock. Lou scheduled bar mitzvah lessons in addition to his Hebrew school obligations, but the opportunity to talk baseball with Altman mitigated the experience of learning Jewish liturgy.

In 1955—5715 on the Jewish calendar—Lou celebrated his bar mitzvah; his thirteenth birthday coincided with the reading of the Golden Calf incident. It was Lou's first public performance, the tremulous cantillation of the Torah resembling his later declamatory *sprechstimme* with a fire-and-brimstone exhortation from God, chanted in a minor key. In bloodstained Biblical prose, Moses descends from Sinai to discover the Israelites worshipping the Golden Calf. He shatters the tablets, then burns the calf and grinds it into a powder, mixing its charred remains with water and forcing them to drink it. He then kills three thousand of the false-idol worshippers in a blazing massacre. In front of family and friends, Lou stammered through the Torah portion with a clangor and foreboding of the punishment he would later mete out to those who believed in other gods. Lou's only god was rock 'n' roll.

To appease his parents, Lou was forced to go to Hebrew school for the rest of the school year to get his bar mitzvah certificate, the synagogue's policy to prevent students from dropping out if they had an early birthday. He suffered through it. Lou wouldn't return to his Jewish roots for decades. Yet with junior high and Hebrew school behind him, Lou continued to struggle to find any catharsis in the land of suburban plenty, where an embarrassment of riches compensated for what he felt was a hollow center; more obstacles awaited him in high school.

Adolescence brought with it a host of problems—the social anxiety, alienation, and hostile behavior characteristic of teenage psychology was heightened to an extreme degree in Lou's slow transition to adulthood. "In social situations he withdrew, locking himself in his room, refusing to meet people. At times, he would hide under his desk. Panic attacks and social phobias beset him," his sister, Merrill Weiner, recalled. "His hyper-focus on the things he liked led him to music and it was there that he found himself." Lou's relationship with his parents rapidly began to deteriorate as his behavior became more erratic and contrarian. Weiner described their father as "a controlling man who never mastered flexibility—not unusual in those days. . . . He resorted to old techniques, setting rules and yelling. Nothing worked. . . . As much as he probably thought he was trying to protect Lou, he only made things worse."

Lou and his father only found common ground in one area. Now that Lou was a man in the eyes of the synagogue, his parents reluctantly agreed to indulge him when he began begging for a guitar. Lou bought a twelve-dollar acoustic Stella, and the Reeds found a music teacher who taught beginning guitar in the back of a local music store. Sidney dismissed Lou's fascination with rock as a passing phase of early adolescent angst that would soon resolve itself—Sidney expected his son to one day inherit the family accounting business—but he was in for a deafeningly rude awakening.

In Lou's first lesson, the teacher began plucking along to "Twinkle, Twinkle, Little Star," but like many beginning guitar students, Reed wanted to skip over the nursery rhymes. He pulled out a new record, Carl Perkins's "Blue Suede Shoes," and asked to learn the rockabilly hit. The teacher taught him the three basic chords to play along, the rudiments of rock—never mind finger-picking technique—and Reed had the raw material he needed to raise hell at Freeport High School. Three chords turned out to be all he needed to make it through the preteen years, and for the rest of his life. It was his first and last guitar lesson.

As a high school freshman, it was as though Lou had auditioned for *Hamlet* and been miscast in a whimsically upbeat sitcom. Elliot Garfinkel, soon to become Lou's first manager, thought of him as a fish out of water in an affluent high school that valued athleticism and pep over Lou's depressive cynicism. "You know the show *Happy Days*? That's exactly what it was like," Garfinkel says. "It was a wonderful suburban community. There was a small greaser element, but most of the kids wore white bucks, crew cuts, and that kind of thing. It was a great place at that time." Under the direction of coach Bill Ashley, the football team went undefeated all four years Lou was there; it was the winningest team in Nassau County. Despite his professed desire to "play football for the coach" on *Coney Island Baby*, Lou didn't exhibit that spirited bonhomie in high school, instead withdrawing into himself and finding solace in his guitar. "He was a kind of depressed personality, seeing the other side of the public," Garfinkel says. "It was affluent, and he was somewhat critical of that kind of environment. I don't think he was happy with that. He looked more to the seedier side of life."

Lou retreated into solipsistic angst, but in those formative years, his image was still evolving. Though he always wore jeans instead of the more socially acceptable chinos, he conformed to the standard, sporting white bucks—buckskin shoes that signaled upper-middle-class privilege—and kept his hair short in the fashionable conservative style. He became more sartorially controversial much later. Lou also had braces to realign his teeth. His parents hoped that social pressure would straighten him out in the same way. "He grew up in a very nice home, a nice environment," Garfinkel remembers, "but his parents were kind of strict with him." Unfortunately, their son was Lou Reed. "He was a very moody young man. It was tough to get a smile out of him," says Garfinkel, recalling a natural bent that was not helped by regular visits to the orthodontist. "He was very serious, very taciturn, very bright."

Freshman year at Freeport High School was not easy, but the town provided a cornucopia of consumer distractions for an alienated high school freshman. Lou spent afternoons across the street from Freeport High School at Gene's on Grove Street, a family-owned soda shop with three long tables in the back, Vibrock's, a restaurant that was the first place on Long Island that served Kentucky Fried Chicken—Colonel Sanders even appeared in person to set up the frying equipment—and Woolworth's, a department store where Lou bought bags of red pistachios, which he ate habitually. He found a new confidante in Rich Sigal, also Jewish, who came to Freeport High from Roosevelt, a less affluent neighboring town.

As a teenager, Lou was a study in contradictions; his mood could suddenly swing from curtly dismissive to uproariously funny, from fiercely competitive to deeply resigned, from irrational exuberance to abject nihilism, from composing rhapsodic confessional poetry to staring at the cool glow of his family's television in a neurasthenic daze. His saturnine temperament rose with the tides, not dissimilar from his peers, though undeniably more extreme; most of his friends from the adolescent years recall that he shouldered the mounting weight of his emotional struggles with a proportional zeal for what he deemed good music and a crackling sense of humor. "I remember us having a lot of laughs, a lot of good times, a lot of joking. It wasn't like Lou was this morose, morbid guy who was hunched over and ruining his life," Sigal says. The two would play competitive tennis, visit nearby Jones Beach, or go horseback riding; in the spring of their freshman year, they joined the track team together.

On the track team, Lou participated in the pole vault and was a sprinter. Arthur Scheer, a track teammate to whom Lou also gave guitar lessons, remembers him as a good-natured if reserved teen. "He was a good guy, just one of the boys," Scheer says. "Our track was out by the dock at the park, a mile or two away from the high school. After practice, the guys would go to the docks, where they'd have fresh clams, eat a dozen of them, and run home."

As athletic as he was, Lou diverted his attention to music. Soon he and Rich Sigal began congregating in Lou's den to listen to Alan Freed's daily sermon or doo-wop 45s, and tuning in to gospel stations out of Harlem, Lou savoring the unfathomable depths of Mahalia Jackson's sanguine vibrato. "We'd put it on and we'd really listen to every song and evaluate it and comment on it," Sigal says.

Lou also discovered jazz. Starting in high school, Lou nurtured a passion for the hard bop innovations of John Coltrane, taking the Long Island Rail Road into the city to see the sax giant hone his quicksilver style and harmonic innovations at gritty downtown clubs. "We used to go into the city a lot. We would go to coffee shops in the Village and we used to go see Coltrane a lot," says Allan Hyman. Lou was profoundly influenced by the improvisational spirit of the music and intended to do with lyrics what his jazz heroes did on the horn.

This fierce reverence did not translate to Lou's social life, though. "Lou was not a mainstream guy, and he was so far outside the mainstream that it offended some of the guys," Sigal says. He recalls one afternoon in Gene's that illustrated Lou's capricious temper. "You were always very respectful and polite when girls were around, and you didn't use profanity for the most part. In one incident, Lou had just gotten a haircut. A girl walked in, and she saw Lou and commented, 'Oh, Lou, you got a haircut.' And he looked up and he said, 'Oh, fuck you!' which froze us all in our tracks, because you just didn't do that. You didn't say it in front of girls, and you definitely didn't say it to them. But Lou did. That was classic Lou."

Lou never had a girlfriend in high school, but he did go on dates. He concealed any bi-curious tendencies from his friends, and though he often spoke of an insatiable sexual appetite, if Lou was seeking out male partners at this time, his friends certainly didn't know. He was, however, seeking out women from other Long Island towns. "Even though Long Island is one big conglomerate of towns that bleed into one another, you still basically stayed within your own high school group if you dated. Not Lou. Lou said to me one day, 'I like girls with black hearts,'" Sigal says. Rather than follow the standard courtship rituals of the 1950s, Lou had less wholesome designs. "When Lou went out with a girl, he didn't take them out and show them off. He brought them over to his parents' house when his parents weren't around or he took them out to a drive-in where no one would see them, and he fooled around with them. Lou wasn't motivated by having a long-term relationship with a girl. Lou wanted to go out and get a blow job or whatever he was doing with these girls, and get rid of them, and nobody would even see them."

Even as a teenager, Lou blazed a trail for his friends by cultivating a counterculture persona that made it hard to relate to others. "Lou was more advanced," Sigal says. "He was always ahead of us. He would read the Beat poets, Ginsberg and Saul Bellow and people who at the time I wasn't particularly interested in. If we were looking at *Playboy*, Lou was reading *The Story of O*; if we were drinking quarts of beer, Lou was smoking joints."

Unable to find sympathy in this suburban enclave, Lou found it in underground literature; he was a voracious reader, and followed the morally ambiguous path of pushing past the brink of social convention established by kindred spirits that only existed in books. *The Story of O* was a banned French erotic novel by Anne Desclos, published in 1954 under the pseudonym Pauline Réage. In the tradition of the Marquis de Sade and Leopold von Sacher-Masoch—the author of *Venus in Furs*—the narrative is a lacerating critique of sexual politics and dark desires that details the gradual unraveling of a female fashion photographer named O as she is inculcated and objectified by a misogynistic culture and degraded by increasing acts of sexual violence, submission, and sadomasochism until eventually being sold into sex slavery. Before it could be banned, a poor English translation was rushed into circulation by the avant-garde Parisian publisher Olympia Press; across the Atlantic, Lou somehow obtained a copy of the banned book and smuggled it into Freeport, where it could taint the impressionable minds of his peers.

The Beat Generation was just gaining ground in the fall of Lou's freshman year at Freeport High. Jack Kerouac had coined the name of the movement, a nonconformist literary revolution, in the tradition of Walt Whitman's ruggedly electrified free verse; Lou would soon attempt to realize their "New Vision" with the ecstatic rhythm of guitar, bass, and drums. On October 7, 1955, the Beats' poetic father figure Kenneth Rexroth emceed an infamous poetry reading at the Six Gallery in San Francisco, introducing Philip Lamantia, Gary Snyder, Philip Whalen, and Allen Ginsberg, then an obscure avant-garde figure, who gave the first public reading of "Howl."

Ginsberg dedicated his Beat epic to Carl Solomon, another avant-garde poet who he had met at Columbia Presbyterian Psychiatric Institute during an eight-month stay to avoid a jail sentence. In 1950 Solomon immortalized the experience of insulin shock therapy in his *Report from the Asylum: Afterthoughts of a Shock Patient*. Using stark, ecstatic language, Ginsberg's poem documents the descent into madness of his peers at the hands of Moloch, a Biblical deity not unlike the Golden Calf that Lou was already familiar with. Moloch embodied a litany of conditions and institutions that had chewed them up and spit them out—the malaise of the "invisible suburbs" that Lou inhabited and the "invincible mad houses" such as Greystone, where Woody Guthrie was diagnosed with Huntington's chorea, and Rockland, little pockets of hell on Earth that Lou would soon come to know all too well, indelibly etched by Ginsberg's populist mantra, "I'm with you in Rockland."

In 1956 "Howl" was published by Lawrence Ferlinghetti's City Lights books and sent a shock wave through the body politic; Lou relished his copy before the US customs seizure at the beginning of Ginsberg's controversial obscenity trial. Ginsberg, a professed homosexual in a time when sodomy was a felony potentially resulting in a hard labor sentence, embodied the culture of dissent Lou aspired toward. Ginsberg enlivened a motley cast of characters that Lou was shielded from in Freeport: the liminal, reprobate, and unscrupulous, those who operated on the fringe of society, beyond conventional norms. In Ginsberg, Lou had found a kindred spirit. "Modern rock lyrics would be inconceivable without the work of Allen Ginsberg," Lou said after Ginsberg died. "It opened them up from the really mediocre thing they'd been to something more interesting and relevant. He was very brave and he was also very honest—a no-bullshit person."

In its opening lines, Ginsberg shoots through the crucible of the rigid formalism and conventional meter prevailed upon by the old-guard gatekeepers of the canon, the ivory tower academics, and, marshaling a paratactic, stream-of-consciousness poetic style, shatters the tempered glass bottle of American literary modernism so the scent of sex and rebellion permeates the room.

> *I saw the best minds of my generation destroyed by madness,*
>     *starving hysterical naked*
> *dragging themselves through the negro streets at dawn looking*
>     *for an angry fix*

In its untamed rhythm, Lou would soon have the mad inspiration to drag himself up to 125th Street for his own angry fix and write about it in his inimitable howl in "I'm Waiting for the Man." The work of Ginsberg, Kerouac, Neal Cassady, and William S. Burroughs, whose *Naked Lunch* J. G. Ballard described as "the *Alice in Wonderland* of the amphetamine age," soon coalesced in Lou's mind to expose those frozen moments epitomized by Burroughs, "when everyone sees what is on the end of every fork." By then-contemporary literary standards, what Lou knew was mundane. A portal out of the suburbs, these literary watersheds exposed Lou to a forbidden world: sexual indeterminacy, invisible traumas most lacked the guts to write about, and a peculiar madness that could only be treated with a self-medicating drug regimen. Ginsberg planted the seed "to recreate the syntax and measure of poor human prose" and combine it with a rock sensibility, "confessing out the soul to conform to the rhythm of thought in his naked and endless head." Lou later met Ginsberg, one of his spiritual fathers, and they developed a more reciprocal artistic relationship; Ginsberg even listened to Lou's music while he was dying of liver cancer in 1997. Lou gave a eulogy at the funeral.

Inspired by Ginsberg's restless spirit, Lou took his first walk on the wild side one summer in high school when he got a job working at the Hayloft, a gay bar and nightclub that operated discreetly in the neighboring town of Baldwin. Though he mostly concealed his bisexual curiosity from his friends, this experience as a waiter was the only indication. "The Hayloft used to be the butt of jokes. If anybody wanted to make some kind of a disparaging remark, the Hayloft would be the focus," Sigal says. "We would chide Lou about it, but not too much. We said, 'What are you going there for?' He said, 'The money's good.' That was just another chapter in Lou's secret life. Somehow he had a drug source; somehow he would find the girls with black hearts from elsewhere. He had this interest in boys that none of us knew about. That's a whole other image of Lou that I don't know if a lot of people would have picked up on."

Another summer, Sigal got Lou a more socially acceptable job as a grounds attendant at Jones Beach. The outdoor amphitheater attracted major rock acts, which was a perk, though Lou was relegated to a menial role picking up trash at the West Bathhouse.

"For kids in town, that was often their first job. It was like if you live near Disney World, you work at Disney World; if you lived near Jones Beach, you worked at Jones Beach," Sigal says.

"We spent a lot of time at the waterfront. We all practically lived at Jones Beach during the summers," recalls Judy November, at one point Lou's physics lab partner, whom he later recruited for a vocal quartet.

The transition from beach bum to locker room attendant was a rough one, if natural. As soon as Sigal was old enough to be eligible, he got a job flipping burgers at the concessions stand; the next year, he applied for a government-appointed position as a trash collector at the beach, affectionately known as a "shit picker." The summer after his junior year of high school, he was promoted to the role of "key man," a mechanical job sorting out locker problems at the bathhouse. He suggested Lou apply for an entry-level position; Lou would suffer the indignity of being a shit picker, but he could earn some money and they could drive to work together, borrowing

Lou's parents' Ford Fairlane. Lou applied and, with his connection to Sigal, got hired immediately.

"You walked around with an idiot stick, stabbed litter, and put it in your bag, straightened out the benches, and you wore little gray uniforms and little sailor hats," Sigal says. Shit pickers often had to clean up unusual messes in the bathhouse; sometimes "you'd look in the corner and there would be a pile of human feces, and somebody had to clean it up. Well if you were the new attendant, you were going to do it. It was almost like a little hazing ritual for the newbie." It turned out to be more trouble than it was worth for Lou. "It was a real job. There were things like that, that Lou didn't really care for, so he didn't last very long."

Lou took another job that traded raw sewage for the cool comfort of a brick-and-mortar warehouse. At a wholesale hardware dealer in Freeport, he lost the open air, but he didn't have to get his hands dirty. Manual labor for a machine parts manufacturer was a far cry from the harsh sounds he would one day produce in a different type of factory. "I had a job in high school, filing burrs off nuts that had been recently manufactured. And I remember the guy next to me was 30 years older than me saying, 'You know, there is a future in this.' And I couldn't imagine what it could be!" Lou later told novelist Paul Auster. It was his first experience with a metal machine.

Lou didn't know what employable skills he had, but menial labor was unacceptable; he dreamed of being a poet and following in the footsteps of the Beats, but no one on Long Island was hiring juniors in high school for their verse. He had a more unconventional vision of his money-earning potential that eschewed the dull stasis of workaday life—he would start a garage band.

With the advent of television variety shows that provided a visual complement to the alluring sound of rock, teen idol worship was running rampant. In the summer of 1957, Jerry Lee Lewis shocked the nation with his provocative gyrations and ivory-tickling acrobatics on *The Steve Allen Show*, unleashing his inner demons with the rockabilly hit "Whole Lotta Shakin' Goin' On." In December of that year, Danny and the Juniors, a doo-wop quartet from Philadelphia, brought the tongue-in-cheek sex appeal of "At the Hop" to *American Bandstand*. With the cool fire of the cathode-ray tube, the devil in the ears was now burning in the eyes. It was clear to Lou that rock 'n' roll was a gold mine, even if he wouldn't be making television appearances; playing sock hops at the Jewish Community Center would provide more than enough pocket change. He never intended to mix poetry and commerce, but compared to filing machine parts, the choice was obvious.

When Lou entered his junior year, he found coconspirators in Phil Harris and Alan Walters, best friends who were also Jewish, rock-crazy teens and had struck out as wage slaves. They were never friends with Lou, but they sensed that an alliance would be mutually beneficial. "He was kind of a standoffish guy, but he could play guitar really well," Harris says. Phil and Alan were a year older and had the voice but not the guitar chops; Lou had the guitar but not the voice. Phil and Alan had nowhere to rehearse in their cramped family apartments, while Lou, who lived less than a mile away from Phil, had a basement that could be used for rehearsal space. As individuals, the three were not marketable, but as a trio with the combination of singing ability, good looks, and raw ambition, they had the basic ingredients of a 1950s doo-wop group.

It was Harris who approached Lou, suggesting that they form a rock group with Alan for the annual Freeport High talent show. To round out the group on drums, they recruited Howie Wolfe, a friend from Roosevelt. They chose the name the Shades, based on the protective eyewear that Lou would one day imbue with a counterculture edge. With the preponderance of doo-wop groups flooding the charts, they even found a manager in Elliot Garfinkel, who had graduated the previous year and was commuting to Hofstra University. Harris's girlfriend, Karen, was Garfinkel's neighbor. Garfinkel had no qualifications as a manager, but he had two valuable assets: a brand-new white Lincoln Continental convertible and an in with Bob Shad, his girlfriend Tamara's father, who happened to be the director of A&R at Mercury Records.

For Phil, what gifts he possessed in the vocal cords did not translate to hand-eye coordination. He began as a deckhand on commercial fishing boats and parlayed the experience to get hired as a valet for Canadian bandleader Guy Lombardo, a portly but debonair violinist and impresario who had a luxurious waterfront restaurant in Freeport called the East Point House, not far from Freeport High. Lombardo lived across town on the bay, and had a dock in his backyard; rather than drive, he would go to his restaurant by yacht. "Lombardo's whole house was mahogany covered, and he had a big mahogany boat," Harris recalls. "I was what they classify as the 'boat hook' off the front of his boat when he came in for his Friday night show until such time as I grabbed the wrong hook and fell in the water. That wasn't much appreciated by them, so my employment was terminated very soon thereafter."

Harris's string of luck continued when he got hired as a waiter at a Brooklyn restaurant owned by his girlfriend Karen's father. His clumsiness once again got the best of him. "The only thing I was claiming fame to was holding six glasses of water in one shot, until one day one of them dropped out. Of course, that annoyed everybody to beat the band. So much for that," he says.

The Shades began preparing for their talent show appearance, rehearsing a Little Richard routine in Lou's basement. *Here's Little Richard*, his debut LP, had been released the previous March, featuring the hit single "Tutti Frutti," a manic romp with a hypersexualized undertone and the immortal lyric "A wop-bop-a-loo-bop, a wop bam boom!" They hoped to be the toast of the talent show; they had even begun collaborating on doo-wop songs that reflected the themes of the zeitgeist: first love and heartache. "During our rehearsals, we started writing some songs, so we had a little bit of original music," says Walters. Their music was tame compared to Lou's later output, but he didn't feel comfortable mixing his unvarnished literary affinities with the wholesome veneer of the radio hits.

As the show approached, the Shades began playing house parties in Freeport, and Harris invited Garfinkel to one to see if he would consider introducing the band to Bob Shad. "Shad said to me that if I ever came across a group that was up-and-coming and had potential, that I should share it with him," Garfinkel says. Garfinkel thought that the band was ready, but no one warned the Shades that Shad would be in the audience for the variety show in the high school gym.

"Shad saw us perform, and we were pretty good. We hadn't had a tremendous amount of rehearsal, but we jelled together and we made some good sounds," says Walters.

Yet Harris wasn't cut out to be Little Richard. "I strained the hell out of my voice doing that routine, but from what I understood, it was pretty good. So we went from there," Harris says. After the variety show, Garfinkel met the Shades backstage. "Elliot came back to us and he said, 'Shad is crazy about what he saw up onstage and would like to meet with you guys. Would you like to get a record contract and become famous?' We said, 'Sure, why not? We've got nothing better to do,'" says Walters.

Before signing any contracts, Shad wanted to test their mettle, though. The Shades crammed into Garfinkel's convertible and drove to Shad's lavish estate in Glen Cove, set up their equipment in his living room, and launched into a set of doo-wop covers. "He didn't want to hear 'Rock Around the Clock' and all that kind of stuff because somebody's already doing that," says Walters. They played their best original, "Leave Her for Me," a plaintive midtempo crooner. "He liked what we had, and he said, 'But the drummer's got to go,'" says Walters. They eventually conceded, and agreed to use a studio rhythm section. "Shad said, 'Meet us in the city. Get your parents together. Come in and we'll put together some contracts. I like you guys. I could do something for you.'" They looked back incredulously, but Shad was serious—the Shades had a record deal.

Little did they know, Lou and the Shades were not the first musicians to set foot in Shad's living room; their humble audition took place on ground well-trodden by the likes of Alan Freed and Patti Page, who would sometimes stop by for dinner. Before his career took off, bandleader Billy Eckstine had been Tamara's babysitter. There were countless upstart record producers with little credibility looking to make a quick buck on up-and-coming doo-wop vocal groups, but this was no flimflam scheme—Shad was one of the unsung heroes of the recording industry, and he had a perspicacious eye for talent. Starting out at the Savoy label in the 1940s, Shad supervised recording sessions with jazz legends Charlie Parker, Dinah Washington, and Sarah Vaughan. Prior to meeting the Shades, Shad worked as a jazz and blues producer, advancing the careers of Lightnin' Hopkins, Brownie McGhee, and Big Bill Broonzy; he later produced such progressive artists as Clifford Brown and Max Roach, Cannonball Adderley, and Booker Little.

But Shad's eclectic tastes and business savvy led him to explore wider sonic territory—he also produced Ray Charles, and espoused Charles's belief that "there's only two kinds of music," good and bad. Later, when Shad branched off and formed his Time, Shad, and Brent labels, he signed doo-wop groups such as the Bell Notes, the Genies, and Skip & Flip; and in 1966 he took a risk and produced the debut album by a destitute acid rock band called Big Brother and the Holding Company, with a volatile lead singer named Janis Joplin. The veteran producer immediately recognized which side of the good/bad dichotomy the Shades fell on; even though they were still in high school, Shad saw something special in them.

Shad initially signed the Shades to Mercury Records, but he had designs of his own. He had been orchestrating an exit strategy from Mercury and wanted to form his own labels, provisionally under the Shad and Time banners. He pitched the idea to the Shades, claiming they would be Time's signature artists. They initially balked at leaving Mercury, with its instant brand recognition, but Shad had already signed established acts to Time, including the Rockin' Chairs, who had just released their hit single, "A Kiss Is a Kiss." Shad planned to feature the two groups as a double bill. With the new contract in place, the Shades were ready to record. Only one niggling issue remained: their name had to be changed due to a rights issue with a previously established group called the Shades. They opted for the Jades, so at the age of sixteen, Lou was already jaded.

The four arrived at the recording studio in Manhattan, a small space with baffled walls and glass partitions, to record "Leave Her for Me," and the melancholic B-side, "So Blue," a faster, more danceable heartbreak tune; both used the ubiquitous doo-wop "ice cream changes," the basic chordal structure of the 1950s sound. To provide some ballast to the inexperienced Jades, Shad enlisted upper-echelon studio musicians: saxophone giant King Curtis, the tenor man behind "Yakety Yak," to inject the requisite growls and honks and guitar icon Mickey Baker, of "Love Is Strange" fame. Lou had met one of his guitar gods. "And I was trying to study the Mickey Baker guitar chord book, same Mickey Baker. There's no way. He could stretch from here to here. It was unbelievable," Lou later recounted.

It was rare for such a young group to record in the studio; Harris stood on a milk crate to reach the microphone, but stature aside, they had logged enough rehearsal time in Lou's basement that the session went off without a hitch. "We did half a dozen takes and it was a go," Walters says. "It was a hell of a record."

The hormone-fueled frenzy of adolescents navigating the cutthroat milieu of the recording industry and grappling with the first blush of small-town fame never affected the music, though. "Leave Her for Me" exuded a pastoral yearning, uncharacteristic of Lou's dark side, which was tempered by the collaborative effort. When Harris crooned the opening verse in his tremulous tenor and Lou strummed the first open G chord, the dalliances with "black-hearted" women and adolescent angst were washed over by palliative harmonies:

*Take away the sunshine, take away the trees*
*Take away the rosebuds that bloom in the spring*
*Take all the blossoms, all I ask is one thing*
*Leave me my baby, please leave her for me*

As Lou and Alan came in on the gang vocal refrain "Leave her for me" after the first verse, as sincere as it was for the other two, it was inescapable that for Lou, this was more of an imitative exercise in songwriting than an outlet for his irreverent confessional poetry. Despite the evolving proclivities that would one day permeate his lyrics, Lou had to learn the fundamentals of rock composition before he could find his own voice. Besides, at the time it seemed that the commercial and the purely artistic spheres had to be kept separate. He would take much greater artistic risks later, but this one paid off.

"Leave Her for Me" was an instant hit. "It became a WINS pick hit of the week. It was doing absolutely fantastic. My uncle was in Las Vegas in the casino gambling, and he called me up and said, 'Your song's playing!' Yet they never saw royalties due to payola and record hijacking schemes. It played very little in the metropolitan area but played big-time in the South," Garfinkel says. "I was rather naive at the time and really didn't know the business that well." Lou eventually did receive royalties: $2.68 for "So Blue" and $0.78 for "Leave Her for Me." Their ambition was not fazed by the lack of financial success, though—Lou inscribed a photo of the Jades performing with a jocular note to his bandmate Alan, "May we make much bread."

Based on the strength of their single, Garfinkel booked the Jades on a dance program hosted by Alan Freed. The 1958 broadcast was couched as a battle of the bands, with the winner getting booked for a recording session. They didn't win that night, but Lou had at least realized a pipe dream of being played by the legendary DJ—not long before Freed was let go from WINS and indicted on charges related to his ongoing payola scheme. "Freed was kind of a drinker. As a matter of fact, he drank all the time on his show. That didn't help his image, but he was what he was, and very good at that," Harris says. "We got involved in payola. That's probably why we never did anything more than the one show with him."

The meager royalties for "Leave Her for Me" came from its sole play on *Swingin' Soiree*, a nightly program on the WINS prime-time block hosted by Murray the K, the on-air name of Murray Kaufman, the silver-tongued impresario who would later be known for promoting the Beatles on American radio. Kaufman wasn't in the studio that night, though.

"They called me up and said Murray the K is gonna play your record tonight," Lou later recalled. "We all tuned in to WINS, 1010 Loves You. We're listening and listening and listening, and finally on comes Murray the K, except it's Paul Sherman. He says Murray the K is ill tonight, and I can't fuckin' believe it, right. My big moment. So Sherman played it. He was an asshole. Not that Murray the K wasn't an asshole, but if you're going to have an asshole play it, you want the biggest."

The band did have one memorable encounter with Murray the K, though. Similar to Freed's dance programs, Kaufman hosted live performances on Long Island. The Jades were invited under the condition that they lip-synch the performance along with the record. "Murray the K arrived in a helicopter, and everybody stormed the thing," says Harris. "He stayed for about half an hour, gets in a helicopter, and goes."

Garfinkel began booking shows at venues along Long Island's North Shore ranging from American Legion posts to beach clubs in Lido Beach to Jewish Community Centers. Most of the appearances took place at shopping malls, often on a double bill opposite the Rockin' Chairs. The Jades generally donned white jackets and string ties, and often lip-synched their performances so venues could avoid soundchecks and live mixing. When they got tired of mouthing the words, they would stop on street corners on the way to shows and do impromptu sets. For Lou and the group, it was the biggest thrill of their lives. "We would pull into the shopping center all sitting up on the back of Elliot's white Lincoln Continental. The girls were screaming like crazy, ripping our ties off and tearing at our shirts," says Walters.

Most of their shows consisted of banal commercial displays, but some veered into rougher territory. At their debut performance at the Highway Inn, a dive bar that attracted biker gangs passing through Freeport, Lou butted heads with the local color. The spangled shirts the band wore didn't help; the world was not yet ready for glitter. "Lou almost got us killed that night," says Walters. Like the other venues, the bar insisted that the Jades lip-synch, but Lou wanted to rock, creating an overdub effect. "Lou, the arrogant son of a bitch that he was, had to sing out loud and was blasting out on his guitar, when something happened on the jukebox." The record started skipping, and the barflies began throwing bottles. "Lou was screaming at them, antagonizing them," Walters says. When the stream of bottles subsided, the band quickly packed up and drove off. "We had to stand by one of those stupid fences to keep the bottles from killing us," Harris recalls of the night. "But we did all right. They seemed to enjoy what he did, even though they were throwing bottles."

Their modest success came at the expense of behind-the-scenes rancor, though. The Jades never saw eye to eye on the direction of the group, and with Lou, the youngest member, attempting to claim a leadership role, they began to unravel. "We could have gone a long way off of that record as a catapult to other, bigger things, but it just wasn't in the cards. The personalities clashed so badly. I mean violently badly," says Walters. For a staunch nonconformist like Lou, he couldn't even compromise with the members of his own group. They couldn't even agree on dress code at the costume store in Hempstead; unfortunately for a 1950s doo-wop group, uniformity was key.

"It was monumental to pick out three shirts that looked the same," says Walters. "The 4G's in Hempstead is where all the groups would go and buy their outfits. You would go in there and buy all of these avant-garde, garish shirts and pants; black pants with blue insets on the sides, and iridescent shirts with sparkles. The fights that would go on inside there because Phil and I thought this was a great shirt, and Lou had to have something totally different. Whatever we liked, he hated. Whatever he liked, we didn't want. We could never agree on anything, not even stupid shirts."

The backstage resentment made it impossible to continue. The Jades were destined for flash-in-the-pan fame. At one rehearsal, Alan and Phil walked into the basement to discover Lou in the buff, soaking himself in buttermilk as a home remedy for a rash. "Why would he have stayed like that as opposed to putting his drawers on? But he seemed to be rather comfortable having us view him soak his balls in buttermilk. He was a strange guy," says Walters. Yet becoming a one-hit wonder at sixteen proved to Lou that he could make it if he tried. "Lou was a depressed kind of guy. He was always somewhere else mentally. He was never really focused on us as a group. It was almost like I was the chauffeur and Phil was his valet. He tolerated us. But I guess he kept it together because he got something out of it also," says Walters. "He was tenacious, very focused, but he was a dick." Lou had effectively torpedoed the Jades. In the first of Lou's many career suicides, the three made the difficult decision to disband.

After the Jades split up, Lou would have one more collaboration with Phil Harris, who decided to launch a solo career under the name Bobby Randle—another Phil Harris was already an established singer. He wrote a love serenade to his then-girlfriend, Karen, who had introduced the Jades to Garfinkel. In 1959 Harris recorded "Karen" for the Shad label, with Lou contributing the instrumental arrangement, featuring Mickey Baker again. The B-side, "Walking in the Shadows," a mournful breakup ballad, was the first single written by Gerry Goffin, who went on to marry Carole King in August of that year and to pen countless *Billboard* hits at the Brill Building. It was Goffin's debut, but it was Harris's final recording.

In the fall of 1958, Lou returned to Freeport High for his senior year and focused on putting together another group for the talent show. Going from Murray the K back to the school variety show was a clear regression, but Lou needed to keep playing. He recruited Judy Titus, his physics lab partner and the captain of the cheerleading team, Rich Sigal, and John DeKam. With Lou on guitar, they practiced several songs; they went by the name the C.H.D. "We were thinking, what can we come up with to fool the school administration so we can say something a little off-color and they won't know what it is? We thought that was really slick at the time—it stood for Dry Hump Club backwards," Sigal says. "Keep in mind, we're talking about different generations here. In our day, dry humping was a pretty big deal, if you could reach that base, and most of the time you didn't." Lou also formed the Tree Toads, an instrumental group that consisted of him on guitar, Steve Brown on guitar, and Sigal on harmonica.

One day, he took Rich down to his basement and gave him his original Stella—by that time, Lou had upgraded to a Gretsch—and taught him a three-chord E progression and a four-chord C progression, the basic harmonic scaffolding of the 1950s sound. It was more chords than Lou felt were necessary. "He said, 'All you need is one chord. Two is pushing it, and by three you're getting into jazz,'" Sigal says. "I said, 'But I know other chords. I learned them on my own. And Lou said, 'You don't need 'em.' Lou was a minimalist, I guess. So we had the two guitars, and with seven chords, we started a band."

They started by playing on the street, and planned to work up to the school talent show. "Once Lou taught me how to play guitar, we took our guitars into the Bowery and hung out with the bums," Sigal says. "Lou always scared the shit out of me when he drove. Lou's the kind of guy who'd be driving the car and he was more interested in tuning the radio." After Sigal felt more comfortable finding his way around the fret board, Lou filled in the rest of the rhythm section; Allan Hyman had a drum set, and Lou's cousin Bobby Futterman played bass. Sometimes Jerry Jackson, one of the stars of the football team, would sit in on lead vocals. Lou named the new band the Valets, and they quickly had business cards printed: THE FINEST IN RHYTHM AND BLUES, THE VALETS: HERE TO SERVE YOU AND YOURS. Along the bottom, the cards also listed the phone number of each band member as a furtive method of getting dates; they were the only students at Freeport High School with business cards. "We played at parties, bars, beach clubs, never making much money, and playing for as little as plates of spaghetti," says Sigal. Playing house parties in Freeport was a long way from Murray the K, but rock hadn't lost its luster—it never would—and it allowed Lou to continue honing his guitar technique.

Lou continued writing songs, but without the Jades he couldn't get another record contract. "I used to go up to Harlem with all these songs after that to try to see if I could get the Jesters or the Flamingos or the Diablos to record one of these things that I was writing out on Long Island," he later said. He was unfazed, though; he had pretensions of becoming a serious poet, not a rock star, and with college looming, he shifted his priorities away from doo-wop fame to joining the underground literary canon.

Lou had his sights set on a college campus as far from Freeport as his parents would condone. Hyman suggested Syracuse; not only did they already have friends attending, the campus was three hundred miles away in Upstate New York, with twenty thousand students and a reputation as a hotbed of creative activity. They arranged a campus visit during their senior year. "We drove up to Syracuse with Lou's father," Hyman says. Lou and Allan also met two girls who were prospective students at the Hotel Syracuse, where they were staying. "We ended up going to my room, because Lou and I were staying together and his father had his own room," Hyman says. It provided a glimmer of the freedom that lay ahead in college. "We said, 'This is where we're going to go.' So that's what we decided to do."

After graduating from Freeport High, Lou had finally earned the diploma that could grant him his long-awaited exodus from Freeport, but his freedom would be hard-won. Beneath the surface, he was grappling with clinical depression; on top of his radical mood swings and brusque demeanor, his homosexual urges did not help reassure him that, even for a teenager in

1950s Long Island, this qualified as remotely normal. Under the supervision of his parents, he sought psychiatric help. The psychiatrist thought it might be schizophrenia and recommended swift and decisive action—electroshock therapy. His parents reluctantly agreed. There would be no stay of execution; treatment started immediately. According to his sister, it was a decision that would ultimately "set into motion the dissolution of my family of origin." Faced with accusations of poor parenting from the psychiatric community and with a limited understanding of genetics, Lou's parents were wracked with guilt; they felt they didn't have a choice but to comply. "My parents were like lambs being led to the slaughter—confused, terrified, and conditioned to follow the advice of doctors. They never even got a second opinion," Weiner recalled. But it was too late.

Lou would at times attempt to downplay his predicament. "I was just a little depressed and it was a dumb doctor," he later said. Yet shock treatment in the 1950s would be at best emotionally scarring, resulting in severe memory loss and a grueling recovery, and at worst, irreparably damaging, both physically and psychologically. With the course of treatment prescribed and his fate sealed—eight weeks at Creedmoor Psychiatric Center—Lou had no recourse but to grin and bear it.

The decision to move forward had nothing to do with homosexuality; though still classified as a mental disorder in the DSM, Lou's particular diagnosis eluded the doctors. Yet whatever it was, the psychiatric community had a ready cure. "My parents were many things, but homophobic they were not. In fact, they were blazing liberals," Weiner said. "They were caught in a bewildering web of guilt, fear, and poor psychiatric care."

Yet when word of Lou's treatments began to circulate, outsiders believed the insidious rumor that it was an attempt to "cure" his homosexual urges. "None of us knew Lou had leanings towards boys. It was never discussed," says Sigal. "I only found out about it after the fact, when I read that his parents had given him the shock treatments. I never knew about that either, so that was part of Lou's secret life."

Part of his friends' absence from his life during such a critical moment was circumstantial; they had all left for college. Hyman went to Syracuse, where much to his chagrin, Lou wasn't there. Inexplicably to Hyman, Lou had enrolled at NYU's Bronx campus. "He had a whole bunch of issues with depression that he was dealing with. There was a rumor going around, and I never believed it, that his mother and father decided he should have electroshock therapy because it would cure his tendency toward homosexuality, which was ridiculous, because at that point in time, at least, he never indicated to me that he was gay or anything like that," Hyman says. "In the context of the time, it's not something that people would communicate." Lou finally admitted why he hadn't gone to Syracuse, though. "We spoke usually once or twice a week, and he said he was getting these electroshock treatments, which I found unbelievably strange, but he said it was helping him with depression," Hyman says.

The treatment was barbaric, partially due to understaffing and intense overcrowding at Creedmoor. According to Dr. Irwin Mendelsohn, who began his residency at Creedmoor in 1960, shortly after Lou was there, electroshock therapy was a last resort. "It was mainly used to treat people who were considered in serious danger of suicide," Mendelsohn says. Anesthesia was limited; patients were generally conscious during treatment. "It was mostly muscle relaxants to prevent fractures. I think the person was pretty aware of what was going on." Compared to the other mental institutions in the state, Creedmoor had developed a reputation as the final resting place of the unfortunate souls the New York City government deemed its most deranged untouchables. "A lot of it was not so much treatment; warehousing was the term that comes to mind," says Mendelsohn. "Many of these people were very delusional, very sick, paranoid, depressed, and there wasn't much that could be done. They were not candidates for psychotherapy, for the most part, and they were abandoned by their families."

Lou's parents hadn't abandoned him, but he felt they had knowingly led him to slaughter, even if they didn't think they had a choice. Creedmoor was plagued by bureaucratic inefficiencies, inhumane treatment, and brutality endured by the thousands of inpatients sequestered within its concrete walls, some of whom were tortured artists. In 1947 the virtuosic jazz pianist Bud Powell had faced more than a year of shock treatments at Creedmoor; in 1967, Woody Guthrie would die there. But Lou was determined to survive. Creedmoor was only his beginning.

# 4

After they wrapped Lou in a bedsheet and placed him on a wooden gurney, the doctor attached two electrodes to his temple and inserted a rubber bite block. This would prevent him from biting off his tongue when the grand mal seizure was induced. No anesthetic was administered, no muscle relaxant. The doctor paced back to the machine, then the two trembling orderlies, barely out of high school and only a year older than Lou was, laid across his chest and knees to brace him for the shock to come. He had read *Frankenstein*; now he was living it. The doctor flipped the switch on the metal box, the size of a small amplifier, and Lou Reed, who had up to that moment in his life been an acoustic being, became quite literally electrified.

It only lasted a few seconds, but the excruciating pain of the convulsions was far more than any seventeen-year-old suffering from the usual maladies of existential angst and heartache was able to bear. If the orderlies had not stabilized his body during the seizure, he would have broken his back. When he regained consciousness from the haze of high voltage, his thoughts were a howl on the low and high frequencies that he would later channel into a real amplifier, but through that deafening white noise one thought remained clear—he would have his retribution.

Yet the aftereffects of electroconvulsive therapy (ECT) made retaliation impossible in the short term. "I watched my brother as my parents assisted him coming back into our home afterwards, unable to walk, stupor-like," Weiner later recalled of the treatments. "It damaged his short-term memory horribly and throughout his life he struggled with memory retention, probably directly as a result of those treatments."

The doctors had assured Lou's parents that the talking cure would not be enough to prevent recidivism. According to the medical community, Lou's aberrant behavior would have to be shocked out of him. With ECT, the doctor had explained, Lou might not abandon the guitar, but he was confident that a battery of twenty-four tiny electrocutions could work wonders. So while the rest of Lou's peers were mowing lawns and wooing women at drive-ins, Lou spent the summer after high school in and out of a mental hospital.

For the family, it was devastating. "Each of us suffered the loss of our dear sweet Lou in our own private hell, unhelped and undercut by the medical profession. The advent of family therapy unfortunately was not yet available to us," Weiner said. Making matters worse, they all suffered alone. In an era when mental illness was stigmatized and kept a family secret, Lou initially concealed his debilitating condition from his relatives and friends. Within and without the home, Lou's battle with ECT would remain an open secret, never to be discussed, a specter that would haunt the family forever.

Creedmoor was the closest thing to hell in Queens. It opened in 1912 in Queens Village as the farm colony for Brooklyn State Hospital, taking as its founding principle the prevailing notion that a pastoral environment could have therapeutic effects on New York's certifiably insane. Yet Creedmoor could not have been farther from pastoral. Though Creedmoor committed only thirty-two patients when it first opened, by the mid-1950s the overwhelming influx of the mentally unstable flooding its campus had expanded the number of residents to roughly eight thousand, a figure that far outpaced increases in the medical support staff.

Equipment fell into disrepair, naive orderlies were often forced into supervisory roles in overcrowded wards with up to 150 patients, and those who were relegated to the dank padded rooms faced deleterious conditions and criminal levels of abuse and neglect. Creedmoor's reputation was tarnished by a dysentery outbreak in the 1940s, rapes, assaults, riots, and random acts of violence; for Lou to spend his summer in that horror house, even as an outpatient, was not only cruel and unusual punishment, it branded him as a pariah and a lunatic. To say that someone "belonged at Creedmoor" was an insult at the time. Apparently, by 1959 standards, Lou did. His parents and by extension civilized society objected to his defiance—even then, he refused to play by anyone else's rules, and as punishment for breaking them, he faced an adolescent's worst nightmare.

The punishment solidified Lou's unflappable spirit of rebellion. Even the gruesome history of ECT conjures images of torture. The treatment was first conceived of by Italian psychiatrist Ugo Cerletti, who was inspired one day at the butcher when he ordered a cut of meat that had not been prepared, and was sent to the slaughterhouse to have it cut fresh. There, the butcher ran an electric charge through a cow to induce a seizure, knocking it to its knees and incapacitating it. This allowed for greater precision when slitting its throat. Cerletti connected this grisly sight with the prevalent belief that epilepsy and schizophrenia could not coexist in one person, postulating that therefore inducing a seizure could reduce or eradicate psychosis.

The epiphany was deeply flawed but clear—he would use the butcher's animal slaughter technique to cure mental illness. Following many animal deaths in the test phase, Cerletti settled on the proper dosage and began experimenting on humans, finding that his theory worked, if only by often rendering his patients lifeless drones, sometimes causing irreversible brain damage and compression fractures in the vertebrae.

Though he later renounced ECT as an abomination, Cerletti was nominated for a Nobel Prize for his work. By the early 1940s, electroshock began to be referred to in medical circles as "annihilation therapy," and was widely practiced under Mussolini to treat intractable wards of the state. Doctors fled the fascist government for the United States and imported ECT with them.

Lou made it through his first electroshock treatment; there would be twenty-three more sessions. He would be back at Creedmoor in two days. To deal with the medically induced trauma, Lou might have found a kindred spirit in J. Alfred Prufrock, but the treatment made it impossible to read. It had been a moment of paranoia that forced Lou to question whether it was he that was crazy or everyone else, and it wasn't him.

Lou had already embraced the counterculture, but electroshock secured his allegiance to the underground. If he wanted to escape, he would have to do it himself. No one, not anyone in mainstream society at least, would do it for him. He would later dedicate his life to exposing the seamy underbelly beneath the sanitized reality presented by the mainstream, eternally distrustful of any authority figure, especially any record executive, after he had seen authority be so wrong. To do it he would harness the power of rock 'n' roll.

Rock conventions at the time were insufficient for this purpose, so Lou molded them into a more violent tool. That summer at Creedmoor, Johnny Horton's foot-stomping country ramble "The Battle of New Orleans" topped the charts; in August, Bobby Darin's rendition of "Mack the Knife" hit the airwaves. Lou could not relate to Horton's countrified ramble or Darin's polished veneer. The sound and fury he heard had more in common with the avant-garde experimentation of jazz artists making waves in the under-ground—Cecil Taylor, Thelonious Monk, and Ornette Coleman.

Yet what truly captured his heart was the sound of Alan Freed, god-father of rock 'n' roll. Now in his last days at WINS, the disc jockey had defined the genre and first introduced the syncopated rhythm and thump of black music to white America. The radio kept Lou alive that summer. Hypnotized by the mellifluous voices of doo-wop, Lou sought refuge in the lovelorn poetry of Johnny Ace, the Diablos, the Jesters, Shirley and Lee, Alicia and the Rockaways, and Doc Pomus, the songwriter of "This Magic Moment" and "A Teenager in Love"—which Lou would later cover—who found a mouthpiece in the Drifters and the Bronx Soul of Dion DiMucci. Doo-wop was Lou's first love—it was the sound of freedom—and it would stay with him forever.

Lou would soon bridge the wide gap between the clean, diatonic rock of the 1950s, avant-garde jazz, drone music, and minimalism to form his own underground sound. In doing so, he would liberate rock from its tacit restriction to the hoary themes of love, lust, and heartbreak, and use his amplifier as a weapon to express the profound alienation that reached a zenith at Creedmoor. Lou cut to the bone. Unlike Dion, his voice wasn't smooth, but he didn't care.

So for the rest of the summer, he returned to Creedmoor. Yet despite the overwhelming attempt to silence his voice, he knew that no institution could hold him. He had been shocked into it; he would shock himself out.

That summer was a blur. After he completed the battery of treatments in the fall of 1959, Lou began an extensive period of post-shock treatments at the Payne Whitney Psychiatric Clinic on the Upper West Side, attending weekly sessions where a Thorazine regimen was supervised. He would have to postpone his matriculation at Syracuse indefinitely; New York University had a Bronx branch not far from Payne Whitney and a commutable distance from Freeport.

Unlike Creedmoor, Payne Whitney had an appealing facade that belied the incapacitating malaise of the post-shock treatments that awaited him. Patients roamed through a well-landscaped courtyard and student nurses greeted him with an officious smile, in pale-blue scrubs.

Despite appearances, Payne Whitney was more reminiscent of the sterile sanitarium in Ken Kesey's *One Flew Over the Cuckoo's Nest*, published two years later in 1962, than the near-penitentiary-style horrors of Creedmoor.

In 1954 Robert Lowell endured a lengthy stay at Payne Whitney to deal with what would later be described as bipolar disorder—crippling periods of depression and euphoric spells of mania; Marilyn Monroe and monologist Spalding Gray would also spend time there to deal with similar issues.

The shock therapy dulled Lou's memory, and the post-shock treatments numbed his senses. With Sigal off at Alfred University and Hyman at Syracuse, Lou had also lost his band. For Lou, the experience was a torment, but beyond the psychosomatic miasma, he was spurred on by the saving grace of his brief stint at NYU and Payne Whitney: access to the city's thriving jazz scene. The soundtrack to Lou's Payne Whitney post-shock treatments consisted largely of two of his favorite artists, Ornette Coleman and John Coltrane, who were busy pushing conventional jazz harmony to the next level. Coleman released *The Shape of Jazz to Come* in October 1959, destabilizing the diatonic center in the seminal free-jazz album; two months later, heralding the fearless experimentation of the 1960s, Coltrane released *Giant Steps*, building increasingly complex harmonic architecture for his virtuosic improvisation out of earlier innovations in bebop.

"When I was going to college I would go down into New York and I would trail Ornette's quartet around—Billy Higgins, Charlie Haden, Don and Ornette," Lou later recalled to Sylvie Simmons. "I couldn't afford to go in, so I would listen through the window and I heard 'Lonely Woman,' and that changed my life. The harmonies, that was it. There's not a day goes by when I'm not humming 'Lonely Woman.'" Lou eventually performed alongside Coleman and on a separate occasion, with Don Cherry, his trumpeter; little did Lou know, an experimental saxophonist and composer who would play an instrumental role in his life had already played with them: La Monte Young.

Lou was not lacking for literary inspiration either. In July 1959, between the waking nightmares and dreamless sleeps during his time at Creedmoor and Payne Whitney, a shocking, illicit book insidiously wended its way into New York via Paris: William S. Burroughs's novel *Naked Lunch*. Lou was unable to focus on a linear narrative, but Burroughs's prose, informed by his experiments with myriad mind-altering substances that led to the frenetic cut-up technique, could be consumed in any order—backward, forward, or upside down. *Naked Lunch* was essentially a postmodern choose-your-own adventure through a disturbed psyche, the intersection of narcotics-fueled erudition and oneiric noir that fired a point-blank kill shot at the establishment. Not only was it the call to arms that Lou needed, it mirrored his liminal shadow land of sedated semiconsciousness.

"Without Burroughs modern lit would be a drama without a page, a sonnet without a song and a bone without gristle," Lou later said. "Burroughs alone made us pay attention to the realities of contemporary life and gave us the energy to explore the psyche without a filter. Without Burroughs there is nothing."

Encouraged by Ginsberg to publish his incendiary tome, Burroughs managed to get the manuscript in the hands of Olympia Press, the intrepid Paris publisher that had dared to circulate *The Story of O* earlier that decade. With a suggestive title inspired by Jack Kerouac, an episodic narrative, and an unapologetic deconstruction of a fixed gender binary, *Naked Lunch* presaged the end of an era of postwar austerity and conservative values, the culmination of a revolution the Beats had fomented from the underground. Burroughs was also openly gay following the accidental shooting of his second wife in 1951 and subsequently chose a road not taken by many. Lou was determined to follow in his sordid footsteps.

*Naked Lunch* is set in the dystopian future city of Interzone, a corrupt police state overrun with degenerate addicts, detectives on the take, and sadistic doctors hell-bent on eradicating homosexuality. In muscular, kaleidoscopic prose, Burroughs articulated the themes that would drive Lou's early songwriting—junkies chasing their next fix, deviant sexual behavior, and an unsparing depiction, in crackling urban vernacular, of life as it is lived on the streets. Lou saw his own experience with the mental health industrial complex reflected in the chilling Dr. Benway, a maniacal distillation of the pernicious and deeply flawed logic that consigned Lou to the mental ward and tranquilizers. As in the rumor that circulated about Lou's treatment, Benway fixates on "curing" homosexuality under the auspices of public health:

> "Take the matter of uh *sexual deviation.*" The doctor rocked back and forth in his chair. His glasses slid down onto his nose. Carl felt suddenly uncomfortable. "We regard it as a misfortune . . . a sickness . . . certainly nothing to be censored or uh sanctioned any more than say . . . tuberculosis. . . ."

For Lou, it was as though a page had been ripped from his own diary. In *Naked Lunch*, Lou found the pulpy inspiration to write "I'm Waiting for the Man" and "Heroin." The Man, described as a "glowering super-ego," appears repeatedly, a dualistic symbol of moral decay in a faceless bureaucracy and the relative anonymity of the black market, a controversial dichotomy that Lou eventually appropriated in his songwriting. Before Lou learned it in Harlem, he learned the lesson in Burroughs's Interzone:

> "Sit down. The Man is four hours late. You got the bread?"
> "Yes. That is, I got three cents."

Lou was more than familiar with drifting in and out of sleep on the Long Island Rail Road, but Burroughs woke him up to the possibilities of fiction to get at the truth. He finally had the inspiration to escape the fetters of his troubled youth. It would be several years before Hubert Selby Jr.'s *Last Exit to Brooklyn*, but with the critical mass of Ornette Coleman, Burroughs, and Ginsberg, Lou decided to stake a claim to his own literary ambition. He began devising his own exit from the plodding feedback loop of Payne Whitney, committed to leaving Freeport. It was 1960; Robert Lowell had just won the National Book Award, splitting American poetry into the "cooked" and the "raw." Lou's brain might have been cooked, but his voice was still raw. He filed an application to transfer from NYU to Syracuse University and was immediately accepted. For Lou, the 1960s had finally arrived.

# 5

It was the fall of 1960, and Lou was wearing out the grooves to Ornette Coleman's *Change of the Century*, playing "Ramblin'" and "Free" on loop. Dwight D. Eisenhower was finishing his second term. Nikita Khrushchev banged a shoe of indignation against a lectern at the UN General Assembly, but John F. Kennedy's candidacy injected some much-needed idealism into the Cold War zeitgeist. Lou packed his guitar, jeans, and meager school supplies into the trunk of his father's Ford Fairlane, and the family drove the 280 miles to Syracuse through gale-force winds as Hurricane Donna ravaged the coastline. A change was in the air, and they could hear it on the radio; Elvis had recently returned from his tour of duty, and "It's Now or Never" was supplanted on the top of the charts by Chubby Checker's "The Twist," leading to the eponymous dance craze. But the cultural establishment was slow to adapt. It was banned by some high schools across the country, and as late as 1962, when "The Twist" resurfaced, it was forbidden in Catholic schools in New York after Bishop Joseph A. Burke declared it "un-Christian." It faced similar censorship when Lou arrived in Syracuse, but Lou was ahead of the beat.

Syracuse, with its pastoral quadrangles and laissez-faire liberal arts curriculum, presented a palpable shift in environment. With twenty thousand students from all walks of life and easy access to alcohol at the Orange, the campus bar, where the drinking age was eighteen, Lou was in paradise. The 1960s were barely underway and Eisenhower's fiscal, cultural, and sartorial austerity trickled down to campus politics. Lou once again represented an affront to the crew cuts, white bucks, and skirts, but Syracuse attracted a thriving liberal arts subculture hostile to the status quo. He reunited with Allan Hyman, who was thrilled to welcome his hometown friend to the frigid campus. "It used to start snowing at the beginning of November, way before Thanksgiving, and we wouldn't see the ground until April," says Hyman. "It was always snowing."

At Syracuse, Lou had the same blank slate that greeted him when he moved to Freeport, only this time, a subversive subset of his peers were more sympathetic to his artistic temperament and distrust of authority. "His crowd was a very different crowd," Hyman recalls. "Lou was hanging out with a group that was on the beatnik side, different than the average fraternity guy." Though there were jocks and conservatives on campus—Greek life dominated the social scene—a bohemian enclave thrived at Syracuse. Yet not everyone was so sympathetic. Lou became an ROTC trainee, wearing a perpetually wrinkled military-issue uniform that didn't win him any points with the commanding officer. His stint was brief; rumors circulated that he was dishonorably discharged for holding a gun to the platoon commander's head.

He found an ally in his eccentric roommate, Lincoln Swados. Swados came from an affluent Jewish family and, like Lou, faced the tacit expectation that he eventually go into the family business, which in his case was law. His father, Robert O. Swados, was a World War II veteran and a prominent attorney in Buffalo who served as general counsel to the National Hockey League, but Lincoln had his sights set on literature. Swados only left the room to attend class, and spent the rest of his time writing an epic novel late into the night. Lou began writing poetry at a manic pace, even scribbling on the sheets, which became a linen palimpsest he could then never wash. Within the first month of living together, they were both completely nocturnal.

In their fervor, rules of decorum went out the window; together, they were on a path to the mutually assured destruction of their dorm room. "You couldn't see him under his bed. He would be under like five hundred pounds of pistachio shells," says Hyman. Rich Sigal noticed the change in Lou when he and a friend came for a campus visit. Sigal arrived in the evening at the appointed time, but no one answered the door, which was left unlocked. They let themselves in and flicked on a light. "The bedroom looked like it had just been robbed. If you went into somebody's drawers, took everything out and threw it to the ceiling, and let it fall down, that's what it looked like. There was stuff on top of stuff. There wasn't a flat surface anywhere," Sigal says. "I'm looking at the bed, and the bed was only partially made and the sheets were gray, not because they were gray sheets, because they'd never seen the inside of the washing machine. And there's a hand sticking out." It was Lou, comatose after a long night of writing. "He said he stays up all night and goes to bed in the wee hours of the morning and sleeps all day," Sigal recalls. "That was his normal routine. How he got a degree is anybody's guess."

Meeting Lou's roommate presented another shock. "Lou says, 'Swados.' Then he says it louder. Finally Lou says, 'Swados! Stop playing those goddamn drums!'" Sigal says. Yet there were no drums to be heard. "And all of a sudden this figure materialized in the center of the room. When you met Swados, it was not like you just shook his hand."

Lou began his campus conquest by starting a show on WAER, the college radio station. WAER mostly split its airtime between the American songbook and the classical canon, but Lou had designs to change that tradition. He approached the station manager, Katharine Barr, a Zeta Tau Alpha sorority girl, who agreed to give him an evening slot, unaware of what she was signing up for. Lou's show, *Excursions on a Wobbly Rail*, took its name from "Excursion on a Wobbly Rail," a cacophonous track from iconoclastic jazz pianist Cecil Taylor's 1959 release *Looking Ahead!* Lou's eclectic DJ style consisted of excursions through the sonic worlds of Archie Shepp and Ornette Coleman, the doo-wop of his youth, and whatever din he could dig up in the station library.

Hyman used to make prank phone calls to the station when Lou was on the air. "I used to play stunts on him all the time," Hyman says. "I would affect a different voice, and I would call up and I would tell him that I wanted to hear some obscure jazz album. He would say, 'I'm not playing that *dreck*. It's awful, disgusting, and I will not play him.' And I said, 'I'll tell you what. If you don't play him, I'm going to wait for you outside the station, and I'm going to kill you.' We would have these fights on the air, and he'd be yelling and screaming. He would say, 'I'm gonna kill you first, you stupid!' He wouldn't say *bastard* or anything, because you couldn't on the air." It was the last time in his life Lou would censor himself, but apparently it was not enough.

Due to faculty and administration complaints, including one alleged report that Lou belched during a public service announcement for muscular dystrophy, *Excursions on a Wobbly Rail* was canceled. Yet that didn't stop him from causing a stir on campus. Hyman suggested that Lou rush Sigma Alpha Mu—Sammy—the predominantly Jewish fraternity he had joined the previous year. Sammy was composed of Jews and other students who didn't cohere with the white-bread image of traditional Greek life; the frat also had several African American members of the Syracuse football team.

"The movie *Animal House* is very similar to my fraternity, but certainly Lou didn't want any part of that at all," Hyman says. "Lou said, 'What are you crazy? Why would I want to do that? I think they're a group of assholes,'" Hyman says. Nevertheless, Lou agreed to attend one rush event. He arrived at the fraternity house in a stained shirt, ill-fitting suit, and tie with one too many knots. "He looked like somebody who lived on the Bowery in Manhattan—like a homeless person," says Hyman. "When I saw him, I was horrified. I knew he did it just to be provocative. So he walks into the fraternity, and all conversation stops. They didn't view him as Lou Reed the rock star, they looked at him like, 'Who is this bum that just walked in?'" Hyman tried to pass it off as a joke, but the rush committee didn't find it amusing. One member approached Lou and said, "'If you decide that you want to be a member of this fraternity, I'm going to blackball you. There's no way you're getting into this house. I just want you to know that,'" Hyman recalls. "So Lou says, 'Why would I want to join this fraternity? You are a member of this fraternity, and you are a fucking asshole.'" When the guy tried to have Lou ejected, Lou refused to leave. "He systematically insulted everyone else in the room. It was the single most embarrassing moment of my time at Syracuse," Hyman says.

Hyman later returned the favor on spring break when he and Lou got stopped in the middle of the night for speeding on their way back to Syracuse from Freeport in Hyman's new Jaguar sedan. The officer took them to the house of a local justice of the peace. "He wakes up this justice of the peace, and she comes down in her bathrobe. The cop says, 'Emma, we've got a couple of wiseass college kids here from Syracuse,'" Hyman says. "She said, 'Just a minute,' then she changes out of her pajamas and into a bathrobe and says, 'Court's in session.'" The officer looked at them with the stone-cold sobriety of a moonless night in Utica. "'How do you plead?' I said, 'Not guilty.' The justice of the peace says, 'OK, not guilty. You have to put up $500 bail,'" recalls Hyman. "Now $500 in those days was like $10,000." Hyman made a deal with the justice of the peace—he would return to Syracuse and collect the money from his fraternity brothers, and leave Lou in the house as collateral. "Lou said, 'You can't leave me here!'" Hyman says. "I said, 'Then both of us are going to stay in jail for two months.'" Hyman sped off, and Lou watched the sun come up with the justice of the peace. After an interminable wait, Hyman finally arrived to bail him out. "I went back and said, 'I was thinking of leaving you here, by the way,'" Hyman recalls.

It was the only time Lou got caught but not the only time he broke the law. Unlike in Freeport, where marijuana was in short supply, Syracuse provided easy access. In the early 1960s, the city supported a bustling manufacturing sector that included General Electric's Electronics Park, the headquarters of Smith Premier, makers of the Smith Corona typewriter, and Carrier, the world's largest air-conditioning company; this in turn created a working-class population that established a thriving black market. Lou could descend into the bowels of Syracuse—the campus abutted a less affluent neighborhood that many considered dangerous—and buy pot on almost any corner. It was a smoking habit Hyman found shocking at the time. "We thought people who smoked pot were drug addicts. Nobody was doing it," Hyman says. "People in jazz and the music world were doing it, and at the time that was very avant-garde."

Lou and Hyman also made a go at solicitation one night. "He calls me and says, 'I have a guy who can get us laid.' I said, 'Really? Are these hookers?' He said, 'Yeah. We have to go meet this guy,'" Hyman says. "We're waiting, and he finally does show up, and he says, 'It's going to be twenty dollars. Lou paid him, and the guy never comes back," Hyman says. Getting laid was not as easy as scoring dope. So Lou ultimately turned to the most powerful aphrodisiac he knew: he formed a band.

He recruited Hyman as the drummer, and Hyman recruited bassist Richard Mishkin, guitarist Stephen Windheim, and saxophonist Bobby Newman from his fraternity. They called themselves LA and the Eldorados, taking Lou and Allan's first initials and cribbing the Eldorados from the eponymous doo-wop group, whose 1955 hit "At My Front Door" rose to the top of the charts. Donald Schupak, another fraternity brother of Hyman's, served as the band's first manager, and began booking frat parties on campus. Sometimes, Lou would play with Steve McCord, in addition to occasional collaborations with fellow Syracuse students Felix Cavaliere, who would go on to form the Young Rascals, Garland Jeffreys, and singer-songwriter Nelson Slater. Before long, LA and the Eldorados began playing in nearby campuses in Upstate New York, including Colgate, Hamilton, and Cornell.

"I never thought it would amount to anything, but Lou always knew it would at some point," says Hyman. They mostly played covers, including

"Night Time Is the Right Time," "Twist and Shout," as well as songs by the Marvelettes and Jimmy Reed, whose 1961 single "Bright Lights, Big City" was a band favorite. Eventually, they included the Beatles and Bob Dylan on their set list. In the tradition of the Jades, LA and the Eldorados wore glitzy costumes that Lou hated. "We wore black vests with gold lamé, usually with black jeans and white shirts underneath. That was our thing," says Mishkin. The official band vehicle was Mishkin's 1957 Chrysler New Yorker, complete with menacing fins, push-button transmission, and a custom white and red paint job with the band's name emblazoned on the back and flames on the hood.

It was Lou's own songs that got them in trouble. "The stuff that Lou was writing at the time was not well received," Hyman says. "It was not music that was heard on the radio." Lou always insisted on playing "The Fuck Around Blues," an inflammatory shuffle that got them kicked off the stage. "People were just not ready for Lou," Hyman says. "'The Fuck Around Blues' did not appeal to a lot of the sorority girls who were then attending those parties."

Lou wasn't out to please the clients, or anyone else. He would frequently show up to band engagements late or not at all. "He'd be totally and completely willing to blow off a band job because he just didn't feel like playing, or he would do a Miles Davis and just turn his back to the audience," says Hyman. "You'd have to go down to his room and drag him out, which I did on numerous occasions." In order to stay on the fraternity circuit, they would change their name to get rehired, sometimes going by Pacha and the Prophets.

For their highest-paying gig, LA and the Eldorados were booked to play Friday and Saturday night for homecoming weekend at St. Lawrence University, 130 miles north of Syracuse. The headline event was on a boat, and Lou suddenly decided he was feeling seasick. "He said, 'I'm not going to play on a boat. What are you, crazy? I'll get electrocuted,'" says Mishkin. "I said, 'Lou, we don't have a choice. They're paying us more than we have ever been paid.' So he takes his hand, makes a fist, then he bashes it through a glass door. This is Friday night, and he really cut himself. And he said, 'Now I can't play,'" says Mishkin. They rushed him to the hospital, where he got stitches; Mishkin insisted that he play the show, with or without the use of his hands. "I said, 'You're gonna sing. You can't play guitar for shit anyways, so get up there and sing,'" says Mishkin.

If Lou wasn't the problem, the elements were. After a show at Colgate in nearby Hamilton, New York, they got waylaid by a blizzard. "It got to the point where we couldn't go any further and we had to stop. Obviously, staying in the car was not an option, because we'd freeze to death or die of carbon monoxide poisoning, so we got out and we walked," says Mishkin. "We could see a light in the haze, and we walked to this hotel. There was a bar downstairs and there were some old townie types." Manager Donald Schupak began schmoozing with the locals. "Donny tended to exaggerate, and he told a story about when he was in the war. Now this is the '60s, and we're twenty or twenty-one, and he's talking about it as if he was in World War II." Schupak regaled them with war stories until closing time, then asked if they could crash in a spare room. "They said the hotel was booked, but we could go over to the courthouse and sleep in the jail," Mishkin recalls. So that's where they slept.

When Lou returned for his sophomore year, within a week, he met Shelley Albin. Shelley was a freshman fine arts student from a Chicago suburb, and Lou was instantly drawn to her. "We met my freshman year at Syracuse, about a week after I got there, through another person he knew that gave him a ride," she says. Shelley was cruising down Marshall Street, the main drag in Syracuse, riding in the passenger seat, when the driver recognized Lou and decided to offer him a ride to his dorm. Lou and Shelley's chemistry was electric. Shelley had migrated east to escape her staid Jewish, Midwestern upbringing and break some rules; Lou was already the consummate rule-breaker. By the time Lou got dropped off, they both knew that it would not be their last ride. An hour later, he called Shelley in her dorm and awkwardly asked her out.

Lou had never had a steady girlfriend, but he feigned experience as best he could. Yet Shelley was not convinced; it was ultimately Lou's sensitive core, sense of humor, and creativity that won her over. "Somebody said that it was their impression that he was very interested in girls and kind of a lady-killer in high school. That was not my impression at all," Shelley says. "He was cute."

The two became inseparable. Shelley was Lou's first muse, a role she was never comfortable with, but he also inspired her art in turn. They would play basketball together, and Lou began serenading her with his guitar, harmonica slung around his neck in the style of the folk revival. Lou and Shelley even wore each other's clothes. Police and campus security kept a constant vigil at the girls' dorms—university housing was never coed—mostly to discourage reprobates like Lou from having midnight assignations with girls like Shelley. "I had a 9:00 curfew in a big dorm," she says. At the forbiddingly named Mount Olympus, men were not allowed past the lobby; any brazen attempt at trespassing would be met with the wrath of Zeus. Yet Lou could never resist the temptation of his spunky Aphrodite.

"If you wanted to go away for the weekend, you had to have a note from your parents, and the person you were visiting had to be a relative. If you wanted to sneak in and out, you had to have somebody who could open the door without the alarms going off." So the couple learned to be stealthy until the following year, planning trysts in friends' dorms, cars, even entwining themselves in bushes; the risk of not getting caught added to the thrill of the assignation. "They had police all around—police in the lobby, police outside, and they would get you. I was suspended for a messy room." Had they suspected what her association with the self-professed bisexual rocker entailed, she might have been expelled. The transgression only made it more fun.

"When I knew him at the very beginning, he was terrific and warm. That's not the Lou Reed people know or think of, but that's the Lou Reed that I knew then," she says. "He was incredibly creative and really interesting and a romantic at heart, a total romantic in the sense that Byron was a romantic." For Lou, Shelley was like a prism, an effect Lou later wrote about in "I'll Be Your Mirror."

It was Lou's first great love. "People say 'I'll Be Your Mirror' was for Nico, but that's my conversation with him," Shelley says, recalling the moments that inspired the song. Yet Shelley had an inkling early on that their blissful romance could not last. "I was a Midwesterner, very naive, who grew up with not abuse, but really an authoritarian parent. You did what you were told—shut up, no opinion—so I was an easy mark," she says. "Anybody more uppity wouldn't have stood for it for a minute, and it is basically very difficult to offend me, and very, very difficult to surprise me with something." When Lou wasn't attempting to provoke Shelley past her aggravation threshold, he was prone to depressive funks. "I think he really did thrive on being down. I think that's when he did his best work," she says. "And if he wasn't unhappy or depressed—I wouldn't say depressed—if he wasn't unhappy or having some kind of terrors, he would do whatever he had to, to be unhappy." She also realized that Lou had a knack for creating a mystifying persona. "It's very Lou-like to come up with something that can't be proved. It builds his persona, which he was always doing, and I don't say that meanly," she says. "He was very good at it. He was very clever, but I don't see him as such a slick guy." Despite these signs, they were in love.

After their first year together, Lou and Shelley visited each other's families. Lou got to introduce his parents to the nice Jewish girl they had always hoped for, so to start out, Shelley's arrival in Freeport had a mollifying effect on the tense family dynamic. "His father was extremely nice to me. Warm, kind of a twinkly-eyed, friendly, outgoing guy," Shelley recalls. "His mother, the same—very warm. They were very clearly of the era and the time." Shelley had heard Lou demonize his parents, but that was not quite her experience. "They were both quite mystified by Lou, and Lou really played the spoiled Jewish prince," she says. "If you don't get all the attention, you do something outrageous till you're going to get it, and if you could terrorize them so they're afraid, even better." Their house in Freeport was surprisingly mundane, as opposed to the Eugene O'Neill drama she expected. "Lou was really a totally normal middle-class kid—totally normal middle-class house. Somebody said, 'What did his bedroom look like?' Well, like any other bedroom. I think it had knotty pine," she recalls. "There was nothing unusual that would say, 'Here's a dark, convoluted person that's going to write "Heroin."'"

While Lou's family warmed to Shelley, he seemed to want to sabotage the introduction. "When I saw him at home with his parents, he was trying to be unpredictable, make them nervous," she says. "But his father increased his allowance, because he said, 'Oh, you can't have a girlfriend like that and not have a better allowance,' which of course, Lou never shared because he was a total tightwad." Lou tried to convince Shelley that his father was a tyrant, but she just saw a carbon copy of Lou. "I can understand how someone would get frustrated with Lou and yell at him, if you were his father. And he would try to be aggravating and effeminate in front of his father," Shelley says. "He looked exactly like Lou, and Lou looked exactly like him, and was built kind of the same. So he wasn't some big, strapping marine sergeant type of a father." Nevertheless, with Shelley acting as a buffer, the Freeport visit provided the most effective diplomatic détente Lou's family had experienced in years.

Lou's visit to Chicago was not as auspicious. He instantly antagonized Shelley's father. It didn't help that Lou did not make any effort to look like a presentable prospect for his daughter. "When he came to visit me between my freshman and sophomore year, his hair was just barely over the top of his collar. People thought that was horrible, really far out. You have to put yourself that far back. It was a different era," Shelley says. Shelley's father was a dyed-in-the-wool liberal, and Lou decided to talk politics. "He offended my father by pretending to be sympathetic to Bill Buckley and conservative, and he tried to portray my father as being evil and domineering, which my father was not," Shelley recalls. By the end of the weekend, Lou was asked to leave; it was clear that Shelley's family never wanted to see him again, and that close family ties and her relationship with Lou were mutually exclusive.

When they arrived back on campus that fall, with the civil rights movement gaining ground and the folk revival in full swing, Lou began antagonizing the local authorities. "The cops were after him because he annoyed them for who knows what reason, and he would emphasize his pseudo-gay or bisexual behavior near them just to piss them off," Shelley says. "They would like to have arrested him or beaten him up a little bit, because they were like Chicago cops. They were itching to get at him, but they had no real reason. They didn't like the intellectuals on the campus." The school's demographics didn't help his cause, either. "They thought they were going to show these smart-alecky Long Island, New York, Jews. So Lou would poke that around as much as he possibly could."

Tempting fate, Lou began dealing marijuana on campus, mostly to fraternity brothers, and Shelley would sometimes help. She spent all her time cocooned at Lou's apartment, with a German shepherd–dachshund mix they named Seymoure. Over time, they developed a routine. Lou would go down the hill from the university, listen to the gospel music in the Baptist church, occasionally stop at an R&B club called the 800, and when his hair got too long, visit a black barber shop that knew how to handle his unruly curls. He would then hit the bar, where he could score or sell his product. Sometimes Shelley would come along; in that case, they would add a stop at the nearby Jewish restaurant. "We would eat franks and beans and mushroom barley soup," she says. "He would never pay, even with his increased allowance." What they couldn't score in Syracuse, they would get from trips to Manhattan. Otherwise, they would send away for pot by mail. "It was like five dollars for a whole grocery bag," she says.

Storing the drugs was tricky business. "He didn't keep it in his place. He kept it in my dorm, where I never was," she says. "So here's my loving boyfriend, and he would say, 'Go deliver a bag to so-and-so.'"

Lou got his straitlaced friend James Gorney involved in the operation. One autumn night, Lou unexpectedly knocked on his door with a strange request. "He said, 'I have a very big favor to ask you. Do you have a storage locker in this building?' I said, 'I do.' He said, 'If I gave you something to store for me, would you be willing to store it?' And I said, 'Yeah.' But he said, 'I'll need to bring it over immediately,'" Gorney recalls. Ten minutes later, Lou returned with a medium-size suitcase. "'I say, 'What's in the suitcase?' And he said, 'Well, I guess you can open it up. I trust you.' I opened it up, and I would say there were about two kilos of marijuana in it," Gorney says. Never having smoked, Gorney was intrigued. "He said, 'If you would keep this for me for an indefinite amount of time, you're free to partake of the contents.' So that was not entirely a good thing for me, because I was supposed to be preparing my master's thesis that semester, and I really wound up spending most of that semester in a haze," Gorney says.

By that winter, Shelley's nerves were shot from the mind games Lou had increasingly been playing. One night after a show with LA and the Eldorados, Lou began taunting Shelley, saying he was going to go and cheat on her. She snapped, walking off into the snow with Lincoln in tow, who tried in vain to console her. "When I left Lou early on in college, I knew I never wanted to be living with or married to or raising kids with a rock star or a famous person who used you all the time," she says. "I didn't want to constantly be having one kind of aggravation or another. It's just too much work for what you get." It was a bitter breakup on both sides, but the romantic she had met the first week of freshman year was nowhere to be found. "He's got his gentle side, and he's totally creative and he can be a lot of fun, but he was also pretty nasty for quite a while, and he used people and treated people really terribly, and I approved a lot of that and I added," she says. "He never understood how I could possibly leave him, and then, how could I stay away?" Lou thought the relationship could withstand high levels of toxicity, but Shelley had to extricate herself, even if it required the nuclear option. "I don't know what made me have the brains to get out of it," she says. "I think it was strictly instinct."

Lou channeled his heartbreak into the arts. He had a brief brush with theater, directing an English-language translation of Spanish surrealist Fernando Arrabal's *El Cementerio de Automóviles* (*The Car Cemetery*), a 1958 avant-garde adaptation of the crucifixion story centering on a banned jazz musician. While Swados played Sinatra on loop and toiled away at an epic novel, he and Lou began devising plans for an underground campus literary magazine. In the spring of 1962, they launched the *Lonely Woman Quarterly*, a campus publication spearheaded by five Syracuse sophomores: Lou, billed as "Luis" Reed, Swados, Joseph McDonald, Karl Stoecker, and Jim Tucker. Tucker lived in a dorm upstairs from Lou, and introduced him to one of his high school friends, Sterling Morrison, who occasionally came to Syracuse to visit. Tucker's younger sister, Maureen, was a seventeen-year-old high school senior about to graduate from Levittown Memorial High School.

In the May 11, 1962, issue of the *Syracuse Daily Orange*, the *LWQ* was officially announced: "Five authors in search of a campus publication in which to express creative writing turned out their own mimeographed magazine this week," the article read. In opposition to the *Syracuse 10*, the mainstream literary magazine that "seemed like the *Saturday Evening Post*," according to Swados, the *Lonely Woman Quarterly* adopted a more freewheeling editorial style. Swados went on to claim that the title derived from supposed beat poet "Henry Strindler," citing the line "The Lonely Woman has a big nose and satin sheets," though the title more likely derives from Ornette Coleman's *The Shape of Jazz to Come*, which opens with the plaintive "Lonely Woman," one of Lou's favorite songs.

The nineteen-page loose-leaf collection consisted of madcap short stories, poetry, and psychedelic illustrations; Stoecker drew the cover image of the titular lonely woman. The *LWQ* was printed on a mimeograph that belonged to Gus Joseph of the Savoy restaurant, which used the machine to print menus, and sold for twenty-five cents an issue. The five editors would regularly congregate at the Savoy, a diner where the avuncular owner welcomed the campus intelligentsia. "The Savoy was a restaurant where we all hung out most of the day," Shelley recalls. "It looked like a regular place with booths and tables, but everybody treated it like a living room. We'd play guitars in there and sit in the booth and make out, take a nap, do your work, have coffee."

Swados advised students interested in sending material for consideration to hand-deliver it. "Just drop by the Savoy and look for those customers who look literate," he told the *Daily Orange*. Swados stipulated that the *Lonely Woman Quarterly* was optimistically billed as a quarterly but would "not appear regularly," claiming that "We have no deadlines to meet and no board to answer to." As for material, Swados was clear. "The magazine doesn't contain great literature," Swados said, "but it has material in it that couldn't be printed elsewhere on campus." Inspired by Henry Miller's *Tropic of Cancer*, the *LWQ* was a fiery riposte against the Young Americans for Freedom, a conservative campus group.

Lou wrote the first entry in the *LWQ*: "He'd always found the idea of copulation distasteful, especially when applied to his own origins. His mother would never do that. No. No, she wouldn't," Lou wrote. Another untitled short story by Lou narrates a morning-after tale of debauchery in Greenwich Village, waking up next to "Isabell," whose "painted lips parted with a now decadent look of sensuousness, lips that had seen things, now parted and twitching, giving forth early morning breath." Lou depicts a day in Greenwich Village at the San Remo Cafe, "a square box-like structure on the tail end of MacDougal Street, complete with big green signs and old barber shop quartet type lights." Located at 93 MacDougal, the iconic literary hub was featured prominently in Kerouac's *The Subterraneans*, thinly veiled as the Black Mask, where the legendary Beat once suffered a drunken beating. The "Remo" was a longtime front for the mob that had been overrun by artists and intellectuals. Allen Ginsberg met Dylan Thomas there, and Warhol began gathering a critical mass before renting out the Factory; Lou had also wandered in on occasion.

Lou's short story contains a set of guidelines adapted from the "Hebraic Vision," Lou's collegial version of the Ten Commandments—"How can you deviate if there's no norm and that's half the fun," "be Victorian dear friend and attack the boxlike structure," "metamorphisize in extenuating circumstances," "feel the joy of guilt," "break with the tintinabulary logic of your mind," "enter the chaos," "be strong and truthful without pretensions," "disbelieve," "I'm the worst of the worst, the phoniest of the phony, the weakest of the weak, the strongest of the strong, setting up new settings for the old, new mores for the sacrosanct." He had come a long way since Hebrew school.

The second issue of the *LWQ*, printed on May 23, 1962, featured two contributions from Lou: "Mr. Lockwood's Pool," a macabre fantasy and sexual dalliance with a centaur written in the style of Charlotte Brontë, and "Michael Kogan—Syracuse's Miss Blanding," a withering critique of the head of the Young Americans for Freedom. Lou's devastating lampoon characterized its subject as "reptillian," having "recently asserted his obese shape to the extent of slithering on all fours into the waiting arms of the conservitive bastillion," with an "American flag placed neatly up his rectum." Spelling was never Lou's forte, but his acerbic wit was sharp.

"That got it banned," Stoecker recalls of Lou's op-ed. "They told us we couldn't sell it on school property."

Swados's two contributions to the second issue were cryptic cries for help. A poem titled "The Nightingale" opens with the narrator "Lost in the land of nighttime / I have crashed into trees / the bark has scratched my skin," and a short piece of fiction titled "Well Goodbye Syracuse." With his mental state deteriorating and the administration cracking down, the *LWQ* sputtered to a halt after its second issue at the end of the academic year. Swados had struggled to register for classes, and if he attended class at all, he had become too fixated on writing his Great American Novel to complete the coursework. Professors competed with the Greek chorus of voices in Lincoln's head that had been steadily rising from a murmur as he teetered precariously between brilliance and madness.

"Lincoln was a terrific guy. Very bright, very sharp, but I don't think any of us knew how he was at the time," Shelley says. "Lou copied a lot of his shtick, although they were both genuinely similar. They were both kind of off-kilter in the same way, and Lou was very protective of him." Yet Lou couldn't protect Swados from himself. Lincoln was put on academic probation, and his family was notified repeatedly until they decided the situation demanded a visit.

Lincoln's family arrived on campus to discover a pizza box stuck to the ceiling, his sister Elizabeth later recalled in the *New York Times*. "Lincoln looked pasty and thin. He confided to me that he was writing a novel and had time for nothing else," she wrote. "Several months later, my father received an almost book-length letter from my brother describing himself as in a helplessly disoriented state. He was unable to go to classes, unable to leave his room. The voices in his head were directing him to do too many different things. My father showed the letter to several psychiatrists, who recommended that Lincoln be hospitalized immediately." Robert Swados decided that Lincoln would take an indefinite leave of absence. Psychiatrists were unanimous in their diagnosis—schizophrenia. Seeing no other recourse, he committed his son to a mental institution. Lou was heartbroken. Sadly, this was the beginning of the end for Swados, but not the last Lou would see of him; soon they would cross paths in an underground farther south.

When Lou arrived for his junior year in the fall of 1962, he found a new face on campus: the short story writer and poet Delmore Schwartz. By the age of twenty-one, Schwartz had been hailed as the brightest literary light of his generation, the best among a crop of young writers including Saul Bellow, Karl Shapiro, and Randall Jarrell. Bellow's *Humboldt's Gift* is a thinly veiled roman à clef for Schwartz, whom he dubbed "the Mozart of conversation." When *In Dreams Begin Responsibilities*, Schwartz's first collection of short stories, was published in 1938, poet and literary critic Allen Tate praised the work as "the first real innovation that we've had since Eliot and Pound." In 1959, Schwartz won the Bollingen Prize for the poetry collection *Summer Knowledge*, but unlike his now more famous peers, Schwartz had consigned himself to relative obscurity, a fallen prince whose literary ambitions were never fully realized due to lifelong struggles with undiagnosed mental illness and the battery of substances he used to self-medicate.

By the time he arrived at Syracuse, a forty-nine-year-old shell of his former self with the liver of a much older man, prone to spells of delirium, his youthful magnetism and incandescence were all but extinguished. In 1957 Schwartz's estranged wife, the novelist Elizabeth Pollet, had become alarmed by his increasingly psychotic behavior—she compared their marriage to "living on the side of a volcano"—and wrote him a letter insisting that he get psychiatric help. Pollet mentioned the critic Hilton Kramer in passing, and Schwartz, paranoid as he was, assumed they were having an affair. Schwartz began stalking Kramer until he showed up at Kramer's residence at the Chelsea Hotel brandishing a gun. Kramer had Schwartz committed to Bellevue, where he was strapped in a straitjacket and diagnosed with "acute brain syndrome." He was released after friends amassed the necessary funds for him to enter rehab at Payne Whitney. Schwartz responded to the outpouring of support by threatening to file a baseless and psychotic lawsuit against Kramer, Pollet, Saul Bellow, and William Styron.

Schwartz drifted from one cold-water flat to the next as his psychosis deepened. Nevertheless, his reputation preceded his paranoia, and Schwartz was invited to the 1960 Kennedy inauguration, though he moved so frequently that the invitation never reached him. He also attended the infamous party in November of that year where Norman Mailer stabbed his wife Adele with a penknife; Mailer was committed to Bellevue. Having descended headlong into regressive narcissism, Schwartz interpreted the near-fatal stabbing incident as somehow intended to thwart him. Soon thereafter, Schwartz's psychotic episodes worsened, and one night, he smashed all the windows in his Greenwich Village apartment. He landed in Bellevue again, where he became convinced that the doctors were trying to kill him; he would have rather died than go back to life in a straitjacket.

In the aftermath of this debacle, he parlayed what remained of his reputation into a teaching post as Syracuse. Just as Lou had gravitated to Swados, he found an instant mentor in Schwartz, who quickly became convinced that Lou could fulfill the literary promise that had once eluded him. In Schwartz's first semester, he taught a course nominally focused on Milton, though in reality devoted to the work of T. S. Eliot, whose landmark poems "The Waste Land" and "The Love Song of J. Alfred Prufrock" served as a springboard into a broader examination of the poet's oeuvre. Lou, who already considered himself the prototypical Prufrock—a pair of ragged claws and an amplifier—albeit less timid and perhaps more of a nonconformist, was mesmerized.

When Schwartz entered the class, his postnasal drip, amphetamine-induced tremors, and frequent hallucinatory delusions would suddenly fade away. The classroom was the only place where there were glimmers of the brilliant poet he once was. "Schwartz would wear a jacket and tie, but it always looked as if he had literally been sleeping in it for a week," says James Gorney, who took the class with Lou. But outside of class was a different story. "Schwartz was without any question bipolar," says Gorney, who later became a clinical psychologist. "Rumpled, snot on the sleeves, nose running incessantly. He always looked as if he were coming in off an all-nighter; mismatched socks and shoes often. He was in pretty rugged shape. He was a very damaged, wounded person, and clearly involved with all kinds of substances, but there was a nobility about him that still shone through."

Schwartz took frequent naps in the graduate student lounge, and sometimes harassed the administrative staff, but he was electric in class. Rather than lecturing, he read poems aloud from his own heavily annotated editions. "When he would start to read a T. S. Eliot poem, there would be a transformation," Gorney recalls. "It wasn't this broken-down guy who almost looked like a bum anymore." Lou seized on Schwartz's captivating classroom performances; he captured the immediacy and vivacity of the moment that Lou strove for in his music. "I had the sense at the time that Lou was looking toward Schwartz almost as a father, maybe the father he wished he had," Gorney says.

As inspiring as he could be to Lou, a false move could result in instant poetic justice. Early on in the semester, another student, Murray Levith, questioned Schwartz's perspective on modern poetry. "The class was a mixed one, with both undergraduates and graduate students, and Schwartz asked me (scowling) if I were an undergraduate," Levith, who was a graduate student at the time, recalled. "'I hope you're not a teaching assistant,' he said. I swallowed hard and affirmed that I was. 'Pity your students.'" Schwartz's withering critique was enhanced by the fact that he smoked in class. "Schwartz smoked cigarettes like no one I have ever seen. He positively drank the smoke, sucking on the cigarette like a straw," wrote Levith. Levith recalled that he would deliberately lean his umbrella against the doorknob and laugh maniacally when late students interrupted the class. Yet Schwartz's disciplinary severity was tempered by whimsical insights: he alleged that "the Metropolitan Life Insurance Company did an actuarial study and discovered that yes, 'April is the cruellest month,'" and compared Milton's paradox of free will in a divine universe to the National Safety Council's accurate prediction of holiday weekend death statistics. Nevertheless, Levith is unsparing in his criticism of Schwartz as a professor: "He was awful." But Lou believed in him.

Much of Lou's education with Schwartz took place outside the classroom. Lou, Gorney, and Schwartz began continuing their discussions over rounds of drinks at the Orange on Marshall Street, where Schwartz would regale them with conspiracy theories about the Rockefellers, how President Roosevelt had arranged for the safe extraction of Freud at the suggestion of his psychoanalyst, and the dirty secrets of major poets. Schwartz's paranoia was legendary. He had an ongoing vendetta against Elizabeth Allen, the English Department secretary, after he became convinced that she was sneaking into his apartment and leaving pornography all over the bed; she kept a hammer behind the desk in case Schwartz ever acted on his physical threats. Lou didn't care, though. "Lou was like a disciple sitting at his feet," Gorney says. "He would look at Schwartz with a worshipful look in his eye. He was riveted on Schwartz." Schwartz, in turn, was riveted by Lou. Philip Booth, another poet-turned-professor, and Robert Durr, a young scholar of metaphysical poet Henry Vaughan with an abiding interest in Thoreau and the psychedelic experience, had also become convinced of Lou's talent for creative writing, but Schwartz was his greatest champion.

"He was crazy about Lou," Shelley says of Schwartz. Lou and Shelley had periodically resumed contact, and Schwartz was adamant that she steer

Lou away from music, where he saw little artistic merit, especially in rock lyrics, and push him toward an MFA. "I was supposed to devote my life to making sure that Lou became a writer and not a rocker," Shelley says. "That was a constant discussion. But Delmore was already in his own world." Of the after-hours gatherings at the Orange, she was not as impressed. "I wasn't drinking, so I'm the stone-cold sober one, and he wasn't sounding quite so wonderful all the time," she says. "Somebody would eventually have to make sure that he got back home and pour him into bed."

For Lou, Schwartz's excesses made him all the more brilliant. On one occasion, Schwartz, Lou, and Gorney rallied around the Beatles' "I Want to Hold Your Hand," which had just arrived on the jukebox of the Orange with the British Invasion. Despite Schwartz's disdain for rock music, he liked the Beatles. "It was so catchy that Schwartz went up to the jukebox, put in a bunch of change so the song would play about five times in a row, and the three of us just started singing it along to the record together," Gorney says. "It was joyous and amazing and wonderful, and something you never forget for the rest of your life."

One night at the Orange, Schwartz said something that would stick with Lou for the rest of his life: "I'm gonna be leaving for a world far better than this soon, but I want you to know that if you ever sell out and go work for Madison Avenue or write junk, I will haunt you."

The following semester, Schwartz taught a course on James Joyce's *Ulysses*. Schwartz had a knack for illuminating even the most difficult passages. "Schwartz would say, 'Well, if you read through a passage and you don't understand it, the next thing you do is you read it aloud, because you can often get the meaning from the music when you hear it, and if you still can't understand it, have three or four drinks, and then read it aloud, and then you'll really understand it, because most of *Ulysses* was written while Joyce was in one stage or another of intoxication,'" Gorney says. Toward the end of the semester, Schwartz brought in his tattered copy of *Finnegan's Wake*, Joyce's dense, nearly incomprehensible final novel, which he had been puzzling over for decades, a task well suited to Schwartz's paranoia. "The bindings had come loose. It was held together with string. As he unwrapped it, on every page, in several different colors of ink, there were no margins left," Gorney says. "He had been poring over this for twenty or thirty years, trying to decipher it. And he spent some time reading sections, and he had deciphered it."

Lou resuscitated the *Lonely Woman Quarterly* one last time. Printed in April 1963, the final issue was distributed off campus that May at the nearby Syracuse Book Center. This issue signaled a maturation of Lou's artistic voice. It was also the first time the *LWQ* credited him as "Lou Reed." Lou's story, "And What, Little Boy, Will You Trade for Your Horse?" imagines Lou or his likeness, David, an angst-ridden Byronic hero, trading the hallowed halls of academia for the grittiness of Manhattan, a self-imposed exodus from the bourgeois pedigree he has inherited. In the story, David encounters subway prophets, Times Square prostitutes, a Margaret Keane exhibit, illicit pornography vendors, and a middle-aged barfly who ultimately sexually assaults him. Lou described the volume as the debut of his "vociferous underground" in the introduction to the final issue. Yet there was something unsatisfying about the written word, which was not as immediate as the guitar and the amplifier. It began to dawn on him that he could combine his two passions.

Lou reached out to stalwart producer Bob Shad. Now more confident in his singing voice, he trekked to the city with new material, "Your Love" and "Merry Go Round," both ostensibly inspired by his rocky romance with Shelley. "Merry Go Round" was punctuated by female vocal backgrounds, surf rock guitar fills, and an earthy Rhodes solo:

> You said that we would never part,
> but baby went and broke my heart
> You wound me up and then you put me down

"Your Love" featured a honking tenor saxophone solo that paralleled Lou's guttural vocals:

> I never thought I was a real whole man till your love
> I used to run around and get as catch can till your love
> well now, don't you know you set my soul on fire

Yet Shad never released the singles. Lou realized that he had passed the age of 1950s teen idolatry; his gravelly voice lacked the tenor resonance of Frankie Valli and the Four Seasons, who had charted with their breakout hit "Sherry" earlier that year. Lou would have to go a different way.

In the summer of 1962, artists such as Joan Baez, Dave Van Ronk, and a twenty-one-year-old folk songwriter who had just had his name legally changed to Bob Dylan formed a critical mass around clubs like Gerde's Folk City. By the spring of 1963, Dylan had entered the mainstream with *The Freewheelin' Bob Dylan*, his sophomore release on Columbia. "Blowin' in the Wind," "Masters of War," and "A Hard Rain's A-Gonna Fall" blew everyone away. By October 1963, the fall of Lou's senior year, Dylan had performed at Carnegie Hall. His next show was at Syracuse. On November 3, 1963, at the University Regent Theatre, Lou and Richard Mishkin clambered into the theater to see the kinky-haired, cipher-like persona behind the voice of his generation. He performed the title track off his forthcoming album, "The Times They Are A-Changin'." For Lou, seeing Dylan live was revelatory.

"We really loved Bob Dylan," Mishkin says. "We would sit around in Lou's apartment and learn the chords and fingerings to every one of his songs." Not only did Dylan have a nontraditional singing voice and a quirky style and phrasing to match, he didn't have the typical good looks of a star. He was also a Jew. Despite all this, Dylan became the yardstick that his contemporaries were measured against. He never let the times shape him; he shaped the times. Lou idolized Dylan and aped his rhythm guitar style, but soon jettisoned the harmonica to avoid comparison to the throngs of campus Dylan imitators.

Three weeks after the Dylan concert, on November 22, 1963, John F. Kennedy was assassinated in Dallas. It was a moment of hysteria, disillusionment, and tragedy. Lou was a senior in college, with no clue where he was headed after graduation, having alienated the only person he had ever truly loved, and having lost his closest friend to psychosis. Now the president had been shot. He resorted to heroin.

Lou didn't get introduced to the drug until January of his senior year, though he had already written early versions of the song. "Heroin got him," Shelley says. "I don't know when he really started it, but it was my boyfriend whose little brother came from out of town and brought it in. It was available in the so-called ghetto and available around but not really that common," she says. "He didn't know that I knew Lou, and he came back one day and he said, 'Oh, I met this cool guy and I shot him up with heroin for the first time.' Whether that's true or not, I'm not sure, but I know my boyfriend's little brother was shooting up everybody he could." By June, Lou contracted hepatitis, but he didn't let on to Shelley, who had finally given in and gotten back together with him.

Before long, old problems resurfaced. Shelley didn't want to be a part of Lou's artistic persona or take part in the real-life stories behind his increasingly sordid material. "If you get involved with a writer or an artist, he'll use you as much as possible, and that kind of comes with the package, whether you like it or not," she says. "People would always say, 'Oh, you're his muse,' and I would say, 'Thanks. I'd rather not be.'" Nevertheless, Shelley became the basis for numerous songs over the course of Lou's early career. "It's not a pleasure to be the muse or the so-called muse. And he was very good at tweaking it, and nobody knows what's real or not," she says. "It's not complimentary necessarily. It's way beyond anything we have control over. It's nice when it works out well and you look good, but not when you don't, which is more often than not."

As graduation crept closer, Lou eked out the necessary coursework, got his diploma, and prepared to move home. Some claimed Lou was not allowed to attend his graduation due to infractions with the university, the law, or both, but Shelley recalls that Lou did not attend of his own volition. If the Syracuse police finally thwarted the elusive campus dissident, it was part of the already blurred line between Lou and his growing myth; somehow, it was true even if it didn't happen. In reality, there would be no cap and gown, no "Pomp and Circumstance," but Lou didn't like Elgar anyway; he didn't rock.

Shelley went home after spending a few final strained weeks with Lou and vowed they were done for good. "He used to say, 'I can control heroin, I can control it. I can take a little here and there.' When I went home for the summer, he called me and said, 'By the way, I've got hepatitis.' So I had to go and get a shot," Shelley says. It was the end of their relationship.

So with the vague notion of applying to MFA programs and deeply ambivalent about the next step, Lou cleaned out his cluttered Syracuse apartment and went home to Freeport. He had no girlfriend, no job prospects other than the standing offer to work for his father, and no money. With nothing but a guitar, some amplifiers, a dog named Seymoure, and a raging case of hepatitis C, Lou began plotting his next move; if he didn't get drafted into the Vietnam War, he had a foggy notion of where his future lay. He would become a writer or a rocker, but not an accountant. Whatever he did, Lou would make it in the city on his own terms. He was an adult now, or something like it. Yet there he was, right back where he started, perched on the platform at Freeport station off the Sunrise Highway, waiting for the Long Island Rail Road into Penn Station.

Off in the distance, past Route 495, was his blinking green light. There, nestled in the Lower East Side at 56 Ludlow Street, John Cale, Tony Conrad, and Jack Smith were making combustible art. Only thirty miles away, out on Long Island, Lou lay in bed, jaundiced, with no appetite, listening to the radio. He couldn't resist the allure of New York—the scene at Gerde's or the Vanguard, the dive bars, the shooting galleries in the Meatpacking District, and the artistic circle gathering around an idiosyncratic upstart named Andy Warhol. But he couldn't just move out of his parents' house and dream his way into the city. Lou needed a plan, and he needed to know someone.

# 6

On July 2, 1964, weeks after Lou returned from Syracuse, Lyndon Johnson signed the Civil Rights Act into law, legally banning the institutional discrimination of Jim Crow. It was the year of *Mary Poppins* and *My Fair Lady*, but also the biting satire of *Dr. Strangelove*; Kenneth Anger was finally gaining critical acceptance for his avant-garde film *Scorpio Rising* and Andy Warhol was shooting his first screen tests at the Factory, as well as a little film called *Blow Job*.

As the country began to shed its bigoted past and remove the cultural flak jackets of the baby boom generation, the US Supreme Court began a glacial drift to the left. The Warren Commission concluded its investigation into the Kennedy assassination, while the court reconsidered its obscenity ruling on Henry Miller's *Tropic of Cancer*, finally allowing the sordid novel to circulate thirty years after its 1934 initial publication in France. The same publisher, Grove Press, published *Last Exit to Brooklyn*, the debut novel of Hubert Selby Jr. The titular outer-borough road sign, nonlinear narrative, and unvarnished depiction of illicit sex and drug use captivated Lou, an escape from the dreary postgrad return to the suburbs. More than anything else out there, the arrival of Selby on the literary scene inspired Lou to appropriate the same style of gritty prose for his songwriting.

That summer, Diana Ross and the Supremes logged their first Number 1 hit on the *Billboard* pop charts, "Where Did Our Love Go," beginning a reign of consecutive chart-toppers that included "Stop! In the Name of Love," "Baby Love," and "Come See About Me." After decades of segregation, race riots, then benign neglect, the Motor City rose from the ashes of wrought iron and steel with a softer touch: Motown, the brainchild of impresario Berry Gordy, with his stable of hit-makers in Hitsville—Marvin Gaye, Stevie Wonder, the Temptations. The Beach Boys scored their first

Number 1 hit with "I Get Around," giving rise to a slew of imitators. The latest entry from the British Invasion came with the Animals' "The House of the Rising Sun," along with a new tune from the Beatles, "A Hard Day's Night," the theme to their debut film.

As Lou lay bedridden in Freeport, wasting away in a hepatitis-induced malaise, the radio and the television his only consolation or exposure to the outside world, he absorbed the wide range of styles; there was the horn-infused funk hybrid emanating from Motown, the Beach Boys' barbershop-style close harmony, basic snare hits and electric guitar rising out of the California surf, and the harmonically rich rhythmic pulse of the British Invasion. Lou had already begun writing "Heroin" and had been honing his own underground aesthetic, but he had nowhere to perform; he didn't have a band. Lou was too hard-edged for the quaint folksiness of Gerde's, and there was no Max's Kansas City.

But Lou had more pressing problems; first he had to evade the draft. Military intervention in Vietnam was escalating, and like other recent college graduates, Lou was called to appear before the draft board that summer. If the hepatitis didn't grant him an exemption, homosexuality certainly would; failing that, he could file as a conscientious objector or trigger-happy lunatic, plead insanity, or all of the above. He arrived bleary-eyed and disoriented, the effect of several 750-milligram doses of Placidyl, an anti-insomnia sedative. After ten minutes, Draft Board No. 4 in Freeport had seen enough. "I said I wanted a gun and would shoot anyone or anything in front of me," Lou later recalled. "I was pronounced mentally unfit, and have a classification that means I'll only be called up if we go to war with China."

Having dodged the draft, Lou set about planning his ascendancy on the New York literary scene. He read *Writer's Market* and studied submission guidelines for the major American literary journals. "*The New Yorker* rejected me. That's when I wanted to be a *New Yorker* poet," he said. "But later it dawned on me—who wants to be published in these magazines anyway?"

At home, Lou's creative aspirations were taken with a grain of salt. He faced pressure to accept his father's perennial offer of stable work as a clerical worker in Freeport, but Lou wasn't ready to settle for a milquetoast career as Walter Mitty so soon after graduating. He drifted through a string of local rock gigs to create the dubious illusion of postgrad initiative and stave off the seeming inevitability of becoming his father until he could find work as a writer, musician, or both.

Then Lou got a call from Donald Schupak. Before returning to law school in the fall, the erstwhile manager of LA and the Eldorados had landed a summer job with Terry Philips, a young record executive at Pickwick International, a budget label with enough commercial traction that demand for product exceeded the speed of production. A job as a tunesmith-for-hire in Queens was not how Lou intended to carry the torch of the literary outlaws he idolized, but he wasn't exactly starting any revolutions from his parents' house.

The Pickwick ethos was epitomized by the name, a literary reference to *The Pickwick Papers*, the first novel by a twenty-four-year-old Charles Dickens. Each installment of the serialized novel sold for a shilling, and featured a rotating set of Pickwickian narrators, who chronicled their run-ins with unforgettable characters. Pickwick appropriated the model, a literary pastiche of style and form, for the pop music industry, ripping off Top 40 hits with an uncanny imitation, selling the product at a fraction of the price, and hiring his own set of Pickwickians to work alongside him at the brick-and-mortar Long Island City song factory. Pickwick recycled the hits of the British Invasion and began shipping them back to England, where they were sold at wholesale prices. The Dickensian name and eclectic sounds obfuscated the true origins: a whitewashed, industrialized concrete box in Queens. The business model was simple—by playing small ball, they could manufacture runs. Pickwick was the songwriting equivalent of a farm team.

The concept of a collective of young Turk songwriters under one roof churning out new material was nothing new. Across the East River, at 1619 Broadway in the Midtown Theater District, an elite group of major league songwriters were penning the source material for Pickwick's catalogue. The Brill Building, named for an upwardly mobile haberdasher who had bought the eleven-story edifice, housed upstarts Carole King, Neil Diamond, and Phil Spector, songwriters who were heir to the mantle of Tin Pan Alley. Holed up day in, day out in cubicle-like booths with a piano, they wrote hit after hit. Record labels, music publishing companies, studios, management offices—they were all housed in the vertically integrated Brill Building. Legendary producer Don Kirshner was not competing with Pickwick, he was competing with Motown; Pickwick was a barnacle on the back of the whale. Gerry Goffin, who might have crossed paths with Lou when Jades bandmate Phil Harris recorded his lone solo hit, "Karen"—Goffin wrote the B-side—worked for Kirshner. But Lou had landed at Pickwick.

Pickwick was coincidentally founded in 1950 by a Syracuse alum, Cy Leslie, a bottom line–minded executive who had entered the recording industry selling prerecorded greeting cards on the Voco label. With the 33⅓ LP format ushering in the album era and gradually supplanting the 78, Leslie moved to disrupt the market with ninety-nine-cent knockoffs and cut-rate reissues. If LPs, which afforded the length required for a concept album, were the musical equivalent of a novel, Pickwick offered the equivalent of paperbacks. "We can't go below 10 songs per album and still sell it," Bob Ragona, Pickwick national promotion manager, told *Billboard* in 1967. "Even for 99 cents, the customer wants something." In other words, Pickwick needed content.

Leslie met Philip Teitelbaum, a young Brooklyn-born Jewish songwriter who had adopted the nom de plume Terry Philips, and had the moxie and vision to propel Pickwick forward. Philips wasn't plucked from obscurity; he had to fight for his shot. "Growing up in East New York–Brownsville, I was the only white kid in my class. Every day I had fistfights with the black guys because I had blond hair that women would die for," Philips recalls. When Philips was fourteen, his father, a gambler, had a sudden reversal of fortune and moved the family to the more affluent Belle Harbor section of Queens. Caught between two worlds, Philips quickly began gravitating toward the sound of jazz that practically reverberated from the streets. "I was somebody who always liked avant-garde shit. I liked blues, but my big love was jazz. I used to sneak in to see Dizzy and James Moody, my two heroes. At sixteen and seventeen, I was going to see Monk and Miles Davis, and one of my future artists, Larry Young," Philips says. After graduating from NYU, he was invited to a party at tunesmith Jerry Leiber's house and, despite his lack of musical training, had enough social lubricant to lose his inhibitions and sing with the jazz trio that was playing. Leiber and his songwriting partner Mike Stoller had written or cowritten dozens of hits, including "Jailhouse Rock," "On Broadway," and "Stand by Me." Swept up in the moment, Philips serenaded Leiber's wife, actress Gaby Rodgers, on "It Could Happen to You," a ballad Frank Sinatra had memorably recorded.

"I got drunk enough that I got up there. I sang, and I killed it," Philips says. The next day, he got a call from Leiber, who fortunately was looking for a songwriter. "'You sang to my wife last night. If you weren't drunk I probably would have punched you. You were singing to her like she was single,'" he recalls Leiber saying. "I said, 'She's a gorgeous woman, and she liked the way . . .' He said, 'She loved the way you sang.' He said, 'Do you want to give it a shot to be a songwriter?' And I said, 'Well, I can try to write something, and I'll send it to you.' He said, 'No, I want to know if you want to work for me.'" So Philips was hired by Jerry Leiber and Mike Stoller, who paired him with a rising talent they had just signed: Phil Spector. "The first guy they had signed was Phil," Philips says. "So basically, I was learning with one of the top talents in the country."

Philips and Spector became roommates, moving into a studio apartment on Eighty-First Street between York and First Avenue. "Our beds were separated by a nightstand. We didn't have a real kitchen. Phil and I were tight. We wrote together, we produced together, and we lived together," he says. They began associating with other up-and-coming songwriters: Burt Bacharach, Mort Shuman, and Wes Farrell. Philips and Spector wrote a handful of songs together, including "World of Tears" for Johnny Nash, and at Leiber's encouragement, Philips released several singles under his own name, among them "Hands of a Fool," "Fear," and "Dream Time." Philips even worked briefly with Paul Simon, whom he met at Associated Recording Studios, where Simon had become "one of the top demo singers in the business," Philips recalls. Before Simon abandoned his stage name, Jerry Landis, he and Philips wrote together. "The worst song that Paul and I ever wrote was called 'The Blob.' It was based on the movie." (The 1958 science fiction film's theme song was written by Burt Bacharach and Mack David; this was an unreleased song inspired by it.)

Soon, Philips branched out into producing when he discovered Jay and the Americans, initially known as the Harbor Lights. Philips met Kenny Vance when he was Kenny Rosenberg; their mothers belonged to the same B'nai B'rith, a Jewish service organization. "I changed them to Jay and the Americans, because the lead singer at the time was a young kid named Jay Traynor, and the Americans was because I was with a young woman from American Airlines, so to be a hero, I named the group after her." Philips brought the group to Leiber and Stoller, looking for support for his maiden voyage in the control room, but Lee Eastman, their attorney, advised them to take sole production credit. Jay and the Americans had to choose. "I basically tore up my contract so they could get a shot," Philips says. It wasn't the last time he would throw out a contract at his own expense.

Philips planned his exit when he got an offer to work at Pickwick. "They approached me and asked if I wanted to start a label with them. And that became Pickwick City Records," Philips says. "But the reason I did it was because they promised me I could do the type of things I wanted to do."

As the LP market exploded, Pickwick rapidly expanded. In 1964 economy albums accounted for a $30 million market share, of which $6 million belonged to Pickwick, with Leslie anticipating that the label would command $7 million of the burgeoning market by 1965. In order to actualize this optimistic projection, he created countless subsidiary labels under the Pickwick umbrella that catered to niche markets, attempting to stake out a piece of the pie: Bridgeview was exclusively pop, home to the Foxes, the Wonderfuls, and the Chick-letes; Design released budget soundalike albums and reissues of Christmas, big band, and country music; Bravo did everything from polka to Tchaikovsky to *Havana at Midnight*; there were also Cricket, Grand Prix, Hurrah, and International Award, all of which would sometimes release the same album simultaneously with different packaging. Not missing any opportunity to capitalize, Leslie began operating through more than thirty regional distributors and arranged for advertising content to appear on the album covers. For his reissue series, Leslie negotiated international licensing deals for a song, with the likes of Soupy Sales, Billy May, Patsy Cline, and Johnny Cash. He also bought advertising space in up to one hundred publications, with a national campaign poised to attract skinflints from coast to coast.

One two-page ad in *Billboard* for Pickwick/33 featured the handwritten signatures of dozens of country and blues stars—including Johnny Rivers, Floyd Cramer, Hank Locklin, Johnny Mathis, Lightnin' Hopkins—scrawled across the top. "What are these names doing on $2 records? The same thing they're doing on $3.98 records," the ad read. "Belting out great pop hits. Blowing, strumming and stomping jazz classics and country and western favorites. Giving new life to symphonic classics." Pickwick promised solid vinyl pressings, high-embossed packaging, and the exclusive "Pinch Back Spine" for easy stacking. This product was designed to fly off the shelves with the reckless appeal of ham at half price. "We've got dozens of famous recording artists nobody ever heard of . . . on a $2.00 record," the tagline brazenly announced. Lou was about to get a shot at becoming one of those famous no-name artists.

The formula of combining aging crooners looking to get more mileage out of timeless but out-of-print releases, newly birthed stars with a trove of unheard-of B-sides, and fledgling talent slumming it in the vast no-man's-land outside the Brill Building proved hugely lucrative. Soon, business was quietly booming at Pickwick, and with Philips having recently gotten engaged, he was in need of some new recruits to shoulder the mounting workload, but he wanted someone who could thread the needle between the Tin Pan Alley–style songbook and the avant-garde sound he intended to foster on Pickwick City. Philips had to placate Cy Leslie and Pickwick vice president Ira Moss, who focused chiefly on profitability, but they understood that their business model necessitated some experimentation, vision, and risk-taking as they excavated untapped corners of the market. The Pickwick model resulted in an odd symbiosis: thrifty hucksters doing anything for a buck and visionaries too ahead of their time to make one. By hedging their bets with low-risk reissues, Pickwick's money men sometimes allowed Philips to roll the dice with unconventional voices like Lou's. So with the understanding that they hedge their bets on a quota of bankably derivative tunes, Leslie gave Philips a chance to explore the outer rim of rock.

Philips was the right man for the job. "Cy Leslie liked me personally. We came from the same background. We were both Jewish, and he loved how tough I was. Cy was tough, but he was six foot six. I was five foot seven and just as tough," Philips says. "Despite being talented and being a wild man, I was a very good businessman. I came from a business background, and I understood that people were paying us, and I never lost sight of that." For most, the business world and the avant-garde were mutually exclusive, but Philips was a rare breed of executive. Not many industry insiders were looking to sign someone like Lou, but Philips was one of a kind. All he had to do was find him. Unable to attract the vaunted talent sequestered off in the Brill Building, or even come close to offering a cushy Brill salary, he turned to the same reliable pool he had drawn from to find Jay and the Americans: Jewish geography. Philips's cousin, Leslie Silverman, knew he was looking for artists and called to suggest Lou as a prospect. "She said, 'This guy can't sing, he can't play, but I know you're gonna love him, because lyrically, he's got this funky kind of sound,'" Philips recalls. Suddenly, his cousin's boyfriend's unemployed friend from Syracuse who once had a regional hit single five or six years before was music to his ears.

That September, Philips heard that Lou would be performing in Syracuse, and on a crazy hunch, he decided to make the long trip upstate in the Pickwick station wagon. It was a particularly cold early fall, with temperatures dipping into the thirties, but Philips kept driving. "As we were driving up, the door handle froze, and we drove all the way from New York City to Syracuse," Philips recalls. "We get there, and I went to some kind of bar or coffeehouse, and I heard Lou with a group. And I immediately saw what Leslie was talking about. I just said the same thing—he can't play, sings like shit, but his sound, his feeling touched me. So here was my opportunity on the first label I had, and I signed Lou Reed as my first artist."

Unlike Teitelbaum, Rosenberg, or Zimmerman, who had all committed the act of erasure often necessary for assimilation into American mainstream culture, Lou had an early advantage. Teitelbaum had too many syllables for rock stardom; the audience liked syncopation in the beat, but not in the name. Rock stars required a crisp cadence and a certain unassuming grandiosity. The fewer the syllables, the better; as the charts had revealed, the fewer the names, the fatter the paycheck. Pat Boone was good; Elvis was great; Cher was divine. The market made an exception for Harry Belafonte. The listening public would even accept a black Jew if his name had the ring of Sammy Davis Jr., but a mouthful like Cherilyn Sarkisian (Cher's given name) was too unambiguously ethnic. And so, for that matter, was Rabinowitz, but Lou's father had already taken care of that. Lou Reed was one letter shorter than Lou Rawls.

"When I signed him, I knew he was a punk. And Leslie's boyfriend had told him, 'Don't mess around with Leslie's cousin. The mouth you have to everybody, he'll knock you out,'" Philips says. But like Bob Shad, Philips saw something in Lou.

Back in New York, Lou rode the commuter line into Penn Station and took the subway to Pickwick to sign his contract. Long Island City was an industrial area, home to the dregs of society and an infinite sprawl of cement debris, chain-link fences, and unmarked warehouse buildings with rolltop gates. The nearest subway station was a ten-minute walk toward the Queensboro Bridge overpass, immortalized a few years later by Simon & Garfunkel's "The 59th Street Bridge Song (Feelin' Groovy)." Only this was the wild side of the bridge. Lou strode past a flophouse motel with hourly rates, the seedy River Park, home to the seedlings of an insidious drug problem, and the towering Queensbridge Houses, a red-brick building complex constructed in 1939—the largest public housing project in North America—situated along the heavily polluted East River, where the worst US oil spill of the twentieth century seeped into the groundwater. It was kind of a dump, but it could be Lou's dump.

The Pickwick Building was a desolate one-story unit located at 8–16 Forty-Third Avenue, at the corner of Ninth Street, a block in from the river, but close enough to smell it wafting in. To get to the studio, Lou was greeted by the administrative staff working the reception area, then led through the front office, into the dank warehouse, where metric tons of vinyl product were crammed onto pallets, and finally to the back, where he was met by Philips, flanked by an Ampex recorder. Lou was expecting Terry Philips, patrician record executive, *Billboard* ninety-nine-cent man, sworn enemy of true art; what he got was the pugnacious creative force behind Pickwick, and a disarming smile with a firm handshake that belied his springy tuft of blond hair.

As long as Philips held up his end of the deal, Cy Leslie gave Philips carte blanche for hiring personnel. Leslie knew that to succeed in the cut-throat record industry, Pickwick had to diversify; Lou knew that for once in his life, he had to compromise to get a foot in the door. In Lou, Philips had found his wild man to fill out the Pickwick songwriting team: Jerry Vance, whose real name was Pellegrino, Jimmie Smith, and Lou, with Philips acting as a buffer to the label. Together they were Lee Harridan Productions, a division of Pickwick International. Lou and Philips settled on a modest weekly salary, and he started working immediately. So Pickwick International spread across genre—as they branched out into the children's market, they also hired Lou Reed.

Following the signing, Philips drove to Freeport to meet Lou's parents. "His father wanted to meet me and I drove out to Freeport," Philips says. "I was paying him on a weekly basis, which his father and mother were relieved by. They were like kissing my ring, because they couldn't believe it. Of course they knew what an asshole he was, what a punk, and what a wise guy." At first, Lou couldn't believe it either. "He didn't have anything together. He was sad. He was this insecure guy. He didn't even believe in his own talent, but the same guy couldn't stop writing that which he believed in," Philips says.

Lou's inner turmoil was evident immediately. "He would come into work stoned every day, because he was the king, as I found out, of pills," Philips recalls. "I could never figure out what he took. Lou was very bright, and he was taking pills that I think doctors didn't know about." Recognizing Lou's self-destructive artistic process, Philips indulged Lou's behavior to encourage his talent. "We used to have to pick him up off the floor each day; he had to be taken to the emergency room twice. Nobody would have gone near him but a wild man like me," Philips says. "Cy Leslie would come in and they would go crazy. And I kept saying, 'You've got to understand, this guy is special.'"

At first, Philips tried to impose some discipline, but he quickly saw how that would backfire with Lou. "I backed off totally, and let him do his own stuff," Philips says. Lou churned out track after track from the bunker-like studio rooms with a pickup and a pencil. Pickwick afforded him the opportunity to perfect his compositional fundamentals, an education in lieu of graduate school. By the following winter, on the verge of 1965, Lou had lent his voice and his lyrics, often anonymously or under a pseudonym, to countless Pickwick tracks. One 1964 compilation album had Lou appearing alongside Neil Sedaka, Johnny Rivers, and the Four Seasons, with lesser-known material from the marquee names and four slapdash entries from the fictional band the J Brothers, who were Lou and the in-house Pickwick staff. "Ya Running but I'll Getcha" was a cloying rockabilly tune with a heart-broken lyric. The track perhaps conjures Shelley, who was still at Syracuse, and engaged to another man.

> *Why you runnin' around*
> *And why you puttin' me down*
> *I'm telling you things will turn out right*
> *And I'll be with you day and night*

A phony billing below Neil Sedaka B-sides was the harbinger of what Lou might become but never would, lest he be haunted by Delmore: a sellout. There was Lou on soul knockoff "Really Really Really Really Really Really Love" by Spongy & the Dolls. There he was again on the Shirelles-esque single "Soul City" by the Foxes. And there he was yet again opposite fresh-faced country star Ronnie Dove on *Swingin' Teen Sounds of Ronnie Dove and Terry Phillips* [sic] with "Flowers for the Lady" and "Wild One." The latter track featured a heavy backbeat, gang vocals, a driving bass line, and a slaying guitar background:

> *They call me the wild one, that's what they say*
> *When something happens, way will come my way*

*But nothin' that they try to do will keep me from havin' fun,*
  *so let 'em*
*Call me the wild one*

But it was too wild for Cy Leslie, who demanded a more commercial budget album. "I wouldn't say fuck you to him, because I really liked him. I said, 'Cy, please. This is so wrong,'" Philips recalls. "He basically said, 'If you want me to keep on financing Pickwick City Records, you've got to do it.' In order to keep Lou's pill-taking ass and get him his weekly paycheck and allow him to write, I had to compromise my—not his—I compromised my integrity."

The resulting album was the budget record par excellence: *Soundsville!* The concept behind *Soundsville!* was simple: take listeners to Soundsville, a Bizarro version of Motown's Hitsville, with an uncanny imitation of every style on the *Billboard* charts. Each track got an illustrative graphic on the cover: "the sounds of Nashville," "the sounds of Detroit," "the sounds of Hot Rod," "the sounds of Surfing"; all coming from seemingly discrete regional bands, but in fact laid down by Lou and the guys in marathon sessions in the Long Island City studio. It was as tacky as Epcot. Yet there was something off about *Soundsville*—Lou cast a dark shadow on every track, even when he wasn't singing. Could it be Lou's doleful touch that darkened the sounds of the West Coast on "Teardrop in the Sand," gracefully intoned by the Hollywoods? The spoken-word break, channeling Skeeter Davis's "The End of the World," could wilt the Byrds' blooming flower: "You know, once I was so happy, I loved the whole world, and now there's no more fun in surfing without my little old surfer girl." There is no hint of Lou on the comparatively giddy "Wonderful World of Love," but could that be the glowering cadence of his lovelorn lyrics and gloomy guitar coming in from Soundsville, New York, on the Hi-Lifes' "I'm Gonna Fight"?

*You want my girl, but I'm gonna fight, yeah, I'm gonna fight*
*Fight for her love, the love that I need*
*For I won't let her go*

What about the unseasonably brisk chill dampening Jeannie Larimore's low-tide sound of surfing on "Johnny Won't Surf No More"?

*Johnny won't surf no more*
*And I'm the one to blame*
*For me he went out too far*
*Oh, oh what a shame*

It is unmistakably Lou's warble caterwauling in from London with the Roughnecks on the anxiety-riddled "You're Driving Me Insane." He had never been to England, but the radio taught him more than enough about the British Invasion:

*The way you walk can carry me on*
*The way you talk you put me on*
*The way that you rattle your brain*
*You know you're drivin' me insane*

There is Lou again, this time with the Beachnuts, stranded on Soundsville's island of existential dread on "Cycle Annie," shredding the sweat-stained guitar break; in addition to Philadelphia's Liberty Bell, a flotilla of forlorn surfboards, and a warbling biker gang, Soundsville is apparently home to a green-eyed monster:

*Now little Cycle Annie she has got a guy name Joe*
*And he follows her around just everywhere she goes*
*Now I ain't sayin' nothin' baby, I ain't sayin' that I mind*

Despite its dopey parti-colored cover, *Soundsville!* was the most pessimistic, depressing $1.98 direct-to-supermarket piffle ever sold. Lou missed Shelley, and it didn't only bleed into his work; her conspicuous absence cast a pall over everything he did. Lou was a rock Orpheus willing to descend to Hades for his Eurydice, but he now found himself up the River Styx without a paddle. In sum, he was twenty-two, and like all twenty-two-year-old boys other than the select few whom the gods had smiled favorably upon—Simon & Garfunkel (who had succeeded despite the unusual name), Brian Wilson, Sonny Bono—he labored under the ego-crushing delusion that he was an abject failure.

But as 1964 came to a close, Philips gave Lou an opportunity to be himself. The '60s gave birth to a slew of dances, many of them holdovers from the previous decade as the sexual revolution went through its awkward stage on the way to maturity. It was as though the fox-trot, jitterbug, and Charleston could no longer contain all the raging hormones, but neither could the Twist. The dance craze itself had spawned its own hit with Cannibal & the Headhunters' "Land of 1000 Dances." A whole dance floor taxonomy had emerged. Beyond the Monster Mash and the Jerk, there were dances about transportation—Goffin and King's Loco-Motion, Archie Bell's Choo Choo, and Marvin Gaye's Hitch Hike; dances about food—James Brown's Mashed Potato, Andre Williams's Greasy Chicken and Bacon Fat, which had separate greasy moves; and a menagerie of dances about animals—Major Lance's the Monkey, Chubby Checker's the Pony, and Rufus Thomas's the Dog. There were dances named for African tribes—the Watusi—and one imported from Finland—the Letkajenkka, which was shortened to the Letkis. The one thing these dances had in common was that they were all danceable—until that point.

Fashion also ran on this type of fad, with kitschy trends as ridiculous as they were impractical. In 1964 ostrich feathers were the rage in haute couture; by late 1965, the cover of *Vogue* featured actress Elsa Martinelli draped in a pluming ostrich feather hat that sprang right from the pages of Dr. Seuss. On October 6, 1964, Eugenia Sheppard published a syndicated column lampooning the new style, and Lou happened to stumble on it one night while he was smoking a joint. "Look at all the ostrich that was floating around Paris. . . . Those stiff, beautiful brocades are strictly for sitting," Sheppard wrote. "Even some of the crepes, unless they're very bias, tend to go dead on a dance floor. As for the skinny, wool evening dresses, they're so chic, but after 10 hard minutes on the dance floor, the girls just have to give up." As the THC hit his bloodstream, the thought of a gaggle of ostrich-festooned debutantes sidelined by their senseless dresses was too ironic to pass up. Lou had his dance move.

The Ostrich was more craze than dance. Lou cribbed the bass line from the Crystals' "Then He Kissed Me," a 1963 single that epitomized Phil Spector's wall of sound aesthetic, which Philips had learned from the man himself. Lou tuned each string to the same note, his first experiment with what he called "Ostrich tuning." It opened with six strings of D and some of the most violent tambourine hits in rock history. "OK, I want everybody to settle down now. We've got something new we want to show you, man. It's gonna knock you dead when we come upside your head. You get ready?" Lou yowled. "Everybody get down on your face, man." Falsetto gang vocals came in with the refrain: "Do the Ostrich!" And then Lou announced the steps, or step: "Hey, put your head up, upside your knees. Do the ostrich! Yeah, yeah, yeah. Now you take a step forward, you step on your head." Having explained the move—essentially a curb-stomp—Lou began to hoot at the top of his lungs. "The Ostrich" had gravel, guts, adrenaline, and some seriously dark gallows humor.

"I was as much of a wild man as he was and maybe more," Philips recalls of the intoxicated recording session. "We had a one-track Ampex, a big, big mother, and we started to do a jam, and they stopped. I said, 'Wait a minute! Don't stop. Let's do this and see where it goes.' We did it on one mic. I kept saying, a little closer with the mic, a little farther, and the minute I heard it right, I knew that was it. And 'The Ostrich' happened. I made it the first release on Pickwick City Records."

To persuade Pickwick to release "The Ostrich," it took a businessman's finesse and an idiosyncratic vision, but Philips had both. "The truth was, Cy Leslie didn't see what I did," Philips says. "I said, 'This is something so exciting. Eventually, I'm telling you, kids will get with it.' Of course, I was only like twenty years off." They called the fake band behind "The Ostrich" the Primitives. The record proclaimed without a trace of irony, "Pickwick City: Where Things Happen," and for one of the first times at Pickwick, with "The Ostrich" and its similarly transgressive B-side, "Sneaky Pete," things really did happen. "We probably sold four copies, but we got tremendous play on college and avant-garde stations," Philips recalls. "That was something the guys at Pickwick weren't interested in, but I knew that those stations saw Lou immediately." Somehow Philips managed to convince Pickwick to roll the dice with a promotional tour in the hope that they could break something truly original. There was only one problem: despite all the studio clanging on the record, Lou's backing band for "The Ostrich" was not nearly primitive enough to be the Primitives on stage.

Pickwick's faith in the commercial viability of "The Ostrich" was perhaps misplaced, but having been given the green light, Philips set out to recruit a band. The concept was risky but not original; across the country, producer Bob Rafelson was busy casting the Monkees, a made-for-TV gambit, but Philips was looking for a different type of band. Instead of a casting call,

Philips went the Pickwick route. He and Jerry Vance caught wind of an Upper East Side house party that promised to attract the bohemians who might put a face to Lou's gritty single.

Down in the East Village at the same time, a recent Swarthmore graduate, David Gelber, introduced two young women to his long-haired, avant-garde musician neighbors. By coincidence, the girls happened to be on their way to the same Upper East Side shindig as Philips and decided to take Gelber's neighbors along. The East Village and the Upper East Side had nothing in common but their latitude. For the two men, it would be an anthropological field study and an exercise in proletarian scare tactics; they might even bed a millionaire heiress.

Far above the streets on the Upper East Side, the two intellectuals were the people in attendance who fit the part Philips was casting. All he needed was a look. Anyone could bang a tambourine, whether they could keep a beat or not, and with Lou's Ostrich tuning, it was easy to strum along to the cacophony. If need be, the band could lip-synch to the record for the promo tour. So with that in mind, Philips struck up a conversation.

One was a prodigy violist on New York's avant-garde scene with a classical pedigree, a member of one of the most commercially inaccessible ensembles downtown had to offer, La Monte Young's Theatre of Eternal Music. The other was an underground filmmaker with no musical training to speak of. With the promise of a paycheck, Philips arranged for them to come to the Pickwick Building, along with a "drummer" of their own choosing. Satisfied that he had found his Primitives, Philips was ready to leave. So with the same unerring eye for talent that had given Lou Reed his start, Philips had discovered Tony Conrad. He had also discovered John Cale.

"Cale hit it off with me. Tony and Walter did, too, but Lou was a punk," Philips says.

"The Ostrich" was destined to be the Primitives' first and only single, a commercial flop. Yet Pickwick's failure to manufacture a band had a silver lining. Through the label's misguided attempt to create the Monkees, Pickwick had unwittingly given birth to the Velvet Underground.

Cale and Conrad convened in Long Island City, bringing along their unkempt sculptor friend Walter De Maria, another La Monte Young associate, where the newly minted Primitives were introduced to Lou. Pickwick presented a seven-year contract, which they adamantly refused to sign. Pickwick agreed to move forward, though, and after a few haphazard rehearsals—one of them at De Maria's Bond Street loft, where they rehearsed material from *Soundsville!* and a song called "Why Don't You Smile Now," one of Cale's sole Pickwick songwriting credits—the four were soon booked at the Hotel Riverside Plaza on West Seventy-Third Street.

A former Masonic lodge built as a replica of King Solomon's Temple, the Riverside Plaza was an ornate Neo-Romanesque high-rise boasting a three-story lobby with an Italian marble staircase; a four-thousand-seat auditorium once hosted Benny Goodman, and in 1965, Claes Oldenburg premiered *Washes* in the swimming pool. Yet whoever picked the Riverside to unveil the Primitives must not have known that Solomon's Temple had already been destroyed.

The Primitives continued wreaking havoc in New Jersey high schools. The four renegade rockers packed into the Pickwick station wagon, full of rented instruments, heading for a parochial school. Expecting the Beach Boys, the confused students looked at the hirsute Welshman, the pale Jew, and their two bohemian associates with the bewilderment of the deer that disrupted local traffic; "Johnny Won't Surf Anymore" made sense, but they just didn't get it when Lou started lip-synching along to "The Ostrich" with its uncannily canned applause track. "Lou took something because he was nervous. He always got incredibly nervous when he performed," Philips recalls.

It was a throwback to his days with the Jades, minus the flying beer bottles. It did not go over well. Yet Philips maintained his belief in Lou. "I was so convinced that the kids would get them that despite the fact that people said, 'Terry, I love you man, you're a great talent, but are you crazy? This kid is shit. He can't sing,' I said, 'I'm telling you, the kids are gonna get with this,'" Philips says.

On the car ride home, due to the combination of uppers and the downer of bombing onstage, Lou was more insolent than usual. "He somehow got fresh with my wife. We were in the car, and I smacked him in the face and banged his head against the glass. I said, 'Say one more word and I'll kill you,'" Philips recalls. "I loved his talent and I loved his vision and I loved his craziness, but his punk mouth I couldn't take for one more minute without really hurting him."

Shortly thereafter, Lou and Philips decided to amicably part ways. "It seemed in those days, as talented and smart as I was, I was always letting people get out of their contract," Philips says. "I did it with Jay and the Americans, and I did it with Lou. It wasn't in my DNA to say, 'But I've got that contract.

I'm gonna fuck you.'" Philips knew that Lou had perfected "Heroin" during his stint at Pickwick, but he later decided not to take any action. "I could have gone to ASCAP and BMI, and I could have nailed him on 'Heroin,' claiming that he wrote it when he was working for me. Nobody wanted to go near a thing like that, but I wanted him to do the kind of shit that I loved," Philips says. "So I let them go, and as they say, the rest is history."

It was at this juncture that Lou reached out to Delmore, sending a letter that voiced his career frustration, weighing the option of filing an application for an MFA, as Schwartz had long hoped he would. Yet Lou harbored a strong sense that there was nothing he could learn in school that he couldn't learn on the streets, and if he was going to fulfill the literary promise that had eluded the man he considered his "spiritual god-father," he would have to work strictly outside the academy, without any institutional support.

After five months in Long Island City, Lou quit his job and sacrificed his weekly paycheck for an uncertain future. Lou was at a crossroads; he considered joining the folk revival wave and sent out demos to several scrappy, liberal folk labels. Some of his songs made it as far as London, where Miles Copeland considered them before ultimately declining. Lou was on an upward slope, but it felt like a plateau. How he would make ends meet without a stable salary remained unclear, but Lou found himself in a Catch-22: he didn't make enough money at Pickwick to leave home, but to make more he had to overcome his shaky self-confidence and strike out on his own.

Lou was having a quarter-life crisis, but amid the drugs, sex, and depravity, he knew he had to leave Freeport as soon as possible. He had to write, and to really go for it, he had to be in New York. Lou signed the letter and sent it to Delmore's cold-water flat. Whether Delmore ever responded doesn't matter; it was more of a prayer than a plea for help. Schwartz was not in a position to help anyway. Syracuse had let him go, and he was rapidly withering away as he spent every last penny at the bar. Shelley was about to leave Syracuse, too, and though she was continuing on to her master's after graduation, she was moving to the city to be with her husband, who had finished his doctorate and been hired to be on the faculty at NYU's Sociology Department. Shelley was moving to New York. Why couldn't Lou? He didn't have a job or any starter money. All he had was an address and a guitar. So with nothing and everything to lose, he packed a bag and headed for 56 Ludlow.

# PART II

# THE VELVET UNDERGROUND

# 7

Fifty-Six Ludlow Street was a grimy five-story walk-up on the Lower East Side between Grand and Hester, an edgy block populated largely by artists living in bohemian squalor, junkies, and derelicts; the smell of fresh-baked bialys and Chinatown stir-fry mixed with the pungent odor of festering garbage. It contained all the raw ingredients that formed the 1960s avant-garde. John Cale lived with Tony Conrad on the top floor of the exposed-brick building in a cramped one-and-a-half-bedroom tenement apartment; Conrad took the bedroom, Cale sprawled out in the other half, which was really the living room. Cale dropped a tattered mattress under the window, looking out on Ludlow, a block away from a high school with a 40 percent dropout rate (it used to be a jail); they split the twenty-five-dollar-a-month rent, and subsisted on milkshakes and canned stew, curbing their appetites with junk.

A scene out of Puccini's *La Boheme*, the chipped-paint railroad apartment had no heat or hot water; in the winter, they burned crates and furniture in the fireplace to keep warm and stole power from their neighbors. "As we struggled, the apartment took on the aesthetic of a coal mine," Cale recalled in the *Wall Street Journal*. Coming from a coal miner's son, the comparison was apropos. As a safety precaution, they repurposed exposed bedsprings as window guards, so it also resembled a prison cell, but rather than keep them in, it would keep the commercial world out. "The bedsprings let in light and air and kept the bad guys from entering off the fire escape. The bedsprings symbolized everything—danger, edge, minimalism," Cale recalled.

It wasn't without music; barbershop quartets would sometimes rehearse on the front stoop across the street, with the thump of R&B blasting from radios downstairs. Yet the encroachment of these eccentric early gentrifiers was not met with open arms. The two out-of-place Beatniks regularly dodged rocks that neighborhood kids hurled at them because their long hair reminded them of the Beatles. By 1964, 56 Ludlow had become a de facto arts collective for the Fluxus movement; Italian underground filmmaker Piero Heliczer, poet Angus MacLise, Jack Smith, whose sordid film *Flaming Creatures* had caused a riot when it was seized by the NYPD at its 1963 premiere, and Warhol superstar Mario Montez all cut their teeth there. "The entire neighborhood was dark—except for the solitary bulb burning in the tea merchant's window on the ground floor," Cale wrote. "No matter how late I came home, the guy was always sitting in that window in the pale yellow light. It was eerie, but it fit the whole scene down here." With its leaky plumbing and gun-toting landlord, it was a hellish paradise for Lou compared to the cabin fever of Freeport. Across the East River in Long Island City, he was late to the party.

Born three thousand miles away from each other a week apart, the chain of events that brought Lou and John Cale together is a phenomenon of avant-garde butterfly effect precipitated by the flap of a finger—Aaron Copland's. John grew up in the industrial Amman Valley in Wales, the son of a coal miner and a teacher; he hoped to transcend the yoke of his upbringing with an affinity for classical music. After playing viola in the National Youth Orchestra of Wales, Cale studied music at London's Goldsmiths College. In the summer of 1963, he was brought to Tanglewood, the arboreal summer home of the Boston Symphony Orchestra in the Berkshires, on Copland's recommendation. Rather than return to London, at the end of the summer Cale moved to New York, where he soon came into the orbit of John Cage. That September, Cale played piano in an eighteen-hour continuous performance with Cage at the Pocket Theatre of Erik Satie's *Vexations*, which, though composed in the late nineteenth century, had never been properly performed (it fit on a single page of sheet music, but Satie's written note stipulated that the minute-long piece be played 840 times in succession). The following week, Cale appeared on the CBS show *I've Got a Secret*, where the panel guessed his connection to the other guest, the only audience member who attended the performance from start to finish. Warhol had also attended, but only had a fifteen-minute attention span; they wouldn't meet again for two years.

Now with a higher profile, Cage introduced Cale to La Monte Young, whose Theatre of Eternal Music included another avant-garde luminary: Tony Conrad. Conrad was a violinist who had studied math at Harvard and went on to become an early computer programmer; creatively stifled, he joined the avant-garde in New York as a musician and later branched out into film, where he carved out an international reputation as a structuralist video artist. But first, Conrad joined La Monte Young's Theatre of Eternal Music, a vanguard collaborative that built on the innovations of Cage and prefigured the drone aesthetic, focusing on intonation and sustained pitch to explore the harmonic possibilities of sound, which the ensemble called "Dream Music."

Young was a saxophonist and composer from Los Angeles who had worked with Ornette Coleman and Don Cherry—Lous's heroes and future collaborators—before migrating east. Though he settled in New York, his musical taste continued its eastward migration; he began exploring the Indian Carnatic tradition, and soon formed the Theatre of Eternal Music, later referred to as the Dream Syndicate, due to the oneiric, trancelike quality of their work. Young, often credited as one of the fathers of minimalism, developed many of his concepts during performances with the Dream Syndicate in meditative genuflection.

The Dream Syndicate incorporated improvisation into classical music, causing a paradigm shift in the conventional notion of a composer that represented a direct attack on high art. With Marian Zazeela, Young's wife, Angus MacLise, a poet and mystic, and Billy Linich, eventually the Dream Syndicate's sound infiltrated contemporary pop, classical, and jazz, even though they performed privately and rarely disseminated any recordings. The quintessential art music ensemble, the drone aesthetic of the Dream Syndicate spread insidiously, like a collective dream, and not on traditional commercial channels, eventually influencing Karlheinz Stockhausen, and also the Velvet Underground.

When Billy Linich left the group, committing himself full-time to Warhol's Factory, where he was christened as Billy Name and appointed archivist and de facto foreman, John Cale replaced him. Early in 1964, Conrad asked Cale to move into his apartment to lower their living expenses; they did whatever they had to do to get by, which by the end of the year included a stint at Pickwick. Cale and Conrad's brief tenure with Lou and the Primitives seemed like an aberration in an otherwise pristine record of disruptive anticommercialism, but the group chemistry was volatile enough that they decided to turn their fake band into a real one. A week after the debut performance of the Primitives, Cale appeared with the Dream Syndicate in a piece called "The Tortoise Recalling the Drone of the Holy

Numbers as They Were Revealed in the Dreams of the Whirlwind and the Obsidian Gong, Illuminated by the Sawmill, the Green Sawtooth Ocelot, and the High-Tension Line Stepdown Transformer." It was time for a louder transformation; minimalism was about to meet rock.

"For me, what it stood for was basically one sign of a general collapse of high cultural social identities," Conrad recalls. "It was a strong marking post in a system of changes that was going on at that time."

At first, they didn't even have a name. After a truncated promotional tour culminating in a TV spot, the Primitives disbanded; De Maria and Conrad went their separate ways, while John and Lou began intently working through new material. They kept Conrad's ethos—"Be primitives naturally"—but otherwise started from scratch as John and Lou hunkered down around the mess of wires they used to power their tiny amps. There was no incentive to find a moniker that could encapsulate their new sound; record deals and airplay held no sway. They were after a sound, which would soon give birth to the art-band phenomenon but initially proved elusive. Were they folk with risqué lyrics? Rock with an attitude? Minimalists with an amplifier? It took time before Cale, who was crucial to the development of minimalism, realized how the earthy aesthetic of the Dream Syndicate could inhabit the concrete thrum of their nebulous new band. Fifty-Six Ludlow was their tenement factory before the Factory.

To make money and just for kicks, the duo resorted to odd jobs culled from the *Village Voice* classified section: they gave blood and posed for smutty tabloid ads. "My picture came out and it said I was a sex maniac killer that had killed 14 children and tape recorded it and played it in a barn in Kansas at midnight. And when John's picture came out in the paper, it said he had killed his lover because his lover was going to marry his sister, and he didn't want his sister to marry a fag," Lou later recalled. Sometimes, on their way to score heroin in Harlem, they would play on the street outside the Baby Grand, a club not far from the Apollo. Partially inspired by the habit they shared, they adopted the name the Falling Spikes.

One day up on Broadway, around 125th Street, John and Lou began performing some of the material they had been honing in the hovel on Ludlow. As outdoor buskers, they had to perform acoustically, but that didn't stop them from attracting a sizable Harlem audience with change to spare, especially only blocks away from Columbia University. As the crowd grew, an NYPD officer stopped them and shut down the show. They hopped the subway and set up downtown on Seventy-Fifth Street, where the duo attracted Elektrah Lobel, a mercurial actress-musician, and recruited her to join the band; she and John also started sleeping together.

They began rehearsing "Wrap Your Troubles in Dreams," a song Lou wrote in the vein of totemic American folk songs, and booked several shows at the Cafe Wha?, an old Bob Dylan haunt in Greenwich Village. The trio never caught traction, though, partially because Lou objected; Lobel strummed the guitar so vehemently that her fingers started gushing blood in the middle of performances. The Falling Spikes played wherever they could, occasionally joining the legendary Fugs to form another impromptu group they called the Transcendental Simulematic Orchestra. Lobel's tenure was short-lived, though; by March, she had been cast as Raul Castro in Andy Warhol's *The Life of Juanita Castro*, a gender-bending critique of Fidel Castro's revolutionary family. As John and Lou approached their twenty-third birthdays, Angus MacLise returned to 56 Ludlow from abroad. They began gathering for informal rehearsals as their tastes drifted farther away from folk.

They changed their name to the Warlocks (incidentally the same name as an early incarnation of the Grateful Dead) and began accompanying experimental silent films by the coterie of underground filmmakers at 56 Ludlow and its environs: Jack Smith, Stan Brakhage, and Piero Heliczer. The underground milieu was a hotbed of creative production, an eclectically contentious atmosphere that inspired a collapse of conventional genre and form into a permeable spontaneous construction. Lou and MacLise collaborated on a manifesto for the band: "Concerning the Rumor That Red China Has Cornered the Methedrine Market and Is Busy Adding Paranoia Drops to Upset the Mental Balance of the United States," a madcap, stream-of-consciousness sketch of their ferocious blend of avant-garde jazz, John Cage–influenced classical, doo-wop, and the Great American Novel. "Western music is based on death, violence and the pursuit of PROGRESS. . . . The root of universal music is sex. Western music is as violent as Western sex. . . . Our band is the Western equivalent to the cosmic dance of Shiva. Playing as Babylon goes up in flames."

Fueled by methamphetamine hydrochloride, heroin, and a regimen of various uppers and downers that were then in circulation in the Village, the Warlocks began their sorcerers' revolution against the more sanitized, clean sound that at the time was monopolizing the market they categorically boycotted. With paranoia rising and the Vietnam War gaining ground, the developing atmosphere of distrust in the political zeitgeist had outpaced the rock that was publicly available. Lou, John, and Angus occupied that niche.

By mere happenstance, Lou and John bumped into Sterling Morrison, whom Lou had met at Syracuse, one day on the subway. Morrison was on his way to an English class at City College—though only five months younger than Lou and John, he had taken the scenic route to his degree—studying medieval literature and reading Tolkien voraciously. Lou invited him to 56 Ludlow to jam; he brought the pop of Mickey Baker, the blues influence of Dr. John, and a lifetime of Catholic guilt. It was a meeting of the minds, the perfect alchemical combination that would soon transform the raw elements of heroin, grit, kinky sex, and endless nights into the Velvet Underground. By early spring, Lou, John, Sterling, and Angus had been tapped by avant-garde patriarch Jonas Mekas to improvise the soundtrack to a Piero Heliczer film at Launching the Dream Weapon, a multimedia happening at the Film-Makers' Cinematheque. Behind the projection screen, separated by cascading veils and psychedelic lights, the four coalesced for the first time; they had risen above their limitations by going underground.

In May, Lou and John convinced Pickwick to let them come into the studio to record. Even though Lou had unceremoniously terminated his contract, Philips sensed that he might be on the verge of a breakthrough. Lou went to Long Island City one last time to lay down several tracks, including "Heroin," which he had been developing at Syracuse but never recorded. Filled with trepidation, he stammered through the first take.

"Good performance," said the engineer. "Do it again. You blew some words. Can you do it again?"

"Oh, Jesus Christ," Lou said.

"It's not like a performance, baby. You're in a recording studio. You don't want to do it down?"

"No, I'm just trying to figure out if I can do it," Lou said. "Can I run out and get some water?"

Lou stormed out of the studio, had a drink, and got himself together. He went back in and started strumming, with John laying down a minimalist bass line. Lou had a tremulous quality to his voice, an unmistakable apprehension, but by the third verse, he was raining down fire and brimstone, as much as an unsure twenty-four-year-old could. Lou imbued the guitar with a folksy twang, a sound he had clung to as he shook off the yoke of Dylan:

*While that heroin is in my blood, and that blood is in my*
*head*
*And thank god I'm good as dead*

The recording conjured the folk revivalism of Village troubadour Dave Van Ronk, whose 1963 Prestige album *Dave Van Ronk, Folksinger* included the old chestnut "Cocaine Blues," with the refrain, "Cocaine run all 'round my brain." Eventually, Lou would pursue a grittier sound, but not yet. In addition to his folk-inflected sacred cows, the repetition of God, invoked repeatedly for satirical effect, highlighted a ham-fisted nihilism that would wane as time wore on, yielding a more cynical, agnostic, and decisively ungrateful closing lyric: "And I guess I just don't know."

The sound they were striving for began to crystallize in the ensuing two months in marathon rehearsals at 56 Ludlow; they also finally found a name that would capture its essence. One day they found a book on the shelf in Conrad's abandoned room, a paperback pop psychology exposé he had apparently picked up in the street: *The Velvet Underground*. Published in 1963, the same year as Betty Friedan's *The Feminine Mystique*, the pulpy chronicle of bedroom behavior during the sexual revolution distorts second-wave feminism to by turns valorize and deplore the kinky fetishes of married couples behind the velvet rope of bourgeois society. Written by Michael Leigh, almost certainly a nom de plume, the book intended to sensationalize the Swinging Sixties—"Here is an incredible book. It will shock and amaze you. But as a documentary on the sexual corruption of our age, it is a must for every thinking adult." The cover depicts totems of sadomasochism: a stiletto, whip, leather mask, and a key for a key party. The title represented everything they stood for; they had even been working on Lou's musical adaptation of Leopold von Sacher-Masoch's *Venus in Furs*. "It was perfect," John later recalled of the book. "There was nothing velvet about the underground world we were living in, that's for sure." There was something velvety about their aesthetic, though, at least initially. The band that would loudly spawn a quiet revolution had a gradual fermentation process.

In May 1965 they recorded their first demo. Lou even mailed it to his parents' house in Freeport, resorting to the postmark as "poor man's copyright," never opening the package. Its contents remain a mystery. Then, in July 1965, they were polished and ready to record a demo they were prepared to disseminate, the first formal tape of the Velvet Underground, committed to the Wollensak reel-to-reel they kept in the apartment. "Polished" is not a descriptor that would ever apply to the Velvet Underground, but that unvarnished stream-of-consciousness creation did not emerge as a fully formed Venus from the East River of their dreams. Like Kerouac, it took enormous effort behind the scenes to affect that level of spontaneity. "In the fifth-floor apartment in '65, Lou, Sterling, and I combined the music of Erik Satie, John Cage, Phil Spector, Hank Williams, and Bob Dylan. The result was a new form of rock—more about art than commerce," John recalled. Yet their initial stabs at originality were a product of their cultural moment, more folk than anything else. It would take time to find a voice that transcended stylistic imitation outside the folk-dominated status quo.

"Venus in Furs" was played in the Scottish folk ballad style of Simon & Garfunkel's "Scarborough Fair," which was circulating around the Village folk scene at the time. It has a similar chord progression and a minor mood; though Lou had written the lyrics, in keeping with the pastoral setting they were aiming for, John sang it in his Welsh brogue, Lou accompanying with a lilting guitar backdrop. From the opening lines, the lyrical delivery contradicted the dark subject matter: "Shiny, shiny boots of leather, whiplash girl-child in the dark" had all the chivalric charm a ballad about sadomasochism could possibly have. "Prominent Men," a socially conscious anthem that betrayed Lou's political side, was never released on a studio album; it sounds like an outtake from Dylan's *The Times They Are A-Changin'*, which was released in January 1964 and produced by Tom Wilson, who would soon help mold the Velvet Underground. Dylan was about to go electric; so were the Velvet Underground, but not yet. Lou opens his ballad of unrest with a plaintive harmonica wail and rhythm guitar, taking lead vocals. Channeling Dylan, he never sounded so nasal. John joins on the heavy-handed chorus:

> *Prominent men tell prominent stories*
> *Prominent men tell prominent lies*
> *Prominent men kiss the ass of Dame Fortune*
> *Prominent men will tear out your eyes*

"I'm Waiting for the Man" features the band's take on the Holy Modal Rounders, the folk duo that had broken in 1964 with their self-titled debut. Rather than "Blues in the Bottle," though, Lou was looking for a more powerful fix than his twangy guitar and harmonica would suggest. In contrast to the two-part close harmony, John at one point disrupts the hootenanny with an inchoate viola frisson that agitates for a harsher sound. The song wasn't clicking; they recorded it three times. An upbeat rendering of "All Tomorrow's Parties" entered the realm of the Byrds, who had just released *Mr. Tambourine Man*—the title track itself a Dylan cover—weeks prior to the Velvets' demo.

By the second verse, Lou could tell that the vocal harmonies were not coalescing. He registered his frustration. "And what costumes shall the poor girl wear to all tomorrow's parties," he sang. "Fucking shit!" After eleven takes, they quit trying to perfect it. They just couldn't turn the Velvet Underground into the Byrds.

"Heroin" closely resembled Lou's Pickwick demo—he had solidified the lyrics—and John had finally figured out how to bring the Dream Syndicate to the Velvet Underground; his viola drone skated over the top for most of the track. The Velvets had found their voice; to prevent the inevitable creep of stylistic imitation, "the band had a ten-dollar fine if you played a blues lick, because it wasn't legit," Lou later recalled. There was only one missing but crucial element on the demo: a drummer to mark the fluctuating tempo; "Heroin" needed a bass drum, the palpitating heart of Lou's bracing masterpiece of disaffected youth. Beyond that, they needed something more percussive, preferably more reliable than Angus, who marched to the beat of a different drum than anyone else in the universe. They were about to find it.

They had another missing link: no manager. John pooled his meager resources and took the demo to London, where he hoped to galvanize the Velvets' American invasion. Through a contact with Marianne Faithfull, he attempted to send the tape to Andrew Loog Oldham, the manager of the Rolling Stones, to no avail. Through another tenuous connection, he tried to get it into the hands of Brian Epstein, who managed the Beatles, but it fell into the slush pile. Before Epstein died of a drug overdose in 1967, he and Lou shared a taxi together; Lou pulled out a joint, and Epstein bestowed his toke of approval, but nothing came of the brief meeting. The Velvets demo made its way through various back channels, but the Velvet Underground failed to gain traction in the UK. There would be no magic bullet overseas; their shot of visibility would remain inextricably linked to the underground.

Late in the fall of 1965, avant-garde filmmaker Barbara Rubin began cajoling her friend Al Aronowitz to attend some of Heliczer's multimedia installations and hear the Velvets. Heliczer had upgraded from his cramped tenement on 56 Ludlow, moving to an expansive loft a few blocks away at 450 Grand Street, which was more conducive to the happenings he hosted. Aronowitz was a journalist for the *Saturday Evening Post* and later penned the Pop Scene column for the *New York Post*; he was a pioneering rock critic and exponent of the New Journalism who covered the Brill Building in a brash, personal style that presaged *Behind the Music*. He was also a friend of Kerouac and Ginsberg.

Notably, he had just introduced the Beatles to Bob Dylan. In other words, Aronowitz had the type of high-profile connections that could break a band, having cemented a reputation as an active trendsetter on the scene he so avidly covered. Rubin was released from a mental institution in 1963, and quickly came to work for Jonas Mekas at the trailblazing Film-Makers' Cooperative; by the age of seventeen, her controversial film *Christmas on Earth*, originally titled *Cocks and Cunts*, had subverted norms and challenged the puritanical status quo; featuring psychedelic camera movements and gratuitous nudity, one scene depicts Warhol superstar Naomi Levine in the buff, covered in body paint, with a superimposed vulva taking up the screen. Soon, Rubin attracted the attention of Warhol himself. The event Rubin encouraged Aronowitz to attend was a screening-cum-filming of Heliczer's *Venus in Furs*, inspired by the eponymous Velvets song. Never definitively completed, the film employed self-referentiality to comment on forms of mediation, exposure, and representations of the body in mainstream culture from within and without. Aronowitz came, and so did a CBS news crew. Aronowitz liked what he heard, and agreed to manage the band. In early December, John took his final bow with the Dream Syndicate; after his instrumental work as an unsung hero of minimalism, he would be replaced by one of its key progenitors: Terry Riley.

By early December, Aronowitz booked the first paying gig for the Velvet Underground; they would begin at Summit High School in New Jersey's Passaic Valley—Philip Roth country—and it wouldn't pay much, only eighty dollars for the whole band. They didn't receive top billing either; that went to the Myddle Class, a local folk-rock act that had caught Aronowitz's eye. Tickets cost $2.50; at the bottom of the concert flier, in small print, the Velvets were listed under "Also appearing on the program" after the Forty

Fingers, another regional act under Aronowitz's wing that was destined for obscurity. Through their newly acquired manager, the Myddle Class had signed a songwriting deal with Goffin and King, who at the time were writing for the Monkees, and collaborated on "Free as the Wind," the first of several singles. Superficially, the Myddle Class resembled the Velvets' early demos, but Lou and the band were about to cross the Rubicon. First, though, they had to avert a crisis.

Angus refused to show up for the gig. "You mean we start when they tell us to and we have to end when they tell us to?" he said. "I can't work that way." Beyond his unwillingness to compromise his integrity for any amount of money, and especially not twenty dollars, MacLise also felt that the aggravation of transporting heavy drums to New Jersey outweighed the show's creative merit. He promptly quit the band. With little time to spare, the remaining three members brainstormed potential drummers; they didn't know anyone willing or able to fill in until they could find a more permanent replacement. Then Sterling remembered. "Oh, Tucker's sister plays drums," he said. Maureen Tucker, the twenty-one-year-old younger sister of Lou's *Lonely Woman Quarterly* colleague Jim Tucker, lived with her parents in Levittown after dropping out of Ithaca College, working as a data puncher for IBM by day and playing drums in a garage band by night. Suddenly, she was a prospect. They immediately hopped on the train and headed for Levittown.

Moe Tucker was not a trained drummer. "I couldn't play a perfect roll for a million dollars. I didn't know how, and I didn't want to know how," she later recalled. She adopted an intuitive style based on her two idols, Bo Diddley and Nigerian percussionist Babatunde Olatunji, whose "Akiwowo" opened and closed Murray the K's radio broadcasts. In 1962 Moe sold candy as part of a fundraiser to bring Olatunji to Levittown, and after a concert in the school auditorium, even got his autograph. She combined the second-line stomp and clave of Bo Diddley's shuffle with Olatunji's tribal syncopation to lay down a behind-the-beat rhythm that oozed rock 'n' roll. She also played standing up. After a brief audition in which Lou determined that Moe could keep a beat, they hired her on the spot and ran through the brief set list.

Booking the Velvets as an opening act was like chasing grain alcohol with club soda. "Nothing could have prepared the kids and parents assembled in the auditorium for what they were about to experience that night," wrote Rob Norris, who was one of the students in the audience. Dressed in black turtlenecks, behind sunglasses—with Cale adorned in what could only be described as silver bling—they were taboo even before they drew blood with the first note. Moe Tucker, in her pixie haircut, looked like an androgynous Ringo Starr. Finally equipped with a sufficient sound system, they turned it up to eleven, feedback be damned, and launched into the opening machine gun hits of "There She Goes Again," a quote appropriated from Marvin Gaye's "Hitch Hike." In Brechtian tradition, they were hurling proverbial stones into the audience; most couldn't identify with the lyrics, which were decidedly beyond allegory. The Velvets flew in the face of the wholesome platitudes of the current top of the charts, the Byrds' rendition of "Turn! Turn! Turn!," which allowed listeners to project their fuzzy moments and lost loves into the song. Lou did not allow this. He laid no claim to axiomatic universality, but rather a radical voyeuristic subjectivism; "Venus in Furs" was a story most had not read, and for $2.50, it was coming at them at an ear-splitting seventy-five beats a minute. They didn't just break the fourth wall; they shattered it.

"It swelled and accelerated like a giant tidal wave that was threatening to engulf us all. At this point, most of the audience retreated in horror for the safety of their homes, thoroughly convinced of the dangers of rock & roll music," Norris wrote. "Venus in Furs" took care of the rest of the prudes. The more intrepid (and those whose parents weren't there to chaperone) walked closer into the maelstrom. When Lou announced their closer, "Heroin," and Moe Tucker began pounding the bass drum into submission, it was clear the title bore no final *e*; no one was expecting *Jane Eyre*.

Backstage, the sweating Myddle Class were furious. John tried to apologize, but the damage had already been done. "At least you've given them a night to remember," said Aronowitz. As a consolation, he invited everyone over to his house for an after-party. As Lou signed a lone autograph as he was packing up, it was evident it would be the first and last time the Velvet Underground would be invited to play at a high school.

"It didn't really seem like the band was ever going to make any money or go anywhere else," says Martha Morrison, Sterling's then-girlfriend, whom he later married. "It didn't seem like a big thing. They were serious, and we believed in the band, but the money was never even mentioned really. They just wanted to play." Sterling had little self-confidence in his style, which did not match the cleaner aesthetic of his peers on the folk scene. "I knew how much he cared, and he would always ask me afterwards, 'How was it? Was it awful?'" Morrison says.

It didn't help that they had little to no external validation or commercial success. So when Aronowitz gave them their next gig, a two-week residency leading up to Christmas at the Café Bizarre, a club a few blocks from Washington Square Park in the Village, they felt no incentive to placate the management. The club's name was a bit of a misnomer; allegedly a former stable belonging to Aaron Burr, it cultivated a gothic atmosphere featuring cobwebs and oak paneling with a fishnet-clad waitstaff caked in Victorian makeup—Cale's spectral viola matched the décor. The club catered to tourists looking to experience the Village and an audience of underage locals, and served coffee and ice cream and hosted fledgling rock acts.

A barker outside drew in the crowd. It was the first club to introduce folk to the Village—Dave Van Ronk's basement fee dovetailed with the low-rent business model—mutually beneficial until the artists got a better offer. To maximize space for customers, the band was crammed into a tiny area in the back of the club; Moe only had room for a tambourine, which would become a permanent part of her drum kit. They played five to six sets a night till closing, and were paid five dollars each, in addition to food; after they finished, the band went to Chinatown or Luna's in Little Italy for a midnight snack. For want of six hours of material, they sometimes resorted to "Roll Over Beethoven"; it would be the last time the Velvets covered Chuck Berry. "The impression I had was that nobody was listening. There might be some people sitting around having coffee, but no interest at all," says Martha Morrison. "They were just out, and that was the band."

Unfortunately, at least one person was listening: the club manager, and he did not like what he heard. But before their residency ended, the Café Bizarre welcomed its most bizarre guest ever: Andy Warhol.

# 8

The Velvets got their big break out of a bad business deal. Barbara Rubin had convinced Paul Morrissey, Warhol's right-hand man, that he should consider the Velvet Underground as a possibility for the Factory house band. As central as he would be to the story, at least initially, Warhol had little interest in signing an unknown group. Warhol had a reputation as a prolific album cover artist, having worked on the packaging for albums by Vladimir Horowitz, Count Basie, Thelonious Monk, Kenny Burrell, and others, but branching out into music management was beyond his expertise. Yet at this critical juncture, Warhol's infamy as agent provocateur far eclipsed his net worth, and Morrissey felt it was time to capitalize on the name. Broadway producer Michael Myerberg, who had produced the first Broadway production of *Waiting for Godot*, approached Morrissey, soliciting Warhol's involvement in a nightclub he planned to open in an airplane hangar in Garden City, Queens, to be tentatively called Andy Warhol's Up.

Morrissey was skeptical of the venture but saw an opportunity to manage a rock group he could then install at the club for a cut of the profit. Myerberg gave the green light, and within a week, Morrissey took Factory associate and multi-hyphenate artist Gerard Malanga to shoot some footage of the band at the Café Bizarre. Morrissey was immediately convinced, and approached them on a set break. They denied having a manager—they only had a verbal contract with Aronowitz—and jumped at the offer to work with Warhol. The symbiosis seemed natural; the Velvets' sardonic wit, blatant hostility toward the established order, and twee intellectualism was Warhol's stock-in-trade.

Having established a relationship with Warhol, the Velvets used the remainder of the Café Bizarre residency to develop new material, often performing the same song repeatedly. In particular, management objected to the macabre "The Black Angel's Death Song," which opened with a shrill viola pedal ostinato; despite the club's haunting décor, Lou's lyrics were too lugubrious. It was not in the Christmas spirit. Having already forced the Velvets to play Christmas Eve, the club demanded that they also play New Year's. On December 30 the manager told them that if they played "The Black Angel's Death Song" one more time, they would be fired. So they did.

At Warhol's Factory, they would have a larger performance space, less managerial interference, and much wider exposure. Their equipment also got an upgrade. Warhol had an endorsement deal with Vox that would finally provide the quality amplifiers they needed: a Westminster, a Super Beatle, and megatons of reverb. The next day, Warhol arrived with an entourage: Rubin, *Village Voice* cofounder John Wilcock, quintessential Factory girl Edie Sedgwick, Donald Lyons, Morrissey, and Malanga, who was so transfixed by the cacophonous din that he began gyrating uncontrollably in an eroticized improvised dance. With a nod of assent, Warhol granted his papal imprimatur, and the Velvets were officially baptized the next big thing. Yet they would never play at Myerberg's club, later renamed Murray the K's World—he reneged and hired Lou's former Syracuse collaborator Felix Cavaliere and the Young Rascals. Warhol, though, always utilitarian, was not one to throw the baby out with the bathwater.

As if validating the critical mass that had gathered around them, on New Year's the Velvets had their first shot of national visibility. On the *CBS Evening News with Walter Cronkite*, correspondent Dave Dugan profiled the Factory milieu in a segment titled "The Making of an Underground Film," featuring Heliczer, Mekas, Brakhage, Warhol, Edie Sedgwick, and the Velvets. The Factory group gathered at punk godfather Danny Fields's apartment to watch the broadcast. "Not everyone digs underground movies, but those who do can dig 'em here," Dugan began. It soon cut to swirling 8mm footage of Lou, John, and Sterling, shirtless with psychedelic body paint and white pancake makeup. "Some underground films have been criticized for dealing too frankly with such themes as sex and nudity, but many movies such as this one may simply seem confusing." The segment then turned the lens to Warhol's landmark film, *Sleep*, juxtaposing its six soporific hours with a raucous dance scene at the Factory. "Andy, why is it you're making these films?"

"Well, it's just easier to do than painting. The camera has a motor and you just turn it on and you just walk away. It tapes all by itself."

"Is there anything special you're trying to say in these films?"

From behind his trademark frames and shock of platinum hair, Andy responded with a classic piece of Warholian popism. "Uh . . . no."

The Velvets rang in the New Year in Warholian style at Harlem's Apollo Theater at a Bo Diddley show; Diddley had just released *500% More Man.* After a few martinis, Sedgwick left with Cale, who—now definitely too sexy for his classical pedigree—had wasted no time in wooing the most alluring Factory girl. Suddenly, Lou found himself swept up into the Warholian vortex, subsumed by a narrative bigger than himself; for the first time in his life, he had unwittingly joined a movement, and Warhol was the irresistible force to Lou's immovable object. Soon, they had Factory nicknames: Lou was Lulu, John was Black Jack. It was 1966, and the wind had changed.

When Lou awoke on January 1, 1966, the MTA had gone on strike, shutting down the subway, but for the first time, he was already right where he wanted to be. "The Sounds of Silence" was all over the radio; folk had finally gained mainstream pop acceptance only months after the Velvets had abandoned the genre. Across the Atlantic, an eighteen-year-old singer named David Bowie was preparing to release his first single in the United States. And Lou was experiencing an artistic rebirth. He was captured in eleven of Warhol's nearly five hundred iconic screen tests, an informal compilation of the decade's counterculture celebrities and avant-garde luminaries from Dali to Dylan to Duchamp. One features Lou suggestively brandishing a Coke behind sunglasses, in another he's savoring a Hershey bar, then lasciviously biting into an apple, but the first screen test—three minutes of head-on Lou in chiaroscuro—captures the ephemeral image of callow youth. It's coy, not menacing; wide-eyed, not grimacing; sober, not drug-addled; Keats, not De Quincey. He even blinks.

The Factory door greeted visitors with a sign: ABSOLUTELY NO DRUGS ALLOWED. So the stairs became a shooting gallery: methedrine, Seconal, Thorazine, every manner of barbiturate and amphetamine, available without a prescription. To be there was to not be fully there, or to be really out there, or only half there, depending on what was there at the time.

If there was one drop of innocence left in Lou, it was frozen out at the Factory. Named for the tin foil and high-gloss paint that Billy Name installed as its avant-wallpaper, the Silver Factory was a low-rent, five-story industrial building that had primarily been occupied by the People's Cold Storage and Warehouse, and though no longer refrigerated, retained the frigid residue of liquid ammonia. The overhead was low, and though the people-watching was free, little else was; the Factory even had a pay phone. The fourth-floor loft had been home to a furniture upholsterer, so Warhol reupholstered its deteriorating walls and windows; Name procured the infamous red Queen Anne sofa on the streets, discarded in front of the YMCA next door. The plush, libidinal curve is featured in the 1964 film *Couch*, in which Beat poets Jack Kerouac, Allen Ginsberg, Peter Orlovsky, and Gregory Corso gambol around the eponymous Factory centerpiece. Lou had a large butt imprint to fill.

Name, Warhol's official photographer, captured all the Factory goings-on on his 35mm Pentax; he literally lived in the closet of the Factory but was decidedly out. He converted one of the Factory bathrooms into a darkroom. Lou entered Name's frame regularly, but most of the action transpired off-camera. On a methedrine kick, Lou, Billy, and Mary Woronov would frequent gender-bending havens like the Stonewall Inn and rave in polymorphous, polyamorous glory until closing time, which was usually at 4 AM, then continue raving at underground after-hours clubs till dawn. They weren't nocturnal; their circadian rhythm pounded a constant four-on-the-floor. With the sun up, sunglasses on, they returned to the Factory to finish it all off with a climax. "Lou would just jerk off, get off, and then get up to leave, so I had to say, 'Hey, wait a minute, I didn't come yet,'" Name later recalled. "So Lou would sit on my face while I jerked off. It was like smoking corn silk behind the barn, it was just kid stuff. There was no rapture or romance involved." There, in the psychoanalytic space of the Factory, Lou could express himself without judgment; no one would think of mandating electroshock in one of the only places in New York outside the yoke of heteronormative culture.

Despite the anything-goes milieu, the Factory ran on friendly competition. At the pansexual house of blond ambition, Lou also had to contend with the sycophantic, the foppish, and the just plain weird among the Factory denizens, Warhol's coterie of superstars—Candy Darling, Holly Woodlawn, Brigid Berlin, eventually Joe Dallesandro—to emerge as more than background music for Warhol's never-ending theater in the round. For Warhol, it was life for art's sake; he even enlisted Moe's IBM typing skills to transcribe the twenty-four-hour tapes of Warhol superstar Ondine that became *a, A Novel*, his 1968 day-in-the-life chronicle of the notorious speed freak modeled after James Joyce's *Ulysses*. Lou never quite fit in at the Factory; he was never sure if he wanted to smile or sneer at all the wan faces, and effected a lip-curling combination of both, existing in the liminal sphere between nihilism and nostalgia, hyperbole and subtext, thought and expression, refusing to be pigeonholed or sensationalized by a single descriptor. In short, he was not a joiner. A flaneur witnessing and participating in the antics of the outsized Factory eccentrics, Lou paced the concrete floors with a notebook in a state of bemused detachment, documenting the myriad grotesqueries for later use. He became the Studs Terkel of the Warholian underground. The Factory, a bizarre Disneyland of the avant-garde louche life, inoculated Lou against extravagant displays of emotion; soon, he had ice running through his veins, among other things.

Lou found a Factory ally in Barbara Hodes, a budding fashion designer who had dropped out of Cornell to accept a scholarship at Parsons, and who was then making ends meet by selling her handmade crocheted dresses at Betsey Johnson's Paraphernalia. She was Lou's first New York girlfriend, given a rare glimpse past his hardened exterior during that formative period. "There were definitely two sides. There was the side that was needy, clingy, romantic, and then there was the side that was a complete jerk," she recalls. On "I'll Be Your Mirror," Lou reflected this yin and yang persona, inspired by an interest in astrology. "Lou always told me that 'I'll Be Your Mirror' is about the sign Pisces, and about its liquidity and duality," Hodes says. His dual nature made relationships volatile. "Anytime he got close to something, he seemed to blow it up." But it was difficult to get that close to anything at the Factory, where objects in Lou's mirror were farther than they appeared, at once original and mass-produced.

At first, Martha Morrison and Moe Tucker couldn't take the chaos of the new environment. "Moe and I were horrified left and right. I remember one day hiding in the bathroom at the Factory, and the bathroom was worse than what was going on outside, all the drawings on the wall in there," says Morrison. The latrine in question depicted a constantly growing pen-drawn priapic orgy that would make de Sade blush; beyond Duchamp's urinal, this silver *O* was the perpetually backed up scatological Toilet of Sadomasochism. Yet through this carnivalesque environment, by turns celebrating and negating the notion of authenticity in a postmodern world, Warhol created a frenetic assembly line for his trademark mechanized pop art in an age of mass reproduction. Everything got flattened into a deracinated image, but inside the Factory, people could be exactly who they were, in three glittering dimensions.

"Andy was quiet and friendly, always working. We used to have to walk between those silk screens. They were all over the floor," says Morrison. "We were sitting around waiting to find out where the party was usually. That's why we went there."

The party wasn't always at the Factory. In November 1965, Warhol had received a stern missive from ELK Realty, his landlord, effectively banning all future parties. "We understand that they are generally large parties and are held after usual office hours," the letter said. "Further, we feel that a congregation of the number of people such as you have had may be contrary to various applicable government rules and regulations and also might present a serious problem with the Fire Department regulations." Clearly, they didn't realize that Warhol did some of his best work after business hours.

Fortunately, though, in December 1965 a new late-night venue opened that immediately welcomed the displaced Factory crowd: Max's Kansas City, a two-story bar and restaurant in Union Square run by Mickey Ruskin. Max's quickly became the United Nations of the city's thriving avant-garde scene; Robert Rauschenberg and Willem de Kooning, William S. Burroughs and Allen Ginsberg, and Garland Jeffreys and Philip Glass would gather at Max's to eat, drink, and break the fire code. Patti Smith and Iggy Pop would soon make their way there; shortly after moving to the city, a young Debbie Harry became a waitress. Warhol and his retinue colonized the elite back room, where dilettantes from the jet set went on a gender bender. Its gritty live shows were legendary. "Max's, before they played there, was our hangout, with really good steaks and really good ice cream balls and loads of fun," says Martha Morrison. "That's where we saw everybody. We went almost every night. Max's was like the clubhouse." For Lou and the band, it was a nonstop party, hopscotching between the Factory by day and Max's by night.

By January 3, 1966, Warhol and Morrissey had exerted managerial control. They appreciated the Velvets' material, which resonated with Warhol's antimaterialist wretched excess, but felt that the band lacked the panache and star power of a convincingly charismatic frontman. If they were to play the Factory, they needed a face that embodied it. After some quibbling, they presented Nico, a statuesque, nearly six-foot-tall blond German model-cum-singer with an elusive Vermeer-esque mystique.

Born Christa Päffgen, Nico was a teenage sex symbol, modeling for *Vogue* and Coco Chanel before turning her ear to rock, wending her way through the beds of a constellation of stars—Brian Jones of the Rolling Stones,

Dylan, and Jim Morrison among them. Nico was rock's Helen of Troy. She recorded Dylan's "I'll Keep It with Mine," which he originally wrote for Judy Collins and evidently repurposed as an uninspired collateralized folk tribute to their brief tryst; eventually, an infatuated Leonard Cohen wrote the unrequited-love song "Take This Longing" for Nico.

Yet nature was not as generous in other ways; Nico was deaf in one ear and, as a consequence, sang everything slightly flat, imbuing her haunting delivery with a discordant expressionistic melancholy. Warhol referred to her as "an IBM computer with a Garbo accent." Despite her Dietrich-esque style, Nico's inconsolable loneliness only heightened her otherworldly beauty— Leonard Cohen later referred to her as "the apotheosis of the Nazi earth mother"—with a tortured artistic soul that complicated what her perfect cheekbones might have otherwise suggested. She was so achingly beautiful that Federico Fellini cast her as herself in *La Dolce Vita*, his psychosexual meditation on the hedonistic life of aesthetes inhabiting a proto-Warholian Roman demimonde. In 1962 she had a son, Ari, following an affair with French actor Alain Delon. She raised Ari as a single mother, mostly eschewing the film industry for the rest of her career. Her dream was to sing, her breathtaking beauty both a blessing and a curse; "I have no regrets, except that I was born a woman instead of a man," she claimed.

Nico quickly became a muse for Warhol and Morrissey, starring in *Chelsea Girls*—the two men's documentary on the bohemian world surrounding the Hotel Chelsea—*The Closet*, and *Imitation of Christ*. Realizing Nico's musical aspirations, Warhol and Morrissey demonstrated their Corman-like production ethos, taking advantage of a mutually beneficial opportunity by slotting her into the Velvet Underground. At twenty-seven, she was the oldest in the group, though this did not necessarily confer seniority. Issued as a nonnegotiable directive, Morrissey's gambit was met with mixed antagonism and charged sexual tension; Nico was the anode to their cathode that created an instant high-voltage jolt of electric polarity. As a lifelong practicing Catholic—Warhol made near-daily trips to the Upper East Side Church of St. Vincent Ferrer, often with his beatific mother, Julia, and volunteered at a church-run homeless shelter—sex was not the object. For Warhol, between his religious devotion and homosexual orientation, cognitive dissonance became a pervasive trope, and Nico injected just a little more dissonance into the Velvets. By adding Nico, he had made the minute adjustment that transformed the Velvet Underground from art-pop into pop art. The Velvets had no choice but to accept the towering flaxen-haired chanteuse, but as a détente, it was unanimously decided that she would always remain a separate entity appearing *with* the Velvet Underground, not a part of it, with Lou continuing to sing most of the songs. Lou also decided that he had to have her.

In their first rehearsal with Nico at the Factory, the Velvets were equipped with decent amplifiers and were ready to run through material, looking for something well suited to their new counterpart. After running through "Venus in Furs," "Heroin," and several others, they decided to give Nico a shot at "There She Goes Again." From "She's down on her knees, my friend," it was not working out; she barely made it through the first verse before stopping. They would need to write something new that would play to Nico's strengths; Warhol suggested Lou write a song about Edie Sedgwick as "femme fatale," the type of offhand remark he would frequently make to stir the creative juices, and Lou wrote one with Nico in mind, marking the first time he used an augmented chord. "All Tomorrow's Parties" also fit the dadaist ennui of Nico's delivery; they were slowly finding a rhythm.

That night after rehearsal, the band reaped the first rewards of their newfound benefactor. Clambering into a bus, they braved the forty-degree weather and took a ride to Roosevelt Raceway on Long Island for the opening of the racing season. In addition to hobnobbing with Salvador Dali, they had their first mention in the *New York Times*, which described them as "Warhol's jazz group."

On January 13 they continued to make waves, playing their first gig with Warhol in an unlikely setting: the New York Society for Clinical Psychiatry's annual gala at the gilded Colonnade and Grand Ballroom at Delmonico's Hotel, blocks from Wall Street. The staid organization, some 350 strong, had invited Warhol as the keynote speaker, partially as a clinical case study, but after he and the Velvets were invited in, soon the inmates were running the asylum. Warhol, dressed in a bespoke suit, Billy Name, Malanga, Sedgwick, Rubin, and cameraman Danny Williams had artistic designs of their own for the evening, which was dubbed "the Chic Mystique," pitched as an exercise in sociological disruption and Freudian refraction, "a kind of community action-under-ground-look-at-yourself-film project." The Velvets were about to collide with genteel society. Following cocktail hour, opening remarks began. Some referred to the event as a "spontaneous eruption of the id" and "a repetition of the concrete quite akin to the LSD experience," a sentiment echoed by the director of psychiatry at Bellevue.

"Creativity and the artist have always held a fascination for the serious student of human behavior," the program chairman said; that night, the patients analyzed the doctors. Roast beef with string beans and fingerling potatoes were brought out as the Velvets took the stage, a silent torture film being projected onto them as they unleashed a high-decibel Jungian apocalypse; Lou had more than his fair share of pent-up rage at the psychopharmaceutical industrial complex. Malanga and Sedgwick started provocatively flagellating themselves with a leather whip as Rubin raced around the room conducting her own Kinsey study. According to the *New York Times*, the evening emptied out fast. "It was ridiculous, outrageous, painful," said one of the psychiatrists. "Everything that's new doesn't necessarily have meaning. It seemed like a whole prison ward had escaped." The Velvets considered the evening a smashing success, scorched retinas and all; the '60s had happened, and they wanted everyone to know.

Many people were already aware, and the reactionary conservatives were not happy about the decay of traditional moral values. On January 21, 1966, *Time* published an unsigned editorial titled "The Homosexual in America," a vitriolic jeremiad against degeneracy and the collapse of culture. It marshaled André Gide, W. Somerset Maugham, and the Bible to condemn empathy or tolerance for homosexuality and its impact on American life, claiming that "growing permissiveness about homosexuality and a hedonistic attitude toward all sex have helped 'convert' many people who might have repressed their inclinations in another time or place." Anonymously, the author writes that "increasingly, deviates are out in the open, particularly in fashion and the arts," appropriating Cold War anxiety by describing the underground as a "Homintern." Adding to the appreciable irony, Leonardo and Michelangelo are anomalies, the Greeks a misreading of a political contingency spurred by sexual frustration. Conversion therapy is strongly recommended, and attempts to conflate the civil rights movement with gay rights vehemently decried. It concludes with a simple reminder that homosexuality is a form of mental illness; it would remain in the DSM until 1973, and if the anonymous author had his or her way, forever. "It is a pathetic little second-rate substitute for reality, a pitiable flight from life. As such it deserves fairness, compassion, understanding and, when possible, treatment. But it deserves no encouragement, no glamorization, no rationalization, no fake status as minority martyrdom, no sophistry about simple differences in taste—and, above all, no pretense that it is anything but a pernicious sickness."

Warhol responded fast. Refusing to remain underground, he booked an appearance with the Velvets and the Fugs on talk show host David Susskind's program on WNTA, New York's public television network. Abandoning any pretensions of civility, Warhol and his retinue wreaked havoc on the sleek studio, as Rubin and Williams pranced around with a camera documenting the unapologetic media disruption; Malanga made liberal use of his props; Fug Ed Sanders rhapsodized about cunnilingus; the stench of pot permeated the room. It was mass hysteria on the small screen. Susskind curtailed the interview before all hell broke loose. Though the genial interviewer had the best of intentions—several years later he would become an early gay rights activist—he served as a figurehead for conservative heteronormativity who symbolized the established order's tacit attempt to repress the American identity crisis within. With no double jeopardy, they penetrated the mainstream. For Warhol, the revolution would be televised.

Yet Warhol's transgressive public act was just a coming attraction for the next happening, with the Velvets front and center. For one week in early February, he hosted Andy Warhol, Up-Tight, a psychedelic multimedia presentation that was out in the open, glamorized, surreal, irrational, and above all, sure to convert the uninitiated. This time, the Velvets got top billing. Staged at the Film-Makers' Cinematheque, performances were twice daily, three times on the weekend. Over a kaleidoscopic light show by Danny Williams, Warhol projected *Lupe*, his impressionistic biopic of "Mexican spitfire" actress Lupe Vélez, an Edie Sedgwick vehicle. Dispelling any doubts as to the Velvets' rank in the Homintern leadership, they opened with "Venus in Furs," a live soundtrack to overlapping silent projections of Warhol's *Vinyl*, based on *A Clockwork Orange*, *Symphony of Sound*, a filmed Velvets rehearsal, and other cinematic curios, as Malanga and Sedgwick danced in hypnotic rapture. It would be one of Sedgwick's final appearances with Warhol; within weeks, she dramatically severed ties altogether and began a downward spiral that ended in her premature death five years later.

That night, as Lou intoned the opening lines of "Heroin," Malanga pantomimed the lyrics; he held a spoon over a lit candle, produced what appeared to be a hypodermic needle, used his belt to tie off, shot up, and gyrated around the stage in an ecstatic dance of death. It was an antiauthoritarian act of martyrdom against the status quo, a sin for humanity's sins, and the ultimate cure for an uptight society. To reeducate the inculcated, Warhol immediately decided to take the show to college.

For Rutgers Uptight, their second attempt to foment an anarchist revolution in New Jersey, tickets were slow to sell, so hours before the performance, Warhol and his band of pranksters descended on the cafeteria in New Brunswick. Before long, a security guard called for backup; Barbara Rubin caught the whole uproarious scene on camera. They immediately sold the remaining eight hundred tickets. That night, the Velvets appeared in white, as ultrasonic avenging angels; by the end of the evening, someone had pulled the fire alarm, but the overwhelming din of the Velvets drowned it out.

Warhol then set his sights on the Midwest. He rented a bus and set out for the University of Michigan Film Festival in Ann Arbor, where they had booked an appearance in March. No one could drive; Nico was deemed the most qualified, and took the wheel for the six-hundred-mile perilous journey. Up-Tight sent shockwaves through the crowd, especially the innocuous-sounding "Melody Laughter," an incessant recursive feedback loop, and the deafening "The Nothing Song," which consisted of nothing but a psychedelic vamp followed by thirty minutes of uninterrupted minimalist feedback, piercing overtones, and strobe lights. In Shakespearean times, "nothing" was a euphemism for death, female genitalia, and that little death we call an orgasm; for the Velvets in Michigan, it was all of the above. Having traumatized the University of Michigan, they were ready to go home. On the long ride home, they made a pit stop for burgers and were almost arrested by local authorities.

Back on their home turf, the Velvets played an informal event at Paraphernalia, the modish Madison Avenue boutique that employed designer Betsey Johnson, who had graduated from Syracuse with Lou. Johnson had been hired to design sleek, fierce costumes for the Velvets; that night, she also met her future husband, John Cale. Johnson custom-tailored the outfits to the band's polarized personalities. "I always made John his black canvas suits with big hunks of ruffles and bows coming out, which were gorgeous. And Lou wanted his crotch to be big, so I would always cut him a crotch," she later recounted to *Women's Wear Daily*.

With the costumes ready, Warhol had several days to prepare for the opening of Myerberg's club in Garden City; Up-Tight had been a dry run for Warhol's ill-fated venture, the raison d'être of his collaboration with the Velvets. The week prior to the opening, the deal fell through. Not one to throw anything out—even Brillo pads became pop art—Warhol and Morrissey took out a monthlong lease at the Dom, the Polish National Home, which was rented out for Polish weddings and, on this occasion, the Velvet Underground's extended residency.

Located between Second and Third Avenues on a bohemian block of St. Mark's Place, the site was no stranger to avant-garde sonic mayhem—the Fugs played the bar downstairs—but Warhol felt it was time for the underground to come up. He and Morrissey began feverishly working to transform the Open Stage at the Dom into an interactive, adrenaline-fueled nightclub in the span of a week. Morrissey took out an ad in the *Village Voice*: "Come blow your mind. The Silver Dream Factory Presents the first ERUPTING PLASTIC INEVITABLE." The next night, Friday, April 1, 1966, at 9:00 PM, it erupted—this was no April Fool's joke. The psychedelic light show eclipsed its previous seizure-inducing luminosity; *Kiss*, *Blow Job*, and several other films projected simultaneously titillated the disoriented, grokking revelers; superstars Ingrid Superstar, Ronnie Cutrone, and a relative newcomer, Mary Woronov, joined Malanga with his torture chamber of sadomasochistic props; Nico stunned in a white pantsuit; the Velvets, all in black, donning sunglasses to shield their eyes from the neon flares, simply killed.

The EPI was a visual and sonic cornucopia, an eye-opening opiate of the huddled masses; by 2 AM opening night, not only minds were blown—the Dom had effectively exploded. Renamed the Exploding Plastic Inevitable, within the first week, the EPI had grossed $18,000. During the course of the disturbing spectacle, Lou almost got electrocuted onstage and someone walked off with Moe Tucker's drums and Lou's Gretsch; tomfoolery was to be expected. This was a happening. Warhol stayed for opening night, but after that fiat lux moment, on Saturday, the pop-up scene creator rested; he had to be up early for the Sabbath. "Andy and his mom went to church. I remember Saturday nights at the Dom, Andy would leave at midnight, go buy the *New York Times*, and go home to his mother," recalls Hodes. "Andy would always say, 'You have to bring home the bacon.'"

The EPI, for all its Day-Glo hedonism, was still a business venture. Lou and the band, as well as everyone else involved in the production, were paid a flat rate, about $100 per performance, which was sustaining, but not rock star money. Morrissey and Warhol knew that if they wanted to be true contenders in the music industry, they would have to expand beyond ephemeral East Village happenings and create something more permanent. So the Velvets would have to record an album.

# 9

Unlike the band's earlier demos, *The Velvet Underground & Nico* was largely recorded at breakneck pace under deleterious conditions. Always a bit of a skinflint, Warhol hedged his bets and only allocated about $1,000 for studio time. As the Velvets didn't have a record deal, Warhol contacted Norman Dolph, a middle management Columbia Records executive and part-time disc jockey and art collector about coproducing the album on spec; he agreed to barter for art and even chipped in for studio time.

Warhol was unfazed by the fact that Dolph had never produced an album. They booked four days at Scepter Studios on West Fifty-Fourth Street, a midsize label that had recorded Dionne Warwick, the Kingsmen, and even the Isley Brothers' "Twist and Shout." Whatever happened, they had no time for a learning curve. When they arrived on April 18, 1966, the chances of making rock history looked dim. Scepter Studios was a cramped, dilapidated hole in the wall, its equipment in a state of shabby disarray that made Pickwick look state-of-the-art—but true to their lo-fi origins, they played it by ear.

Dolph brought in John Licata, a Scepter engineer, to prevent any hiccups. Warhol, a music industry neophyte, adopted a laissez-faire approach antithetical to the censorship prevalent in the recording zeitgeist; he was the banana that ripened other fruit, quite literally in this case. The cult of personality surrounding Warhol existed mostly in negative space—it was what he didn't say that mattered. "He was like the guard dog," Lou later recalled. "Andy said, 'Don't change anything, leave it alone, just do exactly—the exact same thing you're doing; don't let them near it.'" He would periodically drop in for a half hour, toting the tape recorder that was practically a fashion accessory, listen to the playback, and blithely remark, "Oh, that's fantastic."

Most of what they laid down in the free-for-all recording at Scepter ended up on the album's final mix: "Run Run Run," "The Black Angel's Death Song," "European Son," "Femme Fatale," "All Tomorrow's Parties," and "I'll Be Your Mirror." They agreed it had to be perfect, without any postproduction tweaks. Nico lobbied to be featured on lead vocals on more than the latter three, but to her chagrin, the Velvets would barely even approve those. After a series of fruitless attempts at "I'll Be Your Mirror"—no matter what, the Germanic chanteuse could never conjure the image of Shelley, on whom the song was based—Nico burst into tears. She nailed the next take. Warhol liked her haunting delivery so much that he suggested pressing the record with a prefabricated groove that would repeat the eponymous lyric in a sonic infinity mirror. "European Son," an atonal wall of sound that grows out of a Chuck Berry riff, pushes the limits of rock as the Velvets pay tribute to the tradition and usher in a brazen new era of savage feedback and minimalist experimentation. The eight-minute tone poem has two terse stanzas, followed by an instrumental Sturm und Drang fracas:

> You killed your European Son
> You spit on those under twenty-one
> But now your blue clouds have gone
> You'd better say so long

Bidding a violent farewell to the sanitized rock of the past, the primordial sound and fury emanating from the amps overwhelmed the lyrics. It was a tactile clarion call that shattered its blues structure; in-studio Foley created the sound effect when Lou and John dragged a chair across the floor and dropped a mirror. Lou dedicated the song to Delmore Schwartz, who despised rock lyrics. Schwartz, who had moved to New York after his teaching position had been terminated, was in a permanent state of hallucinatory intoxication; Lou hoped he would appreciate the homage. Yet the resulting acetate failed to get any serious traction, mostly due to its taboo subject matter. When the band gathered to give the master its first spin at 33 St. Mark's Place, the apartment shared by second-generation New York School poets Anne Waldman and Lewis Warsh, it seemed entirely possible that the album would never make it beyond the insular demimonde they inhabited. It would be almost a year before it was finally released.

Warhol did manage to use his cache to persuade MGM to sign a modest record deal with the Velvets, though; as an incentive, he agreed to do the cover art gratis. For $3,000 and royalties, they had their first mainstream success. Tom Wilson, a visionary MGM A&R executive, would be peripherally involved in their first two albums. Wilson, a black Harvard graduate from Waco, Texas, transitioned from radical collaborations with Sun Ra and Cecil Taylor to Frank Zappa and the Mothers of Invention, Dylan, and the Velvets; his hands-off approach allowed the band the creative liberty that made them original. Yet the album struggled forward in fits and starts. Before any final arrangements could be made for its distribution, Warhol booked the Velvets in Los Angeles and put them on a plane.

For their planned two-week stint at the Trip, a short-lived venue on the Sunset Strip, dubbed "Hollywood's hippie hangout" by the press, the Exploding Plastic Inevitable met with horror, disdain, and downright revulsion. Prior bookings included the Temptations, the Byrds, and the Rising Sons; the Velvets residency followed the Four Tops. Bright-eyed, bell-bottom-clad girls flocked there hoping to see teen idols but encountered what looked like a group of undertakers and sounded like the breaking of the seventh seal. None of the plastic people in California could comprehend Malanga and Woronov's lithe, bullwhip-wielding interpretive dance.

On opening night, the Modern Folk Quintet opened with their down-home ramble, drawing from a catalog of folk spirituals including "Swing Low, Sweet Chariot" and the pastoral "It Was a Very Good Year," antithetical to the Velvets' blood-curdling howl of defiance; they only appreciated one type of flowering plant. When the Velvets came on, the audience was expecting "Kumbaya"; instead, like a Looney Tunes punch line, they were dropped off a cliff into an existential void.

Despite any errors in marketing, the band's L.A. debut at the Trip sold well, but the bookers were left with buyers' remorse. Jim Morrison was one of the only attendees who appreciated it. When disparaging scuttlebutt didn't sink them, the media fallout took care of the rest. "It will replace nothing except suicide," Cher reportedly told Sonny. *Variety* described the proceedings as "a three ring psychosis." Only the *Los Angeles Times* attached a silver lining to their tepid review: "Not since the Titanic ran into that iceberg has there been such a collision as when Andy Warhol's Exploding Plastic Inevitable burst upon the audiences at The Trip Tuesday. For once a Happening really happened, and it took Warhol to come out from New

York to show how it's done." Yet promising a slice of cake and delivering a slice of life was considered false advertising. In California, the factories used a different kind of tinsel and made different kinds of movies; all *Blow Job* and *Doctor Zhivago* had in common was a pair of lips. Amid all that smog, the Velvets couldn't breathe.

The Velvet Underground never made it to the first weekend in L.A.; the Trip got shut down by the police on the third night due to suspicions of drug-fueled obscenity and problems with their liquor license (though the club had more illicit substances circulating on the floor). Rather than consider the West Coast tour a sunk cost, they stayed on in hazy limbo; due to a union technicality, they were contractually required to remain within the sprawling city limits in order to be paid their full fee. Taking advantage of the reprieve, the Velvets set up in the Castle, a palatial mansion in the Hollywood Hills where Dylan and Ginsberg had once stayed. There, Lou's relationship with Nico flourished; they also took the time to rerecord several tracks at TTG Studios with Tom Wilson.

"The town itself was dead. The pool, the luxury, I enjoyed that, but I remember walking out one day to get some beer, and there was nobody anywhere," says Martha Morrison. "And I said to the guy, 'Where is everyone?' And he said, 'No one walks here.' So I said, 'I'm going back to Brooklyn.'"

Before heading back east, though, in late May the band got booked in San Francisco at the Fillmore by promoter Bill Graham, a former Holocaust refugee who instantly disliked Warhol. "It wasn't so much us against the world; it was us against San Francisco," Moe Tucker later wrote. "The hippies out there hated us and we didn't like them too much either." According to Tucker, as they went onstage, Graham looked at them with a straight face and said, "I hope you fuckers bomb." Frank Zappa and the Mothers of Invention opened with their brand of gonzo psychedelia, closing their set with "Call Any Vegetable." Lou was nonplussed; as a dyed-in-the-wool East Coaster, he hated the Grateful Dead, Jefferson Airplane, and any group in any way affiliated with West Coast hippie culture. "He's probably the single most untalented person I've heard in my life," Lou later said of Zappa. "He's a two-bit pretentious academic, and he can't play rock 'n' roll because he's a loser." (Always mercurial, Lou would later give Zappa's Rock and Roll Hall of Fame induction speech.) With a simple headline, the *San*

*Francisco Chronicle* issued the most contemptuous review of the tour: THE SIZZLE THAT FIZZLED.

Demoralized and exhausted, the group flew back to New York. Disappointed by her low profile with the Velvets, Nico booked some modeling work in Spain. Within a week, Lou checked into Beth Israel Hospital with a case of hepatitis; the unflagging EPI tour would have to continue without him at Poor Richard's in Chicago. The band recruited Angus MacLise to fill in on drums, with Moe playing bass. Angus paid Lou a hospital visit to let him know, but Lou did not mince words—Angus was in no way getting back into the band on a permanent basis. Soon after playing Chicago, EPI lighting designer Danny Williams committed suicide.

In July Lou was dealt a crushing blow. At fifty-two, Delmore Schwartz had alienated all of his friends with increasing acts of paranoia—he accused Lou of being a CIA spy the one time he came to visit. He had gradually become part of the shoddy scenery in the Village, blending in with eroded park benches in Washington Square Park or huddled over a beer at the White Horse Tavern, the literary haunt where Dylan Thomas drank himself into a stupor before dying at the Hotel Chelsea.

"Still I see only in a glass darkly and vaguely," Schwartz wrote in the margin to a letter. It was at the White Horse that he took some of his last frustrated looks into that glass as he raged against the dying of the light. Like Thomas, Schwartz did not go gentle. At the Columbia Hotel, a Times Square fleabag, he frittered away his final days high on amphetamines, drinking himself to death, alone. On July 11, 1966, delirious at three in the morning, Schwartz decided to take out the garbage but accidentally got off on the fourth floor on his way back up. He had a heart attack in the hallway; a neighbor unwittingly misconstrued it as a late-night burglary attempt. When the police arrived, they found the unconscious poet bloodied and disheveled in the hall. He died in the ambulance on the way back to Bellevue. Schwartz's untimely death was a self-fulfilling prophecy, laid out in no uncertain terms in "Sonnet: O City, City":

> *Being amid six million souls, their breath*
> *An empty song suppressed on every side*

It took two days before his body was identified at the Bellevue morgue by a reporter who recognized the name of the former literary wunderkind. When

Malanga visited Lou at the hospital to report the news, Lou immediately checked himself out to attend the funeral, disobeying the doctor's orders.

Alongside 175 mourners at the Sigmund Schwartz Gramercy Park Chapel in the East Village, Lou paid tribute to his mentor. Dwight MacDonald, the *Partisan Review* editor who first published "In Dreams Begin Responsibilities," delivered the eulogy. Dressed in black, Lou attended the interment ceremony at Cedar Park Cemetery in New Jersey; only about half a dozen people were there to say kaddish. Schwartz didn't live to hear "European Son." Mourning the loss, Lou resigned himself to the artistic pickle he would inhabit for the rest of his life: not only would he have to contend with the specter of MGM pushing for creative compromise, but he also had to ward off the ghost of Delmore, which would haunt him if he ever made that choice.

# 10

As cold comfort after Schwartz's death, the Velvets' debut single was released on Verve, "All Tomorrow's Parties" with "I'll Be Your Mirror" as its B-side. In 1961, MGM had bought Verve from jazz producer Norman Granz and, under the supervision of Creed Taylor, began expanding into bossa nova and more commercial titles. The label won a Grammy Award for Album of the Year in 1965 with tenor saxophonist Stan Getz and Brazilian guitarist João Gilberto's *Getz/Gilberto*. With Taylor at the helm, Verve signed rock artists with a penchant for improvisation that might be dismissed from more mainstream labels, adding the Blues Project, the Mothers of Invention, and the Velvets to a roster that also included the folksier sound of the Righteous Brothers.

Then the EPI tour picked up again, with stops in Provincetown, Boston, Cincinnati, West Virginia, Detroit, Canada, Philadelphia, and Cleveland, where Lou's sister, Bunny, was a student at Case Western Reserve. Most important, the Velvets met with producer Tom Wilson to discuss their long-delayed debut album.

Wilson demanded another Nico vehicle, and at Warhol's suggestion, Lou, Cale, and Morrison wrote "Sunday Morning" during all-night writing sessions; they soon recorded it at Mayfair Studios in New York. Though intended as a rumination on paranoia—not only a generative trope for the band but also foreshadowing for tension to come—the breezy song exudes the soft textures of afterglow; for Lou, introducing ironic lyrical contradictions juxtaposed with melodic harmony would be a recurrent compositional device. "Watch out, the world's behind you" captures a willful paranoia complicated by the denial that it matters. Perhaps the intermittent sexual relationship between Lou, John, and Nico, reminiscent of Francois Truffaut's *Jules and Jim*, can explain the song's uncanny disparity between the harmony and the lyric. Lou ultimately takes lead vocals on the track, which was released as the Velvets' second single. "Sunday Morning" failed to find any chart success, but rather than accepting defeat, the Velvets continued to rock on their own terms, liberated from the yoke of studio intervention. As a cult band, they had already been "discovered," yet they were still discoverable for the privileged few.

The commercial dead zone also freed them up to pursue other projects. At the behest of Warhol, Lou wrote a fiery screed on the state of litera-ture and the music industry in the "Fab" issue of *Aspen* magazine, the self-proclaimed "first three-dimensional magazine," which Warhol had been tapped to guest-edit. With the Vietnam War conducting one search-and-destroy operation after another, Lou took the rare opportunity to make an explicit political statement. "All the bastards that you were supposed to feel sorry for and fight wars for were screaming, 'Look at the freaks in Central Park with transistors up their heads,'" he wrote. "The colleges are meant to kill. Four years in which to kill you. And if you don't extend your stay, the draft, by and for old people, waits to kill you. Kill your instincts, your love, the music." Lou skewered Robert Lowell, who had won the Bollingen Poetry Translation Prize in 1962, claiming that "the only decent poetry of this century was that recorded on rock-and-roll records." True to his doo-wop upbringing, Lou's favorite rock-poem released that year was not "Paint It Black" or "Yellow Submarine" but "Stay with Me" by Lorraine Ellison. Rock was the only live wire for Lou. "Writing was dead, movies were dead. Everybody sat like an unpeeled orange. But the music was so beautiful." To Lou, it wasn't that rock could be poetry; poetry was rock.

Across the pond, Lou's missionary zeal for rock converted at least one angry young man yearning to make it new: David Bowie, who received a copy of the Velvets' unreleased album. "Everything I both felt and didn't know about rock music was opened to me on one unreleased disc," Bowie later wrote. "With the opening throbbing, sarcastic bass and guitar of 'I'm Waiting For The Man,' the linchpin, the keystone of my ambition was driven home. The music was savagely indifferent to my feelings. It didn't care if I liked it or not. It could give a fuck." Soon, Bowie began covering "I'm Waiting for the Man" in concerts. The Velvets had just found their biggest fan.

At the dawn of 1967, Lou was about to turn twenty-five, and the Velvets were contemplating what was next as their long-awaited album seemed to be lying dormant and unreleased in some studio vault like a defused bomb. Nico enlisted Lou as an ancillary sideman on her debut solo album, *Chelsea Girl*, strumming alongside Jackson Browne, the eighteen-year-old troubadour she had left him for. Nico still got the lion's share of the Velvets' media coverage, with the rest of the band jammed into a footnote, a source of constant conflict that bubbled beneath the surface.

Beyond a brief stint at the Balloon Farm, the successor to the Dom, the Velvets themselves were back to playing low-paying college gigs at Williams, Tufts, and the Rhode Island School of Design—oftentimes sans Nico. Lou had not set foot in a fraternity house in years, but like sharks starved for the big fish, they had to keep moving.

When *The Velvet Underground & Nico* was finally released on March 12, 1967, it flew way under the radar. Maybe it was being sandwiched between the bubblegum pop of *The Monkees, More of the Monkees*, and the Technicolor psychedelia of *Sgt. Pepper's Lonely Hearts Club Band*—both chronologically and stylistically. Maybe it was Warhol's infamous come-hither banana hanging ominously on the cover. Or maybe it was the incriminating press quotes inexplicably selected for the inner sleeve—"non-stop horror show," "a savage series of atonal thrusts," "the product of a secret marriage between Bob Dylan and the Marquis de Sade." Regardless, the album's failure to launch set off a wave of paranoia and cynicism that would ultimately end in a breakup. New York had let them down.

The risible *Village Voice* ad's tagline was too tongue-in-cheek: "So far 'underground,' you get the bends!" Like divers out of their depths, most of the critics suffered from compression sickness. In his *Voice* review, Richard Goldstein, one of the band's most ardent supporters, pivoted like a shoulder-shrugging Mets fan, opening by damning with faint praise: "The Velvet Underground is not an easy group to like." And though he gave the album a cautious thumbs-up—"this album has some major work behind that erect banana on the cover"—he dismissed some tracks as "pretentious to the point of misery."

A testament to the album's genre fluidity, jazz critic John Szwed reviewed it in *Jazz*, belittling the genre cross-pollination and dissonant polyphony as "rather tedious" and concluding that "something is lost in the translation." The *Chicago Daily News* condemned Lou as a menace to society, Baudelaire filtered through a storm drain: "The flowers of evil are in bloom. Someone has to stamp them out before they spread."

Mostly due to its risqué content, radio stations wouldn't advertise it, and the album itself got limited airplay; Murray the K gave "Heroin" one spin and never again, and Bob Fass at WBAI was a sympathetic ear but refused to play a seven-minute expressionistic chronicle of a mainliner's dark rendezvous with Mr. Brownstone. From the perspective of the black-and-white cultural gatekeepers who valorized or stigmatized nearly everything, no one seemed to grasp that Lou's lyrical conceit was not glorifying drug abuse or kinky sex, but reporting it, filtering the unstable postmodern condition through the lens of life on the Bowery. Just as the censors had once condemned *Adventures of Huckleberry Finn*, across the airwaves, the album was largely blacklisted.

Not even Warhol's enticing banana could stimulate sales; *The Velvet Underground & Nico* was an unmitigated flop. Consumers preferred lower-hanging fruit, but the Velvets slowly amassed a small but passionate fan base. As Brian Eno would later claim, "The Velvet Underground's first album only sold a few thousand copies, but everyone who bought one formed a band." While it faltered at home, the record reverberated in small pockets across the Atlantic, though, wearing out its grooves as far as Vietnam, where active-duty soldiers recorded "There She Goes Again" in a makeshift recording studio in a tent, and to Czechoslovakia, where a dissident group called the Plastic People of the Universe, spurred by the rise of liberalism during the 1968 Prague Spring, would eventually play it for a young poet named Vaclav Havel.

In America, though, it died on the vine. Reviled in the press, shunned by the radio, the false start relegated the Velvets to a rarefied underground; they became the prototypical cult band you've never heard of, fostering an exclusionary elitism and an unsentimental irony free of the good vibrations that dominated the rock renaissance. Yet behind the forbidding scowl lay an insecurity and a yearning to let others in. Self-consciously apolitical, the Velvets, and Lou especially, were Marxist in the Groucho sense.

The album release itself was plagued by another kind of dysfunction. Warhol's iconic cover, the stark phallic image of a banana, culled from a supermarket ad, with the arch double-entendre PEEL SLOWLY AND SEE printed in small type, required a special printing machine that delayed the release indefinitely. Sometimes a banana is just a banana; this was not one of those cases. To allay any doubts, Warhol was insistent that the banana be peelable, revealing the denuded fruit underneath. When it finally reached distribution, Eric Emerson, one of the EPI dancers, was furious after he saw his face superimposed over the band on the back cover photo, and threatened to sue Verve for copyright infringement. No sooner was the album released than the label recalled it, forced to airbrush Emerson out, lest they incur the costly reissue expense of using the custom-printing machine again. Even the recall contributed to the growing myth of the Velvet Underground, the constitutive absence of the band you had to be there to see, if they were there at all. Evidently, the record industry was not ready for Warhol's album as autonomous art object, but moreover, the stalled release and tepid response proved beyond a reasonable doubt that the world was not yet ready for the Velvet Underground.

Like the Dream Syndicate or the detonation of a V-2 rocket, the Velvet Underground's influence was felt even before it was heard. In eleven jarring tracks, the Velvets embodied the infinite messiness of city life with its eight million stories under a streamlined grid—alienation, ontological dread, memory and desire, existential loneliness, love and death—such intense, electrified feeling, expressed in only three chords. Unlike nearly everything else in the mainstream, the Velvets refused to whitewash Marvin Gaye or Chuck Berry and suture the inchoate fragments into a palatable whole consistent with bourgeois repression, but as a result, they remained marginalized on the periphery of the hegemonic monoculture; it was the price of playing against the grain. Unlike the pervasive clichés on the radio that exuded moralizing conviction and a lack of self-doubt, Lou moved from point A to point A, the only one with the chutzpah to start a song with "I don't know" and finish it with "I guess I just don't know."

Unfortunately, mainstream music was lagging behind literature's leading edge, but the poor reception and media backlash didn't stop the Velvets from proving that the sterile intellectualism of high art and the libidinous rhythms of rock were not mutually exclusive. Yet within the emergent canon of rock, Lou redefined what the genre could be. The received narrative dictated that the rock star was either Bacchus or Pan: the rapacious reprobate or the rustic truth-teller, the Rolling Stones or the Beatles, Jerry Lee Lewis or Buddy Holly, and undeniably, unequivocally a white male. Unconventional voices like Van Morrison, Jim Morrison, Frank Zappa, and Ray Davies challenged that false dichotomy, but no one was quite like Lou. He was convincing but not infallible; he had stage presence but suffered from high anxiety, a powerful center that masked deep insecurities, crises of confidence, fears of impotence, a cynicism wrapped in ambivalence, and hyperbolic doubt of everything, even himself. If being neurotic was cool, Lou Reed was Miles Davis.

For Lou, the moral bedrock of civilized society was actually a house of cards, and he couldn't stand the rank hypocrisy that permeated the culture. Beneath it all in the underground, a revolt against the unqualified smugness of paternalism quaked and pulsated, an assault on the inevitability of heterosexual love and marriage and the repressive insistence on a monolithic system of inconsistent ethics. No one could tell Lou what to do, because the truth was, no one knew. It was rock as resistance—even against itself. Just as Warhol's banana was pop art as irreducible object, the Velvets, like the minimalists, were forever searching for the irreducible, primitive ur-sound of the city that could shock words into meaning and encapsulate a totality of expression, never quite getting there. For the Velvet Underground, it was all about the journey; there was no destination.

The next stop was at the Gymnasium, which would inevitably be where the Exploding Plastic Inevitable reached a percussive ground zero. As *The Velvet Underground & Nico* infiltrated Prague, Warhol—himself the son of Czech immigrants—contacted Sokol Hall, a Czech recreation center and gymnastics training facility on Seventy-First Street in the sleepy Yorkville neighborhood that rented its space on weekend nights. Several Olympians had trained there—the official motto was "A sound mind in a healthy body"—but for the month of April in 1967, the Velvets broke the noise ordinance several times over as unsound minds in unhealthy bodies performed a more sensual gymnastics. Two decades before the Velvet Revolution would topple the communist regime, the band led a final revolt of their own in New York. That was the plan, at least.

Even at two dollars a pop, hardly anyone attended the Gymnasium residency shows. Warhol himself had flown to Cannes, where Nico and his coterie planned to invade the film festival while the Velvets stayed at home. Yet the poor attendance allowed them to test out new material; they never bent to commercial demands and wouldn't stand on ceremony, but the flagging audience provided more of a reason to embrace their avant-garde influences—Ornette Coleman, Cecil Taylor, La Monte Young, with a Bo Diddley beat—as they hurtled inexorably off the rails into the no-man's-land of prog rock.

The Gymnasium shows proceeded with Warhol in absentia. Warhol had booked the Dick Hyman Trio and clarinetist Tony Scott—the former a pioneer on the Moog synthesizer and the latter a clarinetist who had worked with Billie Holiday and Max Roach—to present what he billed as "The complete spectrum of sound." For their final show on April 30, advertised as "National Swinger's Nite," "the wildest swing-in the East Side's ever seen," the Velvets planned to unveil their most incendiary track yet. The band turned up to resonant frequency for "Sister Ray," initially known as "Searching," which was loosely based on a black transsexual Lou had met in Harlem depicted in the style of Hubert Selby Jr., with the harmonic influence of Ornette Coleman, opening with a blues vamp on two open chords.

Coleman's genre-defining 1961 album *Free Jazz: A Collective Improvisation* coined the term "free jazz," and though it consisted of one thirty-seven-minute continuous take, it couldn't be contained by one side of an LP. Like Coleman, Lou always showed the underside, and with the collective improvisation of "Sister Ray," imported the paradigm into rock with a track that, in live performances, generally exceeded the bounds of twelve-inch vinyl. When the screeching mic feedback filled the cavernous hall as Lou went for the jugular, it was clear this sister wasn't intended for commercial consumption:

> *I'm searching for my mainline*
> *I couldn't hit it sideways*
> *I couldn't hit it sideways*
> *Just like Sister Ray says*

Almost no one was there to hear it, but the band didn't care; for the Velvets, the medium was the massage—cultural theorist Marshall McLuhan even cited them in the book whose typesetting error coined the malapropism of the title—and it didn't have a happy ending. If, as McLuhan claimed, Warhol's happening was a global village that collapsed space-time, at the Gymnasium, the psychedelic electromagnetic spectrum entered an ultraviolet range above the ears of the few intrepid villagers; the minority who were receptive left with popped eardrums.

In May there would be one final happening for the Exploding Plastic Inevitable. At the Scene, the boisterous Forty-Sixth Street club managed by impresario Steve Paul—weeks before the Doors began their legendary run—the Velvets tuned up with a sense of bittersweet relief; after a protracted adrenaline rush, the party was finally over. They had lost Danny Williams along the way, and Nico was in Ibiza on a modeling gig, but the EPI was going out with a literal bang. As Malanga, Woronov, and Cutrone danced their last waltz, the throngs of would-be superstars rushed the stage, losing all inhibition. It was a moment of Warholian synchronicity as the crowd had their fifteen minutes of fame. The Velvets wouldn't play New York again for years. For Lou, as always, it would be a long way home.

It was not the only major departure for the Velvets; tired of playing in Nico's shadow, Lou made the executive decision to fire her from the group. The dissolution had begun as her affair with Lou petered out. Nico refused to play mind games, and the lacerating self-consciousness that made Lou great lyrically often made him irascible and controlling, with a hair-trigger temper and an Othello-sized jealous streak; her general aloofness and hopscotching relationship with John only made matters worse. Tensions had already boiled over. "When it fell apart, we really learnt how Nico could be the mistress of the destructive one-liner," John later recalled.

"I remember one morning we had gathered at the Factory for a rehearsal. Nico came in late, as usual. Lou said hello to her in a rather cold way. Nico simply stood there. You could see she was waiting to reply, in her own time. Ages later, out of the blue, came her first words: 'I cannot make love to Jews anymore.'" Having already slept with Dylan, it was unclear if Nico meant that she would no longer be sleeping with Lou or that she would never sleep with Leonard Cohen, but the point, its dubious anti-Semitic gravity notwithstanding, was driven home. After Lou broke the news that he was going to fire her, the band had no significant objections; after all, she only sang three songs and had already embarked on a solo career, yet seemed to cannibalize what little press the Velvets got. Having concluded the Big Apple was rotten, with the banana album seemingly destined for the compost heap, the time was ripe to go their own way. As the Summer of Love was heating up, Lou dumped the Velvet Underground's most beautiful member to heighten their overriding aesthetics of ugliness; for the Velvets, it would be a summer of piss and vinegar.

Now on the rebound, they decided to give New England a shot. Steve Sesnick, a fast-talking manager they had met in Los Angeles, contacted the Boston Tea Party, an underground club in Boston's South End that shared a space with a local spin-off of the Film-Makers' Cinematheque. "Today it's a pricey area, but at the time it was pretty decrepit," recalls Steve Nelson, the club's former manager, who got involved in the club while a student at Harvard Law School. Nelson first encountered the band at a fundraiser for the *Paris Review*; George Plimpton greeted guests at the door, but nothing made more of an impact than the Velvet Underground.

The Tea Party was located in a converted colonial-style Unitarian church built in 1872, and served no alcohol; it was refashioned as a brick-and-mortar church of rock, and the congregation came for the music. There were no chairs; when people got tired of standing, they sat on the wood floor. "It was soft drinks and music," Nelson says. For two dollars and fifty cents, people of all stripes could hear Led Zeppelin, the Byrds, and soon the Velvets in an intimate environment.

Sesnick called and booked them immediately. "Sesnick always lived up to whatever the booking was, but he had a tendency to, let us say, exaggerate," says Nelson. Before anyone notified the club of the band's recent personnel change, posters were hastily drawn up: ANDY WARHOL'S NICO AND THE VELVET UNDERGROUND. With the Velvets facing yet another printing debacle, the Boston Tea Party's ad-hoc solution was to black it out, Nico's name occluded by a cartoon headless torso. Nico, Morrissey, and Warhol flew into Boston and arrived midway through their set, but Lou was poised to make a bold public statement; like Martin Luther burning the papal bull and splitting from the pope, Lou wouldn't let Nico onstage. Yet the audience didn't seem perturbed to only see what was initially billed as Nico's backing band; the Velvet Underground was not the Famous Flames. The Tea Party's light show didn't compare to the Exploding Plastic Inevitable, but for the first time, the projections accompanied the Velvets and not vice versa.

"For their very first gig, it was the Velvet Underground as a rock band, all on their own," says Nelson. Over the course of two weekend shows, after a heavy dose of "Sister Ray," "I Heard Her Call My Name," and the methamphetamine-inspired "White Light/White Heat," it became apparent that the riotous Boston crowd, a melting pot of progressive intellectuals—among them a teenage Jonathan Richman—was more amenable to the Velvets' brand of cerebral rock than the navel-gazing New York scene. In contrast to the statuesque Factory crowd, the Bostonians gathered at the Tea Party even danced.

"The place was packed for the Velvet Underground. They really had a big following," says Nelson. "They were raw at the Tea Party. They could have been forgotten in five years, but at the time, there was a feeling that there was something special about them. I didn't have any dream of what would finally come about." As a stand-alone act, the quintessential New York band rose to fame in, of all places, Boston; it was a paradox tantamount to the Yankees (or more apropos, the Mets) selling out Fenway Park.

Having solidified a regional reputation and a loyal fan base, Lou then did the unthinkable—he fired Warhol. After a year and a half of constant pandemonium, both sonically and intravenously, Lou inexplicably decided that it was time to move on to a new illusion. So he severed ties with another father figure. Lou would later describe the fateful meeting in "Work":

> I fired him on the spot, he got red and he called me a rat
> It was the worst word that he could think of
> I'd never seen him like that

It did not end amicably. Warhol demanded to be paid 25 percent of the royalties for *The Velvet Underground & Nico*, whatever meager sum that amounted to; he would never see the money. It was a love-hate relationship—Lou revered Warhol—but it seemed increasingly that, like the iconic images he mass-produced in silk screens until eventually moving on, Warhol had gotten bored of the band. The band reacted with shock, but Lou, never a diplomat, could brook no argument. Despite the brevity of their tenure with Warhol, Lou would remain inextricably linked to the father of American pop art for the rest of his life. Like Lot fleeing Sodom, everything that happened during that indefatigable year of transformation would all be irretrievably lost behind him; by the end of 1967, the crumbling Factory, leaky plumbing and all, would be condemned and torn down. The Factory relocated to Union Square, blocks from Max's.

Returning to their avant-garde roots, in June, the Velvets performed alongside John Cage at a benefit for modern dance icon Merce Cunning-ham—Cage's closest collaborator and lifelong partner—at minimalist archi-tect Philip Johnson's Mies van der Rohe–inspired Glass House in New Canaan, Connecticut. For the Country Happening, the crowd gathered on the lawn of the transparent estate, and following the premiere of a Cage-Cunningham collaboration, the Velvets cast the first stone with "I'm Waiting for the Man," a reaction to similar aesthetic concerns that stemmed from coarser origins. With Malanga cracking the whip, the well-heeled benefactors couldn't help but dance the starch out of their suits. It would be the Velvets' final participation in a Warhol-produced event. On the ride home, they unanimously decided to hire Steve Sesnick as manager.

# 11

Rather than turn down the amps and conform to the mellower sound of the Summer of Love's collective group hug, the Velvets spent the summer of 1967 railing against utopian harmony with a decidedly dystopian deconstruction of genre conventions. Like Captain Beefheart was doing on the West Coast, across New England, the Velvet Underground drew the curtain on a roaring theater of cruelty, using the Boston Tea Party as a de facto home base, bringing the noise to Cape Cod and Philadelphia's Trauma, a folk-psychedelia club near Rittenhouse Square.

By September they returned to the studio ready for a purge. If the banana album was the record as heroin, *White Light/White Heat* was the record as speed. For their sophomore album, they planned to translate their untranslatable amphetamine-laced stage show into two dimensions on vinyl, paring down the material to only the harshest songs for maximum effect; despite their best efforts, the finished product emerged without a crack. Produced by Tom Wilson, and coengineered by Val Valentin, who had collaborated with Art Tatum, Wes Montgomery, and the Animals, and by Gary Kellgren, the engineer behind Nico's *Chelsea Girl*, the album was recorded at Mayfair Studios, blocks from Rockefeller Center, where months before, the Mothers of Invention had recorded *We're Only in It for the Money* and Hendrix recorded "Burning of the Midnight Lamp." No amount of experience or karma could keep the Velvets' needle out of the red as they broke through their own wall of sound.

They arrived at Mayfair with the rabid intent to lay the whole album down in one burning session; it would take about three days, a dazed blur of feedback, distortion, white noise, and uncontrollable leakage. Sterling plugged in his Stratocaster and turned all the way up; Lou beefed up his bionic Country Gentleman with a tremolo unit, preamp, four pickups instead of the standard two, and blaring Vox fuzz boxes; John coaxed cathedral-like banshee wails out of the electric organ; Moe almost broke a few mallets; they didn't always account for a bass. It was a frenzied battle royal—only the loudest would survive.

Wilson, an inveterate Lothario, spent much of the sessions distracted, attempting to seduce a steady stream of women. Standing six foot four, impeccably dressed in au courant parti-colored fashion—antelope suede jacket, horn-rimmed glasses, sporting a mustache and goatee—a visual complement to his blue Aston Martin, Wilson was the smartest, trendiest guy in the room, and he knew it. His great-aunt had been a slave, but he commanded a $100,000 annual salary and had cornered a decent-sized section of the billion-dollar record market; outside the studio, he still couldn't hail a cab, but behind those doors, he was the boss. "You got to show some grip with these cats," he told the *New York Times*, explaining his curt-yet-easygoing approach to dealing with a recalcitrant colleague. "He bit off the wrong piece of chocolate."

With the ability to rein in some of the most intractable artists, Frank Zappa joked that Wilson should run for president, but the Velvets were about to disabuse him of that notion. His managerial style was a subtle but forceful sangfroid, with a proven track record—he convinced Dylan to plug in and dissuaded Simon and Garfunkel from adopting a nom de guerre; he brought Cecil Taylor and John Coltrane together and manned the control room as Sun Ra plumbed the outer limits of the cosmos—but in 1968, he simply sat back as the Velvets laid waste to the Tower of Babel.

"Hey, you cats ready out there?" he said from his perch behind the glass. The Velvets' readiness was not the issue, though; throughout the sessions, form met production value. The engineers mostly hit two buttons—*record* and *stop*—though when to hit the latter was unclear. Mics were left off for entire takes, but at full blasting frequency, it almost didn't matter. The room wasn't big enough to hold them. What resulted from the fracas was a tangled collage, much of it *sous rature*; many of the glitches were left in the final mix. The group adamantly eschewed any semblance of commercial appeal; this was primal scream therapy. The title track was based on a slang term for amphetamine that conflated shooting speed with the meditative healing of occultist Alice Bailey. "The Gift," the combination of a short story Lou had written in his *Lonely Woman Quarterly* days and a blues jam, culminated in Lou smashing a cantaloupe with a wrench. "I Heard Her Call My Name" consisted of five minutes of unadulterated shred, with Lou conjuring Albert

Ayler's savage peals of violence; he later remixed it louder than the already unbalanced studio levels, causing Morrison to temporarily leave the band. The Velvets had never played with more intensity in a studio than they did on the seventeen-minute "Sister Ray." In only six tracks, they had destroyed the world, using noise as a weapon to overwhelm all rational thought—epistemology, phenomenology, and all reflexive facility; having heard that their work was bad in the best way, and certainly beyond unfixable, they rested.

Wilson hosted an interview with John and Lou on his radio show, *The Music Factory*, in advance of the album's release. "A bootless Lou Reed, I might say. This is the first time in two years that I've seen him when he had on a pair of shoes rather than boots," Wilson said. "You're gonna set the whole leather industry back, Lou." Wilson then celebrated Moe as "the only female drummer with a major pop music group." To Wilson, the album broke more than sonic barriers. "Like most things we found out don't matter, sex doesn't matter anymore as far as musicianship is concerned." He then presaged the Velvets as indicative of the recording industry's future. "The fact that the music says something about things, about who we are, where we are, where we're going, where we've been," Wilson said. "It's not fantasy music. It's not, 'If you had a silver horse and I had a golden mule, you know, then we could start an animal farm' or something. It's about real-life situations." Finally, Wilson played a few tracks and mulled over the "little catatonia" the album might induce. Unfortunately for the label, his instincts were right.

In November Verve released *White Light/White Heat*'s first and only single, the speed-fueled title track, selecting the most understated track, "Here She Comes Now," as its B-side. Though narrating a female orgasm, it was the only other cut short enough and sufficiently overdetermined to function above the censors' suspicion; the other sub-five-minute tracks were radio-hostile: "Lady Godiva's Operation," about a fatally botched sex change, and "I Heard Her Call My Name," a lyrical echo chamber culminating in the line "And then my mind split open," giving way to an exercise in screeching fuzz box brinksmanship. Verve knew the single wouldn't break—the whole album was too long, too loud, and too lewd to compete with "To Sir, with Love." It was a hard pill to swallow, or shoot, and the single got banned almost immediately. As 1967 came to a close, Lou took stock—in the span of a few months, he had fired Nico and Warhol, ceased all performing activity in New York, and recorded an album that was designed to fail. As he sang the body electric, the Velvets seemed to be entering a prolonged death agony, but he wouldn't have it any other way.

When *White Light/White Heat* was released in January 1968, it sunk like the Hindenburg. In contrast to the Beatles' *White Album*, released later that year, *White Light/White Heat* was black. The foreboding cover was a monochromatic cobalt, and when viewed at an oblique angle, it revealed the superimposed image of a skull with a sword in it, not unlike Holbein's painting *The Ambassadors*. The few reviews were fairly unanimous in their derisive rebuke; *Melody Maker* called it "utterly pretentious," *Crawdaddy!* claimed the album invoked a "universe of pretension" bogged down by the gravity of the plethora principle, and *HiFi/Stereo Review* concluded that "the put-on proportion is about one hundred percent." Critical consensus emerged that "The Gift," a dark tale of unrequited love turned accidental homicide, reeked of recondite condescension coupled with doom-and-gloom anxiety, and that "I Heard Her Call My Name" doused the listener in proverbial kerosene before completing the effect with the highly flammable "Sister Ray." A full-page ad depicted the band in silhouette, with the ominously gothic invitation to "Come. Step softly into the inevitable world of the Velvet Underground, where there is no now," and "vinyl virgins devour the macabre mind." Even with the eerily perplexing threat of bloodthirsty "vinyl virgins" looming—contagion at the touch of a stylus—the album barely eked out the penultimate spot in the top 200 charts, at 199 for a week. Among the minority who appreciated it was Vaclav Havel, who smuggled it back to Prague as though it were illicit contraband.

"No one listened to it. But there it is, forever—the quintessence of articulate punk. And no one goes near it," Lou later claimed. Yet the few listeners who exalted in its obliterating shriek sensed that, as with all of the Velvets' material, there was more going on subtextually than drugs, sex, and senseless violence. Boston-based *Crawdaddy!* critic Wayne McGuire was one: "Put quite simply, the Velvet Underground is the most vital and significant group in the world today," McGuire wrote, comparing the group to Nietzsche. He later went on to claim that "the most blatant injustice perpetrated by the media on the contemporary music scene had been the virtual black-out on coverage of the Velvet Underground . . . which is musically and mentally at least two years ahead of its time." He was right, but it would take more than one firebrand critic's prognostications for the Velvets to get their due.

In its sensory overload, *White Light/White Heat* tested the limits of the senses. Even before its vinyl sheen was exposed beneath the surface, it announced the contradictions that quaked within with its high-contrast black cover; flush with paradoxes, binary oppositions, penetrations, figurative and literal, and hidden meanings that evaded any attempt to paraphrase and censor, it was poststructuralist rock par excellence. In its anarchic harmonic structure, the fragmentary splicing that exposes the multitrack recording, and its polysemous lyrics, the album mirrors the horrors of urban life—embodiment, disembodiment, nonnormative bodies, a rupturing of the physical self, and ultimately the mind—in a thwarted path to fulfillment. Like gestalt psychology, it operated on the fragmentary nature of consciousness in a fractured world that was becoming increasingly incoherent. Superficially, it expanded the Velvets' ever-widening list of taboos, but Lou knew what most didn't realize, and if they did, refused to acknowledge—beneath the black cover, there were untold depths.

Starting with the title track, the album was the light that blinds, the speed that slows you down. After the initial amphetamine hit, with "Lady Godiva's Operation," the body is the first to go as "the doctor is making his first incision." The relative calm of "Here She Comes Now" concludes the A-side, lulling the listener into a false sense of security. On the flip side, it all gets turned upside down in more ways than one, reaching a psychosomatic climax with "I Heard Her Call My Name," the most chaotic track the Velvets ever recorded. At once a metaphor for orgasm—"I heard her call my name, and then my mind split open"—the disembodiment of the drug experience, and the slippery notion of genre as a whole, the "call" brings the user back from rapture to reality while reconstituting the wall between the self within and the external world without. This was the album's central paradox; in the postlapsarian world of the song, we only experience interconnectedness through the profound dislocation of the body and the mind. Yet despite the apparent futility of raging against the machine, Lou would keep trying to sing the body electric. The fruitless quest culminates with "Sister Ray," in which Lou confronts gender politics head-on and subverts as many social conventions as possible in four verses, the whole time "searching for my mainline." It was the potent image of failing to find a vein that tapped into the universal, even if listeners had never tried heroin. The metaphysical search often lasted up to forty minutes in concert, and didn't end with discovery, but a punishing salvo from Sterling that would leave even the strongest amp exhausted. What was Lou searching for? Spiritual enlightenment, ecstasy, mind-numbing bliss, love? It would be decades before he truly found his mainline, and it didn't come from the barrel of a hypodermic needle.

When the press demonized the album, the label effectively disowned it. This was exacerbated by the fact that Tom Wilson had left to start his own independent production company in Brooklyn, making a critical miscalculation and directing his industry clout into promoting Fraternity of Man's hemp-laced single, "Don't Bogart Me." Without Warhol as a shepherd, the Velvets hardly organized a promotion tour. The week *White Light/White Heat* hit the shelves—its wholesale distribution was minimal—they played a modest release show at the Aardvark Cinematheque in Chicago's Old Town, with nothing booked for the following three weeks. The tour faced another hurdle when John caught hepatitis, possibly from Lou, and landed in the hospital for an extended stay.

Cale had recently gotten engaged to Betsey Johnson, and his illness meant he and his bride-to-be had to postpone the wedding; presaging things to come, the band limped along without him. Creative differences were already driving a wedge between John and Lou, and Cale's sudden absence allowed Lou to experiment briefly with a new direction. At the next tour stop, a college dance at Harvard—not dissimilar to an Eldorados show—twenty-one-year-old aspiring musician Doug Yule saw the band in trio mode; little did he know that months later, he would be the fourth member. Other than several isolated dates at the Trauma in Philadelphia, the Boston Tea Party, and the Kinetic Playground in Chicago, the Velvets had no shows.

Their biggest event of the season was arguably John's wedding to Betsey Johnson that April. Despite a few technical difficulties—at Town Hall, the conservative officials initially refused to issue a marriage license to a woman in a pantsuit, high fashion notwithstanding, and when she returned in a miniskirt, John had forgotten Betsey's corsage—the wedding went off without a hitch, even despite Warhol's presence. Yet it served as a reminder of the Velvets' relative insignificance; other than Warhol, the designer was far and away the most recognizable name in attendance.

The wedding only intensified Lou's lovelorn situation; he had not had a steady relationship in years. To make matters worse, Shelley had left Syracuse and moved to New York after her husband completed his PhD in sociology and got hired by NYU. Living in NYU faculty housing in Washington

Square Village, her apartment was not far from Lou's; she was never far from his thoughts. "He always knew how to reach me, and we would see each other periodically," she says. Spread thin between finishing her MFA at Syracuse, teaching pottery as an adjunct professor at Stony Brook University, and part-time modeling work, she still managed to find time for Lou. Her marriage was already on the rocks, and he provided a link to the past, albeit not an idealized one. "It was out of the frying pan, into the fire," she says. "Stupid of me, but you are who you are. You make the same mistake over and over." Lou made constant romantic overtures to convince her to leave her husband, but despite his remonstrance, Shelley kept their relationship platonic. Lou continued to carry the torch, though:

> *Thought of you as my mountain top*
> *Thought of you as my peak*
> *Thought of you as everything*
> *I've had but couldn't keep*

Shelley was no longer his mirror. "He used to think I should leave and come back with him, but there was no way. I didn't want to be his girlfriend or victim or whatever," she says. "It didn't mean I liked him any less, I just didn't want anything to do with him where he could get me." Sometimes they would surreptitiously meet at Max's. "I had to stay under the radar so my photo didn't turn up and my husband suddenly says, 'What were you doing at Max's last night?'" But these meetings never resulted in rekindling the flame. Lou channeled the emotional dropkick into his songwriting. In contrast to the matter-of-fact narration of "The Gift," the wistful ballad "Pale Blue Eyes" tapped into the roots of Lou's unfulfilled desire. Though Shelley's eyes were not in fact blue, the song's lovesick lyrics burned for her, Lou's version of the unrequited love sonnet.

Lou mined the same reservoir of grief when he wrote "I Can't Stand It," a driving rock plea explicitly invoking Shelley, which gradually worked its way into the Velvets' repertoire. Juxtaposed with "Pale Blue Eyes," the song is not addressed to Shelley but adopts a confessional style, depicting the alienation, squalor, and lost love of an extended adolescence; at twenty-six, it was the next trial in Lou's evolving bildungsroman. Lou's appeal that if "Shelley would just come back, it'd be all right" has a screaming-into-the-void quality; he knows she's not coming:

*My landlady called me up*
*She tried to hit me with a mop*
*I can't stand it any more more*
*But if Shelley would just come back it'd be all right*

But Shelley wouldn't come back. In that particularly cruel, tumultuous spring, in which riots broke out in Harlem following the Memphis assassination of Martin Luther King Jr. and a wave of peace protests in Paris destabilized the French government, Lou mixed memory and desire in his own private wasteland. He wanted to be as far from New York as possible. The Velvet Underground spent the spring in Chicago and Cleveland, where they began playing at La Cave, a no-frills folk club that became a second home after the Boston Tea Party, making an exception to the New York boycott and returning in May to play another Merce Cunningham benefit at the Brooklyn Academy of Music. Gearing up for the summer, the Velvets decided to settle a territorial dispute; after having been tarred and feathered in '66, they would conquer the West Coast. They began with the Avalon Ballroom in San Francisco, opening for Iron Butterfly, which was about to release *In-A-Gadda-Da-Vida* the following week. Unfazed by the high voltage, though, the Velvets returned to the stage after Iron Butterfly finished their electrifying closer and kept the concert going, slaying with one of the longest versions of "Sister Ray" they had ever played.

On June 3, Andy Warhol got shot. Valerie Solanas, an anarcho-communist and radical feminist who articulated her militant ideology in the self-distributed *SCUM Manifesto*, had submitted a script to Warhol called *Up Your Ass*, which dramatized her unorthodox version of social change. Warhol found the material so obscene that even he couldn't produce it, and he later lost it under some lighting equipment (it was eventually found). Spurned and out for blood, the deranged Solanas began stalking Warhol and demanding to be paid for her efforts. Finally, she waited outside the Factory in Union Square with a concealed .32-caliber automatic, and followed Warhol in. At the decisive moment, she pulled out the gun and fired. At the hospital, Warhol flatlined for minutes before he was resuscitated. Solanas turned herself in; she was eventually sentenced to three years in prison on an insanity plea after a psychiatric evaluation determined she was mentally unstable.

Across the country, Lou read about the incident in the paper, flabbergasted. Less than a week later, Bobby Kennedy was assassinated. Eventually, Lou finally called Warhol in the hospital from his hotel. By the end of the conversation, they had reconciled, with no plans to resume their relationship. If anything, Lou was more focused on continental drift.

At the end of June, the Velvets flew to Vancouver, where Sesnick had booked a few dates at the Retinal Circus, a skeevy club with a booming heroin subculture; John couldn't resist. The next day, as they began setting up for the concert onstage, Cale fell off the stage while lifting some equipment bins. They rushed him to the hospital, where an X-ray revealed a broken wrist. Rather than cancel the show, he played bass in a cast. The band didn't mind, but the incident drew attention to the growing conflict between John and Lou; Lou didn't want to share creative control of the group, and began pushing for a less avant-garde approach that placed more emphasis on unadulterated rock and in turn showcased his lyrics.

In early July, the Velvets played the Hippodrome in San Diego, where a nineteen-year-old Lester Bangs was in the audience. Never having seen the Velvets, he later described it as "one of the most incredible musical experiences of my concert career"; Bangs worshipped the band. The future legendary rock critic later wrote a review of the show, which featured "Sweet Rock and Roll," a song that was rarely performed and never recorded. "The lyrics, many of which Lou made up as he went along, seemed like some fantasy from an urban inferno. But it was the chorus that was the most moving: 'Ohhh sweet rock and roll—it'll cleanse your soul,'" he wrote. "That's classic, and no other group in America could have (or would have) written or sung those words." They finished off their West Coast run at the Shrine Auditorium opposite Sly & the Family Stone, followed by a booking with Tim Buckley at the Avalon Ballroom in San Francisco. By all signs, California had become receptive; however, Lou had grown restless with the sound of the band and was about to demand a personnel change.

Back on the East Coast, the band returned to their home turf at the Boston Tea Party. On September 27 and 28, 1968, they played their final shows with John Cale. No one knew that when they closed out their final set with "Heroin," it would be the last time they would play it together as a cohesive unit for decades.

When they got back to New York, Lou convened a meeting with Moe and Sterling at the Riviera Café in Sheridan Square without explaining why.

He issued an ultimatum: either John went, or Lou was going, and taking the band with him. Moe and Sterling were shocked; the decision came abruptly and inexplicably. Like a radioactive isotope, the band had become unstable; in some ways it always had been, yet that same fissionable material defined their explosive sound.

"You mean out for today or for this week?" Sterling said. It wasn't always obvious when Lou was kidding.

"No, he's out. For good," Lou said.

Tables were pounded, voices raised, harsh words exchanged. They quickly reached an impasse. "You don't go for it?" Lou said. "OK, the band is dissolved." Lou wouldn't budge. Begrudgingly, Sterling was nominated to break the news.

He trudged over to John and Betsey's loft on LaGuardia Place and knocked on the door. He stammered through the difficult explanation; John didn't know if he wanted to shoot the messenger or Lou. So John was out of a job, and the Velvet Underground wasn't quite the Velvet Underground anymore.

# 12

Undeterred by John's acrimonious ouster, Steve Sesnick quickly scouted out a replacement. In Boston, he had met Doug Yule, a multi-instrumentalist in the Grass Menagerie, a fledgling local act; the Velvets sometimes crashed at the band's apartment during stints at the Tea Party, and had gotten to know Doug along the way. He also bore an uncanny resemblance to Lou; he was such a doppelganger that Lou sometimes introduced him as his brother. Doug had dropped out of college to pursue the American Dream, and he was about to live it. When Sesnick called, Doug was in the shower. Something told him to take the call, though. Sesnick offered to hire him to play with the Velvet Underground.

Without getting back in the shower, Doug hitched a ride to New York that night, meeting Sesnick and Lou at Max's to discuss the particulars. They had a few days to rehearse and get Doug up to speed before they were scheduled to hit La Cave, followed by a cross-country trip for their biggest booking yet: the Whisky a Go Go in Los Angeles. Fortunately, he only needed to know three chords—getting used to a road crew was easy. He nailed his debut in Cleveland; Lou and Doug stayed up all night at the Howard Johnson's, talking through an early fall cold snap. To everyone else, the loss of John was a lamentable travesty—he was irreplaceable—but Lou kept moving forward regardless. In many ways, Doug fit right in.

Fleeing the early onset of winter, the newly reconstituted Velvets flew to California, returning to the Avalon Ballroom in San Francisco. Days later, they boarded another plane and headed to Los Angeles for their gig at the Whisky a Go Go, where they were on a bill with the Chicago Transit Authority (later shortened to Chicago); Jimi Hendrix and Jim Morrison were among the fans who would eventually assimilate the Velvets' anarchic aesthetic into their own iconoclastic styles. With the confidence boost of Hendrix's approbation, and armed with new material, the Velvets were ready to return to the studio, hoping the third time would be the charm.

If *White Light/White Heat* was the musical equivalent of the interior of a nimbus cloud, *The Velvet Underground* came on little cat feet. Residing within the gothic splendor of West Hollywood's Chateau Marmont, the Velvets set out to craft a self-titled album that would reveal their softer side. With the combination of Sesnick's smooth-talking finesse and the label's plummeting bottom line, the extravagant accommodations ironically slipped under the radar of the MGM brass. Instead of cutting their losses, in 1968, MGM focused many of its dwindling resources on promoting the Boston sound, chiefly organized by producer Alan Lorber; Bosstown would attempt to replicate the success of Detroit's Motown. Groups like Ultimate Spinach, Beacon Street Union, and Orpheus synthesized the folk and avant-garde elements that embodied the intellectual Boston rock subculture, and MGM hitched its wagon to their uncertain success.

Though the Velvets weren't explicitly part of Bosstown, their association with the Boston Tea Party and alternative aesthetic remained consistent with the label's marketing push. Despite the failure of their first two albums, MGM's initial contract with the Velvet Underground had effectively committed the label to producing four albums, obligating the band to record at least two dozen tracks a year until 1971, and the company intended to capitalize on their investment. Even with the shift in band personnel, MGM had high hopes that the Velvets' third album, a mellower effort than their previous material, would surpass the promising sales debut of Ultimate Spinach's self-titled album.

Recording engineer Val Valentin was hired to mix the album at MGM in New York, and Sesnick enlisted Animals guitarist Vic Briggs to produce in Los Angeles. "Vic was always instrumental, and could always get stuff out of you that you really didn't know that you had," recalls Angel Balestier, the TTG recording engineer. Yet Briggs could hardly hear them when they started playing; within three days, the Velvets decided to move on without him and self-produce the rest. If there were any sound challenges, it was due to the studio's enormous size; in contrast to the Velvets' sophomore album, on *The Velvet Underground*, they had perhaps too much space to fill. "This was the old Red Skelton studios prior to becoming TTG," recalls Balestier. "The room could accommodate about a hundred men, and here we are, just this group. But the room had its own character. It was good for them to hear themselves also, so they didn't have to play that loud."

Balestier had honed his craft in New York with legendary engineer Phil Ramone before going to work with Tom Hidley and Ami Hadani at TTG. "The room itself had a portable vocal booth that we could move around the whole room. It was a large room, so you had to baffle it off. We worked on the sound for quite a while, right until we were rolling tape." Part of the difficulty came from the band's equipment. "They had these terrible sounding Vox amps. Lou was trying to get a certain sound out of them, which required a lot of work," Balestier says. "I remember standing out in the studio putting all sorts of mics on them, trying to get a sound. Lou had a certain sound in his head that he was looking for, and we finally got to it by just putting a Shure 545 on the side of the amp." To maximize the sound, placement was key. "We had the amps right in the middle of the room, while the drums were a good twenty feet back."

After ironing out the sound—Balestier employed a similar setup to the albums he had engineered for the Ventures—the sessions flowed smoothly. "They were a pleasant group to work with," recalls Balestier. "They were fairly long sessions, but we were used to it, and the fact that we had an enormous amount of visitors." Tom Wilson, who worked regularly at the studio, would often stop by. "Tom always read his paper in the control room. He was into the series *Batman*, so he'd want to go home early to catch his show, but if you thought he wasn't listening to what was going on, you were definitely wrong," Balestier says. "Out of nowhere, Tom would say, 'What is that I hear?' He was reading, but his heart and ears were really on the session. He was a great producer. He was always impeccably dressed, and you weren't going to get anything by him."

Surprisingly, other than MGM executive Jesse Kaye's occasional visits, the label barely interfered. "Jesse would show up in a suit and give you a piece of candy, and say, 'How are things going?' He'd hang out for a little bit, and then he'd split. We were on our own." By the end of 1968, they had recorded the masters for *The Velvet Underground*.

The band returned to Boston for their first Cale-less show at the Tea Party, where the politically conscious proto-punk Detroit band MC5 was scheduled to open. Steve Nelson's childlike hand-drawn poster illustration depicted the Velvets in red crayon—four smiling kids. "It was deliberately against their image as the bad boys and girl of music, because I didn't see them that way," Nelson says.

Lou was surprised when he saw it. "How'd you know that's what we're really like?" Lou said.

"I know you, I see you. I've been here," Nelson replied.

Nelson saw through the facade of foreboding and ennui, elucidating the liminal line between Lou's onstage avatar and the twenty-six-year-old behind it who lived to rock the house. "There was a separation between Lou Reed the person and his artistic creation, and a lot of people had a hard time keeping those separate," he recalls. "He was an open person, sometimes a little prickly, but anybody who is a great artist probably would be. In a way he was the guy in my drawing—just the kid with the guitar having fun playing rock 'n' roll."

Lou proved the point that night. Prior to the Velvets set, MC5 manager John Sinclair, the founder of the radical anarcho-communist White Panthers and soon the Rainbow People's Party, took the mic in an attempt to incite the audience to overthrow the Tea Party.

"They think they have a right to make money off of this?" he shouted. The three-dollar admission price hardly covered the venue's operating expenses, but Sinclair felt it was three dollars too much. "Kill the pigs! Let's burn this place!"

As the Velvets got onstage, the palpable air of a riot waiting to happen suffused the hall. Lou immediately defused the situation. "I just want you to know, I don't agree with anything that's been said," he said. The Tea Party was their club, and no one was allowed to burn down the house but them. More than the revolutionary spirit, trepidation hung in the air; how would they play "Heroin" without Cale? Doug Yule was one of their own, but no one knew what they would sound like.

"This is a song called 'Heroin,'" Lou said, silencing the debate upfront. Sans viola, the song still rocked.

"From that point on, nobody had any question that this incarnation of the Velvet Underground was still a force to be reckoned with," says Nelson. "People weren't dancing to 'Sister Ray' as much as being bounced up and down off the wooden floor."

Several months later, in March 1969, two months after the inauguration of Richard Nixon, with Apollo 11 gearing up for the first moon landing, Lou turned twenty-seven, and *The Velvet Underground* was quietly released. Prior to its release, Lou had returned to the studio, where he made what was referred to as the "closet mix," an alternate version to Valentin's mix that turns down the instrumental track and plays up the vocals; rather than competing with the heavy distortion of *White Light/White Heat*, the album's focal point was clear—Lou's lyrics. MGM was poised to support a promotional tour, including extensive advertising in print and in radio; all the label needed now was the critical imprimatur. Lester Bangs delivered the verdict in *Rolling Stone*: "The Velvet Underground are alive and well (which in itself may surprise some people) and ever-changing. How do you define a group like this, who moved from 'Heroin' to 'Jesus' in two short years?" he wrote, referring to Reed for the first time as a "death dwarf," a term culled from Burroughs's *Nova Express*. "Can this be that same bunch of junkie—faggot—sadomasochist—speed—freaks who roared their anger and their pain in storms of screaming feedback and words spat out like strings of epithets? Yes. Yes, it can, and this is perhaps the most important lesson of the Velvet Underground: the power of the human soul to transcend its darker levels."

Other critics heaped praise on *The Velvet Underground*. Robert Christgau gave it a cool A; *Creem*, *Melody Maker*, and *Jazz & Pop* were unanimous; Brian Eno claimed it as his favorite Velvet Underground album. Yet critical acclaim was not indicative of commercial results. MGM's marketing plan included several full-page ads—"Why something different? Because: 'What Goes On' . . . their great new single . . . is just that"—and even hired WNEW disc jockey Bill Mercer to record a hackneyed promo. Despite the effort, though, the album's sales were lower than either of their two previous releases. Its distribution was so limited that the Velvets themselves couldn't always find it in record stores in tour cities. The black-and-white cover image of the band in preppy wool sweaters lounging on a couch at the Factory couldn't compete with the psychedelic colors of Tommy James and the Shondells' *Crimson & Clover*. The subtle harmonies and quiet lyrics of "Pale Blue Eyes," though a harbinger of the shoegaze movement, was drowned out by the 5th Dimension's "Aquarius/Let the Sunshine In."

In stark contrast to the white-knuckle fury of their sophomore album, *The Velvet Underground* showed admirable restraint; the former took drugs and mindless sex as its conceit, while the latter aspired toward religiosity and a purer form of love—though "no kinds of love are better than others." It was an album of yearning, a quiet supplication, rising action in the novelistic search begun in "Sister Ray," but reimagined with a redemptive goal.

"Candy Says," sung in quivering vibrato by Doug Yule and presumably inspired by Factory superstar Candy Darling, bemoaned a trifecta of existential maladies those in their midtwenties love to hate: "my body," "the quiet places," and "big decisions." Deceptively conventional, "Candy Says" subtly hints at burgeoning transgender politics, though. Lou posed the album's key question of identity crisis and maturation: "What do you think I'd see if I could walk away from me?" The rest of the album ventured into the uncharted territory of these quiet places in a skeptical attempt to offer some answers—salvation through language, romance, religion—walking away from the hedonistic thrill-seeking and solipsistic anxiety established in *White Light/ White Heat.* Yet the answers still came up short; two albums after "Heroin," Lou still didn't know.

"Some Kinda Love," Lou's paean to pansexuality, reveled in its celebration of carnal desire over impassive thought, replete with a sly reference to T. S. Eliot's "The Hollow Men":

> *Between the idea and the reality*
> *Between the motion and the act*
> *Falls the Shadow*
> *For Thine is the Kingdom*

For Lou, it was the kingdom of the body and the prison of the mind, a seductive rumination on the cognitive dissonance experienced when the mind will boldly do what the body just won't:

> *Between thought and expression lies a lifetime*

Packing megatons of emotion into the sparse lyrics, and under the influence of Schwartz, Lou had reconciled Eliot's "dislocation of sensibility"—the notion that in the modern world, thought and feeling had become unstuck and words divested of their affective power—with an exhortation to experience and feel:

> *Put jelly on your shoulder*
> *Let us do what you fear most*

This recasting of the body as a temple for sensual communion underscored a latent religious sentimentalism, expressed in "Jesus." Lou never converted or considered it, though; the song was never about him, but the creation of a character. With a subdued bass ostinato, no drum part, and a melody reminiscent of the gospel influence Lou had picked up in high school, it was one of the most lyrical tunes he had ever written. "Beginning to See the Light" and "I'm Set Free" continued the theme—"I'm set free to find a new illusion," whether that be the fleeting pleasure of sensuality or religion—but "That's the Story of My Life" challenged social norms with a Factory-made maxim on moral relativism.

The "Billy" referenced in one line of the song, Billy Name, elucidated the unity of opposites at the center of Lou's beguiling lyrics through his pansexual lifestyle; even his enigmatic name was a blank slate that was beyond category. Like Carl Jung's concept of shadow psychology, to Lou, everything existed in a state of yin-and-yang duality, a circular mandala that inevitably returns to itself, a microcosm for the dialectical conflict ripping through the broader culture. It was 1969, and as the '60s were rapidly coming to a close in Day-Glo relief, Lou knew that the illusion of black-and-white moral absolutism could no longer sustain a relativistic culture whose shades of gray had exploded into a dazzling color palette.

This anxiety culminated in "The Murder Mystery," a postmodern, kaleidoscopic collage inspired by Burroughs's cut-up technique that bombarded the listener with contrapuntal left and right vocal tracks, a technique used by the double quartet on Ornette Coleman's genre-defining 1961 album *Free Jazz: A Collective Improvisation*. The Velvets track was a stream-of-consciousness mashup, referencing Warhol's "Candy-screen wrappers of silkscreen fantastic," the Beatles cover "Mr. Moonlight," and the Kennedy assassination opposite nonsensical imagery. Many listeners manipulated the dial to parse out each track; Lou had ostensibly concluded that even after you "read all the books and the people worth reading," that the "real thing is dying." Yet it resisted any attempt to paraphrase; in this vertiginous murder mystery, it was unclear who had been killed or who had done the killing; no body was identified. It could have been the death of innocence, of language, or experience itself in a city supersaturated with information—it could have just been Lou playing with words—but there's the rub.

Like the epic homicidal bender of "Sister Ray," "The Murder Mystery," a nine-minute polyvalent romp, quickly devolved into pandemonium, flooding the auditory field with dadaist lyrics, Procol Harum–like organ drawl, and unintelligible reportorial logorrhea. If the goal was to cram a whole decade onto a few inches of vinyl, it was an unholy mess, confounding more than it illuminated. Though that was par for the course for Lou, who didn't offer any pat solutions or explain away an inexplicable world in his lyrics, like so many of his contemporaries. Instead, he weaved opaque webs of provocative imagery, fragments of thought and expression whose interpretation varied with the listener and seemed simultaneously mundane, sublime, and incomprehensible, just like quotidian life. For Lou, the challenge of finding and creating meaning, differentiating sacred from profane, individual from collective, was his chosen method of mainlining the city. With the Velvets, whose technical abilities were not up to Philharmonic standards, fabricating peace and harmony in the studio from the cacophony in the streets proved an untenable ambition, yet that was precisely the point. Their frustrations and repeated failures to find meaning spoke to a generation of disaffected youth, only writ large by uppers and downers, deviant sex, and a tangle of distortion pedals. But they weren't out of control, or making it up as they went along; like Kerouac, there was always a master plan behind the madness.

With its dual competing vocal tracks, shifting polyrhythms, and broken syntax, "The Murder Mystery" perfectly reflected New York in 1969, a Pynchonian world of enigmatic signs and symbols on the verge of seismic change, where everything got turned upside down, from the "obverse and inverse and perverse and reverse," and so much got lost in the shuffle. Amid that welter of fecundity and decay, it was no wonder narcissism was running rampant; in an era of increasing social marginalization, the personal was political, and as an unsung spokesman of the me generation, Lou, like Walt Whitman, would fight to sing a song of himself, but he was singing for everyone.

The album served as a tepid farewell to that decade of disillusionment, and Lou, the Velvets, and everyone else could only hope for a rapprochement after a decade marked by the Cold War and Vietnam, as well as the less fatal but perhaps equally palpable culture war at home. Lou expressed as much idealism as he had ever in the album's understated coda, "After Hours," a Tin Pan Alley–style duet sung by Moe, aching with the same guileless purity felt at the outset of *The Velvet Underground*. Despite its jaunty rhythm guitar and major triads that could convey a sense of fulfillment or wholeness, the lyrics connote the lack of intimacy and ultimate disappointment of a one-night stand:

> Oh, someday I know someone will look into my eyes
> And say hello—you're my very special one—
> But if you close the door I'd never have to see the day again

As always with Lou, when passing through the crucible of innocence to experience, redemption could only come through love and the belief that it was possible to find it, but he could also serve two masters—Eros and the diabolical god of rock—and as much as he yearned for a love that would calm the raging tides within, he wished the night would last forever.

Although *The Velvet Underground* never took off nationally, the Boston fan base reacted with fervor. The Velvets played their mainstay, the Boston Tea Party, as well as a date at the Woodrose Ballroom, a new venue started by Steve Nelson in a rural roadhouse. They hopscotched between the Tea Party and Woodrose for most of the spring and summer, at one point sharing a bill with an up-and-coming act called the Allman Brothers Band.

Within the same week, two events shook Lou's world: the Stonewall riots erupted from the underground, setting off the fledgling gay liberation movement, and Brian Jones died prematurely in his backyard pool. The Rolling Stones founder was only two days older than Lou—who dabbled in astrology—and his death forced Lou to question his own mortality. But the tour didn't stop; the Velvets were in Philadelphia at the Electric Factory, then the Grande Ballroom in Detroit, and Chicago's Kinetic Playground.

In Chicago, they shared a weekend bill with the Grateful Dead, each night a battle of one-upmanship to see which band could play the longest set; there was no clear victor. Searching for a new audience and aiming for the college demographic, Sesnick booked the Velvets at Washington University in St. Louis. Amid the sold-out audience at the packed indoor gym, a taciturn law student and guitarist named Robert Quine lost his Velvets virginity and taped the whole thing. Quine would soon become one of the most prolific Velvet Underground bootleggers, but more important, he would fundamentally alter electric guitar vocabulary—perpetually shrouded by a pair of sunglasses—through collaborations with Richard Hell and the Voidoids and Lou himself; for the moment, though, sans shades, he was just an awestruck student taking a much-needed study break.

In May 1968 the Velvets had returned to the studio on West Forty-Fourth Street in New York for a series of recordings with Record Plant cofounder and audio engineer Gary Kellgren. "Andy's Chest," "Ocean," and "Foggy Notion" were among the dozen or so tunes recorded. No one seemed to know the exact purpose of these sessions; the band had conflicting views as to whether they were done as demos for an eventual fully realized album that might never materialize, a haphazard collection of previously unrecorded material that MGM intended to one day release in some form, or merely a sly ploy orchestrated by Sesnick to extricate themselves from their contractual obligation to MGM while honing newer songs on the company dime.

It was a time of upheaval for everyone involved; the Velvets were still easing into their new lineup, while MGM was undergoing a corporate restructuring and regime change. Regardless of the purpose, these sessions fulfilled the band's contract to MGM that they record a certain number of songs every year, but after the hat trick of commercial flops culminating with *The Velvet Underground*, their relationship with the label had grown mutually toxic. MGM decided to fold on their bet on the Velvets; whatever the dubious intention behind the collection of tracks laid down at the Record Plant, many of them remained unmixed when the contract was voided. The label ultimately declined to release them in any form until years later, making the call to hold them in the vault rather than spending any more on promotional costs they might never recoup. The Velvet Underground had lost the support of their label and didn't want it anymore.

As their momentum flagged, they kept on moving forward. The summer of '69, a rock festival in Upstate New York was approaching, but the Velvets were not on the schedule for Woodstock; being in the right place at the right time was never their style. They played two festivals that summer: the Toronto Pop Festival, featuring Chuck Berry, Sly & the Family Stone, Blood, Sweat & Tears, and the Band; and they were the headliners at the Hilltop Pop Festival in Lowell, Massachusetts, where Van Morrison was also performing. Two weeks later, their peers descended on Woodstock; though the Hilltop festival got better weather, it was another sign that the Velvets had still not broken into the mainstream.

They staggered on through the fall, playing small venues in Philadelphia, Minneapolis, and finally, Texas. Though Lou would never perform in Texas with the Velvets again, a series of shows at the End of Cole Ave would be immortalized on *1969: The Velvet Underground Live*—composed of material performed in Texas and San Francisco—and released five years later. On their last night in Dallas, the Velvets proved their stamina.

"Do you people have a curfew or anything like that? Does it matter what time you go home tonight? Do you have school tomorrow? Nobody has school tomorrow? Because we could do one long set or we could do two sets. Whatever makes it easier for you," Lou said. "OK, then this is gonna go on for a while, so we should get used to each other. Settle back, pull up your cushions, whatever else you have to do that makes life bearable in Texas." They then brought a little bit of Harlem to Dallas with "I'm Waiting for the Man." When Lou performed an early version of "New Age," he used the original lyrics—replete with a reference to Etta James's "Something's Got a Hold on Me"—ostensibly dedicated to Shelley:

> *Over the bridge we go*
> *Looking for love*
> *I'll come running to you*
> *Hey baby, if you want me*

Their live set burst with allusions to his old flame: "Pale Blue Eyes" and "Over You," in which Lou claims to have gotten over her, though perhaps the rock star doth protest too much:

> *Typically when I had it*
> *Treated it like dirt*
> *Now naturally, when I don't have it*
> *I am chasing less and less rainbows*

They closed out with two Shelley-inspired tunes: "I Can't Stand It" and "I'll Be Your Mirror." More than a thousand miles away, she still lingered on his mind. Running on empty, with the aid of a battery of substances, the band had perpetuated a Herculean tour, but like Wile E. Coyote in midflight over the precipice, gravity was starting to catch up with them.

The Velvets closed out the 1960s on the West Coast, with residencies in Los Angeles, San Francisco, Portland, and the Attic in Eugene. On the last leg in Oregon, Velvets roadie Hans Onsager left $3,000 worth of equipment on the street; when they returned to retrieve it, it had been stolen. Worn down from a rigorous touring schedule—they played seventy uninterrupted shows—and with little to no money saved, they went home. From Christmas to New Year's, they played a run at Philadelphia's Second Fret, a cramped folk club without a liquor license. Lou spent the last days of the decade crashing on a waiter's floor and singing to a small but passionate crowd. It was what he lived for, but the adventure was wearing thin; so was he, his bell-bottoms and boots taking a harsh beating. He could only hope that he would fare better in the next decade; as the cloud nine of free love gradually yielded a reign of cynicism and distrust, things were looking up for a new era of Lou.

# 13

The 1970s were destined to get off to a slow start, though. Aside from a two-week run at Chicago's Quiet Knight, the Velvets' touring schedule had begun to thin out. Moe was pregnant, and as her belly expanded, it became increasingly difficult for her to reach the drums. Furthermore, relations had soured with MGM, and Sesnick began shopping around for a new label. Over the past two years, the label had sustained $18 million in losses, and could no longer support the Velvets. Executive Mike Curb stepped in as MGM president and quickly mobilized the struggling label to streamline and sanitize its roster by cutting eighteen acts, most of them complicit in the proliferation of drug culture. Curb's push to quash the association between drugs and rock was lauded by Nixon, but before MGM could dump the Velvets on charges of indecency, the band dumped them.

Ultimately, Ahmet Ertegun, the president of Atlantic Records who had rejected the Velvets' debut album, agreed to sign them on the condition that they produce an album "loaded with hits," ignoring their abysmal track record. By mid-April, they were hunkered down in the Columbus Circle studio, churning out *Loaded*. Working with Geoff Haslam, a British recent hire who had just worked on Ornette Coleman's *The Art of the Improvisers*, Adrian Barber, a producer and musician with a Beatles pedigree, and Shel Kagan, the former promotion manager for Prestige International who had produced Lightnin' Hopkins and Ramblin' Jack Elliott, they were poised to limit track length and balance a radio-friendly aesthetic with the same uncompromising attitude they had applied to their previous albums.

The material for *Loaded* was the apotheosis of the Velvets' street aesthetic, a raw, pure distillation of the redemptive power of rock over the weight of nihilism and despair. To Lou, rock was the ultimate drug; it allowed him to mainline the real. Opening with "Who Loves the Sun," a heartbreak tune that harks back to the Jades' "Leave Her for Me," the album set its more cathartic tone with the second track, "Sweet Jane." It might have been one of the greatest rock songs ever written, but when they entered the studio, fame wasn't the goal; "Sweet Jane" vibrated and pulsed with the indomitable spirit of rock:

> *But anyone who ever had a heart*
> *They wouldn't turn around and break it*
> *And anyone who ever played a part*
> *They wouldn't turn around and hate it*

Lou set "Sweet Jane" in the prerock, industrialized world of the early twentieth century, beset by mechanistic adherence to moral convention: the "rules of verse" poets used to rely on, the early-model Stutz Bearcat sports car, Tchaikovsky's "March of the Wooden Soldiers," and a series of antiquated film tropes—the unblinking villain and the fainting woman.

This confluence of cultural forces militated against the free expression of the two gender-bending protagonists who, after leaving, find acceptance beyond the city limits, established in the bridge, which eventually got cut without Lou's permission. For Lou, this same liberation from the conservative strictures of society could be achieved musically, which he celebrated in the next track, set in the early days of rock radio. The autobiographical "Rock & Roll" burst with the album's central thesis, an anthem for everything Lou embodied:

> *You know her life was saved by rock 'n' roll*
> *Despite all the amputations*
> *You know you could just go out and dance to the rock 'n' roll*
> *   station*

Aiming for hits, some of the less commercial, softer tracks from the *Loaded* sessions got shelved until later rereleases, including "Ocean," "Ride into the Sun," and "I Love You." The band was wary of recording material that had been previously recorded but never released under contract for MGM, but they tempted fate with "Rock & Roll," which was so hit-worthy it was worth the legal risk.

In order to maintain Atlantic's commercial directive, the band seemed to almost lapse into self-conscious, though not malicious, parody of the buoyant pop milieu. Their stylistic pastiche was a paean to the genre conventions that dominated Lou's youth: the cavalier surf-rock rhythms of "Cool It Down," the screaming retort of "Head Held High," and the rockabilly twang of "Lonesome Cowboy Bill," while the band satirized the vapid vicissitudes of celebrity culture on the languid "New Age." Even the straight-faced love song "I Found a Reason," a throwback to the halcyon days of doo-wop, exuded an uncharacteristic air of optimism:

> *Oh I do believe*
> *You are what you perceive*
> *What comes is better than what came before*

Yet Lou deconstructed the album's uncharacteristically optimistic conceit on the soul-drenched blues closer "Oh! Sweet Nuthin'." It was a salve that celebrated the downtrodden; the song employed a chiastic ring structure—a Biblical trope that Lou deployed lyrically and harmonically—to offer a spiritual benediction to the have-nots, with a descending chord progression that ultimately returned to the tonic, a nostalgic meditation on lack, where Lou and the band felt comfortably at home. Sterling played one of his most emotive solos over jubilant gang vocals on the chorus:

> *Oh sweet nothing, she ain't got nothing at all*

It certainly seemed as though they had nothing. Throughout the sessions, they were missing Moe, now on unofficial maternity leave, and had to rely on a rotating set of drummers: Adrian Barber, Doug, Doug's seventeen-year-old younger brother, Billy, who was still in high school, and Tommy Castanaro, a relative unknown. Rather than recording everything live, the drum parts were often recorded separately; the full band was rarely in the studio together. The final product affected the crisp, clean style they were aiming for, but at the expense of esprit de corps. With Sesnick vying to push the band in a more commercial direction, Moe temporarily sidelined, Sterling considering applying to graduate school—he was finishing his bachelor's degree at City College—and Lou's nerves and vocal cords shot, the Velvets were heading for a fall. The Beatles had just officially announced their breakup; it was as though certain things couldn't survive the 1960s.

Then Lou met Bettye. Bettye Kronstad, who actually had pale blue eyes, not to mention cornflower blond hair, epitomized the antithesis of Lou's Long Island Jewish upbringing. She grew up in Pennsylvania and had worked her way into a full scholarship at Columbia. They had little in common but floated in the same concentric social circles. Though Bettye had auditioned to be a dancer for the Exploding Plastic Inevitable, she declined the job—the costumes were too indiscreet—and they eventually met through, of all people, Lincoln Swados, who since leaving Syracuse was in dire straits. When he was twenty-four, Swados couldn't take it anymore; in an attempted suicide, he jumped in front of a subway train. In a twist rivaling Dostoevsky's infamous penal colony brush with certain death, the aspiring novelist lived, but faced a double amputation, losing his right arm and leg. The ordeal put him in a coma for ten days. He was later transferred to the Rusk Institute, a rehabilitation center at NYU, but Lincoln initially refused any prosthetics. Yet the near-death experience and the subsequent trauma could not snuff out his creative flame; incurably optimistic, he eventually enrolled in a creative writing course at Columbia, where he met Bettye, a diffident, quick-witted freshman. The accident would put him in and out of the hospital for the rest of his life.

As fate would have it, one day, Lou and Bettye's hospital visits coincided. With a less than auspicious venue for a meet-cute, Lou was perhaps not as smooth as he would like to have been. Bettye instantly caught his eye when they met in the hallway; Lou approached from behind, concealing heart palpitations behind braggadocio and swagger. "Hey you," he said. "Yeah, you. You're beautiful. Turn around." She looked at him, startled. "What are you doing here?" After a polite but brief exchange, she left.

Though they had barely spoken, Lou had to see her again. "Later on, he asked his friend if he could call me, so I said, 'Why?'" Bettye recalls. "He came on a little à la rock star. That never appeals to me. In fact, it didn't appeal to me at all," she says. "He was kind of arrogant. There's no other word for it, but he was kind of funny, too."

Lincoln persuaded Bettye that Lou's macho posturing concealed the fragile ego of a "nice guy" within, and she begrudgingly agreed to allow him to give Lou her number. He also explained that Lou was a member of the Velvet Underground, but she was not impressed. "At that time, if you listened to music, which I did, you would know who the Velvet Underground were, because they were managed by Mr. Warhol," she says. "I had heard a couple of his songs, but I can't say I was a fan of his. I was more into the Detroit sound, frankly."

Lou's middling rock star status left Bettye unimpressed—as a Columbia student on the front lines of second-wave feminism, she valued intellectual heft, artistic achievement, and a modicum of respect over fame—and it would take more than swagger to win her affections. Bettye had moved to New York two years prior, an outlier on the elitist Ivy League campus, working her way through college as an administrative assistant at Columbia law school while taking classes part-time.

She was living in a penthouse apartment on 116th Street overlooking the Hudson, but with growing unrest spurred by the draft, the idyllic atmosphere soon turned toxic. Her first semester, classes were disrupted by a student revolt that pitted Bettye against the administration, swept up by campuswide protests that gained national headlines. In response to the revelation of institutional ties to the Institute for Defense Analyses, a hawkish consultancy firm that worked with the Department of Defense, and the discovery of a proposal to build a segregated campus gym, radicals from the liberal activist group Students for a Democratic Society organized a strike that soon precipitated the hostile takeover of university buildings. As tensions flared, Bettye was pushed to the fore.

"I somehow got myself involved in the confrontation between the police and the students," she says. "I was in the middle of that, so I was battered and teargassed." By 1970 she had imminent plans to go to Europe with friends. So when Lou began calling, she wasn't exactly the type to be waiting by the phone. He was persistent, though, leaving message after unreturned message. By the third or fourth call, Bettye finally capitulated. "He wanted to know if we could get together, and he was somewhat convincing, so I said OK," she says.

For their first date, Lou agreed to meet Bettye near her apartment at the West End, a dive bar on campus that had served as an incubator for Allen Ginsberg and Jack Kerouac before they abandoned academia; in 1968 it had become a de facto headquarters for the protest organizers. "We talked, and he drank a lot at that time. I didn't drink. I was nineteen," she says. She didn't want to appear inexperienced, though. "I tried to look sophisticated and ordered a glass of wine. He drank cheap scotch. Lou liked cheap scotch." Lou spent the majority of the night discussing his recent trials and travails. "He drank a lot and complained a lot, but he didn't ask a lot about me," she says. "He was upset about the Velvet Underground. He was upset about Cale. I don't think he wanted to be in an argument with Cale, though. I think he kind of liked him." Mostly underwhelmed but not entirely uncharmed, toward the end of the night, Bettye told Lou about her impending travel plans, but under the influence of Johnnie Walker Red, Lou didn't seem to notice or care.

"He was a gentleman, and he insisted upon walking me back, and that was a little interesting because he couldn't walk very well," she says. He walked her to her door and staggered off to the subway. She figured she had seen the last of Lou Reed.

The next week, Lou called again, though. "I'm leaving for Europe," she said.

"When?"

"In a week."

"Well, can I see you the day before you leave?" Lou asked.

Bettye was dumbfounded; she had only met him once, and it was reminiscent of the most awkward scenes in *The Graduate*. Yet she found his temerity oddly disarming. "Do you think I don't have anybody else I'd rather see the last night I'm in this country?" she asked with a hint of sarcasm.

"No, you should see me."

Despite his insistence, Bettye wasn't about to clear her schedule for a guy she had just met, rock star or not. "I'm sorry, but I have other plans," she said. Having shot down Lou Reed as though reshelving an insipid book with a plodding first page, she immediately booked a one-way trip to Europe.

As Lou's love life flatlined in New York, the Velvets continued the three-year grudge against their home city. Sesnick booked the band for another run at the Second Fret in Philadelphia. On Saturday, May 9, 1970, compared to the sold-out New Year's shows at the same venue, only fifteen devotees were in attendance; 150 miles away, one hundred thousand students protested the Vietnam War at the White House. Lou announced that Moe had come down with a cold at a Mets game—they had just lost 1–7 to the Giants—not wanting to admit that their drummer was on maternity leave. Sterling, Doug, and Lou bore their road-ravaged souls in intimate trio; Doug played drums when the tempo called for it, but mostly it was guitar stripped bare, what some would call the queasy hunger of sleep deprivation born of financial necessity and others would call the blues. When Lou intoned the lyrics to "Train Round the Bend" over some of Sterling's most lyrical, heartfelt playing, he improvised a new verse that exuded a deep-seated, Basho-like longing for New York:

> Oh I am just a New York City boy
> Trying to get back home
> Every night I see that train

They closed out the lonely, drumless set with the visceral anthem "Oh! Sweet Nuthin'." Hunkered down in front of the nearly vacant hall, reverb and all, the dirge-like ode to the peculiar satisfaction of having nothing rarely sounded more exultant, yielded starker sonorities, or rang truer to the moment.

As they finished the *Loaded* sessions, it was finally time to return to New York. When the Velvets got booked for an upstairs residency at Max's Kansas City in the summer of 1970, no one knew they were already in falling action; the climax had happened elsewhere, and instead of a triumphant comeback, they had returned for their final peroration. After a three-year odyssey in self-imposed exile—an existential suburbia—the Velvets had finally decided to return home, but in Lou's narrative of Oedipal poetic justice, home signaled a death to the past. With Moe still out of commission, they drafted Billy Yule, who knew the material and was otherwise spending his summer vacation at home in Great Neck, pounding away on his Ludwig drum kit to Keith Moon and Charlie Watts. Willing to work for steak sandwiches, he was hired immediately and quickly brought up to speed; the Velvets' final rodeo would be supported by a high school senior.

From Wednesday to Sunday, they played two sets a night, one at 11:30 and another at 1:00 AM. Tickets were three dollars. On June 24, the first night of the homecoming, Lou downplayed the anticipation with deadpan wit in his typically arch setup.

"Good evening. We're the Velvet Underground. We once did an album with a pop painter. Because we wanted to help him out," Lou said.

"You're doing better without him!" said a fan in the crowd.

Lou counted off "I'm Waiting for the Man," and the packed crowd erupted. They were finally home. At 1:00 AM, a twenty-three-year-old poet from New Jersey named Patti Smith trekked over from the Chelsea Hotel, where she was living with Robert Mapplethorpe. Smith was brought to lose her Velvet Underground virginity by Donald Lyons, who was there at the Café

Bizarre when it all started. Smith had never heard the Velvets before, and after a watershed moment during "Sister Ray," felt inspired to pursue music.

"The Velvet Underground at Max's Kansas City? At first I thought it was some kind of joke," Richard Nusser wrote in his ecstatic *Village Voice* review. "By Friday night, they were at the peak of their power . . . I don't know what effect this will have on their careers, but judging from past audience reactions to the Velvets (and other groups), I would say things are at an all-time high."

Having influenced the Beatles, the Rolling Stones, and Jefferson Airplane, Nusser wrote, their cult status belied the long shadow they cast as the progenitors of a distinctive rock aesthetic that did justice to the genre's black roots but "succeeded in developing their own style without coming off like a pale imitation." Yet in a cruel, ironic twist, as they finally soared in the press, they were far from an all-time high. Little did Nusser know that the Velvets' "culture born of the Long Island Expressway" would end in a trip home on the same cursed road, endowed with the mythic status granted all premature band dissolutions, leaving the scene they helped create, still with such unfulfilled promise.

On July 4 Mike Jahn published a glowing review of the Max's run in the *New York Times*: "The musicians should be seen, more often than once every three years; they make 80 percent of today's popular rock groups seem pointless and amateurish," he wrote. In Paris, Bettye stumbled on the encomium in the *International Herald Tribune*. "I was at a café having my morning bowl of coffee and French roll and reading the *Herald Tribune*. I saw this article about the Velvet Underground and Lou Reed," she recalls. "I said, 'It's that guy?'" She didn't realize it at the time, but she was reading about her future husband.

Having continually obsessed over Shelley—in contrast to the buoyant lyrics of "Over You," chasing Bettye was less a rainbow than a momentary glittering mirage—Lou circled back one last time like a horribly worn tire on an endless highway with no exit. He called Shelley, but this time, the response was unequivocal: like Moe, she was pregnant.

"My being pregnant made him sort of give up," Shelley recalls. Her daughter was due in November. "He was very angry with me and depressed. I had never heard a lot of those songs until many years later. I didn't want to hear them, so I didn't turn the radio on." Lou had to cauterize the wound, but with the glut of media attention, the Max's residency kept getting extended;

the Velvets finally had the recognition they coveted, but it was too late. What should have been a victory lap became an agony, not only because he came face-to-face with the tragic inevitability that Shelley would always remain the Daisy Buchanan of his misspent youth, but because he realized that the condition of his return relied on the tacit expectation that he conform to the debauched image he had abandoned when he left New York, an image that would seal him off hermetically into an intolerable, inert past. And inertia to Lou was a fate worse than death. So he began plotting his exit.

"I hated playing at Max's," Lou later recalled. "Because I couldn't do the songs I wanted to do and I was under a lot of pressure to do things I didn't want to and it finally reached a crescendo."

At the dawn of the 1970s, in the wake of an epochal whirlwind that had radically reshaped the culture, American life had definitively acquired a rock cadence, but having contributed to that paradigm shift, Lou saw that his success had been a Pyrrhic victory. He had lost the woman he loved, and the creative impulse that was the only thing he held sacred seemed to be hanging in the balance. Sesnick pushed for more and more commercial compromise, and Lou, if nothing else, always maintained an unflappable sense of integrity.

At Max's, the Velvet Underground had become enshrined and perhaps embalmed; their cultural impact reached an all-time high as their financial capital dwindled; they were the nexus of working-class rhythms and bourgeois art, an elusive hybrid that actively eschewed the financial reward afforded those who pandered to mainstream tastes. For the Velvets, or what was left of them, the spring of hope would soon give way to a winter of despair; they had everything and nothing; they were going directly to heaven as Lou was going the other way. And the Velvet Underground was coming to an end.

On August 23, 1970, Lou gave his final show with the Velvet Underground, committed to posterity in a scratchy recording on a Sony cassette machine by Warhol superstar Brigid Berlin, replete with ambient noise. She didn't realize the significance of the occasion—no one would until much later. The rambunctious crowd, unaware that a chapter was coming to an abrupt and anticlimactic conclusion, talked through the whole performance; it was a last set list befitting of Jesus's son. For the first time, Lou's parents and sister were there, though no one knew why. "Good evening, we're called the Velvet Underground, and you're allowed to dance in case you don't know," he said. When they played "I'm Set Free" in the middle of the first set that night, it had a new subtext.

*I've been set free and I've been bound*
*To the memories of yesterday's clowns*

"We're gonna do a few songs for this set that we don't do during the rest of the week. Hope you don't mind," Lou said. "We're gonna do a couple of the ballads that we don't get a chance to do now and then." He chanted most of the lyrics to "Pale Blue Eyes"; it was his swan song. He introduced "Femme Fatale" as "a song about somebody who is very, very mean to somebody else. It's understated. It's another way of saying some people have no heart and they don't care what they do to you at all." Soon, the set came to a close. "This will be the last song for the night. It's called 'Lonesome Cowboy Bill,'" he said. As they finished out the set, still, no one knew, not even the band, that what they were playing was more funeral dirge than victory lap.

After saying one last good night before heaping it all on the bonfire of his discontent, Lou packed up his Gretsch and met his family outside on Park Avenue South. He climbed into the car. It lurched into gear and they drove back to Freeport. B. J. Thomas's "Raindrops Keep Fallin' on My Head," Simon & Garfunkel's "Bridge over Troubled Water," or "The Long and Winding Road" might have been playing on the radio, if it was on at all, but Lou wasn't listening. It was a long ride home.

# PART III
# TRANSFORMER

# 14

Brian Jones was dead, Jimi Hendrix was dead, Janis Joplin was dead—all at twenty-seven—and the rumor mill abounded that Lou, too, was playing the great gig in the sky. *Rock* magazine speculated that Lou had finally gone off the rails and suffered a nervous breakdown, the latent aftereffects of electroshock, and was "disconnected from objective reality." Closer to the opposite was true; he had gone back on the rails—the Long Island Rail Road—and was spending his mysterious reprieve from the spotlight as a typist in his father's office, filing 1099s for forty dollars a week. He had made it to twenty-eight, but at a cost. Lou's grandmother Rebecca, who was now eighty-two, had also moved to 35 Oakfield Avenue to live out her twilight years; she and Lou were waiting in abeyance for some final judgment they knew not what; yet despite all the amputations, Lou knew it was only intermission.

The New York he had left behind was not the New York he despoiled in 1965; it was grittier, filthier, and guiltier, and imminent danger always loomed literally just around the corner. Riding the subway meant possibly getting mugged. There were more cops on the streets than ever, but also more corruption; since the Velvets played their first notes, violent crime had more than doubled; there was an average of five murders a day. With his sudden disappearing act, Lou had seemingly committed career suicide, trading in his Gretsch for an IBM Selectric, his spiritual mainline for a coffee pot, and had resigned himself to the workaday life on Long Island he had begrudgingly inherited. But as glorious as it was in its depravity, New York had become a cesspool. It was out of this unglamorous malaise that glam rock would rise.

Lou parlayed the desk job into a copyright power play, though, filing for the rights to all the material on *Loaded*, which Atlantic had released unceremoniously in November. The cover illustration depicted a vacant stairway to the subway; the back featured a nearly empty recording studio, with Doug Yule seated at the piano. The lineup listed Lou third, after Doug and Sterling; hierarchical band dynamics notwithstanding, the move was deliberate. For the rest of its short existence, the Velvet Underground had a new frontman. Lou had fled the underground, flying from one extreme to the next, from the depraved decadence of an adrenaline junkie's playground to the staid responsibility of a milquetoast number cruncher. Compromise was not a consideration; the middle path did not seem possible.

The album itself occupied an instant place in the rock canon: Lenny Kaye dubbed it "easily one of the best albums to show up this or any year" in *Rolling Stone*; in *Creem*, Lester Bangs waxed hyperbolic—"not only a better album than *Revolver*, but beats the last four Dylan albums all to hell"; Michael Watts praised it in *Melody Maker* as "possibly the most important pop record issued in years." It was as though Lou was hell-bent on becoming the Robert Browning of rock—a poet of alternating admiration and derision, pathologically ahead of his time, and terminally obscure. Lou had been lionized, but as always, having finally pushed the rock up the hill, he refused to rest on his laurels. So he consigned himself to resting on the same bed he grew up in; he had broken down all the walls and circled back to wood paneling.

Then Bettye reentered the frame; after six months in Paris, she had returned to New York. In an uncharacteristically decorous move, Lou had Lincoln call her and ask if he could make another romantic overture. This time she had changed her tune. "I was a little more interested in meeting artists," she says. Lou took the train in and met her uptown; they went to the West End again, and even though Lou had moved back in with his parents, he was more successful. "From that point on we just dated."

Every weekend, Lou would take the Long Island Rail Road into the city, or Bettye would take it out to Freeport; thus their courtship began between the city and the suburbs, from walk-up to country club. Soon, they were madly in love. "It was a very different person that I met. He was reflective and quiet. He was writing poetry. I guess he was probably a little depressed. He was kind of lost. There he was back in his parents' home. That didn't bother him that much, but typing was a little silly for him," Bettye says. "He spent most of the time working on lyrics, frankly."

Lou was making an under-the-radar transition to adulthood, a gradual process of individuation away from the Velvet Underground, and with Bettye by his side, it seemed he felt ready to put the past behind him. "He did have quite a heart. The man that I met when I came back from Europe is the man that I like to remember. Although a lot of people say, 'There he was, wasting away at his father's, typing,' but he wasn't really doing that necessarily—he was finding himself," Bettye says. "He wasn't drinking, he wasn't drugging, he was writing. He was gathering himself together, maybe to get back out there again, but he was a serious, reflective, almost teddy bear kind of a man." She had no inkling that before long, the seamier side of rock would come roaring back. "He was a sweetheart, but fame does awful things to people."

As 1970 came to a close, Lou rededicated himself to poetry. If he was going to be a financial failure, he would do it with class. That March, the week after his twenty-ninth birthday, he gave a poetry reading at the Poetry Project at St. Mark's Church in-the-Bowery, unplugged, unaccompanied, and unsung, joining the ranks of literary luminaries from the New York School who had performed at the East Village arts center—Vachel Lindsay, William Carlos Williams, and Edna St. Vincent Millay. The previous month, Patti Smith had given the sacrilegious poetry reading that spawned *Horses*—"Jesus died for somebody's sins, but not mine"—enlivened by the salacious impieties of Lenny Kaye's guitar.

On the bill with Lou, Jim Carroll, a twenty-one-year-old local poet who would go on to write *The Basketball Diaries*, was reciting poems from his recently published sophomore collection, *4 Ups and 1 Down*. To Lou, it represented a literary homecoming; even Allen Ginsberg was there. Lou began by reading lyrics—he always felt that if it didn't work on the page first, it wasn't worth the song—and after "Heroin," Ginsberg gave a standing ovation. Lou proclaimed himself a poet reborn, renouncing all that amplification, and consecrating himself to the gods of verse, lest he be haunted by the specter of Delmore Schwartz, if there was a heaven at all, or perhaps a hell. He read poems inspired by Bettye, his new muse:

> I think I am now in love.
> I seem to have all the symptoms
> (Ignore past failure in human relations—
> I think of Bettye all the time)

The reading culminated with several proto–gay rights poems. Though housed in an Episcopal church, the Poetry Project was the only building in the city outside of the Factory that was receptive to homosexuality—sodomy was still illegal in New York—and rebellious enough in spirit to house Lou. By all signs, Lou had fulfilled his early literary promise; he had begun publishing poems in *Fusion* but soon established firm footing as the quintessential rock poet, appearing over the course of his career in the *Harvard Advocate*, the *Paris Review*, and eventually reaching an apex, publishing in *Poetry*. He would go on to perform at the Poetry Project four more times. That fall, Lou published a series in the *Advocate* under the name Louis Reed, including the lyrics for "Candy Says" and "The Coach and Glory of Love," which he later retooled and retitled "Coney Island Baby."

Lou was tapped to eulogize the recent premature deaths of his peers in *No One Waved Good-Bye: A Casualty Report on Rock and Roll*, an anthology edited by *Crawdaddy!* rock critic Robert Somma. In his essay, "Fallen Knights and Fallen Ladies," he offers a touching memorial to the fallen of his ilk, but also a memento mori focused on the death-defying acts of his career as "formerly vocalist, guitarist and lead songwriter for The Velvet Underground." As he grappled with mortality and the tragedy of those who martyred themselves to the cause—his cause—a visceral sense of inner conflict pervaded the prose, that he was not just writing about the pastness of the past, but about how it would lead to an uncertain future, one that seemed to be writing itself one key at a time as he sat office-bound in front of the typewriter.

"The singer has a soul but feels he isn't loved offstage," he wrote. "Or, perhaps worse, feels he shines only on stage and off is wilted, a shell as common as the garden gardenia. But we are all common as snowflakes, aren't we?" Yet when Lou left the stage, Bettye provided the love and support to help reconcile this paradox. "Those who hate the nine-to-five regimen do not know the blessings that it holds. It masters the mind and protects it from itself," he continued. "We are a race that needs to work." Yet Lou seemed to harbor survivor guilt. "Perhaps I should die after all, they all (the great blues singers) *did* die, didn't they? But life is getting better now, I don't want to die. Do I?"

Through the lens of Janis Joplin, Lou projected his own ambivalent psychodrama onto the page. He had arrived at a fork in the road—one path paved before birth, the other fraught with brambles and overgrowth, not really a path at all, dangerous and bewildering, but a lot more fun. As his menial job was lining his pockets and his literary star was rising, it seemed that fate had other plans. If Schwartz was his guardian angel of lofty verse, there was a little devil pulling him back down to the underground.

Danny Fields, the proto-punk impresario whom the Velvets had met in their Warhol days, began taking Lou and Bettye to informal gatherings on the Upper West Side at the apartment of Lisa and Richard Robinson. The Robinsons were bohemian royalty—he was RCA's A&R "house hippie," the tastemaker tasked with discovering the next counterculture trend, and she was one of the first rock critics to break the gender barrier, writing for *Creem, New Musical Express, Hit Parader*, and eventually the *New York Post*—and they had a large, rent-controlled elevator apartment and access to an expense account. Though they downplayed the scene that unfolded in their living room, the Robinsons' bohemian peers ostensibly passed in and out with a regularity that in retrospect rivaled sitcom implausibility; this urban tribe of the scene's early champions included Lester Bangs—who was writing a Velvets postmortem for *Creem*, "Dead Lie the Velvets, Underground"—Richard Meltzer, and Lenny Kaye, who for a time crashed on the couch. But before they changed the way we think about music as an aesthetic, political, and above all, social phenomenon, they were just a bunch of kids in their twenties who loved to rock the house.

"Everybody would be sitting around on the floor and Lou would be holding court," Bettye says. "This was a way of introducing him back to the music scene." Lou would bring an acoustic guitar and work out new material; at the Robinsons', he quietly debuted "Walk on the Wild Side," the fortuitous by-product of an unrealized musical adaptation of the Nelson Algren novel of the same name, to a notoriously tough crowd. On April 29, 1971, he even had a mellow impromptu reunion with Nico at the Robinsons', performing an acoustic set of duets—"All Tomorrow's Parties," "Femme Fatale," and some of their solo material—for Danny Fields and the gathered cognoscenti.

Lou had been approached by Carmen Capalbo, the Broadway director and producer behind a long-running production of Bertolt Brecht and Kurt Weill's *The Threepenny Opera*, about collaborating on the adaptation of Algren's Depression-era tale of penniless drifters in the Big Easy. It had already led to box office results with the 1962 Jane Fonda vehicle, and Capalbo sought to replicate that off-Broadway. On *Live: Take No Prisoners*, Lou later gave a wry insight into his psychology at the time: the destabilizing insecurities and the grim alternative to the rock life that might not have been so bad.

"The guys who did *The Threepenny Opera*—this is all true—call me up, of all things, they say, 'We think you're a very literate rock 'n' roll person, and after Ray Davies we think you're the person that could take Nelson Algren's book *Walk on the Wild Side* and do like a musical thing for off-Broadway.' I said, 'You gotta be kidding. It's about cripples in the ghetto, man, what are you, out of your mind?'" Lou said. Compared to crunching numbers, it was a prospect, though.

"These assholes want a treatment for a book that's about cripples? I'm the best-qualified person to write a book about cripples in music? Kill yourself, man! It's better than being a garage mechanic, I think. As long as I keep thinking that. But what if it wasn't true? The genie will appear and say, 'Hey, schmuck, it was really groovy all the time being that garage mechanic out in Islip.' I'll say, 'Oh wow. Why didn't you tap me on the shoulder earlier?' ''Cause you wouldn't have listened.'"

The producers allegedly didn't even provide a book—they told Lou to buy a paperback copy and mark an *X* where they could interpolate a musical interlude. Rotting at the accounting ledger, he struggled for inspiration; Lou could only write honestly, and he could only honestly write what he knew. "I had a great title and nothing else, and then they fired me," Lou said. "I mean, they did it really gently. They let me down easy. They said, 'Lou, man, we've got a chance to produce *Mahagonny* on Broadway.' I said, 'Oh, wow, am I crushed.'"

*Mahagonny*, Arnold Weinstein's musical adaptation of Brecht and Weill's *The Rise and Fall of the City of Mahagonny*, closed after eight performances. Lou was no Sondheim, but that brief debacle in musical theater led to Lou's greatest hit. He jettisoned Algren's plot and kept the title, premiering the Factory version on the Robinsons' couch.

On July 3, 1971, while Lou and Bettye were at the Robinsons' apartment, they got the call notifying them that Jim Morrison had died in a bathtub in his Paris apartment. If Lou was having any lingering doubts about plunging back into the maelstrom and leaving financial security behind, Morrison's untimely demise raised them. But the true believers in the vicious potential of whatever Lou might do next were not about to stand idly by and watch him waste away in a cubicle.

With the necessary clout at RCA, Lou and Richard Robinson began plotting the official launch of Lou's solo career. The plan was to have Lou sign to the label and for Richard to produce his debut solo album. It was a seamless transition; it finally appeared as though Lou had escaped Freeport once and for all. Soon, Lou and Bettye got engaged. After a year of living with Lou's parents and saving their money, the couple found a studio apartment on Seventy-Eighth Street between First Avenue and East End Drive. As Lou pondered his transformation into the next incarnation of his onstage persona, Bettye still had her concerns about marrying a rock star—formerly, or soon-to-be—much less an allegedly unstable one. Yet she had experience dealing with a mercurial temperament.

Her father was a World War II veteran who fought in the Battle of the Bulge and took part in the Normandy invasion; he earned a Bronze Star but was injured in combat and spent time convalescing in a military hospital, suffering from what at the time was called shell shock. To deal with the trauma, doctors resorted to ECT. "I was woken up at night by my father's incredible screaming," Bettye says. "But my observation of living with two people who had gone through electroshock treatment is that I don't think they have many boundaries left." So Bettye was predisposed to sympathize with Lou, and besides, they were in love. They didn't rush to town hall, though.

"I had some reservations about the whole fame thing. It changed him, but I was so committed to him at that point," Bettye says. "I wanted to be the girl he married when he was successful rather than the one that they leave after they become successful."

That September the final piece of the puzzle was about to fall into place. Lisa Robinson found herself in the unique position to introduce Lou to one of the untold thousands who bought the Velvets' first album and started a band: David Bowie. He had already released "Space Oddity" and made a splash with *The Man Who Sold the World*, draped in a dress on the cover; now he was signing to RCA and poised for international stardom. Lou was poised for a steak dinner. Unbeknownst to Lou, Bowie worshipped him and Iggy Stooge; he had begun featuring Velvets material in his live set and dedicated "Queen Bitch" to Lou on the yet-to-be-released *Hunky Dory*.

Bowie was under the false impression that they had already met at a concert of the reconstituted Velvet Underground, but he had in fact met Doug Yule. This would all be settled at the Ginger Man, a semiformal restaurant by Lincoln Center that catered to a predominantly affluent, opera-going crowd. Full of ontological dread and self-loathing, fully conscious of the fact that he had taken a wrecking ball to his career, Lou was fueled by one inextinguishable desire—to exhume himself from the premature grave he'd dug and orchestrate a comeback before his thirtieth birthday. He had six months.

# 15

It had been exactly one year and eighteen days since Lou left the Velvets. The moment was indelibly etched in his consciousness. This was his own private 45, and it sent him spiraling into a turntable-like vertigo. Of the two Lous, the iconoclastic former rocker and the Freeport nine-to-fiver, he knew one was an impostor, and the demure man in the gray flannel suit seemed to be staking a serious claim to his fractured identity. But there at the Ginger Man, Lou knew that Bowie might be the key to resurrection.

Yet with each passing day, launching a solo career felt more elusive. John Lennon had done it—*Imagine* had just been released—so had Ringo Starr. Why couldn't Lou Reed? But Lou wasn't John Lennon. He was the frontman in absentia of a band that blazed briefly until its flame frittered out. To a lot of the suits, he was a has-been. Yet Lou felt ready to emerge from his cocoon.

Bowie's manager, Tony Defries; the Robinsons; RCA executive Dennis Katz; Bettye; and Angela Bowie were on hand to make sure everything went smoothly. As legend would have it, Bowie was wearing a black bolero hat that matched a crushed velvet black cape, with shoulder-length red hair, mascara, and eye shadow. This close to Lincoln Center, the sartorially unorthodox demigod might be mistaken for a transgender habitué of the Lower East Side or a supernumerary from *The Magic Flute*. Otherwise, it was just an ordinary dinner. To an outside observer in the après-theater set, it was the stuff of science fiction—a diplomatic meeting between the bleary-eyed, earthbound ambassador to an occult utopia beyond Gene Roddenberry's wildest dreams and its taciturn, dubiously hostile emissary. Lou was a neurotic talker, David the guileless picture of serenity; Lou was a dyed-in-the-wool New Yorker, David possibly not of this Earth; Lou's head was in the gutter,

David's was somewhere beyond where ground control could reach him. But somehow, they clicked.

Quietly chewing his food, Lou was dumbfounded. There he was, a twenty-nine-year-old erstwhile rocker with squandered potential and no money to show for it, sitting before the next big thing, and it dawned on him why he was summoned out of purgatory that night. The dinner had been arranged not in the hope of resuscitating Lou's ostensibly moribund career, but to appease the label's latest acquisition. He could see it in Bowie's starstruck eyes; Bowie loved the Velvet Underground and had fallen under the spell of Lou. But Lou wouldn't fall under the spell of Bowie quite yet.

In December, Lou and the Robinsons went to London to record *Lou Reed*; the title made the split from the Velvets official, but a lot more than Lou went into the record. RCA didn't take any chances and spared no expense; Lou was the only variable. He had taken up residence at the Four Seasons Inn on the Park, living in the lap of luxury on the label's dime, submerged in a sedated stupor. He spent his days in North London at Morgan Studios, where Paul McCartney laid down part of his solo debut and Rod Stewart had recently recorded *Every Picture Tells a Story*, and spent his nights speeding away. To buttress Lou's maiden voyage, Richard Robinson recruited a group of first-call session players as the backing band: Yes's Steve Howe and Rick Wakeman, the pianist from *Hunky Dory*; as well as Clem Cattini, Les Hurdle, Caleb Quaye, Kay Garner, and Brian Odgers. Of the nine members of Lou's new band, five had logged studio time with Elton John, who had just released *Madman Across the Water*. Yet their next project had little in common with "Tiny Dancer."

The material mostly consisted of unreleased Velvet Underground tracks— "Walk and Talk It" and "Wild Child," which explicitly mentions Bettye, were rehearsed at Max's in 1970, with songs like "Ride into the Sun" culled from *Loaded* outtakes. The plodding "Going Down" and the lugubrious "Berlin" were the only tracks not previously played by the Velvets. Lou opened the album with "I Can't Stand It," replacing Shelley's name with Candy. "Walk and Talk It" cribs the opening riff from the Rolling Stones' "Brown Sugar," out earlier that year on *Sticky Fingers*. "Ocean," the piece de resistance, opened with a gong hit, and washed over all that had passed with a totalizing undertow that at once recalled Delmore Schwartz's "In Dreams Begin Responsibilities"—"The ocean is becoming rough; the waves come in slowly, tugging strength from far back"—but also Eliot's Prufrock, Freeport's Nautical Mile, and the Velvets, who had originated it.

Waves foreground the album's dystopian cover as well. Lou reinforced the self-conscious novelistic quality of *Lou Reed* by tapping illustrator Tom Adams to design it. Adams was responsible for countless Agatha Christie covers, but in 1971, he had painted a series for Ballantine's paperback editions of Raymond Chandler. Lou scrapped the original idea of using a photograph of himself on the beach in Freeport with his dog, Seymoure—the Long Island kid stripped down to his roots—for a more surrealistic edge that might evoke *The Big Sleep* or *The Long Goodbye*. For Lou, who defined his compositional ethos as primarily literary, the album represented an answer to the question, "What if Raymond Chandler wrote a rock song?" On *Lou Reed*, even the cover conjured the feel of the eponymous paperback that spawned the Velvet Underground. With a tidal wave about to envelop a Manhattan block, hummingbirds drink the nectar of Lou's name writ large in spiky roses, atop an open Fabergé egg—symbolic of the Velvets—with a dejected duckling staring at the pavement, resigned to the grim fate of the city. Luckily for Lou, ducks can swim.

The *Lou Reed* sessions went off without a hitch—just Lou without the distractions of overproduction that had the potential to bog down a reasonably financed studio album. Despite an invitation to rendezvous with Ziggy Stardust on his home turf, Lou needed Bettye, who was finishing her semester at acting school in New York. "I actually still have a letter from Lisa. She said, 'Can you please come out here,'" Bettye recalls. "In the beginning, Lou would help me, but later on, Lou became dependent." When she arrived, everything seemed under control. "There wasn't any craziness going on. Lou was focused at that point—the drinking hadn't gotten out of control. It was really civilized, and Lou was very pleased with that album," she says. Playing the role of the dutiful fiancée, she began to realize what life with Lou might be like.

"When you are the person that is in his life, when you're the person that he loves or he trusts, it's almost as though you're like a part of him," she says. "There's almost no other way to explain it. You're actually like an arm or a leg and an extension of him. And that's why he has this extraordinary dependency upon you. He needs all his parts together."

After the album was finished, Lou decided to take another look back, though. John Cale and Nico were scheduled to appear at Le Bataclan, a

Parisian discotheque in the Eleventh Arrondissement, named for the Offenbach operetta set in China, an influence carried over to the variegated geometric structure with dormer windows and a pagoda roof. With Lou only a train ride away, he decided to join the reunion for an intimate drummerless performance. Following days of back-and-forth bickering, they all agreed to one show, to be broadcast on *Pop2*, a French television program. The three had not shared a stage together in five years, and though John and Nico remained on good terms—he had even produced her most recent studio album, the phantasmagorical *Desertshore*—Lou was persona non grata. Following three days of strained rehearsals, bad blood notwithstanding, no one knew if they would perform any of Nico's Velvet Underground features, especially "I'll Be Your Mirror." Nevertheless, it was billed as the first Velvet Underground reunion. It was unclear whether a public appearance would elicit hostility or sentimentality, solidify their estrangement or encourage a more lasting peace. Or even whether they would all show up at all.

Show up they did, though. On January 29, 1972, their names were announced and the unlikely trio took the stage before the packed audience of about a thousand rabid Velvet Underground fans. John wore a plain wool sweater over a button-down shirt; Nico donned a flowing calico dress, having dyed her hair back to its original brunette luster; Lou was in bellbottoms, a loose-fitting sport jacket, and boots, his hair hanging over his ears, eyes sunken, cheeks pallid. Seated stage right, with Nico far stage left, he looked like Buster Keaton in the silent classic *The General*, opposite his former lover's unattainable Germanic ideal, barely acknowledging her with even a sideways glance. Forever stoic, she didn't crack a smile as she stared off into some distant vanishing point. "Hello. It took us a while to get here," Lou said laconically. "This is a song about copping drugs in New York." He counted off "I'm Waiting for the Man," played in the French chanson tradition with John sitting humbly at the piano and Lou strumming languorously on an acoustic. Nico just sat there on her stool, frozen like the Venus de Milo, staring daggers at Lou. When he interpolated "waiting for my MainMan" into the lyrics, referring to Defries's production company with Bowie, shaking his head and smirking malevolently, it was clear who was being condescending to whom.

Lou lit up a cigarette, took a long drag, and John began massaging the keys for the doleful intro to Lou's morose dirge, "Berlin," which Lou described as "my Barbra Streisand song." Nico sat with arms crossed, still staring through Lou. To Lou, who had never been to Germany, it was hard not to read Nico, who was German, grew up in Berlin, and stood five foot ten, into this particular performance of Lou's ballad of love gone awry.

> *In Berlin, by the wall*
> *You were five foot ten inches tall*

As sexual tension permeated the expansive space, Lou gazed out at all the wan faces, entranced in a nostalgic remembrance of things past. "Oh babe, it was paradise," he chanted, salaciously running his tongue along his lips, yet he didn't look Nico's way. After the piano break, Lou came back in on guitar with the verse:

> *You know I'm gonna miss you now that you're gone*

Relishing that last lyric, Lou closed his eyes for seconds, then looked directly at Nico, as though finally confronting whatever unresolved issues they had left behind in the brief affair they'd had years before. Still, it had all the markers of an aggressive gesture.

John picked up his viola for "The Black Angel's Death Song," which Lou announced as "a song from our first album that was termed unintelligible, and it very well may be." This was followed with "Wild Child," with John accompanying on guitar, and "Heroin," which elicited thunderous applause. All sans Nico. John played "Ghost Story," a cut from *Vintage Violence*, his debut solo album, then launched into an unreleased song, the clap-along "The Biggest, Loudest, Hairiest Group of All," a folksy elegy about an unnamed hirsute rock group that made a reputation "satisfying crowds, pill-heads, and the rest that come to hear," but had since disbanded and might "make a comeback any day." Could he have been singing about the Velvets? It certainly seemed likely; depending on the show's outcome, perhaps the comeback was an imminent, if remote, possibility. Even through "Empty Bottles," John's glass-half-full love song, Nico still sat silently brooding, though.

Then came the decisive moment: Nico tentatively walked into the spotlight, and Lou began strumming the opening chords to "Femme Fatale." Did she still have the pipes? It got off to a rocky start, though. Lou was playing in the wrong key, and stopped. Nico laughed awkwardly; evidently it wasn't just like riding a bike. Lou then started again, nodding at Nico and smiling impishly. Somehow, Lou himself making a mistake had dispelled the anxiety; Nico didn't miss a beat. Then, in the last chorus, she left out her lines, leaving the men harmonizing, and trained her eyes on Lou for a long, mischievous moment. Nico's lips, whose legendary pout had the severity of an arctic tundra and rarely showed signs of glacial drift, curled into a deep, sanguine half-smile. As soon as Lou met her gaze, though, she looked down and away sheepishly, as though they were in on a secret that neither had been sure the other one remembered. Yet they still hadn't played the song everyone was waiting for.

Frustrating that expectation, Nico played "No One Is There," "Frozen Warnings," and "Janitor of Lunacy," excerpts from *The Marble Index* and *Desertshore*, disembodied sounds that emanated from the composer's existential bottomless pit, rendered with mournful orchestration for harmonium and viola; rarely had despair been distilled so purely. Maybe by Richard Strauss. It was as though she were the Berlin Wall itself, or Dreyer's Joan of Arc burst forth from the screen to indict the true heretics; if Lou was Jesus's son, Nico was descended from Mary Magdalene. It did not exactly set the tone for warm reconciliation.

Then, as the harmonium petered out in its final death agony, she started coughing. Not a little clearing of the throat, not a tickle that could be washed down with a glass of water—a full-on consumptive coughing fit; it would have brought *La Traviata* to a halt. "John, have Nico tell them this is the last song," Lou said. It was a passive-aggressive move; she was standing right there, and could hardly catch her breath anyway. She coughed for over a minute—dead air onstage—as though giving birth to a black lung. "I want to sing a last song now. If I can. I try my best," she said. Then, perhaps defensively, but with a hint of humor, she added, "I don't smoke cigarettes." The fact was, though, Nico's cough was probably symptomatic of a larger problem: heroin addiction.

Though she claimed not to shoot anything during her stint with the Velvets, she had become a hardcore junkie while romantically involved with French film director Philippe Garrel, starring in his film *The Inner Scar*, which used *Desertshore* as its soundtrack. Outwardly, she still retained the uncanny beauty of Munch's *Madonna*, yet her angular appearance and dewy eyes evoked a haunting mortality.

Then Lou strummed the wistful opening to "I'll Be Your Mirror." With great difficulty, Nico delivered the opening lines, gasping for breath, but John and Lou joined in on background vocals to bolster her frayed vocal cords. Yet she managed to muster the fortitude to belt out the closing chorus, which resounded throughout the cavernous space against the open sonorities of John and Lou's harmonizing. Finally, Lou's love-conquers-all ballad had realized its nostalgic mise en abyme structure—looking back into the mirror of the past through the lens of the present, a transient romance forever encased in amber. The song had not originally been written with Nico in mind, but it had taken on a double meaning that memorialized their time together as well as the contradiction of love itself, indelibly etched in memory yet always slipping through the fingers of the lover. They knew they might never play the song together again. In fact, they wouldn't. Perhaps with that foreknowledge, they gave an encore, playing "All Tomorrow's Parties." For John, Lou, and Nico as a *Jules and Jim* ménage a trois, this party would be their last.

# 16

Back in New York, Lou began working on material for his second album with RCA, scheduled to be recorded that summer. He and Bettye moved into a larger one-bedroom apartment on East Seventy-Third Street and First Avenue, which afforded more breathing room to get the creative juices flowing. "I knew all of the songs by heart. I was there when he wrote them," says Bettye. Lou would write late into the night, then have Bettye perform them the next morning; she had experience singing in a Presbyterian church choir, which added a purity but also an irony to Lou's dark edge. "He'd bring it out in the morning and he'd strum it on his guitar and he'd ask me to sing." So "Walk on the Wild Side," "Hangin' 'Round," and "Satellite of Love" had their humble beginnings in a more innocent, ecumenical style before they were transformed by future collaborator David Bowie.

Lou dedicated "Perfect Day" to Bettye, immortalizing a summer night early on in their romance. "We met in Central Park, and I had actually gone for a horseback ride earlier," Bettye says. She had taken Lou riding once, but he couldn't make it out of the corral, so this time she went alone. "Everyone has sangria in the park in the summer, and that's what we were doing. It was romantic and it was a lovely scene. We were very much in love. It was a really nice time during our relationship," Bettye says. "And then afterwards, we went out to a movie and then we went home."

Yet this reverie that kept him "hangin' on," a reference to the Supremes, sublimated a pessimistic undertone that pervaded the otherwise romantic idyll—during the day, something wicked always lies outside Central park. Just as Lou had cloaked paranoia in optimism with "Sunday Morning," he repeatedly inverted the sentimental evening's tender moments by setting the romance in an uneasy minor mood with a descending chord structure that didn't resolve into a major until the ominous closing pronouncement,

"You're going to reap just what you sow." For Lou, in the end, it all went back to black. Despite its consonance, the dark coda portended a fate that Bettye chose to ignore at the time. "When someone writes a song like that to you, there's not much to say about it," she says. "You hear it—'Thank you, it's lovely'—but you don't really talk about it." It was too early on in their relationship to read the writing on the wall, but Lou—a Sherlock Holmes of the heart, addiction and all—had a perspicacity that could slice through treacle, even his own, with a lacerating self-consciousness. "I think he saw," she says. "It was not only to me, but possibly to him. That might have been a little bit of a warning. There was always a twist, but he writes truthfully, and that's what made him good." Yet for the time being, they were still in the throes of young love.

Meanwhile, with interest ramping up in anticipation of the release of *Lou Reed*, RCA A&R executive Dennis Katz began plotting Lou's comeback tour. There was only one problem—Lou didn't have a band. With the album scheduled for release in April 1972 and a limited budget, Katz did the only sensible thing a savvy businessman from the mean streets of Schenectady would: he turned to family first. Steve Katz, his brother, just so happened to be a founding member of Blood, Sweat & Tears and the Blues Project, who had crossed paths with Lou at Max's.

"We never communicated," Steve Katz recalls of his encounter with the Velvets. "They were like heroin street hip and we were pot suburban hip. Our drugs didn't mesh very well."

Incompatible drugs would soon lead to a profitable collaboration, though. With BS&T riding the wave that began with "Spinning Wheel," the jazz-rock outfit would not be available, but Dennis arranged for Fred Heller, BS&T's young road manager, to add Lou into his management umbrella based out of Dobbs Ferry in Westchester. Meanwhile, Dennis began the search for a backing band worthy of the founder of the Velvet Underground. They just didn't have any money to hire any of the session musicians used on the album, or the time to allow a cohesive sound to ferment. Then they got an idea that would bring Lou up by bringing him back down.

Blood, Sweat & Tears employed a gopher from Yonkers, Scott Clark, who would pick them up at the airport and run errands, and Scott had a garage band. The band was four gangly adolescents—Vinny Laporta, Eddie Reynolds, Bobby Rescigno, and Scott—who all went to Gorton High School in Yonkers, and they didn't even have a name. Then Lou's new management team asked if they might be interested in auditioning to play with Lou. It sounded like a shot in the dark, a high school fantasy too good to be true, maybe even a prank. But, just like when Lou auditioned Moe Tucker in Levittown, he showed up at the Rescigno house in Yonkers for an audition. The band set up, full of youthful trepidation, and launched into some original material. "Lou came to the basement, we did the audition and got it!" Laporta recalls. Vinny was only seventeen at the time, in his senior year of high school, with shoulder-length hair and a freshly wrought class ring; he still had braces. But Lou, always mercurial, didn't find all of that entirely unsympathetic. The band was euphoric. "We totally lucked out. We stepped in shit," Laporta says.

Dumbfounded, they drove out to Dobbs Ferry to rehearse with Lou. He showed them the chords, which were simple enough—they played by ear—and the band started to find their groove. "We just added our parts to it, which we would normally do with Eddie's group, and it worked out," Laporta says. Overnight, they had gone from rehearsing in their parents' basement to rehearsing downstairs from Blood, Sweat & Tears.

"We were rehearsing upstairs and they were rehearsing downstairs, and Lou and I got friendly," says Steve Katz. "This is a time when Lou wasn't doing speed or anything. And he was very likable. He was actually shy."

Even though Lou was thirty, the band had more in common with the Jades than the Velvets. In fact, they hardly even knew the Velvets. "I'd heard of the Velvet Underground and I saw a cover of one of their albums," Laporta says. "I saw a picture of Lou and I'm going, 'Oh, yeah, he looks familiar,' not really knowing him, not knowing his music at all, just knowing and hearing the name Velvet Underground, but no clue of what they were about."

The lack of familiarity was not an insurmountable obstacle, though; Lou was starting his solo career with a clean slate, a sound that harked back to his own suburban roots. In a dry run of "Sister Ray," Lou didn't teach them the song at all. "He goes, 'It's one chord—it's in the key of G—and we just jammed on it," Laporta recalls. "We didn't know the song from Adam. We just kinda winged it following him." But the garage band aesthetic dovetailed with Lou's freewheeling style. All they needed was a name, and soon they were given one—the Tots, partially due to the conspicuous age gap between the band and Lou. To wit, Heller once had to write Vinny a note to excuse him from gym class so he could make a rehearsal. "I give it to the coach, and he's walking down the hall and he sees that it's Blood Sweat & Tears stationery, and he turns his head and does a double take, like, 'Who is that guy?'" They were Yonkers' newly minted rock stars. So it came to pass that Lou would make his triumphant return as Lou Reed and the Tots. And the Tots were in for the postgrad ride of a lifetime.

In April 1972 they were booked for their debut at the State University of New York at Buffalo, arranged by student promoter Harvey Weinstein, who would later transition into film. Before shipping them off to Europe, RCA wanted to make sure the Tots could handle the heat. Without a dedicated road crew yet, they transported their own equipment. "So we're moving the equipment in with Lou and I see these guys looking at posters going, 'Lou Reed, who's this Lou Reed? I've heard of a Chuck Reed, but I don't know no Lou Reed,'" Laporta says. "That was our first real gig."

*Lou Reed* came out that month to mixed but mostly positive reviews, yet it was met with commercial stagnation. Naturally, everyone viewed Lou's solo debut in light of the Velvet Underground, which is to say the critics used the Velvets as a yardstick, and the fan base was at best marginal. Robert Christgau gave it a tepid B+, concluding it was "Hard to know what to make of this. Certainly it's less committed—less rhythmically monolithic and staunchly weird—than the Velvets." But others received it as nothing less than revelatory. "This album fits nowhere in the solo singer-songwriter spectrum," wrote Greg Shaw in *Phonograph Record*. "If you had to shove it in, it would come out standing head and shoulders above the rest." Nevertheless, it didn't sell.

It was at this time that Terry Philips reached out to Lou in the hope of wooing him to Perception Records, an independent label he had founded after leaving Pickwick. Three months after *Lou Reed* was released, Philips charted a single with King Harvest's "Dancing in the Moonlight," but he had established a track record producing Golden Earring and a roster of avant-garde artists. In 1971 he had a sleeper success with Wanda Robinson's radical spoken-word album *Black Ivory*, and had released Maya Angelou's *The Poetry of Maya Angelou*, Dizzy Gillespie's Grammy-nominated *Portrait of Jenny*, and albums by James Moody, Astrud Gilberto, Johnny Hartman, organist Larry Young, and Shirley Horn. He began working with Marion "Boo" Frazier, Gillespie's cousin (Philips would later give a eulogy at Gillespie's funeral), opening the doors of Perception to the bebop forefather and a coterie of artists who chafed against the mainstream.

Lou would not be his most controversial artist; he had at one point collaborated with dissident poet Amiri Baraka. Philips had met Baraka when he went by LeRoi Jones, and after seeing his landmark play, *Dutchman*, attempted to adapt it as an album with a background score. This led to a free-jazz recording session in Brooklyn with members of Baraka's Black Arts Movement—with Albert Ayler and Sunny Murray accompanying Baraka's poetry—but it quickly fell apart when Baraka's associates pressured him into reneging on the deal with Philips. Comparatively, dealing with Lou would be easy.

Since parting ways with Lou, Philips had also discovered David Clayton-Thomas, who lived on his couch for a while, but let him out of his contract so he could join Blood, Sweat & Tears. So Philips and Dennis Katz had crossed paths; having also let Lou out of his contract, Philips hoped to validate his early belief in his potential. "I spoke to Katz and I said, 'I'd like to sign Lou. I'm willing to give him a very good deal.'" Yet Lou still had a commitment from RCA for at least one more album and a tour in support of *Lou Reed* before he could consider leaving the major label for Perception. It would all hinge on *Transformer*.

RCA expected Lou to produce a new album by the end of 1972, and despite the sales figures, the Velvets' following overseas would be enough to carry the tour. So he put on a black velvet suit with paisley filigrees, pancake-white face makeup, dark eye shadow, and got ready to plug in; Lou had been reborn as the Phantom of Rock.

The label was reluctant to leverage too much capital on an asset with a long history of not breaking singles. "The early tours were very 'budget,' so we had some struggles," says Barbara Wilkinson, who later became Lou's road manager. "Lou was not demanding about 'frills.'" In addition to hiring a low-budget band, they bought the Tots low-budget gear. As die-hard Allman Brothers Band fans, they wanted Marshall equipment, but they had to make do with bulky Sunn Coliseum solid-state amplifiers. Ironically, the *Lou Reed* tour would be short on feedback, which he would make up for later. "We didn't use any pedals. You can't get distortion out of a solid-state amplifier," Laporta recalls. "We would have gotten something with tubes with a natural distortion and a beautiful sound." They didn't look a gift horse in the mouth, though.

Immediately following Vinny's high school graduation, the Tots prepared to ship out to London. That Independence Day, there were no burgers and franks, but they were freer than they'd ever been in their lives—they boarded a 747 on the Fourth of July 1972. "I had never flown in my life. And the guy that picked us up, he picked up the Stones and the Monkees," Laporta says. "It's like, holy shit! I just graduated high school. I'm in England. It's happening so fast, and it's ridiculous."

Several days later, they were meeting David Bowie backstage at Royal Festival Hall, where he was part of the Friends of the Earth Save the Whale Benefit. Bowie had just released *The Rise and Fall of Ziggy Stardust and the Spiders from Mars*, and was in full Martian regalia, towering above everyone in platform shoes and dressed head to toe in white. The extraterrestrial sight didn't stop the Tots from going right up to him, though. "We got backstage, and Bowie was like, 'Oh, so you're the Tots!' And we're all shaking hands—we're all trying to shake hands with David Bowie. And he's like, 'So many hands!'" At the end of Bowie's set, he invited Lou onstage for "White Light/White Heat," "I'm Waiting for the Man," and "Sweet Jane." Lou had made it to the UK.

Before Lou could headline his debut, he needed power—a lot. An acoustic set might have been hunky-dory for the cavalier French audience, but the Brits expected amplification, and Lou and the Tots lacked the proper electrical equipment. "We were at a diner, just eating and waiting, because we had our amplifiers from America and we needed these transformers," Vinny recalls. "We needed transformers to plug in to convert American current. We kept goofing, going, 'What are we waiting for? The transformer people! We can't play until they get here. It's the transformer people.' I think that's how Lou got the name of the album."

Eventually, the "transformer people" arrived, and on July 14, 1972, Lou hit with the Tots, sharing a bill with local act Brinsley Schwarz and prog rock group Gnidrolog at London's squalid King's Cross Cinema. They even arrived early for the occasion to find a raucous crowd waiting to have their minds blown. "I never knew the term 'queuing up.' We got there early, and they were queuing up already! We didn't come on until 3:30 in the morning," says Laporta. Then it came time to apply the makeup. Lou and the Tots put on a ghastly white veneer, but not Vinny. "There's no way in the world I'm putting makeup on," he recalls. "The other guys did the highlights in their eyes, but I'd run away. I'd go into the crowd, and when it was time for us to go onstage, I'd come up."

By the time they took the stage, it was nearly dawn, yet they still squeezed in a full set before sunrise, drawing from the Velvets catalog and *Lou Reed,* culminating in an ear-splitting rendition of "Heroin." Keith Relf, the lead singer of the Yardbirds, was among the insomniacs gathered to hear Lou's solo UK debut. Photographer Mick Rock stayed up to document the moment, shooting the iconic close-up that would later be used as the cover of *Transformer*. A review in *New Musical Express* touted the Tots as a "very professional young backup band" with a "cleanliness and precision" that belied their youth. Few would guess that Vinny was flinging a mortarboard only the previous month.

Their opening night continued into the following day. "So there's this girl dancing outside, and she's totally naked. And she ended up coming back to our place," Laporta says. As far as Vinny was concerned, what she lacked in clothing, she more than made up for in gear. "It turned out that she had a black Les Paul and a Fender Super Reverb, and she gave it to Lou," he says. "Lou's going, 'This girl gave us this equipment. I can't take this.' Now I'm a youngster, and I said, 'I'll take it! Are you kidding me?'" Angela Bowie even crashed with them. "Angie was hanging out with us for like three days . . . and nights. We were kids, smoking a little weed, had a couple of cocktails, but nothing crazy." One night, they walked into a pub, and there sat Pete Townshend and Keith Moon, throwing back a few pints of lager.

Lou and the Tots then packed their stuff into a tour bus they shared with British singer-songwriter Phillip Goodhand-Tait and began touring the English countryside, playing Manchester, Croydon, and the town of Aylesbury, where a local dog, unfazed by Lou's demonic countenance, ambled onstage and spent most of the set sitting at his heels. Having proven themselves, the Tots flew home to recuperate for a month while Lou recorded his sophomore album under the wing of David Bowie. As they boarded the plane, the Tots knew they'd experienced possibly the coolest postgrad summer of any high school kids in America.

Lou spent August 1972 in Trident Studios in London with David Bowie and Spiders from Mars guitarist Mick Ronson, working on the album that would become *Transformer*. In addition to referencing the mysterious transformer people who allowed Lou and the Tots to plug in, the title exploited the sexualized double entendre on the "trans"; Lou would differentiate himself from his previous incarnation, emerging as an androgynous figure while altering the proverbial voltage of everything that came before. Somehow, he would still be quintessentially Lou, the man who couldn't help but be aggressively true to himself—even in the absence of absolute truth—yet was always transforming, never quite becoming a fixed, knowable, or commodifiable entity that could be pinned down, explained, or reduced to a hit single. Ironically, a hit single was in the offing, though, but on Lou's terms.

With Jacques Derrida's burgeoning deconstructionist theory hanging in the cultural milieu, what would remain consistent and what would be transformed as Lou deconstructed and reconstituted himself was left deliberately opaque, ambiguous, and androgynous. Lou preserved his mystique behind a mask of makeup that offered infinite frames of reference—to the *Phantom of the Opera*, *Frankenstein*, or even Pierrot the sad clown—fabricating a protean rock icon that resisted any pat interpretation and disavowed sexual difference, hegemonic masculinity, religious iconography, or idol worship, flattening glam rock's Day-Glo hedonism into a high-contrast black-and-white image that was anything but.

Lou represented all these things, but like an electrical transformer, he was also none of them, a mere conduit; he was poised for global stardom, but the man behind the mask had vanished. With *Transformer*, Lou had transformed into a symbol, the empty signifier, a spectral representation of himself that allowed him to narrate the New York demimonde as a walking ghost. Beyond the studio walls, Lou was steadily forgetting himself with a little help from his friends at the bottom of the bottle; and with the help of his friends David and Mick, like an existential cross between Frankenstein's creature and Chandler's Philip Marlowe, he was remembering himself as someone else—someone not so good.

Bowie and Ronson were also transformers for Lou. "Bowie was always a fan of Lou's and wanted very much to work with him. He thought he owed him a great deal, so he was more than happy to produce that album, and he was brilliant at it," Bettye says. "He absolutely transformed the kind of music that I heard when he was writing it and I'd be singing it. We'd go over it at home, and the music that Bowie produced—it was just extraordinary—the difference."

The record was recorded over a ten-day period, six hours a day. Aside from enlisting Ronson to play on the album and coproduce, Bowie pushed it in a jazz direction by hiring drummer John Halsey, a session musician and member of jazz-rock group Patto, and bassist Herbie Flowers, who had anchored the bass on *Space Oddity* and with glam rock outfit T. Rex but also had a jazz pedigree. Bowie then called baritone saxophonist Ronnie Ross, his childhood saxophone teacher, who had played with Woody Herman, Ben

Webster, and Clark Terry. Ross barely recognized Bowie when he saw him in the studio. "I walked out with red hair and no eyebrows, and said: 'You probably don't remember me, but you gave me sax lessons when I was ten,'" Bowie recalled. For the unforgettable doo-wop background vocals sung by the "colored girls" on the chorus of "Walk on the Wild Side," Bowie hired female vocal trio the Thunderthighs, who were ironically all white. The jazz feel complemented Lou's lyrical content, which had a figurative syncopation that negated the monolithic message straight rhythm tended to present. Not only was Lou not quite straight, he could swing.

The back cover of the record complemented Lou's liminal pansexual gender play. Shot by Karl Stoecker—Lou's friend from Syracuse who had based himself in London and begun doing fashion photography as well as album art for Roxy Music—the juxtaposed images confounded traditional representations of gender and sexuality. "I did the 'phony' of Ernie and the photo of Gala," Stoecker recalls. He photographed Lou's road manager, Ernie Thormahlen, in an undersized crop top and a biker hat with a comically large banana stuffed down his jeans—now attached to a body but concealed from view, as opposed to Warhol's free-floating priapic icon—opposite *Vogue* fashion model Gala Mitchell in platform pumps, mascara, and a sheer black negligee. Stoecker posed his Rabelaisian subjects in similar salacious positions: the intimidating roadie juxtaposed by the lithe model, emphasizing the same body contours, with one knee bent and their left hands placed on their waists. With Mitchell framed by a neon border, Thormahlen appeared to be looking at himself in the mirror and seeing the paragon of female beauty reflected back. The transformation took place in the black space between them, but also the potential space within.

The effect was deliberate; Thormahlen's T-shirt actually belonged to Vinny. "Ernie was a bigger guy and I was small," says Vinny. "So I gave him my T-shirt and he put the cigarette pack under the arm, and he's dressed up and looking into the mirror. He goes, 'I need a tight white T-shirt.' I'm going, 'Ernie, look at the size of you!' He says, 'That's what I need! I need a tight white T-shirt.'" Lou had finally found a way to collapse the phallic into the feminine.

Much of *Transformer* seemed to hinge on this displacement and refraction of meaning at the core of Lou's murky new persona. Lou accentuated the contradictions inherent in the imagery with chords that clashed with the lyrical content, deploying a technique already present in film editing, anempathetic sound, in which the score undermines the visual or fails to empathize with the character, often creating an alienating synthesis; Stanley Kubrick mastered the effect. Lou had previously honed the effect with "Sunday Morning," and it was epitomized on *Transformer* with "Perfect Day" and "Satellite of Love."

The album opened with the flower hit of "Vicious," a glam rock call to arms inspired by Warhol—the subject of "Andy's Chest"—with nothing stereotypically floral or frilly about it. With a razor-sharp guitar line, this flower was mostly thorn, or perhaps the toxic oleander, but that was the point; amid a historical moment of increasing uncertainty, Lou ruptured cliché with a bracingly vivid series of paradoxical images that characterized the album, approaching the sublime. For "Perfect Day," Ronson arranged an evocative piano part and a string section that underscored the song's quixotic beauty without becoming maudlin, apropos of a rosy retrospection that carried all the signs of perfection yet in reality eluded that impossible ideal.

With *Transformer*, Lou did for rock what Gore Vidal had done for literature in *Myra Breckinridge*, his polymorphously perverse 1968 satirical takedown of patriarchal culture. On "Make Up," he posed the question of what exactly was being constructed or made up. For the song's "slick little girl," makeup served not only as a beauty product, but also as a means to obfuscate the gender binary. Similarly, for Lou and Bowie, gender was a fluid social construct, and this "slick little girl" was not necessarily a girl in the conventional sense, delineated by the song's bridge:

> *Now we're coming out*
> *Out of our closets*
> *Out on the streets*

"Satellite of Love" presented another paradoxical symbol—the remote satellite orbiting the Earth as an ironic symbol of love from a distance, evoking the celestial loneliness of Major Tom in Bowie's "Space Oddity" from a terrestrial perspective. The song's blasé protagonist seems to sit at home alone watching a satellite launch, aware of the open secret of his partner's infidelity, a sentiment that, like the titular image, belies the ascending major chord progression, soaring background vocals, and animated horns that conclude the song. "New York Telephone Conversation," loosely inspired by conversations with Lisa Robinson, and "Goodnight Ladies," yet another reference to Eliot's "The Waste Land," underscored the way meaning and tone are constantly misconstrued in social interactions, especially in New York.

Just as the Mick Rock cover image applied Warholian aesthetics to subtly deconstruct the cult of celebrity, "Walk on the Wild Side," the ne plus ultra of pop gender- and genre-bending, deconstructed conventional notions of gender as a whole. At first listen, it sounded like a typical pop single, but something uncanny lay beneath—it had two bass lines. Herbie Flowers showed up at Trident Studios at 10 AM the morning he was booked for the session with his acoustic and electric bass in tow. He had no clue what he was getting into, never mind sheet music, but for "Wild Side," he didn't need it. Lou tersely explained the bass part.

"It's one bar of C and one bar of F, and one bar of C and one bar of F," Lou said.

The tautology sounded like a Zen koan. "Yeah, then what?" said Flowers.

"Man, it's just one bar of C and one bar of F!"

Flowers figured the acoustic sound suited the song's insouciant shuffle, but then an idea occurred to him that might introduce a multilayered nuance into the vamp. He overdubbed the electric bass line a tenth above the acoustic one in unison to create a polyphonic harmony. "When you combine that with the other bass, it takes on another character," Flowers later recalled. "Lou said, 'That's gorgeous,' because he said it actually suited what the song's about." Twenty minutes later, Flowers had laid down the iconic bass line, a service for which he got paid a double rate—they were paid by the instrument—of seventeen pounds. Like the transgender characters the song immortalized, when the layers were peeled away, there was a doubling down below, but a beautiful harmony emerged through those ostensibly conflicting parts. The censors missed the message, too—the fellatio reference to "giving head" was slipped in more subtly than in "Sister Ray"—and "Walk on the Wild Side" became an international hit.

Lou slyly foregrounded gender-bending and the politics of desire, the crux of the "Walk," which is more of a saunter than a speed walk, amphetamine notwithstanding; the seamy New York underbelly was depicted as a countercultural mecca that subverted the American Dream, fulfilling the utopian promise of a truly free alternative. Though Lou had left the Factory several years prior, the song chronicled the lives of several Warhol Superstars: Holly Woodlawn, Jackie Curtis, and "in the backroom" of Max's, Candy Darling—who had recently appeared in Paul Morrissey's *Women in Revolt*—as well as

Little Joe Dallesandro and Joe Campbell, who was known as "Sugar Plum Fairy," the Factory's main purveyor of "sugar." Campbell was a confidante of Dorothy Dean, the quick-witted *New Yorker* fact-checker who worked the door at Max's and bestowed Warhol's moniker Drella.

On "Wild Side," they each got their own verse, delivered in Lou's declamatory narration over a repeating two-chord structure, the "Amen Cadence," named for its occurrence at the end of most hymns. Now that Lou had some critical distance, this hymn celebrated the freedom symbolized by the Factory as it confronted the artifice inherent in gender stereotypes, sexuality, and pop music itself. The two chords repeat until the song fades out, but over that rigid sameness, Lou uncovered infinite variation and improvisation; so much could be done with just two chords. Rather than present a cohesive whole, each of the song's constituent parts was introduced piecemeal—the strings, the saxophone, the "colored girls" with their ghostly reverb—calling attention to the means by which recordings, like gender, are assemblages.

The track's familiar refrain, "Take a walk on the wild side," was not a heavy-handed exhortation, but a coy invitation, a subtle seduction of the ears, which can't be shut like the eyes or closed like the mouth. While it invited the listener to venture into a world beyond the pale of the tame—yet perhaps living within it—the song was also the walk in itself, an insidious perambulation that had suddenly waltzed into car stereos across the country.

By narrating the visual, Lou forced AM radio to see the marginalized with a pop sensibility that boldly acknowledged a frequently overlooked truth—we are far more alike than we are different, and might even have something in common with "Holly from Miami, FLA."

The 1960s were all about polarities: the freak and the bore, the degenerate and the model citizen, the underground and the elite, the sordid and the sanitized, the innocent and the corrupt, but now that the '70s were in full swing, those strict boundaries had been supplanted by a contrapuntal, more fluid continuum. Yet Lou knew that the boundary was artificial to begin with. "Wild Side" fades out, perhaps unfairly truncating Ross's effortless solo—evincing a come-hither quality—but also suggesting that the song would continue after the engineer pressed stop. The wild side would always be there—society just didn't acknowledge it.

The *Transformer* radio spot played on this notion of deconstructing reality. "In the midst of all the make-believe madness, the mock-depravity, and the pseudo-sexual anarchists, Lou Reed is the real thing," the announcer narrated in his dulcet baritone. Yet Lou knew the dangerous truth that this voice of male authority didn't acknowledge—beneath it all, there was no real thing.

Living that reality or lack thereof took a toll on him, though. As he collapsed the false dichotomy of the gender binary and fully embodied the image of the radical queer-cum-fallen everyman, he began to lose sight of the boundary within that separated performer from performance. With the songs on *Transformer*, all published by Oakfield Avenue Music, Lou symbolically returned to the site of his initial gender confusion—35 Oakfield Avenue in Freeport—and cast off the yoke of his conservative parents. Yet it seemed he had taken the transformation too far. Thus began a slow downward spiral as he gradually transformed into the edgy, intoxicated persona he had created to escape the past. As the tour resumed, it became increasingly difficult to know the dancer from the dance.

Still, Lou held it together for the next leg of the *Lou Reed* tour. For the Tots' first return gig, they played the Carré Theatre in Amsterdam with Jeff Beck, who had released *Jeff Beck Group* earlier that year and was on tour with Tim Bogert and Carmine Appice. Vinny was in heaven, but he was also terrified. "Jeff Beck is my favorite guitar player. I was shitting," he says. "I was so conscious of my guitar playing, and I was afraid to play any Jeff Beck riff." They spent the rest of the European tour in the UK, playing London, Manchester, Glasgow, and everywhere in between; by the time he was done, the staid campuses at Oxford, Leeds, and Essex had been tainted by the scourge of Lou.

The band flew back to New York in time for the release of *Transformer*. On November 8, 1972, RCA unleashed the album that would finally make Lou a star. A censored radio edit of "Walk on the Wild Side" was released in tandem, but most stations opted for the raw and uncut version. Before long, the album rose to Number 29 on the *Billboard* Top 200 chart for 1972, and in 1973, "Wild Side" peaked at Number 16, with an even higher chart position overseas. The reviews were mixed, but it couldn't stop the wave of Lou's hit from washing over the unwashed masses. "This new album is further proof even that Lou Reed has turned into something sicker than a homicidal-rapist-mass murderer-porno editor," read a review in *Creem*. "This album proclaims itself as most masterpieces proclaim themselves: IT GROWS ON YA!!" Writing in *Rolling Stone*, Nick Tosches was not as laudatory, calling the album "a real cockteaser." Though Tosches dismissed roughly half the songs, he remained hopeful that Lou would inject some "good faggot energy" into future material and "just go in there with a bad hangover and start blaring out his visions of lunar assfuck." It seemed many of the critics didn't buy the album's implicit political edge, but critical sensitivity notwithstanding, Lou was heading in that direction regardless.

To deal with his inner turmoil, Lou began self-medicating by drinking himself into a stupor. For anyone who dared to book Lou, it was even a contractual obligation. "In part of the contract, it said there had to be Johnnie Walker Black there at the gig," says Vinny. "When Lou was on, it was fine. If he was bombed out, it was the worst thing in the world. If we'd find a bottle of Johnnie Walker Black, we would hide it. We would literally hide it."

One night, during "Sweet Jane," they weren't all playing in the same key. "Lou had his guitar tuned down. We were in regular tuning, but if Lou played his low E, it would be a D. But he was so bombed he was playing it in like E flat. So if you know what E flat and D sound like together, it was noise," Vinny recalls. "People in the audience wouldn't know." Lou's self-destructive behavior didn't derail the tour, but at home, things were already falling apart.

It was hard to discern whether the drinking was a coping mechanism for the touring or vice versa. "You're going from one city to the next, sometimes in twenty-four hours," Bettye remembers. "Then there's the rehearsal and getting there, and getting to the hotel, and going to the venue and then rehearsing, then coming back, trying to eat but not really, then getting dressed and then going, doing the show, and once you perform a show, you have to come down after it." Touring disrupted Lou's natural circadian rhythm, which was syncopated to begin with. "No performer falls asleep after a show. So they have to come down. And then there would be ridiculous parties, and you'd have to wake up in two hours if you were lucky and get on a plane." Yet at that point, Bettye had already invested so much in the relationship, she pushed forward despite her doubts; besides, above all else, she believed in Lou's music.

Lou and the Tots embarked on a series of test performances in preparation for their mainstream US debut, scheduled for January 27, 1973, at Alice Tully Hall and billed as the "Out of the Underground" show. The day after Christmas, Lou and the Tots performed live on the radio from the Ultrasonic Studios in Hempstead on Long Island, a broadcast that was later released as *American Poet*. Just as he had done previously with the Velvet

Underground, Lou celebrated New Year's in Philadelphia, performing at the Main Point alongside a cappella group the Persuasions. For the *Transformer* tour supporting act, Lou's management hired Garland Jeffreys, his former Syracuse collaborator, who was hot on the heels of his own self-titled solo debut on Atlantic. But before Lou could come out of the underground, he had one more thing he had been wanting to do for a while: get married.

In early January, Lou and Bettye got married in their apartment on Seventy-Third Street. Fred Heller contacted an officiant that would be mutually agreeable, or disagreeable to both of them. "Fred arranged for a Catholic bishop to perform the ceremony," Bettye says. "I was Presbyterian and Lou was Jewish. So I guess Fred thought that would be something in the middle." It was an intimate, modest ceremony, with only Heller and his wife present as witnesses. Neither told their family. "By then, *Transformer* had come out and my father had seen the white face on the cover and had no idea what his daughter was doing," Bettye says. They celebrated the covert nuptials unceremoniously at an informal gathering with Clive Davis and other studio bigwigs, almost a de facto coronation of Lou after the success of *Transformer*. The wedding was brushed under the table. "Everybody was sort of making deals or talking or schmoozing, and we had just been married, so I was on a different plane than anyone else," Bettye says. "Maybe there was a congratulations that went on, but it was a small thing and it was private." Then the newlywed couple quietly flew to Jamaica for a weeklong honeymoon. The scattered pieces of Lou's life had suddenly come together, but the cognitive dissonance between the superficially well-wrought urn of his professional and personal life and the fragments shored against the ruins inside his head made for a delicate balance. Soon, the honeymoon was over.

By the time of the Alice Tully Hall show, Lou had been hyped up in subways across the city as a benighted figure fit for the pen of Gay Talese, whose trenchant *Esquire* profile "Frank Sinatra Has a Cold" could have just as easily applied to Lou, albeit with a different malady.

On January 27 it was pouring rain. Deep in the bowels of Alice Tully Hall, slumped over a dressing room sofa with Johnnie Walker in one hand and a Marlboro in the other, Lou lay like a glazed doughnut next to Andy Warhol, Polaroid perched on his lap as he waited for Lou to give some sign of life. Lou leered silently into the abyss, which leered right back; he had been jittery and then drunk for most of the night, and backstage at Lincoln Center between sets, he appeared even more dazed, gazing into a boisterous theater where beyond the curtain, the expectant voices of throngs of eager teenagers echoed, impatiently awaiting the arrival of their strung-out anti-hero, some partaking in a few surreptitious tokes as the pungent odor of weed grew in the hallowed hall. Warhol was perfectly aware, as was Bettye, that any attempt to inject some levity over the pall Lou cast into the darkness would only result in a withering retort. Lou was turning thirty-one in a month, and he had climbed to the top of the rock ladder; Lincoln Center validated all of the hard work he had done underground with the Velvets, as a poet and a genuine artist, but validation never sat quite right with him.

Nursing a bad case of writer's block, Lou already had mounting pressure from the label to produce an even bigger follow-up to *Transformer*. He was exhausted from rehearsing and touring and honeymooning; putting on and taking off the ill-fitting velvet suit, white foundation, and eye shadow; the unending stream of publicity interviews, radio appearances, and photo ops. He was bloated from the lethal cocktail of nonstop partying, booze, and mood elevators; he felt like a used tire that had long ago worn out its tread. Lou was struggling with a rare condition most would consider the be-all and end-all of American life, a state of being that exceeded Warhol's wildest dreams. But for Lou, it provoked inconsolable feelings of alienation, tempestuous outbursts, existential terror, even dread. Lou Reed was a star. The man had met the myth, and the stage wasn't big enough for the both of them.

"I think he drank too much, frankly, but he did perform," Bettye recalls. Everyone seemed to be having a better time than Lou, including his parents and sister. "I was backstage in the wings—I got him on. When he was finished, somebody threw a bouquet of flowers into my hands, and I took it out to him." Lincoln Center had just been viciously hit by Lou, like it had been hit with a flower.

The Tots buoyed their drunken leader, though, as Yonkers descended on Alice Tully. "We had tons of our local neighborhood friends who used to come see us play locally. They were all the way in the front row, going 'Eddie! Vinny!' And I'm like, 'You're not supposed to do this. This is a Lou Reed concert,'" Vinny says. But Lou was in another world. "My father came, my aunt, my grandmother, and she's like, 'What's that funny smell in the air?' My cousins said, 'They're smoking weed, Grandma!'" Before they hit twenty, the Tots had reached a pinnacle usually reserved for the Chamber Music Society.

# 17

As Woodward and Bernstein began following the money trail, Lou coped with the constant pressure of touring by following the drug trail, and his drug of choice was speed. Bettye not only had the responsibility of chaperoning Lou and keeping him sober enough to make it onstage, she took on the role of lighting designer. "I was interested in lights. He said, 'You want to do the lights?'" Bettye recalls. She had no experience, but the technicians gave her basic training, and she familiarized herself with the lighting plot. "No one knew his songs better than me, so if I could do the lights I was probably the right one to do it. And that was great, but it was a lot of work. That made it a little better for me, because at least I was doing something that I loved." From up in the lighting booth, she had a brief reprieve from the strained relations with Lou.

With their relationship fraying, Lou's infamy only grew. Lou and the Tots headlined in Ohio—where Lou had a huge following—and flew all over the country. Despite the growing tension at home, the tour was not without comic relief. In Boston, where they played Jordan Hall, Lou lay in bed with a cold and Vicks VapoRub smeared on his chest while Vinny cruised the streets with Garland Jeffreys to do a bit of self-promotion. "We go into a couple record stores, and Garland says, 'Hi, would you happen to have the new Garland Jeffreys record?' And they go, 'No,' and he goes, 'Can you do me a favor, can you order that for me?'" Vinny recalls. That night at the concert, Lou's nasal congestion didn't derail his performance. Luckily, no one expected Lou Reed to sound like Sinatra.

Throughout the *Transformer* tour, even the opening acts would soon occupy a vaunted rock status: Bruce Springsteen, Roomful of Blues, and Blue Öyster Cult. BÖC opened for Lou on March 9, 1973, at the Ford Auditorium in Detroit, and the night would live in infamy in the annals of rock history for the first bout of an ongoing literary rivalry that pitted Lou against Lester Bangs, the irrepressible editor of *Creem*. Lester was Lou's most tireless champion—he defended him from the vultures when he was down-and-out, worshipped the Velvets, and cared more about rock than just about anyone on the planet—but as with many artists and their critics, he and Lou had a fraught symbiosis. Lester idealized Lou, and his Jacobinic zeal for everything Lou stood for meant occasionally having to knock him down if an album fell short of expectations.

The twenty-six-year-old rock prophet valorized and vitiated Lou, waxing vinyl in a muscular prose style that adapted the novelistic New Journalism of Tom Wolfe and Joan Didion for a rock audience; dubbed the king of the "Noise Boys"—many of whom had frequented the Robinsons' apartment several years earlier—Bangs found a way to infuse language with a high voltage without ever plugging in. He didn't write with words so much as sparks, and his notoriously savage wit was matched only by his overwhelming physicality.

Execrable and excessive, ungainly but unstoppable, Bangs was a formidable opponent who on a hot day could rival James Brown in a sweat-off, with an idiosyncratic fashion sense that might best be described as Dust Bowl chic, and an anthropomorphic mustache that could eat Burt Reynolds for breakfast. Lester was the epitome of uncool; with a slight glandular problem, his body odor was a distillation of the MC5, *eau de rock*. For Lou, who could pull off sunglasses at night, and was deadly but odorless like carbon monoxide, Lester represented everything he had left behind in Freeport. Yet despite all this, he was possibly the best writer in America. So when they squared off at the Holiday Inn bar in East Detroit, someone was bound to get knocked out, as long as they could stay sober enough to make it through twelve rounds of insults.

But Lou could do two rounds at a time. Double-fisting Johnnie Walkers, he parried one blow after the next, as Lester and Nick Kent, a twenty-one-year-old proto-punk Brit from *New Musical Express*, tag-teamed their verbal jabs. "I'm outdrinking you two to one, you know," Lou taunted. From the corner of their Rust Belt ring, he was dressed in baggy pants and a puffy shirt; they were facing Lou Reed the person more than the leather-clad rock 'n' roll animal. They had him right where they wanted him. Spurred by the cynicism of the incipient Nixon hearings, and the burgeoning gonzo style of penetrating interrogation and subsequent indictment of the cult of personality surrounding rock celebrity, the questions centered largely on sex and drugs, with little attention paid to the music itself. It was as though they were interviewing Charlie Parker about heroin and not about bebop. How did the booze affect his metabolism? Was he aware that he beat Keith Richards in a recent magazine poll on the next rock casualty? How did it feel to corrupt America's youth? What about the gay scene? Lou played along, though, feeding into the mythology of the character that he had created and they wanted him to be.

After the concert, the blowout continued at the Holiday Inn in an intoxicated blur with Lester baiting Lou into absurdity. "I was in the room when that happened. And he was just there with Lester in a corner and I was off a little bit to the side, talking to people who were there," Bettye recalls. "There was a lot of drinking, a lot of snorting, and that wasn't something that I wanted to be a part of." It frittered out in that intoxicated fashion until Lou drank himself into a drunken blackout and someone carted him off to his room.

That November, the article ran in British music rag *Let It Rock*, titled "Lou Reed: A Deaf Mute in a Telephone Booth," culled from one of Lou's most memorable insults of the unforgettable evening, which he probably couldn't remember. Eviscerating in his assessment of Lou's personal peccadilloes, Bangs described Lou as a "bibulous bozo" knocking on death's door, with a "nursing-home pallor" and a "rusty bug eye" as he drank off the shakes. Dippity-do's resemblance to the female anatomy, watermelon farming, and Judy Garland factored into the desultory conversation, as well as a debunking of the notion of universal bisexuality. Idle speculation into Lou's own sexual orientation abounded, along with a pointed suggestion that he resume his amphetamine habit, with Bangs finally concluding that for Lou, it's all a big pity party. Round One was over, and by all signs, Lester had won a Pyrrhic victory—two weeks later, his no-holds-barred style got him banned from the pages of *Rolling Stone* for a snarky review of Canned Heat—but his nigh-heroic attempt to get behind Lou's corroded image only yielded more smoke and mirrors. Rock idolatry by default flattened out the subject, reflecting more about the icon than the man himself. Yet the resounding conclusion was inescapable: Lou was a mess.

"I take drugs just because in the 20th century in a technological age living in the city there are certain drugs you have to take just to keep yourself normal like a caveman," Lou told Lester in a moment of uncharacteristic frankness and lucidity. "Just to bring yourself up or down, but to attain equilibrium you need to take certain drugs. They don't getcha high even, they just getcha normal."

Bettye couldn't deny that Lou was in trouble, but instead of running, she tried to help. "It was clear that Lewis had a substance abuse problem," Bettye says. "I had ended up becoming a policewoman, a nursemaid, and everything else. I didn't like that role, but he said, 'You know, I need you.'"

For the rest of the tour, as with most mind-altering experiences, there were high points, low points, and weird points. On March 24, the day after Springsteen opened, Lou and the Tots played the Century Theatre in Buffalo, where in front of three thousand crazed fans, a Lou lunatic leapt on stage, screamed "Leather!" and bit his rock idol, apparently driven to an act of vampirism by Lou's leather suit.

"I could see Lou's face. His eyes opened wide," Vinny says. "The guy jumped onstage, and he bit Lou's ass!"

Lou would not only perform in an intoxicated state, he would also pantomime it. Unable to escape the pervasive orbit of "Heroin," he began wrapping the microphone cord around his arm and pretending to shoot up. Misconstrued as a junkie anthem, it was originally intended to exorcize his inner demons, but as the pressure of touring increased, Lou gradually embraced the depraved persona the fans craved, perhaps as a cautionary tale. Yet it was only a slight exaggeration of the truth.

"Early on he could drink a lot, later it was speed," recalls tour manager Barbara Wilkinson. "But he always went onstage and performed . . . even if I had to put ice cubes down his back to wake him up!"

Finding it easier to communicate with thousands of concertgoers than with his wife, Lou dulled his rage at the bottom of the bottle. He could only be fully present under a spotlight. "Once he starts drinking he can't stop," Bettye recalls. "And it changes him. It's not good for him. He can't do it—it's destructive. That's sort of where it started getting a little bit out of control, but not outrageously."

Then things got worse. He had become more violent in his attacks on Bettye, and not just verbally. "Lewis eventually became physically abusive, although not for long, man," she says. He gave her a black eye, but she fought back. Soon, it was a cold war of icy indifference, accusatory tirades, and stony silence.

As their relationship disintegrated, Lou was at a creative standstill. "He couldn't write—he was blocked," says Bettye. "He needed to get another album out there in order to honor the contract and it was seriously freaking him out, and when he would freak out he would drink and smoke and snort."

On a tour stop in Toronto, where Genesis opened for Lou, who was living up to his Phantom of Rock persona more and more, he turned to producer Bob Ezrin for inspiration. The twenty-four-year-old Canadian behind Alice Cooper's wall of sound had met Lou during the *Transformer* sessions when Ezrin was scouting for studio space; Cooper had just released *Billion Dollar Babies*, a no-frills shocker that recalled the Velvets' raw grit. "He wanted to do something entirely different. He was afraid of being a pop star," Ezrin recalled. Lou visited Ezrin's house and they had a brainstorming session on the living room floor, discussing how he might return to his underground roots. When Lou played his lackluster new material, Ezrin could see it lacked the pathos of his earlier work.

Then Ezrin had an idea. "You tell a life in two minutes and thirty seconds in a way that almost nobody else can," Ezrin said to Lou. "I love that, but I often find myself wondering afterwards what happened to those people. For example, 'Berlin.' I often wondered what happened to those two people? Where did they go? We should just try and tell a story like that."

They began spitballing ideas for this hypothetical concept album but came up short. "Wait a minute. You wrote it. Let's not tell a story like it. Let's tell that story!"

For the first time in months, Lou's eyes flickered into focus. "Give me a month. I'll be back," he said.

Yet it wouldn't be so easy for Lou to compose with a speed-induced case of writer's block that rivaled Henry Roth's. Then he realized the only viable solution—write what you know. But as always, what Lou knew was not pretty, and his days of wine and roses came with a head-splitting hangover. His only raw material was the pain of his dysfunctional marriage.

As the drug abuse escalated, he still couldn't write, though. One night at a party, it reached a fever pitch. "This girl came out of the bathroom, and I saw him in there and he shut the door quickly. But I saw him sitting on the toilet with a thing in his arm, tied up. He was clearly shooting something. And I lost it, man," Bettye says. "We were not in a good place. But he still needed me. I see hard drugs, and I went out the door. But he couldn't write, and I was kind of between a rock and a hard place. I wanted out, but

I couldn't get out." Despite the unforgivable behavior, something told her not to abandon him. "I believed in him. I believed in his music. I believed in his importance—I loved him—but this was craziness."

That night, Lou didn't sleep, subsisting on the ebb and flow of Johnnie Walker and speed and writing in a hypnotic burst of turbulent creativity. To Bettye's surprise, by the next morning, Lou had produced the songs that would comprise the remainder of his next album, *Berlin*, the star-crossed conclusion to the love story that began as the song of the same name. Much to her chagrin, what she heard described the dissolution of their marriage in lurid detail, but also betrayed the story of her own painful upbringing, especially "The Kids," which paralleled her childhood trauma of being taken from her mother. "He brought it out the next day, and he played it. And what am I supposed to do? Of course it hurt me," she says. "When you're living with a writer, anything they hear is going to be used. No one mentioned that part to me. And I felt so violated."

Coupled with the drugs and the abuse, she couldn't take it anymore. "I told his manager I wanted to leave," Bettye says. Yet Dennis Katz, who at this point had left RCA to become Lou's manager, urged Bettye to stay, for Lou's sake and for the sake of the album.

Lou returned to Toronto with the new material. "He showed up and we sat in the same place on the floor and he started playing songs like 'Caroline Says' and 'The Kids,'" Ezrin recalled. "They gave me gooseflesh. So he gave me the songs and I said, 'OK, now give me a month.'" They went to a small studio in Toronto and hastily laid down the tracks on tape so Ezrin could get to work on the orchestrations.

With a deal for the *Berlin* sessions inked, the Tots had reached the end of the line. On April 20, 1973, at the Santa Monica Civic Auditorium, they played "Sister Ray" for the last time. Ezrin had a bigger studio sound in mind for the album. "He saw us play and he was like, 'These guys are OK,' but he wanted new guys," Vinny recalls. "I can remember being up in the hotel room with Bob Ezrin smoking hash, and it was the weirdest thing. It was like, 'This guy just fired us!' They said, 'You guys did a great job, but Bob wants a new band.'" As they returned to Yonkers, the Tots had been on the ride of a lifetime; they were local celebrities. "When I think back, it's like, damn! I can't believe that!" Vinny says. "I can't believe it happened."

While Ezrin ironed out the details, Lou continued the *Transformer* tour with Moogy Klingman, a keyboardist from Great Neck who would soon go on to be a founding member of Todd Rundgren's Utopia. Less than two weeks later, Klingman had recruited a band, including a drummer that went by the mononym Chocolate, and they hit at Memorial Hall in Kansas City. By the end of the tour in June, Ezrin had finished arranging *Berlin*, which he envisioned as a lugubrious rock opera that would measure up in gravitas with Puccini. To achieve the desired effect, he hired an all-star band of session musicians, including Alice Cooper guitarists Steve Hunter and Dick Wagner, Steve Winwood, Cream bassist Jack Bruce, who imported a jazz feel straight out of Tony Williams Lifetime, drummer Aynsley Dunbar, and an airtight horn section consisting of Ars Nova trombonist Jon Pierson, tenor saxophonist Michael Brecker, and trumpeter Randy Brecker, who later co-led the virtuosic sibling funk duo the Brecker Brothers.

The recording process began at Morgan Studios in London, the same studio where Lou had recorded his ill-fated debut, and later at the Record Plant in New York. Immediately, the *Berlin* sessions were underscored by the thinly veiled roman à clef; Bettye was present, Lou wasn't all there—his perennial Johnnie Walker a constant prop—and their marriage was a shambles, fraught with emotional baggage that he brought into the studio every day.

Yet Lou always treated his collaborators with respect. "It was all written parts, and we came in and did it, and that was it," recalls Randy Brecker. "We went out for lunch with Bob and Lou, my brother and I. Lou Reed seemed like a more normal guy than I thought he was. There was no makeup or anything, and we were shooting the shit."

Even though she wanted to file for divorce, Bettye agreed to stay at least through the completion of *Berlin*. "I always believed in his music, no matter what kind of a person he was," Bettye says. "There was something important about what he was doing, but also, he was opening up rock 'n' roll to a disenfranchised audience—the LGBT community. That was important to me. I did stay to the end because even if it was really painful, even if some of it was rooted in my mother's story and what was going on between us, I did believe in it. There was a rock opera there."

Despite all the speed, *Berlin* was a slow, somnolent burn. Lou's waking nightmare seeped into the studio. The grueling sessions lasted up to twenty hours a day over a twelve-day marathon, often leaving Ezrin in a disoriented, feverish state. By the end, he had gone off the rails, and spent time recuperating in a psychiatric institution. Yet he still felt the macabre tone poem they birthed together was worth the price.

Having promised Lou's management she would stay for the remainder of *Berlin*, Bettye bore the brunt of Lou's erratic behavior. He rarely came home after the recording sessions ended, so she spent most of the time in the hotel, sometimes taking a stroll through St. James Park at dawn. "He would come home and he would curl up next to me and go to sleep," she says. "I know that he went out afterwards and I didn't care. He had to get through it, and he needed me to be there. So I was."

Lou's Kurt Weill–inflected melodrama adopted a cinematic style that even featured ambient sound effects—cheers, a crowd singing "Happy Birthday," all imbued with a languid perversity—as though emanating from a film that would never be projected; Lou's imagistic lyrics provided an imagined visual that reflected the dark collective unconscious. Lou was not just a composer, but an auteur who adapted his anxieties into a visceral filmic experience with a disconcerting voyeuristic immersion usually reserved for film itself. Like the titular wall that framed the album's concept, Lou was not only divided against his wife, but also against himself. He struggled with mood swings, tour-fueled mania, apathy, and a propensity to fall into a bottomless depressive funk that had no backbeat; he was simultaneously East and West Berlin. It was as though Lou had become a bellwether for the moral decay and encroaching nihilism of the broader culture; perched on the periphery of society, he was at that moment a symptom of a national sickness, and *Berlin* might have been, if not an inoculation, at least a form of triage.

Reflecting the theme of entropy as an organizing principle, Ezrin's elaborate production tempered an intricate score with understated arrangements that colored Lou's jaded, melancholic delivery and built to a dissonant frenzy. Glam rock in decay, *Berlin* traded the tragicomic sarcasm of *Transformer* for a decidedly tragic narrative arc. Bookended by the lush solo piano arrangement of the title track and the dismal catharsis of "Sad Song," the descent into sadness took place in the interstitial space. Lou poured what was left of his heart into the fictitious story of Jim and Caroline, two speed freaks living on the edge of society, who spiral into a dysfunctional marriage punctuated by a Eugene O'Neill–style long day's journey, domestic abuse, and the wrist-slitting suicide of "The Bed," which culminates in haunting background vocals. The album reached its most crushing moment in "The Kids," a harrowing child services debacle in which the voices of Ezrin's crying children ring out in abject despair, an effect he elicited by telling them their mother had died in a fatal accident (she hadn't). Lou and Ezrin ironically offered a harmonic resolution to the overwhelming sadness with "Sad Song," heightened with strings and a full horn section. The disillusionment etched into the vinyl announced itself on the cover. Avoiding any false advertising, the image depicted a shattered picture frame, a fall from innocence of the connubial bliss Lou and Bettye had once enjoyed on that ephemeral perfect day. *Berlin* was all about imperfection.

Ezrin's overriding sensibility dictated that even though most people had not experienced Lou's heightened transposition of the streets, or ever taken methedrine, the album's totalizing decadence and ennui would impel the listener to intuit the universal through the particular and the deeply personal. To Lou, whose pancake-faced phantom persona preserved an air of self-effacing humor, the studio served as a de facto confessional booth; the rock opera represented a cry for help and a turn to the dramatic—with the comedy finished, it was as though the mordant clown himself were crying out, "But doctor, I am Pagliacci."

Released in July 1973, the album produced two kinds of detachment—in addition to alienating most of the mainstream audience, it detached Lou from the market-driven sinkhole he wanted to avoid, proving that he had not devolved into a caricature of himself, but was a serious artist working in the medium of rock, still capable of challenging material that didn't play to the lowest common denominator. With polarizing reviews, it left some critics numb, others practically moved to tears. Nick Kent called it "a coup" and the *New York Times* lauded it as one of the "most original rock records in years," but Christgau gave it a tepid C, *Rolling Stone* dismissed it as a career-ending "disaster," and one critic compared Lou's vocals to the "heat-howl of the dying otter." Eventually, *Rolling Stone* would issue an unequivocal reassessment of the album, hailing it as "the *Sgt. Pepper's* of the Seventies," but at the time of its release, Lou had made another commercial flop.

In 1973 the literary and cinematic equivalent of the fatalistic concept album had a banner year, finding critical traction in other mediums, but Lou's Brechtian psychological realism was by and large considered too intense by the critics and had not yet been embraced by rock's elite practitioners. The dysfunctional marriage conceit was well worn by the modernist poets—Ted Hughes published *Prometheus On His Crag* and Lawrence Durrell put out *Vega and Other Poems*. *Zen and the Art of Motorcycle Maintenance*, with its psychotic narrator and obsessive philosophizing, became a bestseller, and Thomas Pynchon's *Gravity's Rainbow*, with its shell-shocked vets and V-2 rockets, went on to win the National Book Award. *Last Tango in Paris* and *Scenes from a Marriage* had cultural cache that translated to box office results. As usual, Lou found himself firmly out of lockstep with his cultural milieu. Though there were albums produced in a similar vein—the Who's *Quadrophenia* was released only months later—it would take years for Pink Floyd's *The Wall*, another Ezrin-produced concept album, Television's *Marquee Moon*, and the Smiths' self-titled debut to gain cultural acceptance for similar explorations into the urban pastoral mode at the core of *Berlin*.

With cynicism and moral corruption reaching a high-water mark that year, the soundtrack to American life hewed toward more upbeat themes. The airwaves were not ready to receive Lou's vision of gloom. Striking a chord in the hearts of listeners required more digestible confections, and Lou's auditory sauerkraut did not sit well with the charts. In 1973 listeners wanted stories of wholeness, not brokenness; romance, not disillusionment; the continuity of life, not the inevitability of death. So as RCA released *Berlin* out into the ether, it had to contend with Marvin Gaye's *Let's Get It On*, Paul McCartney's "My Love," and Tony Orlando and Dawn's saccharine tale of eternal love, "Tie a Yellow Ribbon Round the Ole Oak Tree." Yet by playing against the grain, Lou had proven beyond the shadow of a doubt that he didn't need market success to make his mark. After a brush with pop stardom, he had narrowly escaped the empty excesses of glam rock.

# 18

This anticommercial coup recontextualized Lou as the mercurial, audacious figure he always was, but it also scandalized his already failing marriage. If the album was intended to expel the inner demons that led Lou to lash out at Bettye—*The Exorcist* would be released only months later—it was a disaster, and Bettye decided to push forward with the divorce. She flew to Santo Domingo to obtain a twenty-four-hour divorce, an expedient route to separating that only required one party to attend the hearing. But when she returned, Lou tried to win her back.

"He seemed to take it seriously—'I lost her over this, so if I want to keep her, I'm going to have to not do that anymore,'" Bettye says. "I thought about it for a while, maybe a couple days or a week, then I decided we'd try it again. I thought he'd really gotten it."

With Bettye back in the picture, the *Berlin* tour started gearing up, but in light of the album's commercial failure, Dennis Katz wasn't sure what direction to pursue that would placate RCA and keep Lou's head above water. So he turned to his brother. "*Berlin* was a bomb, and Lou and my brother asked my opinion," recalls Steve Katz. "So I just said, 'What I would do is I think Lou ought to take all of those Velvet Underground songs and release them in a different context—a great band, maybe more of a heavy rocking quintet. And go on the road and record a live show.'" Katz assumed correctly that combining Lou's newfound rock star status with his older material could result in wider exposure for his avant-garde past. "They said, 'Good idea! Why don't you produce it?' So I said, 'What, are you kidding? That'd be great.'"

Steve Katz and Bob Ezrin assembled a band of consummate technicians who could support Lou even at his most inebriated state—Detroit-bred dueling guitar duo Steve Hunter and Dick Wagner, Columbia A&R man and keyboardist Ray Colcord, who had discovered Aerosmith, Indian-Canadian bassist Prakash John, and Finnish drummer Pentti Glan of Bush, whom Ezrin knew from the Toronto scene. Then Dennis Katz called Howard Stein, the promoter behind the Academy of Music on Fourteenth Street and Irving Place, and booked Lou tentatively for a date in December when they planned on recording his follow-up album, *Rock 'n' Roll Animal*.

From the label's perspective, Lou faced tremendous pressure to produce a hit after plunging into the commercial sand trap of the avant-garde, and a live album that would recast old chestnuts presented the most laid-back route back to the green. "*Rock 'n' Roll Animal* was the perfect thing to happen after *Berlin*," says Steve Katz. "I love *Berlin*. It's not something I whistle in the shower, but it's a beautiful record. Ezrin's a genius. But he also had a nervous breakdown afterwards. Lou was like catching a cold. You spend too much time with Lou, you're gonna get a nervous breakdown."

Like a method actor re-creating the affective memory of the moments before a drug blackout, Lou began transforming himself into the eponymous animal at the helm of his next project. Almost immediately, Lou began to make outrageous demands of Bettye. Prior to the opening show at the Music Inn in Lenox, she had to be flown in. "I was an accessory, the kind that he absolutely, desperately needed," Bettye says. "I had been helicoptered in to rehearsals up in the Berkshires, because he couldn't work without me. Other than that, I was the girlfriend or the wife or the ex-wife or the fiancée. People weren't seriously interested in knowing me."

The following week, Bettye and the band flew overseas, where Lou performed at the Scheessel Rock Festival in Germany, skunked it up at the Celebration Garden Party at the Crystal Palace Bowl alongside James Taylor and Beck, Bogert & Appice, and traveled to Paris where he was headlining the Olympia, the iconic venue that once hosted the Beatles and the Rolling Stones. It was easily the most significant booking of Lou's burgeoning solo career.

But his marriage was crumbling. Despite Lou's commitment to reconciling with Bettye and starting with a blank slate, he buckled under the pressure of touring. "In England, it started again. It was a mess," Bettye says. "Then we went on to Paris, and just before we were supposed to leave, I didn't appreciate something that he said and how he was treating me, and I said, 'I'm not going.' He left without me and I went home." Back at the hotel, she called Dennis Katz and announced her imminent departure, asking for a one-way ticket back to New York. Bettye didn't care about the settle-ment—she just wanted out—though eventually, she received back payment for the lighting work she had never been compensated for. She then called William Esper to see if she could reenroll in acting classes at his studio. At twenty-four, after enduring the peaks and valleys of her life with Lou, Bettye had finally decided to reclaim her own life.

As Lou was taking the stage at the Olympia, Bettye left the hotel, dis-traught. It was raining, and she didn't have an umbrella. As her tears mixed with raindrops, a Paris gendarme took her aside at the Arc de Triomphe to see if she needed help. She went home to the hotel, and the next day she boarded a plane to New York.

The show went on without her, but Lou's performance visibly suffered. "The Olympia show in Paris was memorable," recalls keyboardist Ray Col-cord. "There was an opening act, a band called Kracker, and they started at 8:00. They finished at 8:45 and we were ready to go on and Lou didn't show up till midnight. Then the audience was almost entirely music critics and lead singers from French rock 'n' roll bands. It was not a happy crowd." The irate crowd might have thrown wine bottles at the stage, Colcord recalls. "We cranked up the PA and went through the set really loudly."

Gaunt and barely lucid in his leather suit, Lou fumbled through the lyrics, taking frequent breaks to pace around the stage, gyrating spasmodically—when he was standing up. By the time he reached "Walk on the Wild Side" mid-set, he sat slumped on the stage floor, glancing sideways as if peering into some indeterminate time and place. After reciting the first verse in a dazed monotone, Lou proceeded to frantically stroke the microphone as though masturbating. In a later verse, he dropped the mic completely. At one point during "Heroin," he suddenly fell to the floor, an act of metatheatricality that straddled the line between performance and reality, as the guitars surged. Nearly a decade after he wrote it, the lines had finally fermented into their full, tragic resonance.

With Bettye gone, Lou upped his Scotch and speed intake. Days later, he partied all night in Amsterdam, and while appearing the next night in Brussels, he collapsed onstage, narrowly averting an overdose. The cur-tain fell, and Bernie Gelb, the obstreperous sound manager from Dawson Sound, hoisted him fireman-style up the stairs to his dressing room. The rest of the show would have to be canceled. The audience began hurling chairs and screaming in a berserker rage, demanding that the show resume.

Lou and his entourage barely escaped the horde of rioting Belgians, who, distinguished primarily for their waffles, chocolate, and beer, had not been known to riot after the 1830 Belgian Revolution. Yet Lou could bring out the worst in people.

Lou finished the final two weeks of the *Berlin* tour with the Persuasions as a supporting act. At the Glasgow Apollo, after the band's high-wire instrumental introduction, he was so intoxicated that he had to be carried onstage and then carried off at the end of the set; the fans raised a ruckus. "After the show, they showed their appreciation by trying to turn over the tour bus with us in it," recalls Colcord. "They were rocking it back and forth, and they had it up on two wheels till the cops made them stop and got us out of there."

Then Lou received word that on October 1, 1973, his grandmother Rebecca, who was eighty-five, had passed away. He finished the tour anyway, though, and performed what he considered to be the best concerts of the European leg, concluding at the Rainbow Theatre in London. Afterwards, they partied till sunrise. The band was ready for *Rock 'n' Roll Animal.*

One of the first things Lou did after returning to his empty apartment was get a new do. As his personal life exploded, his hair had mushroomed into a dense cloud of curls; now he opted for a streamlined coif, buzzed to a crew cut that radiated angular androgyny, looking like a perversion of H. R. Haldeman on an all-night bender. For the title role of *Rock 'n' Roll Animal*, Lou abandoned the sartorial creepiness of the Phantom and toned down the crepuscular eye makeup; a sad panda no longer, he opted for a modish form-fitting silhouette to suggest a speed freak's feral restlessness. The sinister glint of studded black leather—belt, bracelets, and choker collar—completed the escaped-from-the-Central-Park-Zoo look: rabid sex panther. In the midst of the Christmas season, Lou donned his fiercely gay apparel with a spiritless sneer.

Leading up to the record date, the band rehearsed in New York and the tour resumed with far-flung stops in Toronto, Akron, Philadelphia, Providence, and a show at the Kennedy Center in Washington during a snowstorm. On December 21, 1973, the Academy of Music was packed. Steve Katz and the sound crew worked the board from a Record Plant mobile unit outside. As Lou was unreliable, it was of paramount importance that everything else be impeccable. With the era's superlative rock guitar heavyweights at the helm, there was little cause for concern. When Steve Hunter and Dick Wagner lit into the opening major triad, filtered through MXR phase pedals and an Echoplex, a staggering guitar duel that made instant history, they transformed the venue into a gothic cathedral of black magic. Smooth and effortless, Hunter and Wagner glided through the changes on air, playing foil to Lou's rough-hewn gutter liturgy.

Colcord and the rhythm section propelled the band forward, allowing the guitars to shred. "My job was to provide a solid core with me and the bass and drums so the guitar players could go off and solo whenever they wanted to. They could do dual lines with no guitar playing rhythm and the bottom wouldn't fall out," Colcord says. His souped-up gear was at maximum amplification to compete with the deafening sound. "I had a really hot-rodded Hammond B-3 and a clavinet and a Fender Rhodes, and it was hot-rodded, bi-amped with two Crown DC300 amps, JBL horn drivers, bass speakers, and two Leslies. It was loud because the guitar players were loud, and to be able to hear myself play I needed to have some wattage."

The iconic intro to "Sweet Jane," composed by Hunter, was the first song the band had learned, and by December, it was in top form. "The first time we got together to rehearse in New York was at a rehearsal studio somewhere. Lou wasn't there," Colcord recalls. "So Steve said, 'Well, I have this instrumental thing I wrote.' And in about a half hour, we all learned that intro." At the Academy of Music show, it was incandescent.

Then Lou, attired as leather-clad rock god, ambled onstage as they transitioned into the opening riff to "Sweet Jane," finally home after a grueling, drug-addled year on the road, he was given a hero's welcome. Lou hated the thought that any guitar acrobatics could upstage his lyrics, but the songs were front and center, a testament to the Velvets' towering influence on the rock idiom. No one could upstage Lou; he had an aura, and created an atmosphere just by being in the room.

So after Lou successfully entered the room without incident, the rest was gravy. "As soon as I heard the Hunter-Wagner intro to 'Sweet Jane,' I knew it was a great take," recalls Steve Katz. "It really didn't make any difference what Lou sounded like, because it's not like, 'Oh, Lou Reed's not in tune.'"

Ray Colcord injected "Heroin" with a Baroque organ rubato interlude, and the band amped up Lou's signature song with heavy distortion and a harmonized celestial guitar duet that climaxed in an unhinged chromatic attack. Clocking in at thirteen minutes, it was a full four minutes longer than the Velvets original. They maxed out side one with two tracks. After soaring through "White Light/White Heat," they performed a significantly peppier rendering of "Lady Day." Before the climactic encore, "Rock & Roll," which boasted some of the exemplary guitar breaks of the 1970s, Katz realized that his producing gambit would have legs, but by the thrilling conclusion, he knew he had a bona fide hit.

Ironically, the only difficulties with *Rock 'n' Roll Animal* were technical. "One of the mics went out, and we were missing half an audience track, so we needed to beef it up somehow," Katz says. The thunderous applause notwithstanding, sound engineer Gus Mossler conceived of a solution more reminiscent of sitcoms of the era. "Gus went into the archive room and comes back with a John Denver tape. So half the applause you hear on Lou's album is from a John Denver concert." The *Animal* shows were a far cry from "Take Me Home, Country Roads," but applause has no genre. Prior to the second show, the sound crew shut down the sound system when Howard Stein declined to pay them their fee up front. Strong-armed by the threat of three thousand irate Lou Reed fans, he handed over the cash and the show went on.

"After you buy the album, open the jacket and make sure there's a record inside," read the irreverent ad. "The 'Rock n Roll Animal' is a bitch to contain." Ripe for cranking the speakers up to eleven, *Rock 'n' Roll Animal* was destined to be Lou's highest-charting album to date, peaking at Number 45 on the *Billboard* Top 100, where it remained for twenty-seven weeks. It was unanimously declared a critical and commercial success; three years after the Velvets disbanded, the world was ready for them. Despite all the amplification, though, Lou grew to despise it as its shadow quickly eclipsed *Berlin*. He was wrecked by market-driven success, especially when he felt the market had such bad taste, and as his star steadily rose, he sank into a moonless night of the soul.

Only three days after the unqualified coup at the Academy of Music, while the rest of the North Shore ate lo mein on Christmas Eve, Lou was arrested in Riverhead, a sleepy Suffolk County, Long Island, town, for attempting to fill a forged prescription at a pharmacy. Just as he had spent the wee hours with an Upstate New York justice of the peace back in college, Lou had to rely on his friends to extricate him from the sticky situation. "I took Caesar's Limo to bail him out," recalls Barbara Wilkinson. "It was a vintage white Cadillac that played 'Here comes the bride' on the horn. I think it was all that was available. Try getting five hundred dollars in cash before ATMs!" Lou avoided spending Christmas morning in jail, but he had successfully joined the ranks of rock stars with a rap sheet, even if his minor transgression took place at a pharmacy. After decades of playing the part of the depraved miscreant, sixty miles east of Freeport, Lou had finally lived it. It was a Christmas miracle.

Lou might have had an ulterior motive for his increasingly outlandish behavior. He began to notice some box office discrepancies, and suspected Dennis Katz of fuzzy accounting. Lou knew that Dennis was an avid collector of Nazi memorabilia, and he had a feeling that Dennis was taking advantage of Lou's ostensibly compromised state to surreptitiously skim the funds for a vintage SS uniform. However, Lou wanted to test his theory before leveling an accusation tantamount to character assassination, especially in an industry that relies almost entirely on reputation. He confessed as much to Barbara Hodes. "He said, 'I'm going to act crazier than normal. I want to see how far they're going to go,'" she recalls. "And more and more money kept disappearing." Lou contacted a prominent entertainment lawyer and filed a lawsuit, which he eventually won.

After acrimoniously parting ways with Dennis Katz, Lou hired Jonny Podell, the manic booking agent behind Alice Cooper, the Allman Brothers Band, Crosby, Stills, Nash & Young, and George Harrison's solo tours. Podell was a self-made booking agent who grew up in Forest Hills and cut his teeth with Associated Booking Corp., the legendary agency started by Joe Glaser, Louis Armstrong's lifelong manager. Podell, who cultivated a notorious freebasing habit, had recently left ABC to found BMF Enterprises, a boutique agency that measured up to its nefarious moniker. In shifting management, Lou, having cemented a public image as one of the baddest MFs in the business, had transferred control of his career from the Scylla of Dennis Katz to the Charybdis of Podell. Quickly, the drug-addled charade Lou used to build a case against Katz was becoming a reality.

"Lou took to speed just like that. I think that was his drug. I don't think heroin was ever really his drug of choice," recalls Hodes. "He would stay up for three or four days at a time. It's amazing. He lived on hot dogs and whiskey." Lou's ascetic diet of pure junk food also fed a growing appetite for amphetamine. This was facilitated by visits to Dr. Robert Freymann, the eponymous doctor immortalized by the Beatles' "Dr. Robert" on *Revolver*, a real-life physician with a quietly booming practice catering to celebrity clientele on East Seventy-Eighth Street. Freymann would prescribe a patented vitamin formula: B-12 spiked with a shot of speed, a tonic for the times.

Lou had reconnected with Hodes, who was spending considerable time overseas as a high-end designer. When they overlapped, they would sometimes arrange a European tryst. "Taking him to a decent restaurant in Paris was interesting," Hodes says. By early 1974, Lou had moved into her one bedroom apartment at 45 Fifth Avenue. "I had a list of ten addresses for him," she recalls. "I don't remember Lou ever having a checkbook. I don't know where he got his mail." Considering the unsavory array of residences in Lou's itinerant past, his new digs were a big step up.

Coinciding with the move, he slimmed down and bleached his hair; at one point, his stylist shaved symmetrical Iron Crosses into his crew cut, evoking the Nazi war decoration. "He had a hairdresser on First Avenue in the Sixties, and it was the hairdresser's idea," Hodes says. "He came home one day looking like that and I said, 'Oh, my God!'" Lou's new Aryan-chic look was more bad haircut than calculated joke. Nevertheless, as far as the public was concerned, Lou wasn't pushing the envelope, he was burning it.

On the heels of the success of *Rock 'n' Roll Animal*, RCA had put pressure on Lou to quickly release a follow-up studio album with Steve Katz as producer. Yet changing the experiment but repeating the results seemed unlikely. Having carved out a reputation for breaking the mold, with Lou more than anyone, success could never be planned. And with Lou in no shape to work, the partnership seemed unlikely to yield any inspired creative output. Lou responded by essentially cranking out *Sally Can't Dance* in a speed-induced fever dream, writing it almost entirely at Hodes's apartment. "He jokingly called it 'The shittiest album I've ever made,' and he made it a shitty album on purpose. I don't know why," Hodes recalls. "I had a view straight out to New Jersey. He would sit at the bottom of the bed, and he just made up *Sally Can't Dance*."

There was nothing Katz could do to counteract Lou's willful incompetence. Ironically, he preferred Lou on speed; the anxiety of the comedown had Lou on a short fuse. "When I knew he was coming off of speed, I wouldn't answer the phone. When he's doing speed, it's fine, but when he wasn't doing it, he was really nasty," Katz says. Yet Katz put up with Lou's capriciousness. "I liked Lou. I'm one of the few people who did. I thought he was hilarious. Lou was a real asshole—he was a prick—but I liked him."

To compensate for Lou's emotional absence, Katz enlisted an A-list band with a large horn section including BS&T collaborators Lou Marini and Alan Rubin, as well as Insect Trust multireedist Trevor Koehler, adding background vocals, even including Doug Yule on bass on "Billy." The material was partially autobiographical, but it was as though the Lou who only the previous year had made *Berlin* was a different guy altogether.

When they convened at Electric Lady Studios in the Village, Lou made it apparent that the refrain from "Ride Sally Ride," the opening track, reflected his cold indifference:

*Oooh, isn't it nice, when your heart is made out of ice*

It was a caustic couplet that only Lou could have written. The rest of the album ranged from the strange to the misanthropic, going from bad to weird between tracks in dark gallows humor. "Animal Language" depicted the disturbing speed freak deaths of anthropomorphized dogs and cats, "Sally Can't Dance" the gruesome fate of various incarnations of Sally; "Baby Face" detailed cohabitation problems, while the soporific "Ennui" dealt with adult resignation.

*You're the kind of person that I could do without*

Yet despite Lou's icy heart, "Kill Your Sons," about his electroshock experience, and "Billy," a folksy antiwar ballad on a childhood friend scarred by the Vietnam War, were two of his most affecting tracks. Even on speed, he couldn't mask the pathos, especially when dealing with the subject of adolescence.

However, the recording was a nightmare for Katz. "Lou would be working until four o'clock in the morning and Lou would go in the bathroom, shoot up, and say, 'What's the next track?'" Katz says. "Meanwhile, we're all dying. That was his sense of humor."

Throughout the recording process, Lou was deliberately phoning it in. He proposed that he record every vocal track consecutively in one track, but Katz wouldn't allow it. "Lou wasn't very involved, and I wish he could have been, but he couldn't be, based on what was going on in his chemistry," Katz says. Then, before beginning work on the mix, Katz's house in Rockland County burned down. "I was depending on my engineer and living under duress," Katz says.

With the attention of the artist and producer diverted elsewhere, it seemed the record was doomed. "If it wasn't for the drugs, *Sally Can't Dance* would have been a very different album. Lou would have been more involved. It would have been a Lou Reed singer-songwriter album, instead of a hope-for-the-best album."

Lou also flirted with the idea of producing an album for Nico. She flew to New York, but after several days, it became apparent that their working relationship would not lead anywhere fruitful, exacerbated by the fact that it was already tight quarters in the one-bedroom apartment where Lou was staying. Adding Nico, whose health was in dire straits, presented an immediate obstacle. "He brought her over to the States and she stayed in the flat with us, and she didn't bathe and was just a wreck, and Lou kind of kicked her out," Hodes recalls. The apartment was already too small for the two of them.

Lou encountered a welcome distraction when he met twenty-two-year-old Rachel Humphreys (born as Richard Humphreys), who cut a stunning figure on the city's burgeoning transgender scene, in a basement drag bar called Club 82 in the East Village. The subterranean, cabaret-style haunt attracted a stream of fledgling punk acts on the CBGB circuit—the New York Dolls, Patti Smith, Debbie Harry's pre-Blondie band the Stilettos, and the Miamis. Rachel had grown up in provincial Bridgeton, New Jersey, and San Antonio, and had the combination of self-possession and spunky attitude that instantly grabbed Lou's attention, even though he was in a methamphetamine-induced stupor:

> It was in a late-night club in Greenwich Village. I'd been up for days as usual and everything was at that super-real, glowing stage. I walked in there and there was this amazing person, this incredible head, kind of vibrating out of it all. Rachel was wearing this amazing make-up and dress and was obviously in a different world to anyone else in the place. Eventually I spoke and she came home with me. I rapped for hours and hours, while Rachel just sat there looking at me saying nothing. At the time I was living with a girl, a crazy blonde lady and I kind of wanted us all three to live together but somehow it was too heavy for her. Rachel just stayed on and the girl moved out. Rachel was completely disinterested in who I was and what I did. Nothing could impress her. He'd hardly heard my music and didn't like it all that much when he did. Rachel knows how to do it for me. No one else ever did before.

Soon, Lou moved out of Barbara Hodes's apartment, and he moved in with Rachel. "I really liked Rachel," says Katz. "She used to wear razor blades taped to her dress, just in case she had a bad experience. She was terrific. She was very nice and laid-back, and I think she was very healthy for Lou. And she was very beautiful."

After cosmetology school in Bayonne, Rachel moved to New York. "He did Lou Reed's hair during the tours," recalls Gail Garcia, Rachel's older sister. "That's what he wanted to do—hair. My mom told him, 'If that's what you want to do, that's what you want to do.'" From an early age, the family could tell Rachel identified more with his sisters. "We knew since he was little he was gay. He used to like to play with Barbie dolls and dress up in girls' clothes," Garcia says. It wasn't an issue in the family, though. "He was easy to get along with. He'll give you his shirt off his back if that's the case."

And she did it for Lou. Going into the *Sally Can't Dance* tour, Lou's spirits were higher, boosted by Rachel, but as his drug use escalated, his speak-singing performance style had become in some cases literally one note, a mixture of glottal stops and onstage antics. Nevertheless, Lou hit the UK in staggering stride, supported by a powerhouse band: former Rhinoceros and Iron Butterfly guitarist Danny Weis, who specialized in a style called "chicken pickin'," keyboardist Michael Fonfara, bassist Prakash John, and drummer Pentti Glan. In August, they toured Australia, using bassist Peter Hodgson and drummer Mouse Johnson—both also formerly of Rhinoceros—with AC/DC as the opening act.

The parade of interviews started to become a charade, though; the press didn't take Lou seriously, so he followed suit. As Nixon resigned the presidency, Lou began practicing a different kind of resignation. In Sydney, prior to sold-out shows at the Hordern Pavilion, he faced a barrage of inane questions at a press junket at the airport, which he parried with equally inane, Warholian responses. As usual, the questions were restricted to drugs and sex:

"You said a little while ago that you sing mainly about drugs," one said. "Why do you do this?"

"'Cause I think the government's plotting against me."

"You like singing about drugs. Is this because you like taking drugs yourself?"

"No, it's 'cause I can't carry when I go through customs. I figure somebody in the audience . . ."

"Were you searched by our customs men for drugs?"

"No, 'cause I don't take any. I'm high on life."

"Do you want people to take drugs themselves?"

"Oh yeah, I want 'em to take drugs."

"Why is this?"

"'Cause it's better than Monopoly."

Following more of this pablum, the Australian journalists finally got down to the nitty-gritty. Reduced to the flat stereotype of a degenerate, Lou had been given the choice to play along or come across as an intolerant schmuck, even if he was intolerant of the media's intolerance. He opted for aloof bemusement. "Lou, you sing a lot about transvestites and sado-masochism. How would you describe yourself in the light of these songs?"

Lou cut through the homophobic piffle. "What does that have to do with me?"

"Could I put it bluntly, and pardon the question—are you a transvestite or a homosexual?"

"Sometimes."

"Which one?"

"I don't know. What's the difference?"

"Why do you like describing yourself as this? Why do you think you fit into this type of person?"

"It's something to do."

"Is life so boring to you?"

"No!"

Finally, Lou dispelled a circulating rumor that he had once attacked his British fans after a concert and been arrested onstage on obscenity charges. "Well who writes these things for you, if they're not true?" one said.

Lou delivered the wry punch line: "Journalists."

As the legend of Lou became fact, journalists were more than happy to print the legend.

Playing off this degraded media refraction, the cover illustration of *Sally Can't Dance* depicted Lou as a caricature of himself; framed by a circular red border with cartoonish font, the stylized image evoked the Looney Toons (which Lester Bangs referred to as "Lou-nee Tunes"), with Lou's shock of blond hair, popped leather collar, and aviator shades. Yet the back cover complicated this sanitized vision of Lou as an impish incarnation of Archie, filtered for commercial consumption. The payoff came on the obverse side: reflected in Lou's sunglasses as though sitting across from him, rather than

Veronica Lodge, the image shows Rachel with a five o'clock shadow, smoking a cigarette (which is not just a cigarette), drawn more in the style of R. Crumb. Behind the shades, Lou was still incorrigibly Lou; even while making minor concessions to the mainstream, he maintained his staunch commitment to the marginalized bodies relegated to the underground.

Perched at the intersection of art and commerce, the latter seemed to hold no currency for Lou. With the album released that month, he had no ostensible investment in its success; in fact, he seemed committed to the opposite effect. Yet despite his effort to step on RCA's proverbial feet, like the hapless characters in Mel Brooks's *The Producers*, Lou's surefire flop became a sleeper hit. It peaked at Number 10, dwarfing *Berlin* and even outselling *Transformer*, receiving generally positive reviews. To Lou, the triumph of kitsch over taste represented the ultimate indignity; it was a reluctant profit for a reluctant prophet.

Adding to the camp, a TV spot called "Sing Along with Lou" showed him slouching in a leather jacket and sunglasses in front of a night sky background, with the album's title track playing over karaoke subtitles.

On October 9, 1974, toward the beginning of the US leg of the *Sally Can't Dance* tour, Lou played the five-thousand-seat Felt Forum at Madison Square Garden; Hall & Oates was the opening act. Mick Jagger was there to witness it from backstage. "I gave him champagne," recalls Barbara Wilkinson. "He did not want to be seen, steal any of the spotlight." Some found the show melodramatic, with unintentional religious imagery. "He tied the mic cord around his arm, but somehow looked more like an Orthodox Jew laying tefillin than a chipper tying up," wrote Wayne Robins in the *Village Voice*. For the rest of the tour, Lou pretended to shoot up onstage, sometimes took his shirt off, and sang so far behind the beat that he made Chet Baker look like Bobby Darin. But Lou could do what he wanted. He was selling out major performance venues across the country. Despite his antipathy for *Sally Can't Dance*, Lou was a full-fledged star.

# 19

One man devoted his formidable critical powers to keeping Lou's ego in check: Lester Bangs. Round two of the heavyweight grudge match was scheduled for October 26 at the Detroit Hilton, where Lou was staying before his tour stop at the Masonic Temple, an imposing neo-Gothic structure in the Motor City's historic district. Since their last bout, Lester had trained extensively at the *Creem* offices to build up a tolerance for Lou through endurance drinking and a strict mental toughness regimen. He had also fortified his inimitable walrus crumb catcher.

Lou, on the other hand, was not in fighting form. Though he was notorious for having journalists on the floor in seconds with the devastating one-liners he deployed like uppercuts, Bangs didn't believe the hype. Poised to exploit Lou's weaknesses—which were laid bare in albums like *Berlin*—Lester had studied the mix of arrogance and hostility that masked deep-seated insecurities and a soulful heart. His strategy was to come in swinging, an attempt to use rhetorical force to pummel his rock idol into critical submission for *Sally Can't Dance*, which he deemed a travesty, maybe even a sellout. But Lou was the Muhammad Ali of rock, floating like a psychotropic butterfly and stinging like a drunken bee, if he ever landed on his target. Lester just had to hope he wasn't fated to be the Sonny Liston of critics.

When he entered the eighteen-story Detroit Hilton, Bangs was out for blood, ready to take on his hero, who he affectionately dubbed a "depraved pervert and pathetic death dwarf," a Shylockian "huckster selling pounds of his own flesh," and the apotheosis of "all the most fucked up things that I could ever possibly conceive of." That night, the mythology would end; it was Lester's last stand. "So I was gnashing ready to pound Lou to a sniveling pulp the minute he hit town. THIS WAS IT! THE BIG DAY! THE

ONLY OLD HERO, MUCH LESS ROCK MUSICIAN, LEFT WORTH DOING BATTLE WITH!" he wrote.

Lou sat seething with Rachel and his entourage, livid that Trader Vic's, the formal restaurant on the hotel's first floor, had refused service, enforcing a strict jacket-and-tie policy that Lou was in breach of with his black T-shirt and sunglasses.

"Hi, Lou . . . I believe you remember me," Lester said.

"Unfortunately."

Before Lester could deliver his opening combination, Lou left the ring, though, "muttering something about going to get a newspaper." No one wanted to interrupt dinner and take to the streets of Detroit to find him. "Turned out later he'd gone for a walk around the block and gotten lost," Lester wrote.

After the show, which Hall & Oates opened, Lester and Lou returned to settle the score at the hotel room in front of Rachel and the rest of Lou's coterie. They huddled together, Lester clutching a bottle of Johnnie Walker Black, as they stared each other down, both wearing shades, like the moment of charged stillness before two dogs attack each other.

"Fuck you, I ain't gonna talk to *you*, I'm gonna interview *her!*" Lester croaked.

"She's a he," Lou said, according to Bangs's recollection, "and you ain't int'rv'wing 'm, man."

The rambling, elliptical onslaught that followed perhaps foreshadowed the Rumble in the Jungle, which took place four days later and culminated in Big George hitting the deck in the eighth. It began with petty jabs; barroom-style banter revolving around David Bowie and Iggy Pop, before settling on a long exchange on the particularities of amphetamines—Obetrol, Desoxyn (methamphetamine hydrochloride)—in which Lou unloaded an amateur chemist's degree of knowledge that left Lester spinning.

"Lou, we're gonna have to do it straight. I'll take off my sunglasses if you'll take off yours," Lester said. They followed suit.

The veil lifted, Lester threw his first punch of the night. "Do you ever resent people for the way that you have lived out what they might think of as the dark side of their lives for them, vicariously, in your music or your life?"

Lou blocked it, though, and Lester countered by backing him into a corner on the epistemology of decadence and his infamous onstage antics. Barbara Wilkinson, the de facto ref, attempted to curtail the fight, but Lou wanted to keep on swinging, which he denoted by switching the record to Ronnie Wood's *I've Got My Own Album to Do*, out the previous month, which Lester detested. Lou intended it as a palate cleanser before unleashing his new material—*Metal Machine Music*—but Lester was too far gone for heavy metal.

"In your worst moments you could be considered like a bad imitation of Tennessee Williams," Lester said.

Then came Lou's haymaker. "That's like saying in your worst moments you could be considered a bad imitation of you."

"What do you think that the sense of guilt manifested in most of your songs has to do with being Jewish?" Lester asked. It was three thirty in the morning, and Lou had to wake up the next day to travel to Dayton, Ohio. Following two hours of sparring, it seemed a little late for the Talmud. It was all over. Even though both remained conscious, Lou had won by TKO.

Six months later, the Detroit Hilton filed for bankruptcy and closed its doors for good, as though the residue of bad vibes had spread into other rooms. The fight would later be seen by a readership of 130,000 in a forthcoming issue of *Creem*, dubbed "Let Us Now Praise Famous Death Dwarves, or, How I Slugged It Out with Lou Reed and Stayed Awake," a combination of James Agee and Burroughs. Clearly, Lester loved Lou, or what he represented, but was unsparing in his description of Rachel:

> It was grotesque. Not only grotesque, it was abject, like something that might have grovelingly scampered in when Lou opened the door to get the milk and papers in the morning and just stayed around. Like a dog that you could beat or pat on the head, either way didn't matter because any kind of attention was recognition of its very existence. Purely strange, a mother lode of unholy awe. If the album *Berlin* was melted down in a vat and reshaped into human form, it would be this creature.

This bigoted caricature was the final low blow. Lou's disdain for Lester had gone from mere contempt to out-and-out malice. Nobody but Lou could take down Lou. He seemed to by and large agree with his assessment of *Sally Can't Dance*, though, and began plotting his next artistic move.

Lou and Rachel temporarily moved to the Gramercy Park Hotel, before eventually settling in an upscale apartment on East Fifty-Second Street abutting FDR Drive, on the same block where Henry Kissinger, Shirley MacLaine, Greta Garbo, and John Lennon had lived in luxury. RCA contributed state-of-the-art technology—VCR, camcorder, clocks—to make Lou, Rachel, and the Baron, their genteel dachshund, feel comfortable. But before they could get settled, pressure began mounting for Lou's next world tour. First, he needed a new band.

With jazz fusion in its heyday—Ornette Coleman's Prime Time, the Brecker Brothers, Herbie Hancock's Headhunters, and Chick Corea's Return to Forever all reached a previously untapped crossover audience—Lou forged his own path into genre hybridity with the Everyman Band. He knew it would polarize critics and fans who got off on his more animalistic antics, but he didn't care. The Everyman Band, consisting of tenor saxophonist Marty Fogel, drummer Michael Suchorsky, bassist Bruce Yaw, and violinist Larry Packer, came with a jazz pedigree and a respect for funk that could burn down the house. Based in the Finger Lakes region, they had toured up and down the East Coast for several years, but through Larry Packer's connection to Lou, they finally caught an unlikely break.

Originally a reference to the medieval Everyman plays, the band's name fostered the spirit of collaboration they embodied. "'Everyman' for us meant to be all-inclusive, to have the spirit of tolerance and good nature towards people," Fogel says. Lou, though lacking in good-natured charm, wanted his music to have a more inclusive sensibility conducive to an extended improvised jam.

Together, Lou and the Everyman Band had instant chemistry. "I really liked Lou. He could be really difficult at times, but never with me. We always had a cordial relationship of mutual respect," Fogel recalls. "People who annoyed him, he could really cut down to size and slice them up verbally, but he also had a sweet, gentle, loving side to him." Yet Lou's acerbic wit was perhaps even sharper. "He had an incredible sense of humor. He was not possibly, but definitely, the funniest, wittiest person I've ever been around. And generous to his band personnel."

Lou also hired Doug Yule, with whom he had reconnected on *Sally Can't Dance*, for the tour. After some preliminary rehearsals, the band packed up their gear and flew to Rome to commence the tour. "I never aspired to be a rock 'n' roll musician. I aspired to be a jazz musician and just really a good saxophone player. But when I was playing with Lou, the band was just a kickass great rock 'n' roll band," Fogel says.

The dynamic range was key. "We were capable of huge, coming-at-you energy, but at the same time, with a turn of Lou's head or him raising a shoulder, like an unspoken cue, we would go from this roaring beast to gentle backgrounds," he says. "In Lou's band, dynamics were really something to behold at certain times. It sent chills up and down your spine. There was just an intuitive understanding of what each of us was going to do."

Sometimes the tonal fluctuations onstage galvanized boisterous crowd dynamics offstage. In February 1975 Rome was embroiled in fledgling proletarian riots led by Italy's Communist youth, a continuation of the 1968 Situationist revolts, and a Lou Reed concert represented the ideal revolutionary stage. The radical *autoriduttori* movement, spearheaded by Milan's alternative press, successfully extorted fixed price reductions at concerts under the threat of a populist uprising for noncompliance; the organizers agitated against capitalist access barriers that excluded the masses from the arts. Stoking the flames of protest in Rome, the Palazzo dello Sport stadium workers had gone on strike, so the concert—and mayhem—was postponed till the following week.

In Turin, the tour got off to a peaceably calm beginning. In light of his notorious onstage antics and the Iron Cross that had been briefly chiseled into his hair, protesters anticipated a fascist figurehead they could rail against but were surprised by Lou's ballad-heavy set. "We were expecting a Nazi uniform with dark sunglasses, short blond hair, a McQueen look-alike, but instead we got a quiet boy, curly-haired, with a profile that looks like Capello, the Juventus player," read an English translation of an article in Turin's *La Stampa*.

But the concert promoters weren't able to meet the radical arts revolutionaries' demands in Milan, where evidently they charged full price, and paid for it in full. As Lou arrived, a critical mass of Situationists gathered at the entrance to distribute anti-Semitic leaflets boycotting David Zard, the Jewish-Italian concert promoter. The pastoral Italian folksinger Angelo Branduardi, the opening act, was unable to stave off the brewing conflict. Soon it was time to foment revolution to the soundtrack of sax-heavy renditions of "Sweet Jane" and "Coney Island Baby." After the second song, applause dissolved into a stampede as they ransacked the theater. Rioters in bandanas stormed the stage, brandishing iron bars and cudgels. Others threw bottles, gas cans, stones, bricks, Molotov cocktails, and a miscellaneous barrage of what *La Stampa* described as "bags of various liquids." Two injuries were sustained, chairs wrecked, equipment destroyed. Yet it was only a prelude to the big showdown.

Rome was even worse. For the rain check at the Palazzo dello Sport, it actually started raining as the riot broke out. Carabinieri flooded the stage and shot tear gas into the seven-thousand-strong crowd. Damages to the facility were in the millions. Mixing Lou and Italy was like mixing orange juice and gasoline—sonic napalm.

"They herded us off the stage, brought us down into the bowels of this stadium, put us in a room, and turned off the lights," says Marty Fogel. "People were running up and down the halls screaming, yelling, breaking things. They blamed it on people trying to have a free concert." Lou wouldn't return to Italy for five years.

Shaken, Lou and the Everyman Band boarded the tour bus only to find the Italian driver nodding off on a tortuous road. "It was very late and we were driving through the middle of the night. The bus driver is falling asleep at the wheel, and we're going up into the mountains," Fogel says. "That was my introduction to playing rock 'n' roll with Lou Reed—a riot and a professional bus driver who's falling asleep."

The experience colored the tour as they wended their way through Europe over the next month, without Larry Packer, whom Lou let go after the ordeal in Italy due to creative differences. "Sometimes, we'd take two or three flights a day to get to places," Fogel recalls. They returned to the United States in March and began an extensive American leg of the tour, but Lou still felt weighed down by the unintentional success of *Sally Can't Dance*.

"The worse I am, the more it sells," Lou said of the album. "If I wasn't on the record at all next time around, it would probably go to number one."

So the next time, he wasn't on the record at all. Lou's next album was his most radical experiment to date, a surefire commercial flop. Leveraging the *Billboard* capital he had accrued on the charts, he planned to make an artistic statement more in tune with his anarchist ideals, a wordless avant-garde manifesto so unlistenable, uncommercial, and unintelligible it would be sure to piss everyone off. Inspired by La Monte Young's Dream Syndicate, which he explicitly mentioned in the stream-of-consciousness liner notes that diagonally bisected the gatefold sleeve in typewriter font, Lou harnessed the power of the drone. Through its concentrated, piercing sameness, drone forced listeners to pay attention to the infinite difference of the sound; what was chaotic, unfixed, and always changing in tonality. Pop was ordered and mollifying; drone was disordered and disturbing. But that was the point. Instead of giving them the world as it ought to be, Lou wanted to give them

## This Queen Takes Dictation

Miss Toby Futterman (right) of 139 Dumont Ave., a pert brunette, will be crowned Queen of Stenographers at the Stenographers' Ball Saturday night at the Manhattan Center. Miss Marie Hill (left) of 102-54 43d Ave., Corona, will be a lady-in-waiting. This will be the fourth annual gathering of the pothook girls, sponsored by the United Office and Professional Workers of America. Miss Futterman is employed by the United Lawyers Service.

Lou's mother, Toby Futterman, is crowned Queen of Stenographers at the 1939 Stenographers' Ball. BROOKLYN DAILY EAGLE, FEBRUARY 7, 1939, WWW.NEWSPAPERS.COM

After releasing the single "Leave Her for Me" in 1958, the Jades perform at the Malibu Beach Club, Long Beach, New York. From left to right: Phil Harris, Lou Reed, Alan Walters.
COURTESY OF ALAN WALTERS

Lou's next garage band, the Valets, used these business cards to get gigs (and dates) in Nassau County, Long Island. COURTESY OF RICHARD SIGAL

Lou's band at Syracuse University, LA and the Eldorados, performs in front of the Sigma Alpha Mu fraternity house. 1964 SYRACUSE *ONONDAGAN*, COURTESY OF SYRACUSE UNIVERSITY ARCHIVES

The first issue of the *Lonely Woman Quarterly*, the alternative literary journal Lou cofounded at Syracuse University in May 1962. COURTESY OF SYRACUSE UNIVERSITY ARCHIVES

Lou's ill-fated Syracuse mentor, Delmore Schwartz, author of "In Dreams Begin Responsibilities." COURTESY OF BEINECKE RARE BOOK & MANUSCRIPT LIBRARY, YALE UNIVERSITY

The Velvet Underground puts a psychedelic spin on Mendelssohn's "Wedding March" at Andy Warhol's "World's First Mod Wedding," Michigan State Fairgrounds Coliseum, Detroit, November 20, 1966. Warhol gave away the bride, then filmed the nuptials before signing tomato soup cans. BENTLEY HISTORICAL LIBRARY

Moe Tucker sings "After Hours" at the cramped Second Fret, Philadelphia, 1970. After the show, the Velvets slept on a waiter's floor. PHOTO © GEORGE MANNEY, PHILLY POP MUSIC, WWW.PHILLYPOPMUSIC.COM

The Velvet Underground plays a triple bill with the Nazz, led by Todd Rundgren, and the Colwell-Winfield Blues Band at the Electric Factory, Philadelphia, September 20–21, 1968. PHOTO © GEORGE MANNEY, PHILLY POP MUSIC, WWW.PHILLYPOPMUSIC.COM

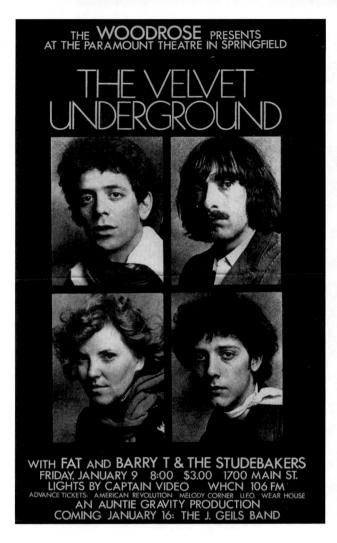

Lou at the Paramount Theatre in Springfield, Massachusetts, January 9, 1970. An eighteen-year-old Jonathan Richman opened. COURTESY OF STEVE NELSON

The Richard Avedon–inspired poster for the Velvets' legendary 1970 residency at Max's Kansas City, their first New York appearance in three years. With Tucker on maternity leave, seventeen-year-old Billy Yule played drums. COURTESY OF STEVE NELSON

Lou in Miami, FLA, 1973, reading *Massage Parlor* by Jennifer Sills. "The true, shocking—and sometimes freaky—story of the sexual phenomenon of the seventies."

Bettye Kronstad, Lou's first wife, Miami, 1973.

Lou's New York sol[o]
debut at Alice Tully
Hall, January 27,
1973. From left to
right: Eddie Reyn-
olds, guitar; Scott
Clark, drums; Lou
Reed, guitar; Bobby
Rescigno, bass; Vinn
Laporta, guitar.
 STEVE ROSSINI/HIGHLAND
DESIGN STUDIO

*Berlin* producer Bob Ezrin.
COURTESY OF BARBARA WILKINSON

From left to right:
promoter Paul
Dainty, Lou Reed,
tour manager
Barbara Wilkinson,
tour coordinator
Ron Blackmore,
Australia, 1974.
COURTESY OF BARBARA
WILKINSON

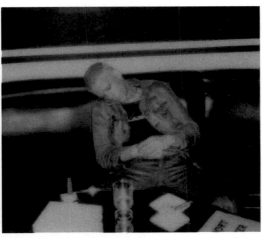

Shots of Lou on the road, 1974. COURTESY OF BARBARA WILKINSON

Lou reads a *Playboy* with Barbara Wilkinson, New York City, 1974. COURTESY OF BARBARA WILKINSON

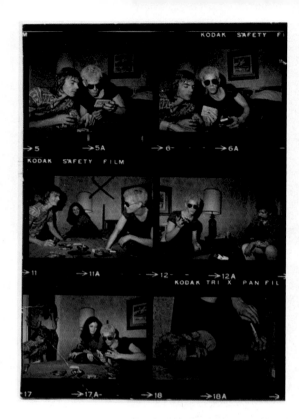

Lou Reed, his transgender partner Rachel, lighting designer Ron Meadows, and others, Adelaide, Australia, 1974.
COURTESY OF BARBARA WILKINSON

Lou brandishes his Ampeg Dan Armstrong Plexi Guitar at the Roxy, Los Angeles, 1978.
DAVID ARNOFF

Nico at the Whisky a Go Go, Los Angeles,
June 1979. DAVID ARNOFF

Lou at the Bottom Line, New York City, June 5, 1979. From left to right:
Chuck Hammer, Moose Boles, Michael Suchorsky, Marty Fogel, Lou Reed.

Lou Reed and Robert Quine at the Palace Theatre, Albany, New York, 1984.
MARTIN BENJAMIN/ROCKSHOTS

Lou on the 1986 Amnesty International Conspiracy of Hope tour, a series of six benefit concerts with U2, Peter Gabriel, the Police, Joan Baez, the Neville Brothers, Bryan Adams, and others. COURTESY OF AMNESTY INTERNATIONAL USA ARCHIVES/COLUMBIA UNIVERSITY CENTER FOR HUMAN RIGHTS DOCUMENTATION & RESEARCH

Lou signs a Honda Elite motor scooter donated to Amnesty for auction, 1986. Courtesy of Amnesty International USA Archives/Columbia University Center for Human Rights Documentation & Research

Conspiracy of Hope tour, 1986. Courtesy of Amnesty International USA Archives/Columbia University Center for Human Rights Documentation & Research

At Vaclav Havel's request, Lou rocks the White House, September 16, 1998. From left to right: President Bill Clinton, Hillary Rodham Clinton, Dagmar Havlová, Vaclav Havel, Mike Rathke, Lou Reed, Fernando Saunders, Tony "Thunder" Smith. COURTESY OF WILLIAM J. CLINTON PRESIDENTIAL LIBRARY

Lou recites "Four More Questions" from *The Raven* as part of the Downtown Seder at the Museum of Jewish Heritage, New York City, 2004. MELANIE EINZIG

A devoted practitioner of tai chi, Lou appears on the cover of *Kung Fu*, June 2003. COURTESY OF KUNGFUMAGAZINE.COM, © 2003

From left to right: Laurie Anderson, John Zorn, and Lou perform collective improvisations at the Festival International de Jazz de Montréal, July 2010.
COURTESY OF DENIS ALIX

From left to right: Dr. John, Lou, and Christian McBride at the Jazz Foundation of America's Great Night in Harlem, 2011. RICHARD CONDE

the world as it was; "passion—REALISM—realism was the key," he wrote. "'Real' rock, about 'real' things." It was a wall-of-sound realism that stripped off the wallpaper and the plaster to expose the brick foundation underneath.

Unlike pop, which recycled the same tropes in a new package just different enough to sell, avant-garde noise music used repetition as a weapon against the repetitiveness of the mainstream culture machine. For Lou, who had just felt the residual effects of becoming a cog in that machine, feedback loops served as an extended metaphor for the way pop replicates itself as a kind of humdrum hall of mirrors. So, with Tony Conrad's experimental film *The Flicker* in mind, he devised *Metal Machine Music*, the perfect sonic Master Cleanse for a guy who refused to sell out, and with the intent of creating rock Stockhausen, sequestered himself in his apartment and started to purge—just a man and his amps pounding away at 5 AM in the garment district.

"Lou bought a couple of tape recorders, took them home, and played with them while speeding his brains out," says Katz. "You couldn't get in touch with him. He came up with an idea of playing a joke on the record company, which I thought was funny, because the record company deserved it."

He created the desired effect with two guitars placed in front of a vast tangle of equipment. There were no synthesizers, just the clangor of machines interacting with each other, like a sentient mechanized band. He tuned the guitars to the same note, employing the technique used on "The Ostrich," positioned them in the feedback sweet spot, and unleashed a fusillade of hisses, squawks, and bleats. The sound and fury he had first experimented with when backed by the Primitives had come full circle, sans drums, vocals, and other people. Unlike pop, which tended to conceal the means of production, Lou enumerated the various tools he used on the back of the record, recipe style, a dyed-in-the-wool gearhead's wet dream: "five piggyback Marshall tube amps," the Arbiter fuzz pedal employed by Jimi Hendrix, and a litany of modulators, preamps, and tremolo units. There was something democratizing about *Metal Machine Music*; technically, anyone could make it if they wanted to, provided they were sufficiently out of their gourds. Lou listed one final ingredient—the chemical formula for methamphetamine.

His experiment in organic chemistry began with a scientific question. What was the sound of speed? Soon, Lou had figured it out: guitars—lots of guitars. Subtitled *The Amine β Ring: An Electronic Instrumental Composition*, easily misconstrued as a lost Wagner epic, it referenced amine, an ammonia derivative used to make meth, β-Methylphenethylamine, meth's positional isomer, and the ring, both a chemical property as well as a sound modulator. An asterisk above the subtitle pointed to "dextrorotory components synthesis of sympathomimetic musics," alluding to D-methamphetamine, a potent psychostimulant and sympathomimetic drug. The results bore the mark of the Faustian bargain Lou had made with his high-frequency drug of choice. "It's for a certain time and place of mind," Lou wrote. That state of mind was evidently speed-induced psychosis, an accelerated heart beating itself into cardiac arrest. If "Sister Ray" was an attempt to mainline the 1960s, this all-consuming wail mainlined the psychedelic confusion and paranoia of the '70s. There was no making sense of it all; *Metal Machine Music* was a massive fuck you.

"He was one of their top artists, so he said 'I want this put out,'" Katz says. "And not only did he want it put out, but as a joke that he played on RCA, he wanted it on Red Seal, the classical label." The label declined to issue it as a classical record—classical comprised a tiny fraction of the market—but the money grab inadvertently raised the stakes of the joke.

That joke was told at the expense of RCA, which shelled out to release the album in four-channel quadraphonic sound, so unsuspecting buyers could experience *Metal Machine Music* in its full ear-splitting glory. Yet it also skewered the industry's bottom-line-over-quality business model, an indictment of capitalist culture at large. It was the sound of rebellion in extremis, everything pop production tried to suppress and smooth over; Lou's metal machine sliced through society's iron cage. Its continuous sixty-four-minute industrial cacophony sounded like the busy hum of industry itself—the caustic grinding of gears rather than the slick finished product at the end of the assembly line. But this was no normal assemblage; the album's rough edges resembled the garbled static a car radio might emit after being recovered from the bottom of a lake, the kind of caterwauling that could make cats homicidal. John Cage had never gotten such wide exposure; Xenakis at least had math on his side. Nothing could prepare Lou's loyal fans for this forcible entry into the now, not even the caveat emptor of a petit mal epileptic seizure warning he included in the liner notes.

Without ever getting played in its entirety, the message was heard loud and clear. For Lou, who was rarely at a loss for words, it didn't even require lyrics; he thought of it as rock distilled to its pure essence, which was anything but pure. It was preverbal but postmodern—its ambient screech defined the concept album that didn't need to be heard to be understood—and Lou fully expected it to be reviled. But that was by design. Exhibit A: the liner notes—"No one I know has listened to it all the way through including myself. It is not meant to be"; "Most of you won't like this, and I don't blame you at all. It's not meant for you"; "This is not meant for the market." What it was meant for was left up to interpretation for the few die-hard Lou disciples and Fluxus fanatics who intuitively grasped the radical underlying ideology and deigned to go all the way.

The intrepid or insane who made it there could spend their entire lives pondering its meaning. Unlike Young's Theatre of Eternal Music, *Metal Machine Music* was truly eternal. Foregrounding the album's immense gravity, Lou had it released as a double-LP—cut up into four "movements," each exactly sixteen minutes and one second—with a locked groove on the fourth side, an intentional glitch he first toyed with on "I'll Be Your Mirror." He listed the infinity symbol as the closing track's run time; its final seconds of interminable death agony would play ad infinitum, an eternity of feedback flashing before the ears, until, like life, the needle was lifted. Lou had a twisted sense of humor.

And the label played the perfect straight man. During the March 1975 leg of the *Sally Can't Dance* tour, RCA released *Lou Reed Live*, a collection of outtakes from the *Rock 'n' Roll Animal* concert. It was an attempt to squeeze every last penny out of Lou, and it served as the ideal setup for his irreverent punch line, which he delivered in his memorable closing line to the liner notes of *MMM*: "My week beats your year." His week sometimes included making *Metal Machine Music*, or preparing for an international tour, and that was just the beginning. Unlike those who would buy the album, though, a week for Lou Reed did not include sleep. Or buying *Metal Machine Music*.

In July, Lou flew to Japan just in time to be out of the United States for the release of *Metal Machine Music*, performing a week of shows in Tokyo and a stop in Osaka. Lou hopped over to Australia, but across the world, he missed Rachel so much that they would sleep with the phone next to their ears so they could hear each other breathing. In August, following one show in New Zealand, Lou canceled the rest of the tour and flew back to New York to cure his homesickness.

Back in New York, Lou discovered that most of those who did buy *MMM* returned it immediately. Three weeks later, it had been pulled from every record store shelf in America. Branded the rock equivalent of Stravinsky's *Rite of Spring*, it instantly secured a place in history as the most notorious album ever released on a major label. If this brazen flip of the bird didn't nullify Lou's creative life, nothing ever could.

All but unlistenable from the label's perspective, *Metal Machine Music* was a sunk cost, its nuclear fallout only good for bad publicity. Some considered it the ultimate sadomasochistic act of self-flagellation, but in its reductio ad absurdum statement, the album made a mockery of the contract between critic and artist and the broader mandate of pop consumerism. Yet the megatons of bad press ironically inured Lou against the media circus surrounding pop stardom; he was above it all, or perhaps beneath it. Whether Lou was the Zeus-like sadist indiscriminately spreading white lightning or rock Hades dragging everyone down to an underworld of white noise was unclear. At the very least, though, he knew one faction would be forced to slog through the whole keening mess: the critics. *Rolling Stone* compared it to "the tubular groaning of a galactic refrigerator." Christgau torpedoed Lou's grade-point average, giving it a C+ and calling it "a blatant rip-off." *Rock Australia* magazine came up with "a dentist's drill battling a pneumatic drill for possession of a tattered moog riff from Tangerine Dream."

Yet contrary to expectation, the critical guillotine didn't fall on every copy—despite the bad blood, Lester Bangs held it up as the Marianas Trench all future albums would measure up against, a piece of art so reprehensibly abominable it had sunk to the darkest depths of brilliance. Lou told Lester that deep in the quadraphonic mix he had buried excerpts from Beethoven's *Eroica*, Mozart, even Bach, but the multifarious layers of white noise harmonics made verifying the claim the type of outlandish assertion that sent Delmore Schwartz into the rabbit hole with *Finnegan's Wake*. Still, his most ardent disciple blasted it from his car window all over the streets of Detroit like the mobile air raid siren from hell. Lou's sworn enemy was one of the only ones who had his back. With *Metal Machine Music*, Lou had committed career suicide, but he had also risen like a phoenix from the ashes of the metal machine.

# 20

Keeping a relatively low profile, Lou had cemented a reputation as the Godfather of Punk, the patron saint of CBGB OMFUG, the grungy venue founded by Hilly Kristal, a former manager of the Village Vanguard. The final *G* stood for "gormandizer," a term Kristal imported from the French culinary tradition to signify the wretched excess inside its desecrated walls. Tom Verlaine and Television, Blondie, the Ramones, Wayne County, and David Byrne's Talking Heads trekked to the Bowery to cut their teeth on its legendarily filthy stage, an incubator for everything punk embodied. Lou and Rachel had begun to frequent the iconic club, where the Rheingold flowed freely and the biohazard of a bathroom trumped the Factory's chrome latrine in its sheer revulsion. Its graffiti-stained walls and dank floor, soaked with bodily fluids, was a haven for roaches, with a small staircase leading to a seat-less porcelain throne of shit, the Parnassus of punk, and half-conscious bodies at the urinals down below pissed aimlessly as they saw the whole abject excremental romp unfold with the pomp and circumstance of Leopold Bloom. Copping a squat at CBGB was a germy initiation into the punk netherworld, more dangerous than a sexual encounter with a random stranger.

It was during a Ramones show at CBGB in September 1975 that Lou and Rachel were accosted by cartoonist John Holmstrom, Ged Dunn, and Legs McNeil, three self-described punk transplants who had fled the suburban plenty of Connecticut for the urban squalor of the Village. In an unsolicited gambit interview for the inaugural issue of *Punk*, a gonzo magazine dedicated to proliferating the burgeoning aesthetic Lou had inadvertently played a seminal role in birthing, they followed him to Mickey Ruskin's Locale. They baited Lou into anger with inane questions, which wasn't hard, ranging from how he liked his hamburgers cooked to his comic book preferences.

Holmstrom illustrated the resulting interview, "Lou Reed: Rock 'n' Roll Vegetable," in addition to drawing a caricature of Lou as a bug-eyed Frankenstein for the cover. His cult status had risen to the level of parody, and no one knew what he would do next to top *Metal Machine Music*.

Yet instead of topping himself, Lou went back to the beginning, plumbing the depths of the old rag-and-bone shop of the heart to find inspiration in the doo-wop of his Brooklyn youth. In October, he entered Mediasound to record *Coney Island Baby*, as much a love letter to Rachel as it was to the nostalgic Coney Island of the mind. Initially planned as a Steve Katz production, Katz quickly dropped out of the session, replaced by recording engineer Godfrey Diamond.

"We did work on *Coney Island Baby* in preproduction. He played 'I Wanna Be Black,' and I said 'I can't do that.' I said, 'I'll Get Shot!'" Katz recalls. "'I wanna be black, I wanna be shot in the spring like Martin Luther King.'" Ultimately, Lou held the track for future use.

The band for the record consisted of keyboardist Michael Fonfara, guitarist Bob Kulick, drummer Bob Meday, as well as Suchorsky and Yaw of the Everyman Band. Diamond learned what he could of the music in a huddle in the Gramercy Park Hotel, and combining a technician's finesse with the kind of hands-free approach that a twenty-four-year-old might workably adopt, he allowed Lou to take the reins. Lou had met Kulick during a tour stop in Toronto; Kulick was performing with disco singer George McCrae, and though disco was anathema to Lou's aesthetic, he liked what he heard. Kulick had almost joined Kiss after responding to their legendary *Village Voice* ad for a lead guitarist, and Lou wanted to give him a chance. He invited Kulick to Mediasound, gave him a vintage Stratocaster, and told him to wing it.

"Should I listen down a few times, make a chart, see what's going on?" Kulick asked.

"That's not what I want. I want you to go out there and just play what you feel to what you hear, off the cuff, no rehearsal," Lou said. "I want off the cuff licks. No thinking. No knowing. If there's a mistake, we'll fix it." For Lou, it seemed there were no wrong notes, only right resolutions. Lou was the anti-Ezrin, a taskmaster when it came to banning processed riffs in favor of an emotional rawness; the goal was to channel doo-wop through an improvisatory approach that harnessed the crazy feeling and visceral immediacy Lou first heard emanating from the radio—the sound of freedom.

"The tunes had a definite form, but unless there was a particular horn line, I was pretty much on my own. I would play what moved me at the moment to play," Fogel says. "In some ways, Lou was kind of like a dictator, but musically, he was not. He just expected people to bring their best effort and put out energy when you were up there and play like a band, not so much a backup band, but really be a band."

The energy Lou was channeling originated in doo-wop. "It's gonna be the kind of stuff you'd play if you were in a bar and you didn't want to hear about it," he told Lester Bangs. "It's the Brooklyn–Long Island axis at work. Like you know the Harptones' 'Glory of Love,' doo-wop, I wanted to rip that off them but not use the song, do my own."

Lou peppered *Coney Island Baby* with this kind of free-associative shibboleth to the halcyon days of doo-wop, emanating from the jukebox of his unconscious. By turns a tribute to doo-wop and a tongue-in-cheek send-up of its sanitized themes, Lou rewrote the 1950s with a liberal edge, the way only he could. Other than the Excellents' "Coney Island Baby" or the Velvetones' "Glory of Love," loosely referenced in the title track, itself a new take on an earlier song he played with the Eldorados, the majority of the songs were Lou Reed interpretations of previous doo-wop hits, often bearing no more than a lyrical trace of the original. The opening track, "Crazy Feeling" was also nearly identical to the title of the first single recorded by Kenny Rogers, the saccharine "That Crazy Feeling," released in 1957 when he was a doo-wop singer. Lou's version is about after-hours transgender love. The chorus to the jaunty "Charley's Girl" ("You'd better watch out for Charley's girl") contains allusions to Lou's own Pickwick cut, "Cycle Annie":

*You'd better watch out for little Cycle Annie*

"Ooohhh Baby," an onomatopoetic staple of the doo-wop idiom, was a hit for the Hollywood Flames, "Ooh Baby Ooh," and for the Teardrops, "Ooh Baby." Lou's version exposed the seamy underbelly of prostitution and vice in Times Square. Taking a cue from Ike and Tina Turner, whose "Ain't Nobody's Business" dripped off *So Fine* in 1968, Lou wrote "Nobody's Business," a riposte to the braying media mob casting aspersions on his private life. He drew from Velvets outtakes as well, recording a version of "She's My Best Friend," amped up with heavy distortion. For Lou, what was past was prologue.

On the title track, the album's languorous capstone, featuring Kulick's spontaneous obbligato guitar echoing Hubert Sumlin, Lou reflected on his ongoing quest for freedom—from commercial mandates, artistic compromise, and social convention. Using the image of "the coach" as a type of metonym for all-American hegemonic masculinity, Lou juxtaposes the football conceit with a more emotional end zone:

> *Ah, but remember that the city is a funny place*
> *Something like a circus or a sewer*
> *And just remember different people have peculiar tastes*

Having escaped the conservative strictures of middle-class society, Lou extended this metaphor to his broader career struggles.

Yet most poignantly, as the mellifluous background vocals came in, Lou seemed to find the freedom and light he'd been looking for in his emotional life in Rachel. Lou experienced the same liberating catharsis he first had listening to doo-wop in an unlikely place, culminating in a sentimental dedication to his paramour: "I want to send this one out to Lou and Rachel and all the kids at PS 192," he sang. "Man, I swear I'd give the whole thing up for you." Despite the prickly veneer, love in its manifold forms was always the answer.

Yet there were many layers to peel back before he got there. He foregrounded this rock star persona with the cover photo, shot by Mick Rock, mugging in a tuxedo and hat that aped the vaudevillian flourishes of Joel Gray in the 1972 film adaptation of *Cabaret*; if Lou was the androgynous Weimar-era Berlin Emcee, that would make Rachel Liza Minnelli. Like the enigmatic character, Lou's public persona concealed a raw emotionalism and sentimentality beneath. Even if he never played football for the coach, and never would, the sentiment exposed a yearning at Lou's core; the patina of hedonism and decadence concealed an idealistic sense of wonder that was now on full display.

Released in January 1976, *Coney Island Baby* peaked at Number 41 on the *Billboard* chart. *Rolling Stone* called it "a career-capping touchdown scored so honestly and directly that almost no one can believe it." Not everyone agreed, though. "This album made me so morose and depressed when I got the advance copy that I stayed drunk for three days," wrote a nonplussed Peter Laughner, who had grown up on the Velvets. It signified a departure from the cagey debauchery of Lou's earlier output, an artistic rebirth that inevitably left some disappointed. But the label was pleased with the album. Lou had previously sunk into debt, partially as a result of *Metal Machine Music*, and RCA was happy to have Lou's third-highest chart performance. However, Lou decided to leave the label on a high note, parting amicably.

Prior to making a clean break, Lou called Clive Davis, the executive who had split from Columbia to found Arista Records, and inquired about the possibility of joining the fledgling label's roster. Davis knew Lou in a social capacity—he once gave him an after-hours tour of the Village underground scene—but knew that Lou's uncompromising reputation might prove intractable. Nevertheless, he agreed to sign him, and contracts were finalized. Yet leading up to his debut on Arista, Lou expanded his range by stepping into the producer's chair for Nelson Slater, a friend from Syracuse.

Lou had reconnected with Slater in San Francisco, and agreed to lend his imprimatur to his first album, *Wild Angel*. Drafting the Everyman Band, in addition to Bob Kulick, the lithe recording captured the free-floating atmospheric effervescence of *Coney Island Baby*, with Lou blending in with the boisterous gang vocals. Lou began incorporating several Slater songs into his live sets, including "Sad About It" and "Complete the Story," but when it was released in March 1976, RCA made only a tepid effort to promote the album. The foreboding Mick Rock cover, depicting a woman gagged and bound by a chain over a red background, undermined any commercial potential, and Lou lacked the clout to put someone else's racy music on shelves. Nevertheless, Slater occasionally joined Lou onstage when tours stopped in the Bay area.

Later, Lou hired Kulick for the *Rock and Roll Heart* tour, but when Lou missed a rehearsal, Kulick taught some of the parts to the band. The next day, Lou discovered to his chagrin that Kulick had familiarized them with the material, and they could therefore rely on reflexive facility.

"You showed them some of these songs," Lou said.

"Yeah, I just figured they'd be ready for you when you came in. We'd be able to play them rather than having to teach it to them."

"I wanted to teach it to them."

"I didn't know that," said Kulick. "I'm sorry."

"So now you have to be fired." There was a silver lining, though—soon, Kulick was playing with Kiss, Alice Cooper, and Meat Loaf. Besides, Lou had begun to embrace his roots in college jazz radio.

For *Rock and Roll Heart*, Lou harnessed the avant-fusion sound of the Everyman Band. Recorded in the Record Plant, from its opening notes, the album embraced a horn-based aesthetic. With Fogel laying down a bright sax intro on "I Believe in Love," alongside the airtight rhythm section of Fonfara, Yaw, and Suchorsky, they explored the harmonic outer limits of the basic chord structure without straying too far from the tonic, the ideal vehicle for the collective improvisation that had always been present in Lou's lyrics. It was stylistic potpourri, blending the Afrobeat syncopation of Fela Kuti's Africa '70, the improvisatory funk of Weather Report, and the smooth, horn-driven sensibility of Miles Davis's electric band, a radical departure from the Hunter-Wagner dueling guitars of *Rock 'n' Roll Animal*.

The nihilism and depravity that characterized Lou's earlier persona gave way to a deeper emotional investment that he had displayed with the Velvets, but with a softer touch. Lou allegedly wrote much of the material in the studio, executing everything from conception to mixing in four weeks. The style-over-substance tracks focused on the Everyman Band's ability to create a mood that evinced the spirit of spontaneity Lou championed in the title track, doing his damnedest to replicate the garbled bravado of Bruce Springsteen's demotic, salt-of-the-earth sound on the recently released *Born to Run*. *Rock and Roll Heart* abandoned Lou's erstwhile insistence on the primacy of the lyric; there were no vocals on "Chooser and the Chosen One," an instrumental fusion track, and Lou even rented a baritone saxophone for Fogel to flesh out the low end of "You Wear It So Well." This tonal shift was evident immediately in the album's opener, "I Believe in Love," which foregrounded a lightly swung saxophone line and jocular lyrics in a major key that preached the gospel of rock with a childlike sense of wonder Lou had not exhibited since "Rock & Roll." Yet it still retained an ironic wink that forced listeners to question where exactly Lou's belief ended and his agnosticism began:

> *I believe in music, music, music*
> *It'll satisfy your soul but*
> *I believe in love*

It was clear that he was doing rock the way he heard it and the way he liked it, whether anybody else liked it or not, even Clive Davis. "Banging on My Drum," if facile in its sentiment and its sole lyric, "I'm bangin' on my drum, boy, I'm having lots of fun," sent the message that Lou was not the egotistical monster the media had portrayed him as, but just a humble neighborhood guy from Long Island living out his childhood dream, only in a much bigger, grittier basement. Ranging from the pulsing groove of the unreleased Velvets tune "Follow the Leader," the buoyant "Rock & Roll Heart," and "Claim to Fame" to the melancholic backbeat of "Vicious Circle" and "Temporary Thing," Lou self-produced the album with a nonchalance that belied the mounting pressure to score a hit on his Arista debut. "A Sheltered Life," a jazz tune about the innocence of life in the suburbs, had Lou doing his best imitation of a Rat Pack crooner and prominently featured Fogel on an extended overdubbed call-and-response tenor saxophone dialogue with himself that channeled complex harmony, technical virtuosity, and a klezmer undertone more befitting the world's coolest bar mitzvah than Madison Square Garden.

Clive Davis lobbied hard for Lou to bolster the production with a string section and other pop frills to transform the title track into a radio-friendly hit, but he refused. Lou would release the album under Arista on his terms only. The critics largely panned it. "Lou promised this would be a rock 'n' roll album, but I call it stuff 'n' nonsense," Stephen Demorest wrote in *Creem*. Christgau gave it a B– in what was becoming a string of shoddy grades, but Lou didn't care about critics. Davis didn't score the hit he wanted; *Rock and Roll Heart* sold modestly, but the tour soon proved that profitability and artistic integrity are not mutually exclusive.

Before the *Rock and Roll Heart* tour kicked off, though, Lou made an impromptu midsummer appearance with John Cale at the Ocean Club, the boho-chic watering hole Mickey Ruskin had just opened on Chambers Street in TriBeCa. With its light installation by sculptor Frosty Myers, the cozy bar had a small stage in the back not much bigger than the Café Bizarre. Lou accompanied Cale on guitar on "I'm Waiting for the Man," alongside up-and-coming acolytes Patti Smith and David Byrne, the latter of whom had recently formed the Talking Heads. The meeting was brief, and frustrated any expectations of a more extensive Velvet Underground reunion. Yet news had spread on the underground grapevine that a Velvets reunion might be in the offing.

"I wouldn't want a steady diet of it. In that type of situation, it's nice to delve into something that existed for real and make it exist again for real," Lou told *Creem* reporter John Morthland. "It is what it was and it was what it is, and the various components by themselves can't be the Velvet Underground. Nostalgia is a very good reason not to do it more than once or twice."

All the focus was placed on the forthcoming tour. The set consisted of a stack of forty-eight discarded black-and-white televisions repurposed from curbsides and second-hand stores all over New York. "I actually went out and helped Mick and Lou gather up black-and-white television sets before the tour started," says Jeff Ross, at the time a twenty-two-year-old guitar tech from Long Island who had landed a gig at Jonny Podell's BMF Enterprises. "I remember driving uptown in Harlem, picking TVs up off the street. There was a place down on Christopher Street just below Greenwich, a TV repair shop, and probably some of them came from hospitals." During concerts, Mick Rock projected looped experimental footage, a postmodern commentary on the gulf between Lou's media-constructed persona and the flesh-and-blood band onstage. Following a year off the road, Lou hit the ground running, playing a string of dates including Akron, Toronto, and New York's Palladium, where anticipation grew for what post–*Metal Machine Music* Lou might sound like. Concertgoers were treated to a rough-hewn, irascible rocker with a propensity to swing like a jazz crooner or a death wish to shred his vocal cords, depending on the song.

Soon Lou felt the need for more guitars in the band and decided to informally audition Jeff Ross. It was not conventional for a bandleader to give his guitar tech a chance at joining the band, but Lou balanced a penchant for drug-induced tyrannical behavior with a strong egalitarian ethos. "I got a call from Lou inviting me up to dinner," Ross recalls. "Lou spent a good deal of time complaining about how he needed a guitar player in the band, and didn't know how to come up with one. He'd been playing with various guys in the city, and they were all too technical, too straightforward, and I was more of a punk player." Lou brought a collection of TEAC reel-to-reel tapes to Ross's apartment, where he had a player. "When we got in, he saw my '54 Les Paul, and he said, 'Hey, man, play 'Sweet Jane.' And I swear, I had no idea what I was doing. I picked up the guitar and started banging on it. And he said, 'Yeah, that's great!' So we hung out, we played I guess through the early part of that winter, and that sort of secured my place in the band." Lou would begin his next tour with Ross on lead guitar.

In November, Lou flew to Los Angeles to headline the Roxy and the Santa Monica Civic Auditorium. At LAX, Fogel happened to spot pocket trumpeter Don Cherry, the Los Angeles native known for his collaborations with Ornette Coleman and Albert Ayler. Cherry had just recorded his first album with Old and New Dreams, a quartet of Ornette Coleman collaborators composed of Cherry, saxophonist Dewey Redman, drummer Ed Blackwell, and bassist Charlie Haden. Cherry was one of Lou's idols. They possessed certain commonalities—an explosive improvisatory energy as well as a history of hepatitis early in their careers. And fortunately for Lou, Fogel already knew him.

Fogel rented a basement practice space on Sixth Street in the Village next door to Cherry's wife Moki's textile studio, though the Cherrys' principal residence was in Stockholm, where they were raising their son, Eagle-Eye. "I'd see Don all the time, and we would say hello. But then one day in 1976, we had just arrived at the Los Angeles airport, just kinda hanging out, waiting for a limousine. And I'm standing by this phone on the wall, and Don Cherry comes walking up to where the phone is. And I'm standing there, and we said hello and started talking, and then he left," Fogel says. "Then we were getting ready to go, and I said to Lou, 'Man, I just ran into Don Cherry out there!' He says, 'Go get him! Go get him! I love him!'" Having once played Cherry on the radio in college, Lou invited him to play with them; the chance meeting led to an ongoing relationship with the free-jazz luminary for the next several years.

So without rehearsing, Cherry played it by ear during a spontaneous set with Lou and the Everyman Band, casting a new light on "Sweet Jane," "Coney Island Baby," and "Charley's Girl," punctuating Lou's hard-rocking style with an organic approach that demonstrated Lou's avant-garde leanings, which had been dormant for years. Like Lou, Cherry could tell a riveting story, but on the trumpet or the *doussn'gouni*, a fretless string instrument from Mali that resembled a kora. Lou easily adapted his scat-like recitative chant for a jazz sensibility, taking a backseat to Fogel and Cherry, who used the basic chord structure as a kind of modal funk and took flight. On "Walk on the Wild Side," Cherry and Fogel mined the song's playful character for a cutting session that sliced deeper than usual. For the next week at the

Roxy, Cherry helped them take it out as far as they could go—and then he left them there.

Following that high, though, Lou ended the tour with a setback. Rachel got mugged and assaulted. Lou called Warhol in distress. "He'd come back from a successful tour, he was a big hit in L.A., but he said Rachel had gotten kicked in the balls and was bleeding from the mouth and he wanted the name of a doctor," Warhol wrote in his diary. "Lou called back and said he got Keith Richards's doctor to come over. I told him he should take her to the hospital. I was calling Rachel 'she' because she's always in drag but then Lou calls him 'he.'" Rachel had been contemplating gender reassignment surgery, but the transgender rights movement had not yet solidified, and not fully understanding the nature of the decision, Lou was adamantly opposed to any operations, a growing source of conflict in their relationship.

Despite any mounting tension in the relationship, to the band, Lou seemed uncharacteristically at peace. "I think that Rachel was the glue holding Lou together, or at least keeping him in the public view in many respects," recalls Jeff Ross. Rachel would sometimes crash at Ross's apartment if relations with Lou got too heated, but compared to his past excesses, Lou was calm and collected. "I know that he doted on her. If there was a light shining, it was the two of them together. It doesn't mean it was the healthiest relationship in the world."

By 1977 Lou's relationship with Rachel had a higher profile in the press. Photos of the couple peppered the cover of *Walk on the Wild Side: The Best of Lou Reed*, a compilation album intended to capitalize on Arista's publicity push. They celebrated their third anniversary at a party in London that spring, documented by photographer Jill Furmanovsky in *Rock Scene* magazine. At Maunkberry's, a gay club near St. James's Park, they toasted over champagne and kissed before cutting into a three-layer mocha cake—"One layer for each year" written in frosting—with their joint initials, "LR," as a cake topper. In "A Talk on the Wild Side," a July 1977 interview with Victor Bockris published in the pornographic magazine *National Screw*, they were the subject of a five-page spread featuring full-color photos by Mick Rock. Yet throughout the tour that led to Lou's next record, *Street Hassle*, beneath the quixotic veneer, there was trouble brewing.

Lou tapped Richard Robinson, who had produced *Lou Reed*, for *Street Hassle*, a mostly live album that would attempt to capture the ferocious energy of Lou and the Everyman Band. Aiming for verisimilitude, they sought out

Manfred Schunke, a German recording engineer who had pioneered binaural sound, in which microphones would be positioned on either side of a dummy head, known as a *Kunstkopf*, enhancing the headphone listening experience. Though the process dated back nearly a century, *Street Hassle* would be the first pop album to use the costly technology.

The tour began in England, where they hit an immediate snag when the London Palladium canceled Lou's March 20 appearance due to the threat of a riot on the scale of the Rome debacle. The Clash's "White Riot," their first single, had been released only two days earlier; the anarchist rumblings of the Sex Pistols, who had recently recorded "God Save the Queen," and newly formed bands like Buzzcocks and Joy Division, were raging across the city. Galvanizing the punk subculture, the Godfather of Punk posed what British authorities perceived as an imminent threat to social order as partisan politics drove a wedge between the conservative supporters of Margaret Thatcher's growing opposition party. So the band began touring in earnest several days later in neutral Sweden, where the local population might be more impervious to the rumblings of Lou Reed.

The night before they left for Sweden, Jeff Ross hoped to catch some rest; it was his official debut as lead guitarist. "I'm beat asleep and my phone rings. It's Lou, and he says, 'Come down right now.' It's three o'clock in the morning," Ross says. "So I go downstairs, and the bar is closed. Lou and Fonfara are there, and they helped themselves to a bottle of Glenfiddich, which is empty on its side, and another bottle of Glenlivet. Lou pours me a big shot. And they're jacked. Lou is wearing a guayabera, with these giant pockets in the front." Ross could smell an initiation ritual on Lou's breath. "In the left-hand pocket of the shirt is a thick stack of plane tickets—all my tickets for the entire European tour. He pours me a shot, and he goes, 'Drink that.' And I was not a drinker. So I drank it, and he pulls the tickets out of his pocket and he slaps them down, and he says to me, 'Are you going to be able to do this?' Put yourself in a twenty-two-year-old head. Of course I can do this! He tells me he'll let me back out and send me home if I say I can't do it. But then he says, 'If you fuck me up, you'll never work in this business again.' That's a quote. I carried that with me afterwards, because I didn't. I didn't understand that I was at the right hand of god. I thought we were all peers. Not really. He could be scarily unpredictable."

The only thing more unpredictable than Lou himself was a Lou Reed audience. Continuing the tradition of breeding civil unrest in cities with a history of nonviolence, the band had some trouble when they headlined in Aarhus, Denmark. The anarchy of the Sex Pistols wasn't restricted to the UK; that year, Danish rock progenitors the Sods, later known as Sort Sol, announced the arrival of punk in Copenhagen. That night, Lou helped galvanize that anarchic movement. Toward the end of the set, during "Berlin," audience members began throwing beers at the stage.

Ross was prepared for safety hazards—the band had had a near Altamont moment in Germany when a rowdy group of Hells Angels threatened to disrupt a show—but he wasn't expecting flying bottles. "Lou was sitting in front of the stage—he had taken to singing intimately to the crowd—and a bottle comes whizzing past his head and crashes into the drums," Ross says. Lou couldn't just shrug it off. "Let me tell you one thing. You police your own," Lou told the crowd. "Listen. Nobody throws a can at me. You understand? You want another song, you take care of your own."

Then came another bottle. "I think his intention was to let it chill out and come back. But I just remember turning around and seeing my guitar tech grab my guitars, scoop them all up, and we all left the stage," Ross says. As they made a hasty exit, the promoter tried to forestall a riot by translating Lou's outburst. "What he did was he got up and basically said in Dutch, 'Lou said go fuck yourselves. You're a bunch of assholes. He's never played for a worse audience.' Whatever riot act Lou had read to them, the guy translates like an absolute dullard, and then all hell broke loose."

Riot police resorted to tear gas and attack dogs to quell the disturbance; equipment was destroyed in the onslaught of half-empty glass projectiles; a cymbal from Michael Suchorsky's drum set got bent in half when a piece of truss came crashing down. The band was huddled backstage like a band of postapocalyptic refugees avoiding the punk-crazed zombie hordes. "It was like *Night of the Living Dead*," says Ross. "The promoter then sent the limos away. The limo drivers decided they were going to split because it was too dangerous, so there were no cars, and we were stuck there. In my memory, it was hours. But it was long enough for them to destroy absolutely every piece of equipment that was on that stage. We were carrying a lot of gear with us, and they turned over a full grand Steinway and destroyed it. They knocked over the lighting towers." When the riot subsided, there were still some remaining fans. "I have a very vivid memory of us ducked down below these industrial windows, with people roaming around outside the building trying to figure out where we were," Ross says. "When we finally got in the car with an escort, there were still people trying to catch the cars. 'There they go!' It was absolutely mad, but it was a really good show."

Following that debacle, Lou decided he and the band had to be armed and ready for anything they could throw at him. "He'd gotten a switchblade, but we'd all gotten switchblades. Whatever Lou got, I got, and I assume everybody got," Ross says. Later on in London, after the performance injunction was lifted, Lou put it to use. "We were playing at the New Vic, and the Arista rep, an English guy, came in. I don't know what he said to Lou, but Lou had that switchblade out and had the knife at his cheek in seconds. This was my school of rock. He had a lot of quick anger. I would bet you dollars to doughnuts that a lot of that came from sleep deprivation and amphetamines, but a lot came from this insecurity he had about who he was supposed to be."

The tour marched on into Germany, where Manfred Schunke recorded live dates beginning in April, muting the audience track to create a cross between a studio sound and a live recording. Lou chose some of his rawest material: "Gimmie Some Good Times" opened with overdubbed dialogue, in which Lou had an epic rap battle with himself and won; the deliberately muddy blues track "Dirt" relied on distortion to evoke Lou's malicious feelings toward Dennis Katz; and "I Wanna Be Black" satirized the racist cultural tropes perpetuated by blaxploitation films and appropriated by white America. It was a rock transposition of the anxieties raised by Norman Mailer's polemical 1957 essay "The White Negro," seizing on the cognitive dissonance and insecurity of being complicit in that cultural theft. Lou had written the song several years earlier but finally recorded the controversial mashup of stereotypes, replete with a too-soon reference to Martin Luther King, penis envy, and Raelettes-style backing vocals. Despite Lou's sense of cultural displacement and self-conscious racial borrowing, he knew where he came from:

> I don't wanna be a fucked up middle-class college student
>> anymore
> I just wanna have a stable of foxy little whores

The band honed the material as they traveled through Europe, but Robinson wanted to make it as gritty as possible. When the tour stopped in London, Richard and Lou, still riding high on whatever amphetamine was available in Germany, decided they wanted to take a cue from the spreading punk movement, having heard an up-and-coming act. "They came back one night, and they're telling us, 'You guys got to play like that,'" Fogel says. "And then he said, 'Rock 'n' roll is noise. Rock 'n' roll is not music.' And I said, 'I haven't spent my whole life preparing to be a really good musician to just start playing noise.'" Fogel decided to quit the band after the tour concluded. In May, Lou concluded that leg of the tour with a homecoming, headlining three nights—May 9–11, 1977—at the Bottom Line, a four-hundred-seat club in the Village where he would cut a live album in 1978. After the Bottom Line, Fogel left the band.

After the Bottom Line shows, Jeff Ross also left acrimoniously; in the breakup, Lou ended up inheriting Ross's Les Paul Junior. Despite his resentment, the tour with Lou allowed Ross to embark on a solo career on the underground scene, ultimately landing a management deal with Chris Charlesworth, who had produced *The Who by Numbers*. "It punted me into the upper echelon of the business. I would have to say, I'm really grateful for my time with Lou. He was fundamental in my own design, and not because I idolized him," Ross says. "As angry as he was, and as frustrated as he was, he felt things more deeply than he could actually express articulately, so instead of doing it with complex verbiage, he simply put it out there—whatever it was."

The subsequent leg of the tour kicked off in France, where Lou had amassed a sizable audience among the burgeoning punk rebellion. The milieu inhabited by "Les Punks," as they were known, crystallized around Lou as totemic father figure. The scene even spawned an all-female punk outfit called Les Lous, and Marie et les Garcons, originally called Femme Fatale, which John Cale later produced. The Velvet Underground's raw sound, which was not always intentional, became a lingua franca for the burgeoning punk scene, even though the newly christened godfather strove to distance what he considered the Velvets' cerebral take on high modernism from the doggerel of some pale imitators. Yet for the most part, he embraced the title. When Elvis died later that month, the punk movement responded by spitting on his proverbial grave. "Fuckin' good riddance to bad rubbish," said Johnny Rotten. "I don't give a fuckin' shit, and nobody else does either." Like an amplified storming of the Bastille, the death of the King happened at a symbolic moment for punk, and Lou was their Robespierre.

Lou concluded the tour by following the punk revolution to Australia, where the Saints, the Last Words, and the Thought Criminals were taking off. Lou received a royal welcome; nearly a decade after the Velvets disbanded, he was finally appreciated as the visionary artist he had always been. Lou's persona as public enemy was now in vogue.

Yet Lou harbored deep ambivalence surrounding his coronation as Godfather of Punk. The punk aesthetic largely centered on shock and awe—making as much noise as possible—but Lou had already begun distancing himself from punk genre conventions. Several months later, Lou paid a visit to Fogel's house in Montclair, New Jersey, to personally ask him to reconsider leaving the band. Fogel relented and rejoined. "I don't think Lou wanted to just make noise," Fogel says. "I think he wanted to create art."

Since Fogel had left the group, that's exactly what Lou had done. When they returned home at the end of the summer, Lou knew that *Street Hassle* needed a transcendent centerpiece. Ensconced in the Record Plant studio, Lou recorded "Street Hassle," a three-part gutter opus with literary pretensions, bolstered by a lush but tasteful chamber string section arranged by polymath Aram Schefrin, founder of the horn-driven rock band Ten Wheel Drive, and a choir of ethereal background singers. Sandwiched in the middle of the album, light on drums and distortion, the title track was the antithesis of *Metal Machine Music*, eleven minutes of pure poetry, pulp fiction elevated to the level of the sublime. In the first suite, "Waltzing Matilda," a transgender woman picks up a male prostitute in a dive bar, with a graphic scene that rivaled Bukowski's most devastatingly cathartic moments.

There was a kind of libertine humanism to Lou's bohemian reportage, a push to follow the heart into whatever dark alleys it led to. The second suite, "Street Hassle," describes the aftermath of a drug overdose in unvarnished verse:

> But when someone turns that blue, well it's a universal truth
> And then you just know that bitch will never fuck again

Lou was just telling it like it is, an abiding truth of life on the edge unfurled with brutal gallows humor, the inherent risk and ephemerality of the thrill chosen over the banality of the humdrum. Ultimately, the corpse in question ends up back on the street:

*And by morning, she's just another hit and run*

The final suite, "Slipaway," featured uncredited cameo appearances from neighboring studios by Bruce Springsteen, who was recording *Darkness on the Edge of Town*, and Joe Perry, who was recording *Draw the Line* with Aerosmith. Culminating with a tale of a jilted lover, Springsteen lays down a heartbreaking verse bleeding with cryptic aphorisms, capped off by a sly interpolation that revealed the mysterious stranger's identity to anyone not yet familiar with his inimitable boozy drawl:

*Ya know, tramps like us, we were born to pay*

The sprawling track closes with a deep yearning—a dirgelike expurgation of unrequited love—but perhaps, as was often the case, Lou was not the lovelorn protagonist pining away; if it was anyone in his life, it was Rachel.

# 21

Relations had deteriorated between Lou and Rachel by the end of 1977, and they fought more and more. The conflict centered on their mutual ambivalence about gender reassignment surgery, which at the dawn of the LGBT rights movement was largely relegated to pop culture references like *Dog Day Afternoon*; the decision was generally misunderstood.

Transphobic activists in the Gay Liberation Front refused to acknowledge a distinction between homosexuality and transgender, considering any surgery a conformist concession to society's heteronormative prejudices. In regard to the surgery, Lou, whose traumatic experience with shock therapy was never far from his mind, vacillated on whether Rachel should cave to what he wrongly perceived as a response to social pressure. "There would be a discussion about sex change operations, and every time Rachel would be scheduled to do that—that's what Lou wanted, as far as Rachel would say—then Lou would back off and say, 'Well why are you doing that? I love you because of the way you are,'" recalls Lydia Sugarman, a friend of Rachel's who moved to the city in the winter and early spring of 1977–78. Lou waffled on what it meant to be a supportive partner. "That would just throw Rachel into a tailspin, to the point where she'd become suicidal."

Sugarman consoled Rachel as her relationship with Lou gradually dissolved. "She was kind of a tragic figure, because she loved Lou so much, and she basically would do whatever he wanted to make him happy, because that would make her happy," she says. "It was so early in the movement, though, there was an emotional and psychological dissonance that was present in the relationship between Lou and Rachel on both their parts."

One day, toward the end, Sugarman took Rachel shopping for khakis and a plaid shirt, a deliberate gender play. "She was tall and thin and larger than life," she says. When she and Sugarman met downtown beforehand, Rachel shocked the passersby with an ostentatious marriage proposal. "She was on the north side of the street and I was on the south side, and she was shouting, 'I love you! Will you marry me?' I was in the whole glow of reveling in finally living in New York."

Shortly thereafter, it was all over. Rachel's identity crisis pushed her to a breaking point. "I got a call late at night from Rachel in a hotel room, suicidal, totally distraught, because they'd had a big argument about gender surgery, and Rachel had no money," she says. Sugarman met Lou at three in the morning at an ATM in the Village so he could cover the hotel, and then she returned to Rachel for suicide watch. "I remember going to the ATM, taking out a couple hundred bucks, and going back to the hotel and spending the night with Rachel, being up all night to make sure that she was there to wake up in the morning." Lou had moved on, and there was nothing Rachel could do.

Whether they wanted to or not, Lou and Rachel's radical and very public relationship had exposed a crack in the heteronormative structure, but the epistemology of the closet society was locked in was yet to be exploded. Queer studies theorist Eve Sedgwick was still in graduate school, and she and her associates wouldn't break down the socially constructed wall of gender and sexuality stereotypes until around the time the Berlin Wall fell. Lou recognized that gender and sexuality varied along the Kinsey scale, first propounded in 1948, but three decades later, society still labeled love and desire in black-and-white terms, putting a strain on their relationship that Lou and Rachel unabashedly ignored. Rachel presented as female, but whether to call her a transvestite, a transsexual, or something crueler, as some critics had characterized her—even the politically correct pronoun usage— was still up for debate. Was Rachel Lou's roommate, boyfriend, girlfriend, partner, lover, all of the above? Patriarchal society demanded an answer, and Lou and Rachel refused to acknowledge the implicit prejudice of the question. Yet the residual effects of intolerance impinged on the complex psychosexual challenge of living firmly beyond the boundary. Feminists and gay rights activists alike frequently excluded transgender politics from the polarizing discussion of hetero- and homosexual identity, and as was often the case with Lou, few precedents led the charge.

Lou and Rachel were out on their own, and along with the usual trials and tribulations of sustaining a monogamous relationship—especially for someone as mercurial and polyamorous as Lou—their relationship problems ultimately proved insuperable. "When you desperately love someone, and you feel that person pulling away, it feels like your whole world is falling apart," Sugarman recalls of her last meetings with Rachel. "I do believe he loved Rachel in his own way, but like with a lot of relationships, it probably became too hard."

Lou had also met Sylvia Morales. Sylvia, a military brat born in England with an itinerant upbringing, had moved to New York to fulfill a high school fantasy with her friend Anya Phillips, a flamboyant habitué of the early punk no wave scene. "We were actually real oddities in high school, because Anya was very fashion conscious and I was this sort of intellectual, bookwormish type," Sylvia recalled in Legs McNeil's *Please Kill Me: The Uncensored Oral History of Punk*. "That's where she and I had made a plan—she was going to come to New York and become famous as a fashion designer, and I was going to be her assistant. It was a very 'Cosmo Girl' type of fantasy, like, 'I'm going to marry a rich rock star, I'm going to know everybody, we'll have all these famous friends who will make records and I'll design the record covers and we'll go on tours and I'll just do everything and I'll design the whole look.'" So that's exactly what they did.

Between tours in 1977, Lou returned to New York, and one night he met Anya at a bar in the Village. Anya, who was an extrovert in the extreme, had no compunction about marching right up to Lou and chatting him up. Before long, Anya brought Lou over to meet Sylvia, inadvertently acting as her wingwoman. "We spent all that night talking and started arguing right away," Sylvia said. "Lou's very, very, very smart and I fancied myself to be very, very, very smart and Lou made some remark that I was not as bright as he was." Cowed by no one, Sylvia was more than willing to take on the battle of the sexes and win, measuring up when it came to literary and artistic know-how. "I was not gonna let this guy think that he was some rich famous rock star that was impressing me."

After that night, Sylvia decided to write Lou a letter; rather than getting his number from a mutual friend, the tenor of their punk meet-cute dictated a more epistolary courtship ritual. She asked Diego Cortez, the artistic agent provocateur who would soon found the Mudd Club alongside Anya, for his address. Instead of writing back, Lou took the more expedient route and called. Before long, they were dating, and Lou came over to Sylvia and Anya's apartment. In the bathroom, he found Anya's diaries, which she placed prominently by the toilet, so anyone looking for titillating reading material could read about her sexual exploits. Lou assumed the diary was Sylvia's and swiped it for later perusal; when Anya saw it had gone missing, Sylvia demanded it back. The small theft only fueled Anya's jealousy, though soon thereafter she coupled up with jazz-punk icon James Chance. But Lou and Sylvia's romance was interrupted when Sylvia and Anya got evicted and Sylvia was forced to go back to Denver to live with her parents.

Before long, though, she was back in New York. "I came back to New York from Denver and I totally didn't have any idea what I was going to do," Sylvia recalled. "So I went to CBGB's and Richard Hell said, 'Oh, come over and rent an apartment in my building.'" Anya, who had moved into a different apartment, begrudgingly allowed Sylvia to use her phone to call Lou and let him know of her return. "He was very happy to hear from me and said that we would meet at Phebe's," she said. Phebe's was a bar on the Bowery not far from where Burroughs had a loft. "But he stood me up that night and I was very angry about it. I called him back and Lou said, 'Oh well, I was going to come, but the guys came over and we had to jam.' I was really furious and told him off and hung up." She intuitively knew that with Lou, she could never give an inch.

"The next morning there was a knock on my door and it was Lou. He'd been waiting outside for hours to get into my building," she said. The building where Voidoids frontman Richard Hell lived didn't have a functional buzzer, and Sylvia hadn't bought a phone yet. "Since I didn't have a phone yet, Lou had been waiting outside for a couple of hours for someone to come out the door so that he could get in. So Lou said, 'Do you want to go to Montreal?' Which is, like, much cooler than saying, 'Do you want to go to the movies?' or something. So I said, 'Sure.' And we pretty much stayed together after that."

When Lou played the Évêché at the Hotel Nelson in Montreal's historic district, an excited fan screamed out, "Take no prisoners, Lou!" With a live a recording at the Bottom Line scheduled for a few weeks later, Lou had the title of his next album.

Meanwhile, *Street Hassle* had been released in February, and though *Rolling Stone* hailed it as "the best solo album Lou Reed has ever done," it didn't sell well, except for in France, where Lou's formidable fan base continued to support their hero. Robert Christgau's assessment was damning with faint praise, claiming that "the production is muddled and the self-consciousness self-serving." He gave it a B+. Lou responded with an entire album.

*Live: Take No Prisoners* was the fierce culmination of the *Street Hassle* tour. Leading up to the live recording, though, bassist Bruce Yaw had departed due to friction with Lou, and the band needed a replacement. Enter Ellard "Moose" Boles, a larger-than-life bassist of African American, Choctaw, Cherokee, and Cajun descent, hailing from Buffalo, with a predilection for ten-gallon hats. Moose was every bit deserving of his epithet. He had been a member of Freeze, a Buffalo-based band that had gone on tour with Gregg Allman after the Allman Brothers disbanded. They were offered a chance to hedge their bets and continue with Allman in California, but Freeze went all in on the ill-fated prospect of a thaw. After the bad bet, Boles resorted to work as a stagehand and bouncer. Then out of the blue, he got an opportunity to audition for Lou. He spent the next few days listening to as much Lou Reed as he possibly could.

Lou's management arranged for Moose to be flown into New York from upstate; it was his first plane ride. He arrived at Lou's apartment expecting to be grilled on "Sweet Jane" and "Wild Side," but Lou never opted for predictability. "He asked me to play something by Marvin Gaye," Boles later recalled to the *Buffalo News*. "Then Lou asked me to go to a local bar and hang out." He got the job. Moose began the *Street Hassle* tour and was whisked off to California, where Lou honed a blistering live set bolstered by guitarist Stuart Heinrich and background vocalists Chrissy Faith and Angela Howell, all of whom had an association with the Everyman Band. In late May, on a rainy Wednesday night at the Bottom Line between Greene and Mercer in the Village, Lou began the set that would become *Live: Take No Prisoners*.

"He's in New York. This is his hometown—it's kind of like his living room, and he could just go and do what he wanted to do," says Fogel. "He was Lou, so if you didn't expect that, I don't know what you would expect, but you had to expect the unexpected if you were coming to a Lou Reed concert."

The album opened with the malevolent hiss of Lou lighting up a cigarette, reverberating in binaural sound. This was Lou, as real as it gets, telling it like it is—unfiltered, uncensored, and off the rails. Lou stretched its ten tracks into a double album with a lacerating comic monologue over a rock vamp, occasionally interrupted by a song. Now that Rachel was gone, the nostalgia trip was over: this was Lou without apology. The public had never seen him this unguarded on vinyl. "I'm gonna quote a line from Yeats," he said. "The best lack all conviction and the worst are filled with a passionate intensity. Now you figure out where I am." He was possibly the only rock star who would unabashedly quote Yeats's "The Second Coming" before unleashing the heavy artillery.

"Watch me turn into Lou Reed before your very eyes," he said. "I do Lou Reed better than anybody, so I thought I'd get in on it. Enough attitude to kill every person in Jersey."

He had rarely put his sense of humor onstage, but Lou's sardonic wit was legendary. "Sweet Jane" included a broad smattering of Henny Youngman–style one-liners vis-à-vis Lenny Bruce. "Are you political, Lou? Political about what? Give me an issue, I'll give you a tissue and wipe my ass with it. We're just here to make out. You bend over and we'll put the head in. If you don't like it then we'll talk about it," he said. Lou was an equal-opportunity offender; nothing was immune. He then mocked Patti Smith's recently released *Radio Ethiopia*, which was also on Arista. "Are we being broadcast tonight? Fuck *Radio Ethiopia*, man. I'm radio Brooklyn! I ain't no snob, man."

On "I Wanna Be Black," Lou riffed on his Jewish roots. "And fuck up the Jews!" the backup singers sang, echoing one of the more tasteless lines in the song. "Hey—you're talking about my people. If I got a people. 'Hey, Lou, you got a people?' Oh, I got a people," he said. "So what's wrong with cheap, dirty jokes, man? Fuck you. I never said I was tasteful. I'm not tasteful." It was a performance that pushed the limits of satire, but Lou never recognized any limits.

In explaining the backstory to "Walk on the Wild Side," he also name-checked Gore Vidal, Mamie Van Doren, Dorothy Dean, and Norman Mailer, the controversial novelist who was also one of the founders of the *Village Voice*.

The *Voice* was the target of what was perhaps Lou's most ruthless jeremiad, a fiery riposte to the critics, singling out critic Robert Christgau, whose reviews in his *Consumer Guide* over the years had consistently given him mediocre grades. "What does Robert Christgau do in bed? Is he a toe fucker?" he said. "Can you imagine working for a fucking year and you got a B+ from an asshole in the *Village Voice*?"

Christgau, for his part, took the bait, as though Lou had planted an elaborate setup for a punch line that would once again ensnare the critics.

In his review of the resulting album, the critic wrote, "I thank Lou for pronouncing my name right," before issuing his grade: C+.

What *Metal Machine Music* did without words, *Take No Prisoners* did leaving no words unsaid. Some found it morally repugnant, others unlistenable; some appreciated its spare-no-excess novelty, while a select few Lou purists extolled the mere fact that he had the chutzpah to exceed the saturation point for bile and the leverage to release it on a major label. Lou wanted everyone to know that he really didn't care what they thought of him, no matter who they were. They could take him or leave him, but Lou would still be there, and he would take no prisoners. It was impossible to go to a Lou Reed show and leave without scorched ears. Outtakes from the album were readily available for a sequel, but this was no *Rock 'n' Roll Animal*. Lou had spent the previous five years extricating himself from the artist-patron hierarchy the record label relied on. Now Lou was beholden to no one—he had escaped the system from within it.

This approach led to *The Bells*, a transitional album of all new material that blended jazz, disco, and a more personal songwriting ethos, with no eye toward a potential market. Following a short European tour, Lou, the Everyman Band, and Don Cherry went to Wilster, a hamlet in West Germany, to record the album in binaural sound at Manfred Schunke's Delta Studios. The pastoral redoubt was a converted farmhouse that included a housing area for the artists with separate rooms, a communal dining area, and "a place to hang out and drink Johnnie Walker Black," Fogel recalls. "And then there was the recording facility, which was really high-tech, but it was in the middle of farm country."

It was there, in the middle of nowhere, that they made one of the great jazz-rock fusion albums. The eclectic compositions included "City Lights," with a nod to Charlie Chaplin, "Families," a meditation on the dysfunctional American nuclear family, and "The Bells," an atmospheric nine-minute free-jazz collective improvisation. No through-line was immediately apparent, but Lou evidently took his inspiration from the eponymous poem by Edgar Allan Poe. Lou later rerecorded it on *The Raven*, his 2003 Poe tribute. Poe's haunting poem employs jingling bells in a kind of swung trochaic meter to chronicle the pleasant "tintinnabulation" that portends an ominous reversal of fortune:

*From the molten-golden notes,*
*And all in tune,*
*What a liquid ditty floats*
*To the turtle-dove that listens, while she gloats*
*On the moon!*
*Oh, from out the sounding cells,*
*What a gush of euphony voluminously wells!*

Lou made sure it had plenty of molten notes. Nils Lofgren, in the midst of a solo career between the dissolution of Grin and joining the E Street Band, cowrote three songs, "Stupid Man," "City Lights," and "With You." The last featured improvised interpolations by Fogel and Cherry. "I did a little horn arrangement for myself and Don, and maybe there would be two beats at the end of the measure, and we were rehearsing the tune, Don was playing this free stuff in those two beats," Fogel says. "I looked at him and I go, 'What are you doing?' And he said, 'Whenever you get an opportunity to take it out, you've got to take it out.' So that's what we did."

The tonal reversal reached its intense peak on the title track, which developed during the sessions. "I was in the studio one night late, just playing the piano and playing part of 'The Bells' that I had composed, and Lou came into the studio and said, 'What's that?' and I explained it to him. And he said, 'Man, that's really great. I want to record that.'" Lou took Cherry's cue and took it as far out as he could, improvising some of the lyrics on the spot. He even asked Cherry to quote part of Ornette Coleman's "Lonely Woman" in the dense harmony of the title track's spectral intro.

On the resulting album, Lou foregrounded the intimate, reflective glimpse into his inner life with the black-and-white cover photo, shot by portraitist Garry Gross, showing Lou, sans makeup or elaborate costume, holding a hand mirror and looking directly at the camera in stark seriousness. Excepting "Disco Mystic," a spectral disco dirge with no lyrics other than the title repeated trancelike ad nauseam, the songs delved honestly into Lou's restless love-longing and myriad frustrations. As always with Lou, *The Bells* took risks, but the expressionistic lyrics dealt more overtly with Lou's persistent themes, though the album abandoned old standbys. Absent were any drug references; the focus was emotional, not the coping mechanisms for emotion that drove Lou to drink.

The time was ripe for a serious cross-genre experiment with free jazz from an artist on the more mainstream side of the aisle; the same month *The Bells* was released, Ornette Coleman was the musical guest on *Saturday Night Live*. In his fearless jazz-rock, Lou got at the heart of the matter, not diluting either genre, and though not everyone understood or appreciated Lou's foray deeper into art-rock, Lester Bangs, despite their disagreements, thought his career had finally reached an apotheosis. "*The Bells* isn't merely Lou Reed's best solo LP, it's great art," he wrote. "With *The Bells*, more than in *Street Hassle*, perhaps even more than in his work with the Velvet Underground, Lou Reed achieves his oft-stated ambition—to become a great writer, in the literary sense." Not that anyone's opinion mattered, but Bangs was right. Of course, the album didn't sell, but on *The Bells*, Lou was no longer playing the role of Lou Reed; he was himself, passionately, with the confidence and conviction to do it fully. After one of the longest periods of adolescent angst and soul-searching, Lou was passing into adulthood, but he had a few inner demons to slay before he got there.

He started by buying a house with Sylvia on a large parcel of land in remote Blairstown, New Jersey, a township of about five thousand in Warren County, situated right on the Pennsylvania border in the Kittatinny Valley along the Appalachian Trail. Lou was seventy miles from his fifteen-hundred-square-foot apartment on Christopher Street in the Village and only twenty miles from the Delaware Water Gap. He and Sylvia would spend three days a week in the city and the rest in Blairstown. Having recorded *The Bells* in a rural environment, the quintessential New York rocker had traded the biohazard of the East River for the rustic tranquility of Blair Creek. He still imported some urban pleasures into his countrified life under the expansive vaulted ceilings of his new home, decking it out with a game room that included a vintage jukebox as its centerpiece. But mostly, they were deep in the great outdoors. Lou and Sylvia lived next door to Camp No-Be-Bo-Sco, a Boy Scout camp where within a year, the slasher film *Friday the 13th* was shot, taking advantage of the eerie Appalachian calm. But the scariest thing to come to Blairstown in 1978 was Lou Reed.

In keeping with the positive vibes, Lou also reconnected with Richard Sigal, his childhood friend from Freeport, who was a sociology professor not far away at the County College of Morris. Lou had mostly severed ties with his hometown friends, but he was thrilled to have Sigal back in his life. When Sigal arrived in Blairstown, he discovered that Lou had replaced the drugs with a variety of other diversions, including an Atari. "Lou loved toys, and had a snowmobile, a pool table, a beautiful old jukebox filled with doo-wop forty-fives, lots of cutting-edge electronics, and a gun," Sigal recalls of his visits. "He told me one day he'd put a round through the living room floor when the gun went off accidently. When I asked him how it happened, he said, 'I didn't think there was one in the chamber.' Famous last words. He also had an 'earth toilet' instead of a septic system." In the winter, Sigal's children went skating on the pond on the property; he helped Lou cut down the perfect Christmas tree.

The change wasn't only social. Lou began expanding his sonic palate to include synthesized textures, but the rest of his band didn't follow him in that direction. Then he met guitarist Chuck Hammer. Lou had first heard his name prior to recording *The Bells*, but they didn't meet in person for months. Hammer had grown up on Long Island, and graduated in 1976 from the University at Buffalo, where he studied with saxophonist Archie Shepp. After graduating, Hammer moved to Santa Barbara with a girlfriend, and began performing on the local scene, but he had loftier ambitions. He had compiled a mental bucket list of artists he wanted to play with, and Lou and David Bowie topped it. On a visit to New York, he decided that the only way it would ever happen would be if he asked; fortune favored the bold.

"I'm walking around Fifty-Seventh Street, and I saw Arista Records, and I just had a brainstorm," Hammer recalls. He wouldn't wait to meet Lou in an elevator, an opportunity that would probably never come. Like Sylvia had done, Hammer opted for the written overture. So he ventured into the Arista offices to write Lou a letter. "They said, 'You can't write a letter to Lou Reed here, but you can go to his manager, Eric Kronfeld, and write a letter,'" Hammer recalls. He walked down to Kronfeld's Times Square office in the imposing Paramount Building on Broadway, where he met Kronfeld's receptionist, who gave him a pad and allowed him to write from the stairwell. "I told him that I thought *Berlin* was a masterpiece, that I loved his music, and I wanted to work with him," Hammer says. "I also told him I was the best unknown guitarist in the country." Hammer left his friend's phone number in New York, thinking Lou would never bother to make a long distance call to an anonymous guitar player, especially when he wasn't looking for one, and left. He didn't expect to ever get a response.

A week later, Hammer's friend called with the news. "My friend said, 'Are you sitting down?' I said, 'No. Do I need to be?' She said, 'Yes. Sit down. Lou Reed just called here looking for you; he said he has a gig he wants to talk to you about,'" Hammer says. When he called Lou, he got his answering machine. "I had never seen an answering machine. The very first answering machine I ever spoke to was Lou Reed's. And his message said, 'Hi, this is Radio Free Brooklyn. Leave a message.'"

Hammer left a brief message, but his roommate insisted he call back with something more forceful. "So I set up my Polytone 102 and my Ibanez hollow-body, and I said, 'It's Chuck again. There's something I forgot to say,' and I just went for it. I played for about a minute. I went out for a beer, came back, and the phone was ringing," he says. "I picked it up and it was Lou Reed. And that was the moment where everything in my life shifted. Completely."

Lou then conducted a preliminary interview. Having been subjected to so many, he kept it short, but Hammer still knew that one slip of the tongue could sink him. "The first question he asked me was, 'Do you take drugs?' I said no. The second question was, 'How far back do you go with my music?' I said, 'I know about the Velvet Underground, but really *Transformer*.' Lou said, 'Good.' He said, 'What kind of music are you playing now?' I said, 'Disco.'" With the Bee Gees' soundtrack to *Saturday Night Fever* dominating the charts, disco was in its heyday, but this was Lou Reed. Little did Hammer know, Lou was working on his own take on disco, which he was about to record in Germany.

Nevertheless, Lou agreed to audition Hammer, provided he abide by several ground rules. "The ground rules were that I come to his apartment at the specified time on Christopher Street. He'd let me in and he would show me where to set up, and I'd set up and I'd play for twenty minutes. After twenty minutes, if he didn't come into the room, I had to pack up and leave, because he didn't want to be in a position to reject me." In November, Hammer promptly sold his Volkswagen for $600 and bought a one-way ticket to New York for the audition. "I set up, playing and playing and playing, doing *Street Hassle*, and Lou Reed's not coming into the room. So twenty minutes go by," he says. But he kept on playing. "I say, 'Fuck this, I'm just going to play something that I wrote.' So I play this thing that has a slightly distorted sound, and Lou comes walking in." Lou didn't want to hear himself echoed back; he wanted to hear Chuck. "He didn't want to hear any riffs, any pre-worked-out things. He just wanted real musicianship, and he demanded that every moment that I worked with him."

Next, Lou asked him for twenty dollars for a taxi to the string of music stores on Forty-Eighth Street. Lou had no cash on hand and wanted to take Chuck to one particular store to show him that he had a custom-made guitar being built that could replicate the texture and tone Chuck was already achieving. With the synthesized sound Lou aimed for on *The Bells*, he wasn't appropriating Chuck's style—Chuck had merely beaten him there. Having covered his creative liability at Chuck's expense, they went back to Lou's apartment and jammed for a while. But Lou didn't hire him. He flew to Germany to record *The Bells*, and without the wherewithal to buy a ticket back to California, Chuck stayed in New York, crashing in a friend's apartment in Queens.

Before long, Hammer had established himself on the scene, though, and even jammed with John Cale, but he continued calling Lou almost daily. Sometimes a contractor doing work on Lou's apartment would pick up, but Lou was gone. As the frost of New York winter crept in, the suspense was killing him. Then one day in late January, Lou answered the phone. He told Hammer to have his manager arrange for him to pick up a Roland guitar synthesizer Lou stored at a sound studio on the Bowery, and familiarize himself with the instrument—it had only been one year since Roland had manufactured the GR-500, its first guitar synthesizer. Lou told Chuck that after that, he should jam with several of the band members before coming to the house in Blairstown for a rehearsal for the *Bells* tour. He had a month to prepare, and he spent the time buffing up on as much of Lou's catalog as he could, spending seventeen hours transcribing and transposing the string arrangement on "Sad Song" for guitar.

While Hammer prepared for his audition, in late January, Lou guest-hosted *Radio, Radio* on WPIX-FM, a local station that sometimes broadcasted live sets at CBGB. It had been what felt like eons since he hosted *Excursions on a Wobbly Rail* at Syracuse, but Lou still had a knack for the medium and a soft spot for the bygone era of AM radio when Alan Freed filled the airwaves with the sound of doo-wop. As unlikely as it seemed that Lou would spin golden oldies, he nurtured a deep-seated love of certain strains of pop. Drawing from his own collection, which he carted with him to the studio, Lou began with "Want Ads" by Honey Cone and segued into Crazy Elephant's "Gimme Gimme Good Lovin'," which Lou claimed "contains the best guitar solo. The man was years ahead." He followed that with Sister Sookie, the Turbans, the Doves, the Ronettes, and lots of Dion and the

Belmonts. "Wow. Wow!" Lou exclaimed. "Really, really. I mean, consider." After all these years, he was still a doo-wop fanatic. "I always thought this music was so romantic," he said. "I get tears in my eyes. I used to be one of those people—I knew the color of the labels. I went all through college, and I can't remember very much from then, but I can recite you rock and roll lyrics. My 'To be or not to be' was probably written by the Doves."

Lou took time to play material from *The Bells* as well. "I am so tired of reading reviews that say, 'Reed's inept lead guitar playing,'" he said. "I don't care if it's inept! What do I care if it's inept? I didn't say it was ept. Jesus, man!" By all signs, Lou was well aware of his mixed reviews. "I make records for me," he quipped. "A bad review from *Rolling Stone* is proof to me that I'm still alive." Then Lou waxed nostalgic about college ROTC; it was a desultory ramble as he drifted back to the doo-wop era. "I was a platoon leader. Can you picture this? I marched them into a fence," Lou said. "I said, 'Let me out.' They put me in volleyball. Then I developed aquaphobia because I failed the swimming test."

Lou continued vamping until John Cale showed up in the studio. "Cale! Grab a seat, John," he said. "Ladies and gentlemen, John Cale has joined Lou Reed for an on-the-air reunion in the middle of New York, Welsh city of the heart." Whatever acrimony lingered between them felt largely dispelled as they hammed it up. After playing Al Green's buoyant "I Feel Good" from *The Belle Album* opposite "It Was a Pleasure Then," a doleful track from Nico's *Chelsea Girl* cowritten by Nico, Lou, and John, the voluble guest host asked Cale a few pointed questions.

"Do you think drugs corrupt children, John?" Lou said.

"No, I think it just pacifies them."

"I think it stimulates them. Well, some people's pacification is a stimulation." Their spirits were high, but anyone expecting a reunion would have to wait a decade.

Meanwhile, Chuck had spent the month woodshedding as much as possible, and as he headed to the most nerve-wracking audition of his life, Lou only added to his anxiety. "I took a Greyhound bus to Blairstown, and when I got off the bus, Lou was waiting there in an open-back jeep," Hammer says. "Lou floors the car full-speed, drives a hundred yards, and slams on the brakes—decides that we're going to stop in the only saloon in Blairstown." At the bar, Lou placed "a typical order, four Scotches and a beer," Hammer says. Only Hammer didn't drink. "I finished maybe one

Scotch and Lou finished the rest of my Scotches, and we're going to his house and we're driving on the wrong side of the road."

At the house, Chuck met Sylvia and the rest of the band—Rachel was even there to return some final items that belonged to Lou. Lou wasted no time with the audition, calling "Sad Song" first. "He turns around, looks at me, and he says, 'You're everything you said you were.' And so at that point I knew I got the gig," Hammer says. The strain of Rachel's presence was kept to a minimum; it was mostly amicable, and Lou was drunk enough that he could easily handle the situation. "Rachel was a beautiful girl, tall and dressed in leather, and Sylvia was standing next to her. At the first break, Rachel comes up to the stage, and she hands him a leather bag. She was returning some of his things," Hammer recalls. "He had already moved on emotionally, because the way she looked that day, she was there to stun. That was the last time anyone saw her on the scene."

With the addition of Hammer, Lou was ready to go on tour with *The Bells*. "My approach was to really play the chords primarily and orchestrate inversions," Hammer says. "Every one of us was a specialist in certain areas. I understand the voicings and the rhythm. Lou chopped the rhythm up," Hammer says, referring to Lou's inchoate rhythm guitar playing. "When I had the records, I didn't understand that he was trying to shake the music up and give it teeth."

At the end of March, they played their first show in Stockholm. Lou was drinking heavily. "Every three days, he went through two bottles of Scotch," Hammer says. "On his own." Two weeks later, at the three-thousand-seat Stadthalle in Offenbach, Germany, Lou caused yet another riot. "After the first section of the set, Lou would do what we'd call the *Berlin* suite. 'Men of Good Fortune,' 'Sad Song,' 'Caroline Says II,' 'The Kids,' and sometimes 'The Bed,'" Hammer says. "Lou insisted on absolute silence. He said, 'If you're not quiet, I'm gonna leave and I'll come back in ten minutes and see if you're quiet then.'" So like a harsh disciplinarian, Lou actually left the stage. When he returned, he faced a heckler, whom Lou had the spotlight technician follow until security officials ejected him.

"He cared about the music to the point where he was willing to risk a riot for quiet so he could play it," Hammer says. But Lou wouldn't get that golden silence. "It was a very deep stage, and out of the corner of my eye, I see a girl come up the stairs from the edge of the stage," Hammer says. The woman lunged at Lou, but at the last second, he sidestepped her. "She fell facedown. He proceeded to drag her across a twenty-foot stage by her hair. You don't go on Lou Reed's stage. Anyway, that's when the riot erupted." People started throwing chairs. "We ran for our lives."

In the dressing room where they hid, the police came, ostensibly to check on their safety, but in actuality to arrest Lou for disturbing the peace. "He was scared, and they actually took him to a jail." Lou was given a drug test, which he miraculously passed, and after spending the night in a German prison, was released on bail the next day. Nevertheless, they figured they'd overstayed their welcome in Germany.

Four days later, on April 10, after a show at the Hammersmith Odeon in London, Lou had one of his most infamous encounters with David Bowie. "We have our sound check and we meet David and we ride back to the hotel on the bus to change," Fogel recalls. "And Lou's going, 'Isn't David a great guy?' 'Yeah, David's a great guy.' 'Really a terrific guy?' 'Really a terrific guy.'"

That night, the British audience was half hoping for the Velvet Underground, the band that inspired the Sex Pistols, or at least *Transformer*-era Lou, not the discordant clangor of *The Bells*. From the glam rock period, the sartorial shift was radical: Lou was wearing jeans and a black vest. But there was only one audience member who Lou wanted to please—Bowie.

"Lou was drunk at the Hammersmith Odeon," Hammer says. During a solo, Hammer spotted Bowie, wearing a Japanese outfit with a big cross emblazoned across it. When the set ended, they exited the stage to meet Bowie, who performed the encore with them. After the show, Lou, Bowie, and their joint entourage went out for Chinese at the Rendezvous, part of a chain of upscale Chinese restaurants. Rock stars rarely frequented the Rendezvous; opened several years earlier, the chain had created a blue ocean market by adapting Chinese cuisine for a genteel British crowd. So what few customers were there for a late-night egg roll could not help but notice when Lou and his entourage, including an enormous man in a cowboy hat, marched into the restaurant. High on the adrenaline rush and ecstatic over his reunion with Bowie, Lou immediately ordered celebratory bottles of Dom Pérignon. Hammer told Bowie how much he had influenced him, and Bowie asked him to collaborate on his next album, *Scary Monsters*; it appeared by all signs that the night was going smoothly.

They began to reminisce, arms around each other's shoulders, almost manic, when Lou's British press coordinator, Howard Harding, walked in with two journalists, Allan Jones and Giovanni Dadamo. So whatever happened next would have a captive audience.

Ostensibly, in a few short minutes, it appeared that the two rock giants might work together again. Then, as Lou asked David about the possibility of Bowie producing his next album, out of nowhere, the celebration curdled like a lemon slice in a glass of milk.

Bowie sat in stony silence, pondering how to respond. Lou stared at him expectantly, waiting for any sign of affirmation. He didn't need Bowie, but he wanted him. "If you clean up your act," Bowie said coolly. Lou sat there seething, breathing heavily.

"Don't you ever say that to me," Lou hissed. "Don't you ever!"

He reached across the table and grabbed Bowie by the lapel of his shirt and smacked him hard on the back of the head with the wrath of a man possessed, returning the unchecked assault on his ego with blunt-force trauma that somehow felt commensurate. "Don't you ever fucking say that to me!" he wailed.

Lou apologized, and conversation resumed. They hugged, then kissed; the diplomatic gaffe had been forgiven. But three minutes later, Lou asked Bowie about working together again.

The Thin White Duke sat motionless, unflinching. "If you clean up your act."

Lou began sweating profusely, in a pugilistic trance as an unholy rage welled up inside of him. "I thought I told you," he said, grabbing Bowie by the shirt again, "never to say that!"

He leapt up and dragged Bowie across the table, knocking the piled plates to the floor, half-eaten bits of food flying everywhere amid the melee. He smacked the back of his head, pummeling Bowie, slapping him, beating the impudence out of the only man with the audacity to impugn his character to his face.

A large hand came down, pulling Lou back. Then another. It was Moose, hoisting him aloft and hauling him away from the oval-shaped table as he struggled to break free and snuff out Bowie's impassive voice, which was still ringing in his head. Up he went, writhing in Moose's mammoth arms, leaving behind him a trail of glass shards as he floated on past the caustic din and into the quiet night.

Back at the hotel, they calmed their nerves with a nightcap. "We might have been doing some drinking, and Lou passed out on the couch. He was dead out," Fogel says. Then, at three in the morning came a knock on the door. "I open the door, and it's David Bowie and his bodyguard, and he wants to fight Lou," Fogel says. Well, Lou is passed out on the couch. He's comatose. There's no waking this guy, not that he'd want to wake up and fight David Bowie anyway. David had no choice, so he left."

For the American leg of the tour, the shows captured the unpredictable intensity of the Bowie incident—Don Cherry joined them for some—but Lou's erratic behavior persisted. Nevertheless, he was always supportive of his band. "He taped everything. If you had a hot night, at the airport he flipped you a tape. I have twelve of those unreleased tapes," Hammer says. One of those nights was at the Roxy in April. "We're in the middle of 'I'm Waiting for the Man.' He says, 'Chuck!' I hit the pedal and went ballistic. After the solo, he couldn't sing. He had to vamp through a whole verse and a chorus before the crowd let him sing," Hammer says. In San Francisco, Lou brought Hammer to his room after the show. "He said, 'You hear this solo you took? You levitated the room.' That is why I love Lou Reed. He gave me my life as an artist."

But Lou's electric stage presence had a dark side. In June, Clive Davis went to see Lou play the Bottom Line. Lou interrupted the middle of his set to have what he later described as a business discussion from the stage with the head of Arista about the lackluster publicity push for *The Bells*. Disco's death knell had already sounded, and the title track would never make it on commercial stations. "Here, this is for you, Clive," he said. "Where's the money, Clive? How come I don't hear my album on the radio?" Lou had to issue a press release apologizing for the outburst, but the writing was on the wall that his time at Arista would be short-lived.

At the end of the summer of 1979, Don Cherry asked the Everyman Band to accompany him on a ten-week tour of Europe, and with the logistics of the *Bells* tour still up in the air, they agreed. Fogel wouldn't rejoin the band after that; the rest of the Everyman Band continued with Lou, but not for long. Soon, they would record two albums for ECM under their own name. But as the leaves began to fall, the same restless energy that led Lou to quit the Velvets had already set the scene for another dramatic departure.

When the tour details were ironed out, Lou prepared for a full-contact assault on Europe at a September show at Columbia University, where he decided to externalize his feelings by smashing as much equipment onstage as he could get his hands on. On short notice, he hired versatile session drummer Doane Perry, later a member of Jethro Tull, to fill in for Michael Suchorsky, who was on tour with the Everyman Band and Don Cherry. At Columbia, the McMillan Theatre only accommodated seven hundred people, and students from all over the campus clamored to get standing-room-only tickets for Lou's take-no-prisoners intoxicated binge. One of them was Suzanne Vega, then an underclassman at Barnard, up the block from Tom's Diner; it was Vega's first rock show. "Suddenly it hit me that I could write about things I had experienced without softening up the edges or apologizing for it or putting it in a nice package necessarily," Vega recalled in the *Los Angeles Times.*

That doesn't mean the show was a pleasant experience—it was more like carnage. "He wrecked two guitars and he was about to wreck a third one, and I waved him back," Hammer says. "He wrecked his own guitar, and he took Stuart's guitar from him onstage during a song, wrecked it, then two songs later, looked at my Roland, which was his Roland at the time, and he was coming towards me onstage, and I just looked at him. This is what was going on onstage. It was great." Lou destroyed microphones, flung lit cigarettes at the audience, and peppered the set with more obscenities than usual. As marijuana smoke wafted through the crowd, he reminded the collegial audience that he had at one point considered applying to the Columbia University's Graduate School of Journalism. Needless to say, as he broke every rule of decorum that sustained Ivy League elitism, Lou was a long way from J-school. He closed the show with "Heroin," using it as an ironic antidrug PSA. He closed with an inspirational address. "Thank God that I just don't care. If I did care, I'd be driving a Dodge in Minnesota. Baby, can't I drive your car?" he deadpanned. "I guess I just don't know." He was drunk and on a bender, but he still had wisdom to impart. And after all the years on the road, he had the wisdom to realize that he still just didn't know.

Yet that was about to change. Lou spent October 1979 touring Europe, and when he came back, scheduled three shows at the Bottom Line during Christmas week. Meanwhile, as the global oil crisis and Iran hostage situation unfolded while Carter's presidency came to a close, Lou began feeling uncharacteristically patriotic. Inspired by Hendrix's *Rainbow Bridge,* he performed "The Star-Spangled Banner." Despite his nihilistic attitude and religious background, Lou began experiencing odd feelings of beatific compassion that could only be described as the Christmas spirit. It was as though he'd seen Marley's ghost, or some divine force that warmed his heart and impelled him to sing Irving Berlin's "White Christmas," embellishing it with a yuletide accent of jingle bells.

On Christmas Eve, Lou was cheerful; by the December 26 show, he was giddy. In a rare show of gratitude, he even thanked the audience for celebrating the holiday season with him, and debuted a new song—"Love Is Here to Stay"—a love-conquers-all anthem about an unlikely couple:

> *He likes Edgar Allan Poe, and she's into Mean Joe Greene*
> *She thinks eating meat's disgusting; he likes hot dogs*
> *She's into gestalt therapy, while est and the rest just make*
>     *him ill*
> *But love is here to stay*

Then Lou made an announcement—he was engaged to Sylvia. Miraculously, he had survived the 1970s unscathed, for the most part, and he was in love again. He also had to confront a new sensation he had not had in a long time, possibly ever. He was happy.

# PART IV
# SET THE TWILIGHT REELING

# 22

It was Valentine's Day 1980, and Lou was getting married. There was no wedding announcement, no chapel booked, no reason for a bachelor party. Despite pretensions of temperance, Lou had cultivated a reputation for decadence in the press, but this wedding was to be free of ostentation—Lou was starting off the decade as a minimalist. Though there was a cake, the signs and signifiers of glam rock and the excesses of his checkered past were planted firmly in the rearview; as he tied the knot with twenty-four-year-old Sylvia, Lou even wore a suit. The ceremony took place on a frigid Thursday with the guests crammed into Lou's apartment on Christopher Street, directly above the Stonewall Inn in Sheridan Square. As weddings generally go, the event hosted unlikely company; in this disparate group, Lisa Robinson found common ground with Sidney Reed. Following the ceremony, the modest reception was held around the block at One If by Land, Two If by Sea, a tasteful restaurant on Barrow Street in the Village.

For Lou, the 1970s had been characterized by speed, but he had resolved, with the influence of Sylvia, to finally slow down. It was time for the mild side.

Albums, tours, and side projects would be undertaken solely at Lou's discretion, on his terms. So even when Paul Simon called to offer Lou a role in *One-Trick Pony*, his upcoming starring vehicle with Warner Bros., Lou had to hear about what the casting commitment entailed before finally agreeing. Simon wanted to cast against type—the Lovin' Spoonful, the B-52s, and drummer Steve Gadd would all showcase their musical talents—but in Robert M. Young's film about artistic integrity butting heads with commercial compromise in the record industry, Lou would never play a note.

Instead, Lou was cast as Steve Kunelian, a major label producer without any taste or artistry, a soulless cipher anathema to everything Lou stood for.

In his scenes, Simon's Jonah Levin, a thinly veiled version of himself, contends with Kunelian's propensity for pop overproduction when an officious, Clive Davis–like executive played by Rip Torn, who introduces the would-be Phil Spector as "very Top 40 oriented," insists that they collaborate on "Ace in the Hole." In the crisis point of the film, Kunelian decides to "open it up texturally" by adding strings, David Sanborn's saxophone, and background vocals, layered in at the recording studio over the course of a montage until the final product no longer resembles the original track. Playing the part with expressionless ferocity, Lou's stoic portrayal recalls a nightmare version of "Walk on the Wild Side," channeling a role he perhaps could have played in real life had he continued at Pickwick and risen up the ranks.

The film coincided with a major turning point in Lou's career; having nearly lost it completely in the preceding decade, in the 1980s, Lou was adamant about exerting control. He signified this shift by gradually distancing himself from the vices and viceroys at his throat—physically, emotionally, and spiritually. After marrying Sylvia, who finally gave him a sense of emotional stability, he moved as far away from the city as possible within a commutable distance, and even began studying tai chi. The '70s had been a series of death-defying acts, and Lou knew that something had to give.

To focus on his spiritual balance, Lou sought out kung fu master Leung Shum, a practitioner of Wu style tai chi chuan, an ancient branch of the internal Chinese martial arts that develops the chi energy source through continuous motion, disciplined circular movements, and mindfulness training. He found solace in a Suzuki motorcycle. "I read *Zen and the Art of Motorcycle Maintenance* and took it apart," Lou said, "and then I couldn't get it back together. Now I'm proud just to take out and recharge the battery without killing myself." As Sylvia enrolled in creative writing classes at Sarah Lawrence College, Lou began dabbling in biofeedback therapy. With his erstwhile caged beast persona characterized by manic bursts and radical mood swings, the new Lou could even control his heartbeat.

Kicking off this departure from the past, Lou also got away from it all immediately following the nuptials. As part of his honeymoon with Sylvia, the newlyweds escaped the deep freeze of New York winter by spending a month recording Lou's next album, *Growing Up in Public*, at Beatles producer George Martin's newly opened AIR Studios in sunny Montserrat, a small Caribbean island with an active volcano. Martin had invested in a state-of-the-art sound board, and Lou decided to sacrifice the binaural technique used for previous releases in favor of the crisp recording quality AIR promised; its tropical locale, compared to his previous experiences in rural Germany, only sweetened the deal.

Splitting his time between lounging at the beachy resort and logging time in the studio, Lou reflected his enlightened perspective with inward-looking lyrics and a psychoanalytic bent. The album brought Freudian analysis, neurosis, and substance abuse to the foreground with an erudite vernacular and emotional honesty that Lou had previously kept ambiguous through an imagistic poetic style. Lou later decided to include a lyric sheet in the liner notes, abandoning a fidelity to rock formalism that would consider detaching the music from the lyrics verboten. Yet on *Growing Up in Public*, Lou concentrated primarily on the page, as rock's longest-standing teenager worked out his final bouts of adolescent angst. In Montserrat, Lou was taking a vacation from the man he used to be, but he was also becoming someone else—maybe someone good.

As his perspective deepened into adulthood, the effects of the transition were manifested in the album's disjointed quality. Michael Fonfara handled most of the music—he took a cowriter credit on all the tracks—freeing up Lou to concentrate on the lyrics. Without Fogel to temper Fonfara's synth-pop proclivities with jazz harmony, and as a result of this collaboration style, a rock musical sensibility permeated the recording. "Lou flipped, and the flip happened at *Growing Up in Public*," says Hammer. "Lou was losing his record contract with Arista. He needed a hit, and Michael was trying to get a commercial band off the ground. So he worked on the songs, and Lou wrote these lyrics that didn't fit. They were narrative to synthpop."

The lyrics to the title track epitomized Lou's transition—"A Prince Hamlet caught in the middle between reason and instinct"—as the album balanced self-awareness and craft with improvisation. In what was a largely rocky farewell to the libidinous, neurotic, unpredictable id and ego at play in his back catalog, Lou still indulged in guilty pleasures of the past. "Some of the songs were written down there, drunk at the pool, certainly 'The Power of Positive Drinking,'" Hammer recalls. "He picked up my '61 Strat in Montserrat, said 'Can I borrow that?' We were sitting there in the studio, and he wrote 'Think It Over' right there on that guitar and then he showed me exactly the part he wanted me to play." These spontaneous creations allowed Lou the dual advantage of an isolated space to map out his artistic future while running interference against any preproduction commentary from the label.

"I mastered the art of recording known as 'capture the spontaneous moment and leave it at that,'" Lou later recalled to Dave DiMartino. "You go into the studio with zero, write it on the spot, make the lyrics up as the tape's running, and that's it. And then you learn the record afterwards." For Lou, albums served as the script for the tours; after recording, the band would have to get off book. But at the album stage, contrary to the sterile production process some labels favored, Lou strove to capture a glimmer of spontaneous humanity. "What I wanna get on my records, since everybody else is so slick and dull, is that . . . moment."

On *Growing Up in Public*, though, the nature of that moment shifted. "I think he kicked open a door to the phase that continued for the rest of his life," Hammer says. Many viewed the album as a roman à clef, but the lyrics were only tangentially autobiographical, diminishing certain qualities and heightening others in a poetic effort to underscore persistent themes that reflected Lou's artistic journey. The bildungsroman structure opened with "How Do You Speak to an Angel," connecting an Oedipal complex with romantic difficulties, embodied by the character's anxiety in front of the titular angel—"How do you speak to the prettiest girl?" He elevated his familial conflict in "My Old Man," detailing a father who beat his mother; though this in fact didn't happen, it condensed Lou's complex relationship with his father from idolization to alienation into one potent image.

"If I was restricted to me, it'd get very dull for me. I create a character— and that may or may not apply to me," Lou said. "Whether my mother's dead or not really doesn't matter, it's the attitude I'm interested in. I wanted to express a view, so I manipulated the events to justify the view."

As much as Lou wrote *Growing Up in Public* in the afterglow of his recent marriage with an alacrity that he rarely matched, and sang predominantly in a major key that reflected a newfound optimism, his lyrics were not lacking in gravitas. He dedicated "Think It Over" to Sylvia, inspired by their recent engagement and subsequent marriage. In the song, the woman takes an impetuous proposal cautiously, opting to "think it over" instead of rushing into things. Lou explicitly quotes *Annie Hall*—Diane Keaton's "la-dee-dah"—to evoke a bittersweet nostalgia for irretrievably lost romantic moments, not that he would cast himself as Alvy Singer. "I thought I had to stick that in a song, 'cause that's too good just to leave in a movie," Lou said.

The closing track, "Teach the Gifted Children," revolves around a plagal cadence and insouciant backbeat, employing vivid imagery to juxtapose the fraught upbringing depicted throughout the rest of the album with the "cool and cleansing water" of another parenting model. Unlike the folksy aphorisms of Crosby, Stills & Nash, Lou finds life lessons in a different branch of Americana. Lou references Al Green's "Take Me to the River," a hit for the Talking Heads, but Lou's version, with soulful background vocals, harks back unmistakably to the gospel pulse of the original. An immersion in Green's river—Lou and Sylvia had seen him live—was Lou's version of a baptism.

"His religion was music, if he had one," Sylvia later recalled. "That was as close to spirituality as I think Lou would ever own up to. That was a religious experience, seeing Al Green."

Though the album didn't sell well, Nick Kent, a longtime chronicler of Lou's peaks and valleys whom Lou apparently loathed, lauded it as a career pinnacle. "*Growing Up in Public* is probably the best piece of work Lou Reed has ever been involved in," Kent wrote in *New Musical Express*. "All human life is there, including yours and mine."

Yet no amount of hyperbole could convince the Arista brass to push it harder. Nevertheless, for the first time in his career, Lou and the label were in lockstep—it was time to abandon his feverish pace and take a long-overdue break from recording.

The tour pressed on, though. Lou began the *Growing Up in Public* tour in the Midwest, followed by Cleveland and a series of shows at the Bottom Line. In early June, Lou jokingly announced his candidacy for president in the 1980 election, running for the Rock and Roll Party, with his band as cabinet. Reagan wouldn't be officially nominated for another month, but Lou promised to declare war on California, where the future president was governor. A rock star with no political experience running on an independent ticket just might have stood a better chance against a staunchly Republican Hollywood actor than the incumbent peanut farmer, but Lou, who could lie about his past but not his ideas, left politics to the politicians. As the election shuttled forward, Lou and the band departed for Europe.

Lou planned on retiring from touring after one last hurrah. Following a five-year boycott of Italy, Lou returned for what he figured would be a final bow. "We were playing for giant places in Europe. Very rarely do I remember playing for less than ten thousand people," Hammer recalls. In Europe, where

Lou had a huge following, they would fill fifty-thousand-person stadiums. "Fifty thousand people in the stadium, all holding lighters," says Hammer. "Lou looked up at that audience and he said he couldn't believe where it went for him. He expressed a sense of awe. And to play 'Vicious' in front of fifty thousand Italian fans at full volume in a stadium, you never recover. That's all I can say. It's not like you go back to your life and everything's great."

After a nonstop month of touring, including one last Communist riot in Madrid, Lou returned to New York for a quiet summer. The band played a string of shows on the West Coast in September, still maintaining a soaring energy level, but Lou had warmed to the idea of a long hiatus. He had signed up to produce Hammer's debut solo record for RCA, but decided capriciously to collapse the project. For Lou, it was a time of great renunciation.

The epiphany came at the Riviera Café, where years earlier he had made the big decision to begin dissolving the Velvets. Regarding his current band, Lou had the nagging foreknowledge and sudden self-awareness one gets when it becomes clear that a working relationship has reached a tipping point, but no one is ready to pull the plug.

"I didn't really know it yet, but the band was already breaking up," Hammer recalls. "I was in the bar with him, and what comes on the juke-box—'Walk on the Wild Side.' I didn't put it on; he didn't put it on. We were silent at the table, both listening, and I'm in the ultimate surreal moment. Lou looks up when the song ends and the saxophone solo came on, and he said something very revealing. He said, 'I can't believe how naive my voice sounds.' Then we sat there and I just didn't say anything. That was a turning point for Lou."

Two weeks after Reagan's election, Lou played his final show with the *Growing Up in Public* band, an uneventful date at the Aquarius Theatre in Los Angeles. Lou had to get off the road or risk death by rock; within the past year, Sid Vicious, Ian Curtis of Joy Division, and John Bonham had all died of drug overdose or suicide. The following month, John Lennon would be assassinated.

Not only was Lou disbanding the group, he decided he was retiring permanently from touring. The Age of Aquarius was over, not that Lou had ever been part of it, supplanted by the age of cocaine, rampant deregulation, and malignant narcissism. With greed at an all-time high, Lou was retreating into a cocoon of temperance and altruism in his rural sanctuary. Yet a voice inside him screamed that nothing in this world is permanent, and that one day, when the time was right, he would be back to reclaim the throne from any unlawful usurpers. Continuing in the path of Siddhartha, Lou had decided to abjure the life of hedonism for a more ascetic existence in New Jersey. He became more introspective, less proactive; more composed, less tempestuous; more content, less restless. Free from the fetters of record label obligations, the pressure to produce the next album, and the emotional drain of constant touring, at the dawn of 1981, Lou seriously contemplated entering a twelve-step program. It was as though he no longer needed all the crutches to get through the day. Lou had finally found his mainline.

After the *Growing Up in Public* tour concluded, Lou recorded one more track with the *Growing Up in Public* band—"My Name Is Mok," composed for the animated feature film *Rock & Rule*, produced by Canadian animation studio Nelvana. The film's plot concerned an aging rock star, Mok, in search of the perfect voice to summon a powerful being from another dimension, and included music from Debbie Harry, Iggy Pop, and Cheap Trick. Though a separate voice actor was hired, Lou provided Mok's singing voice, recording the track at RCA Studios with Sean Fullan, a young engineer who had just recently moved to the city.

Following that project, though, Lou needed a break. He had been on the road almost continuously for the better part of a decade, spending much of that time surviving on booze, speed, and sleepless nights. He was almost forty, and still maintaining an indefatigable pace that would leave many people half his age exhausted after a week.

"He understood he needed to take a break for his health," Sylvia recalled. "We spent about a year and a half in one place, in a country house, but other than that, working was incredibly important to him. It was the focus of his life, and so it became constant work. He was very perfectionistic and very insistent on being good at what he did, and that meant working at it and working very hard, and anyone who ever worked with him would know that."

For the rest of 1981, Lou stopped touring and turned his attention inward. He joined Alcoholics Anonymous and Narcotics Anonymous—there were specialized rock 'n' roll meetings that met in the Village—and committed himself to a life of sobriety. Blairstown was isolated enough to keep him honest. So Lou began the twelve-step program: he admitted he was "powerless over alcohol," "came to believe that a Power greater than ourselves could restore us to sanity," and "made a decision to turn our will and our lives over to the care of God as we understood Him." Well, Lou only worshipped one God, but he suddenly realized that he didn't need drugs to rock.

In spring 1981 Lester Bangs unexpectedly showed up at an AA meeting with Jim Fouratt, a gay rights activist who was active on the rock scene. Lester had left Detroit for New York in 1976, and became one of the rare rock critics who had started a band himself. *Jook Savages on the Brazos*, released by Lester Bangs and the Delinquents, was notable for a mix of rockabilly, punk messiness, and bleak nihilism, with tracks like "Life Is Not Worth Living (But Suicide Is a Waste of Time)" and "Accidents of God." Lester and Lou maintained their grudge, but it seemed their final showdown would be a silent one.

Despite their antagonistic history, Lou now had an ally in the program. "How dare you be here—you're the reason I took heroin!" one group member screamed at Lou, Fouratt later recalled in *Let It Blurt: The Life and Times of Lester Bangs*. By this time, though, Lou understood more palpably that for all that time he wasn't promoting drug use, but writing about the emotional turmoil and failure to cope that led to obliteration by alcohol.

On the road to sobriety, Lou began keeping a compositional journal, but he wanted a new band to do justice to his struggle through rehab. First, he contacted Doane Perry, who had learned all of Lou's material in one rehearsal for the Columbia show, which was conducive to his intentions for the next album. Lou didn't know what it would be, other than that it would be unpredictable. Then Lou met Robert Quine, a friend of Lester's, when Sylvia took him to hear Richard Hell and the Voidoids at CBGB. Instantly, he heard the guitar sound he'd been looking for. After the show, Lou approached the stage.

"You're a fucking great guitar player," Lou said. He had no recollection of Quine, who had followed the Velvets across the country years earlier—in 1969, when he was in law school. They were the same age, and the nondescript balding man in sunglasses didn't look familiar to Lou. Lou didn't have anything nice to say about the Voidoids as a whole but, in his own curmudgeonly way, had nothing but faint praise for Quine, an acolyte of Mickey Baker and Charlie Christian who sounded more like Albert Ayler with a Stratocaster and a Marshall amp. Quine had logged untold hours in the Bay Area dropping acid and spinning John Coltrane's *Ascension* until he reached a point of visionary clarity. He also had a peerless hunger for the music, having spent three years writing tax law for textbook publishers Prentice Hall. He quit his day job and never looked back. No one played like Bob Quine.

In the middle of their first meeting, Quine, who was one of the more inscrutable guitarists ever to pass through CBGB, lost focus for a moment. "Goddamn it, you look me in the eye when I'm talking to you, or so help me God I'll smash you in the face," Lou said. From Lou, they were terms of endearment. Faced with the prospect of playing with one of his greatest influences, Quine snapped to attention. He agreed to join Lou's band on one condition—that Lou start playing guitar again. From that moment, Quine and Lou were tuned in to the same frequency.

All Lou needed was a bass player to round out his stripped-down new sound. Lou's manager called Fernando Saunders, a straitlaced Detroit native who had been playing with Jeff Beck, Eric Clapton, and Steve Winwood. Saunders also had a jazz background and a lithe fretless bass sound that appealed to Lou; he had recently collaborated with guitarist John McLaughlin. "I was this vegetarian carrot juice kind of kid," Saunders said. "My life changed. It was like someone opened this other door." Soon they were all rehearsing together. Saunders's lyrical bass style—influenced by Jaco Pastorius—which Lou referred to as "Fernandizing," played foil to the distortion-heavy dueling guitars of Lou and Bob. Lou treated Fernando's bass lines as a call-and-response dialogue in the low register. "He says something and I say hello back, on the bass, though. So when he says 'Fernandizing,' he wants me to speak, but it is a way of playing," Saunders said. "It's like this slinky kind of harmonics, a more melodic kind of playing, with groove. That's why he asked me to play with him in the beginning, because he likes that I play with groove and melody at the same time."

Lou then hired Sean Fullan, whom he had met in the studio sessions for *Rock & Rule*, to engineer his next album, *The Blue Mask*. Fullan was a California native who had just come off a long stint as an apprentice to legendary recording engineer Glyn Johns. Fullan was only in his midtwenties, but he had been voraciously studying audio engineering technology and styles since he first heard Led Zeppelin as a teenager. Johns, who had produced for the Who and Eric Clapton, taught Fullan how to master technology while favoring a style of acoustic engineering that would provide maximum fidelity to the live sound with minimal interference in the final mix. Fullan had also learned from engineer Chris Kimsey while in Paris as an assistant engineer on the Rolling Stones' *Emotional Rescue*. After Fullan moved to New York from Johns's pastoral studio space in Sussex, he was soon thrown into a studio with Lou Reed, but he was prepared for *The Blue Mask*.

"For the last six months, I was literally in the country, so to be plopped down in New York was very, very daunting, but exciting as well," Fullan says. "This was exactly where I wanted to be, but I had no idea what a bizarre adventure it would be."

In the fall of 1981, Lou called to schedule a lunch at his home in Blairstown to discuss the album in preproduction. "He goes, 'I want you and Bob to come out. We'll have lunch, we'll talk about the record,'" Fullan recalls. "And I'm like, 'How do I get there?' He goes, 'Don't worry about getting there. Somebody'll work that out.'" After listening to every Lou Reed album to prepare for the meeting, that Saturday morning at the appointed time, a car came to pick him up. "I go outside at ten and there's this big stretch limo. I get in the car, and there's this bald guy with sunglasses on," Fullan says. "I go, 'Hi, I'm Sean Fullan, I'm gonna be the engineer.'"

Quine was a brooding loner who kept his own counsel; he wasn't into pleasantries. Even behind tinted windows, Quine never removed his sunglasses. "He wore sunglasses all the time—all the time," Fullan says. "It's like, 'I want to see who you are! Take those sunglasses off. You would never do that with Bob Quine. I would never have dreamed of asking him to take off his sunglasses."

Tampering with Quine's guitar sound was even worse; his stoicism concealed a fury within, but the illusion of pandemonium on the frets was carefully calibrated. "I'm the guitar player," Quine said. "Great. I love guitar players. It's my favorite instrument," Fullan replied. "And then he immediately reciprocated with, 'Well I'm not your normal guitar player. I have a distinct style and sound and I don't want anybody fucking with it.' And I was like, 'That's not what I do. I'll try to get the best microphone the right proximity from your guitar, so don't worry about that,'" Fullan says. For the rest of the hour-and-a-half-long ride along the Jersey Turnpike, Quine relaxed as much as he ever did. Fullan, on the other hand, had no precise sense of what Lou wanted to discuss.

When he saw the Zen rock gardens outside Lou's Blairstown residence, it didn't calm his nerves. "We were completely deer in the headlights," Fullan says. But Lou also wasn't quite sure where the album was headed; he wanted to feel it out. "I was like, 'Are we gonna book some rehearsal time and rehearse?'" Fullan recalls. Lou was unequivocal. "'Nope. Fernando and Doane will nail it, and Bob and I got it,'" Lou said. "They turned to me and said, 'So, um, how do you want to record it?' And I said, 'Well, I just want to record it very open,'" Fullan says.

The key for Fullan was fostering a positive studio space. "The one thing that I learned most about engineering was to create an environment that was comfortable and safe. Everybody can see and hear each other," Fullan says. "There were never any distractions. There were no guests, no friends popping by. There was absolutely no tolerance for drugs or alcohol anywhere near the session."

For Fullan, *The Blue Mask* was more like a sporting event than the drugged-out party one might have expected from an earlier incarnation of Lou. "They had trained for it and prepped for it, studied for it, and there was no messing about," Fullan says. "We would rehearse a couple of times, and we'd record three or four takes."

Lou was more confident than ever, but he had a hands-off approach to leadership that required a downsized band. "He didn't feel that he wanted a lot of opinions and a lot of influence, because I think he'd had that in the past, and it just wasn't who he was. He was ready to take charge and take responsibility, and let the chips fall where they fall," Fullan says.

After playing with Lou at Columbia, Perry knew not to expect much guidance. "What Lou was after was that he wanted us to all follow our initial gut instincts. So as a result, he didn't give us any of the music written," Perry recalled. "It wasn't really discussed that much how we would approach it. He trusted Robert's instincts and Fernando's and mine to serve the music." Following Quine proved difficult but exhilarating. "Sometimes, Robert would just play these solos that were . . . hair-raising. They defied any kind of categorization," Perry said. "He had a real stream of consciousness about his playing, which made every time he soloed entirely different. No two solos were ever alike."

Quine tuned a whole step apart from Lou to distinguish his sound. "The ferocity with which he played—you had to stop what you were doing and listen," Fullan says.

Lou had no interest in producing a hit single; *The Blue Mask* was made with the "spirit of pure poetry." Even though "Average Guy" had radio-friendly potential, he deliberately chose a less commercial take for the final mix. "The fact that it was sounding like something that would air on the radio put him off," Fullan says. "That's not what that song was about, so we picked this mixed tempo—it wasn't slow, it wasn't fast, it was just sort of what he felt that he intended."

There was only one recurrent distraction during the sessions. Late at night, amps at the expansive RCA studio in Midtown would pick up radio chatter from nearby taxi dispatchers. "Every day, it would just appear around nine or nine thirty at night and it would kind of throw us all off," Fullan says. But on *The Blue Mask*, nothing could disrupt Lou's focus.

"Lou turned to me, and he said, 'Fuck it. If it's gonna appear on the record somewhere, it's gonna appear on the record somewhere, and we can't worry about it. We just have to plow on. We just have to make this record,'" Fullan recalls. So in the intro to "The Gun," the phantom hum of two voices was interpolated into the mix. "As we were recording it, nobody freaked out, nobody stopped. And after that was over, Lou just looked at me and said, 'See what I was talking about?'" Nobody at the label said a word about the glitch—the haunting radio static was apropos of the song's overarching theme—so Lou benefited from some uncredited, garbled backing vocals inadvertently provided by two New York City cab drivers.

*The Blue Mask* represented a victory over his battle with addiction, but also a reckoning of the identity crisis that inflected every prior album. He finally felt secure in himself as an artist, and all of the pent-up aggression culminated in a grand catharsis, channeled through some of the rawest lyrics of his career and Quine's savage attack on the guitar. "My House" imagined the ghost of Delmore Schwartz visiting his house in New Jersey, summoned by a Ouija board, having found inner peace in the afterlife:

> *My Daedalus to your Bloom was such a perfect wit*
> *And to find you in my house makes things perfect*

The album charted Lou's struggle with his negative influences, and the triumph of the positive forces in his life. Cravings, withdrawal, and masochistic tendencies course through the album as much as love, nurturing, and creative freedom. "Underneath the Bottle," "Waves of Fear," and the title track detail the sobering recovery process—tremors, night sweats, and all; "The Day John Kennedy Died" is shot through with disillusionment and heartbreak. In "The Heroine," though, a nautical-themed feminist ode for solo guitar, Lou expressed an immense debt to Sylvia for helping him right the ship through the tempest of his addictions. The title's homophonic irony, the album's only hint of self-consciousness, showed how far Lou had come emotionally since he first penned "Heroin." That journey to salvation culminates on "Heavenly Arms," the euphoric closing track, an unself-conscious testament to beatific love dedicated to Sylvia.

"It was a really important song to me," Sylvia said. "That was the genuine voice of Lou—that's how he could express a lot of things in a song."

Sylvia designed the album art, a repurposed image from the *Transformer* photo by Mick Rock, tinted blue. It at once channeled Picasso's Blue Period and a Warhol silkscreen, its simplicity reflective of the album's minimalist orchestration and conversational style. Yet it was also apparent that this was Lou, unvarnished and unfiltered, at the peak of his artistic powers—he had taken off the mask.

Critical consensus emerged that a month before turning forty, instead of having a midlife crisis, Lou had released his magnum opus. "Lou Reed's *The Blue Mask* is a great record, and its genius is at once so simple and unusual that the only appropriate reaction is wonder," wrote Tom Carson in *Rolling Stone*. Robert Christgau finally gave him an A. It was a resounding coup.

Yet the chorus of approval was missing one loud voice—Lester Bangs's. Two months after *The Blue Mask* was released, on April 30, 1982, Lester died on his couch in New York, seemingly of an overdose of Darvon. Quine, who had become close with Lester despite his recording relationship with Lou, was one of the first to hear the news. The next day, he went over to Lou's apartment on Christopher Street in a daze, expecting a grieving session. Lou still held the grudge, though.

"That's too bad about your friend," Quine recalled him saying. In the course of a long tirade, Lou brought up the *Creem* article in which Lester insensitively referred to Rachel in derogatory terms. "Do you understand, Quine—this is a person I was close to. And he is calling her a creature and thing," Lou said. Quine could not understand why Lou refused to forgive him or how he could speak ill of the dead, and decided to gradually curtail his friendship with Lou while maintaining his position in the band. Lou and Quine had the same type of combustible relationship that fueled the Velvet Underground.

Keeping his equanimity in all professional matters for the time being, Quine introduced Lou to Fred Maher, an eighteen-year-old prodigy. Lou hired Maher to mime Doane Perry's part on Lou's first foray into music videos, not counting the live Warhol projections from the Exploding Plastic Inevitable. Six months prior to the release of *The Blue Mask*, MTV aired its first music video—"Video Killed the Radio Star" by the Buggles—and Lou, the technology and media buff that he was, quickly hopped on the bandwagon. The resulting performance-style video for "Women" featured the band onstage, backlit with blue filters, with Lou in a leather jacket and sunglasses, Bob Quine in his typical sunglasses and sport jacket, and Fernando Saunders in a shirt and tie. Lou decided to hire Maher for his touring band, if and when the tour resumed.

Lou's reintroduction into live performance began gradually, but with Sylvia taking over management duties, Lou had a sensible partner who loved him behind his career. Lou's touring hiatus had lasted more than a year, but he increased his visibility by accepting a role in *Get Crazy*, the 1983 musical comedy directed by Allan Arkush. The film was loosely based on the Fillmore East, where Arkush had once worked, and detailed the planning and performance of a benefit for a fictional rock venue. Lou convened Perry, Quine, and Saunders and recorded his contribution to the soundtrack, "Little Sister," a paean to the unconditional love of his own sister, Bunny. Lou had a speaking part as well, playing Auden, an exaggerated version of himself, described as a "metaphysical folk singer" and "antisocial recluse" who "invented the '70s," was "dropped by six record companies," and hadn't left his apartment in years. While turning random bits of phone conversation into instant songs, Auden explains that, like Lou, he worries that marriage has softened his edge, but gets cajoled into performing live when a promoter issues a deathbed request. After an hours-long scenic taxi ride through the city, though, Auden shows up after the audience has left, and performs for the few remaining fans. Perhaps, for all those years, Lou had just gotten lost on the way to the venue.

In late 1982 Lou returned to the RCA studio to record a follow-up to *The Blue Mask*. *Legendary Hearts* was dedicated entirely to Sylvia, who also designed the album art—Lou clutching a chrome motorcycle helmet, seen in a three-quarter shot on the back cover, shot by photographer Waring Abbott. Lou hired Fred Maher as the drummer, retaining Quine and Saunders on guitar and bass, though tension between the two guitarists continued to escalate; like the rock equivalent of Felix and Oscar from *The Odd Couple*, Lou needed control and Quine thrived on chaos.

Emboldened by the reception of *The Blue Mask*, Lou took sole pro-ducing credit—Fullan couldn't come to terms on a contract with Lou's management—and he brought in engineer Corky Stasiak, who had mixed *Rock and Roll Heart* and *Growing Up in Public*. While executing his vision in the studio with absolute conviction, the material itself was racked with self-doubt. If *The Blue Mask* recreated the battle between base desires and loftier types of fulfillment, *Legendary Hearts* turned the lens on a more equivocal set of binaries: true love and skin-deep romance, work and play, sobriety and relapse, patriotism and cynicism. The title track underscored the gulf between the timeless love stories of legend and the ephemeral nature of real-life monogamy, coupled with a sense of performance anxiety rooted in Lou's fear that he could never measure up to Romeo:

> *I'm good for just a kiss*
> *Not legendary love*

This cynicism reaches a climax on "Home of the Brave," an elegiac saloon song dedicated to the downtrodden and lonely, inspired partially by Lincoln Swados, who Lou still occasionally saw in the city. Yet Lou bookended the album with a positive response to the challenge of "Legendary Hearts" on "Rooftop Garden," which found a more practical contentment in life's mundane pleasures. Yet the recording environment was not as comfortable; compared to *The Blue Mask*, Lou was less amenable to creative compromise, especially when it came to Bob Quine.

When Quine heard the final mix, he discovered that Lou had all but mixed him out of the record, apparently deciding that the studio wasn't big enough for two guitars. Quine was irate. "I was in Ohio and I took it out in the driveway and smashed the tape into pieces," Quine later recalled. "I didn't talk to him for a month but he knew what he'd done." Nevertheless, the album became another critical success, yielding two singles with accompanying music videos, and Lou began gearing up for a comeback tour. Quine begrudgingly agreed to stay in the band despite their strained relationship.

On February 25, 1983, frostbitten fans lined up around the block to get into the Bottom Line, where Lou was finally staging his comeback. He had planned a short residency for the last week of February, culminating in a concert film, *A Night with Lou Reed*. Andy Warhol even showed up surreptitiously. The "looky-Lous" began to murmur, as the guttural rumble of the crowd's collective "*Louuu*" summoned the erstwhile Godfather of Punk out of his long hibernation. Everyone was curious—did Lou still have it? Yet no dusting off of the vocal cords was required; if a bit more gravelly than before his retreat to the underground, the heightened bass in his speak-singing only added a dark gravity. As per usual, Lou opened the show with "Sweet Jane," mixing selections from *The Blue Mask*, *Legendary Hearts*, and the greatest hits of the Velvets and his solo career to date. Quine and Lou could kept their problems offstage—Lou still let him enter the Lovecraftian dimension on "Waves of Fear" and "Walk on the Wild Side." Immediately, it became apparent that Lou had not devolved into rusty forgetfulness in his time off, though his new illusion was as raw as ever.

"Lou would turn to Quine and say, 'Quine!' And Quine would make that guitar noise from hell," Maher recalled. Lou insisted that Maher's drum kit be placed on the stage, rather than on a riser as was the tradition; not only did it fuel the improvisatory atmosphere, it allowed Lou to easily find his place if he ever got lost.

Getting lost in a vamp is the musical equivalent of getting lost in a parking lot, but in a Lou Reed song, it was possible. "I hit one note that actually caused me to levitate about half a foot," Lou recalled after one of the shows. "I'm not sure whether it's the pain or pleasure that did it, but it was such a strong sound. It was feeding back and I was following its angle, as it were. It was going that way so I went with it. If I kept following it I would have ended up on some table out there." A week later, Lou made a one-night-only appearance at Studio 54, effectively concluding the American leg of the *Legendary Hearts* tour. Lou may have still had the stamina to maintain the sleepless touring schedule he had grown accustomed to, but not the willingness to compromise his health.

The tour resumed for one week in early September, with a truncated series of shows in Italy. This time there would be no riots, even though the amphitheaters Lou filled had tens of thousands of seats. Two of the shows, one in Verona on September 7, and another on September 10 at the enormous open-air ruins at Circus Maximus in Rome, were recorded and later released as *Live in Italy*. They returned in mid-September, in time for Fred Maher to enroll as a freshman in the architecture program at Cooper Union.

Lou had another album in the works, and scheduled the studio time around Maher's winter break. But during the gestational period for *New Sensations*, the dissonance between Lou and Bob Quine intensified. Days before entering Skyline Studios, Lou fired Quine from the band and decided that he would be the only guitarist on the record.

Unlike his previous two releases, *New Sensations* would not be a quartet album. Along with coproducer John Jansen, who had produced Jimi Hendrix's *Rainbow Bridge*, Lou beefed up the band with backing vocals, electric violinist L. Shankar, keyboardist Peter Wood, and a horn section including the Brecker Brothers, trombonist Tom Malone, and trumpeter Jon Faddis. Lou wanted to maintain artistic control while letting loose on a more pop-friendly outing—"I Love You, Suzanne," an upbeat take on the themes explored in "Femme Fatale," and "My Red Joystick" had a driving four-on-the-floor beat, a facile melody, and frivolous lyrics, with potential for radio play. "I Love You, Suzanne," opening with a spoken-word quote from the Contours' "Do You Love Me," was one of Lou's most danceable tracks. In the era-specific video directed by Tim Newman, Lou proved that at forty-two, he could still bust a move, and that a happy Lou Reed was not an oxymoron.

As indicated by the cover art, an image of Lou controlling a joystick video game avatar of himself, *New Sensations* featured carefree, doo-wop-inflected songs that channeled the bombastic spirit of the age. The title track showed that even though Lou had experienced a veritable anatomy textbook worth of sensations, the city still offered more. Perhaps for the first time, Lou seemed to just be having fun in the studio. Buoyed by Michael Brecker's tenor saxophone sound, "Doin' the Things That We Want To" matter-of-factly extols the virtue of Sam Shepard's recently opened play, *Fool for Love*, and Martin Scorsese's *Raging Bull*. Lou articulated his bold approach on "Fly into the Sun," a rejoinder to the bleaker Velvets song "Ride into the Sun." On the cusp of 1984, Lou had become rock's high-flying Icarus:

> I'd shine by the light of the unknown moment
> To end this worldly pain
> And fly into the sun

Lou was back in top form; with *New Sensations*, he released a nuanced album that captured critics and the mass market. "I Love You, Suzanne" spent weeks on the rock charts. A world tour was in order.

Leading up to the 1984 *New Sensations* tour, Quine swallowed his pride and asked Lou if he could rejoin the band. Lou agreed, and with the addition of Peter Wood on keyboards and occasionally accordion, the tour began in

Denmark and Belgium. Soon, Maher got an offer to join British pop band Scritti Politti, and was replaced by drummer Lenny Ferrari. As the opening act, Lou contacted Atlanta-based new wave band the Swimming Pool Q's, who had just released a self-titled album on A&M. From September through November, they toured across the country and beyond, hitting Boston, Philadelphia, Cleveland, San Francisco, Toronto, and other stops along the way. Toward the end of the US tour, Lou was booked for a TV broadcast of his show at the Palace Theatre in Hollywood, where Bob Dylan happened to be in the crowd. Dylan was blown away by "Doin' the Things That We Want To," and gave Sylvia his stamp of approval; he was inspired to write "Brownsville Girl" with Sam Shepard, which was released two years later on *Knocked Out Loaded*.

Lou then spent December touring Europe, from Stockholm to Barcelona to London. By the end of the tour, relations between Quine and Lou had soured to the point where Quine felt, perhaps a touch paranoid, that Lou was having his microphone deliberately turned down. Quine walked away from the band acrimoniously. Lou had lost a key collaborator, but he had gained something he had been agitating for starting years prior, and maybe always—control over his public, private, and inner life. For Lou, that was the ultimate new sensation.

# 23

It was the lull between Thanksgiving and Christmas when Lou got the call from Wieden & Kennedy. They were a fledgling advertising agency in Portland, Oregon, competing with Madison Avenue, and they had an unlikely proposition—did Lou have any interest in starring in a commercial spot for Honda scooters? The admen had already sold Honda on the idea—worth $12.5 million in billings—but it seemed Lou would be the harder sell. Why would the man who made *Metal Machine Music* even consider becoming a celebrity pitchman?

Wieden & Kennedy was still reeling from the loss of the Nike account, which dropped them due to a lack of edginess. Honda, which was known more for cars in the United States but motorcycles in Japan, wanted to brand their bulky Elite model scooters as a hip alternative to Harley-Davidson, Lou's bike of choice. So in an effort to win back Nike and convince the youth counterculture to start riding scooters, they contrived the edgiest move they could think of: hire Lou Reed. Newbie copywriter Jim Riswold was still in his late twenties, and had grown up idolizing Lou, so he had an ulterior motive for landing Honda as his first commercial.

"Since I can't resist short, pithy answers, the short, pithy answer to 'Why on Earth did you use Lou Reed in a commercial?' is 'I wanted to meet Lou Reed,'" Riswold says. "I had long believed he was the coolest person this side of the Milky Way, and sometime in my youth I had, much to the chagrin of my parents, painted my fingernails black and embarked on a period of less-than-light drug use in his honor."

At the pitch meeting, Riswold jettisoned any elaborate script in favor of something more befitting of the former Phantom of Rock—he pulled out *Transformer* and played "Walk on the Wild Side." It was a bold move, but like the slang-illiterate American censors, the representatives from Honda apparently didn't understand the expression "giving head." Regardless, it had that je ne sais quoi they were looking for. Wieden & Kennedy won the account.

"Celebrities have been used in advertising since time immemorial. However, what I think made the Lou Reed spot different at the time was that it used a persona-non-grata celebrity," Riswold says. "The very things that made Mr. Reed off limits to any sane advertising professional, as well the majority of the record-buying public, are what appealed to me: his outspokenness, his troubles, his twenty-four-hour sunglasses, his choice of subject matter, his grating personality, his ennui, his aloofness, his coolness, his ego, his behavior, his unpleasantness, his sexual ambiguity, his darkness; in short, his Lou-ness."

When it came to approaching Lou, as it turned out, he didn't scoff at the notion. Despite his ostensible antipathy for the mainstream—and the fact that the closest he'd come to celebrity endorsement was drinking a Coke in a Warhol screen test—Lou appreciated the financial support of the advertising industry. Compared to record labels, advertisers were often more generous, and the self-aware campaign concept captured some of the irony of "Wild Side," with a clever tagline.

"I thought it was a terrific idea, a good way to reach people and get my music across," Lou later recalled. "I like trying different things to make people aware of me, because I think they'd like the music if they got to hear it."

Some leveled the charge of selling out, but the subversive Honda spot barely even showed the product, and the gritty footage had the appearance of amateur home movies. "We wanted to push the unpleasantness of Lou-ness even further by making the spot look like Lou shot it," Riswold says. "I think all these elements together made it look and feel like the spot came from the dark recesses of Lou's soul. It became an ad about him that co-opted the scooter. He even commented on that fact in subsequent interviews by saying, 'I thought the ad was good for me because it was about me.'"

Wieden & Kennedy hired veteran director Steve Horn, who shot verite-style footage of the Lower East Side, still a hotbed of drug activity and crime where squatters agitated for low-income housing. In a market saturated by glossy thirty-second spots—a saccharine ad featuring Bill Cosby hawking New Coke, a dyspeptic spot populated by professional dancers flipping over McDonald's toe-tapping special sauce in a parody of *Footloose* and *Flashdance*—truth in advertising was not exactly a premium.

For the Honda ad, though, Horn planned to shoot the first postmodern commercial, a meta-critique of advertising itself. He deliberately underexposed and overdeveloped the film to give it the effect of a Warholian avant-garde experiment, shooting an unvarnished tableau of street life—roving car window washers, ladies of the night, idling police cars, bustling neighborhood barber shops—everything conventional ads tried to conceal. The master reel was brought to Larry Bridges, a talented editor known for his groundbreaking appropriation of high-art film grammar into music videos, who was also a Lou Reed fanatic.

Bridges decided that to do justice to "Wild Side," simply executing the often thankless task of editing, the invisible art, would not reinforce Lou's boundary-pushing mantra to look beneath the surface of things. Instead of discarding the whip pans, 8mm-style flicker, and lens flares that were de rigueur for French New Wave films but would ordinarily undermine the high-budget corporate precision of a network TV spot, Bridges emphasized the glitches and human error behind the camera. To hammer home the slice-of-life message, he incorporated *Breathless*-style jump cuts over Lou's iconic theme. In the final shot of the minute-long sequence, the camera zooms out to reveal Lou perched on a Honda scooter, under a flashing DON'T WALK sign, as he removes his aviators and delivers the ironic tagline: "Hey, don't settle for walkin'." By stripping the song of its political undertone, the ad mounted a subtle, amusing critique of the conventional advertising model from within. Only those who could afford it could take a ride on the wild side; everyone on-screen, though, was still taking a walk.

"In hindsight, I should have used *Metal Machine Music* as the track. It would have made the ad even more oh-so-Lou," Riswold says. "It would have also gotten rid of the rather silly line he says at the end in the only in-focus shot of the whole spot. In the spirit of his great sardonic last line from his liner notes of *MMM*, maybe his line should have been, 'If it's good enough for me, it's good enough for you.'"

The question lingered as to whether it was good enough for Honda, though. At the client meeting, Wieden prefaced the presentation of the unorthodox finished product to Honda's austere marketing manager with a strong assertion. "What you are about to see is important," he said. After the ad played, the agency executives waited with bated breath for Honda's response.

"We need to be *that* scooter company," the marketing manager said.

On the strength of the ad, Nike rehired Wieden & Kennedy, who soon created the "Just Do It" campaign, and *Advertising Age* named Steve Horn Television Commercial Director of the Year. The era of postmodern advertising had arrived. It was so effective that Honda followed it with another iconoclastic cameo, written by Riswold: Miles Davis, leaning on a scooter, trumpet in hand, riffing off his infamously irreverent line, "I'll play first, and I'll tell you about it later . . . maybe." But it was Lou's presence that ushered in advertising's birth of the cool. Despite the sea change it caused in advertising, Honda's scooter sales stagnated. Nevertheless, Lou got to finally cash in on "Wild Side," a copywriter got his wings, and the viewing public got a quintessentially Lou-like welcome to the world of consumerism during commercial breaks from *Mr. Belvedere*.

It wasn't the only time in 1985 that Lou and Miles came together to support the same cause. Lou's foray into advertising coincided with an even more unlikely beginning—a walk on the altruistic side. Spurred by Michael Jackson's sprawling "We Are the World" campaign, Steven Van Zandt, the guitarist in the E Street Band, approached Lou and a slew of other artists, including Miles, Bruce Springsteen, Bob Dylan, Afrika Bambaataa, and Kurtis Blow, to join Artists United Against Apartheid, a human rights activism project in protest of the South African apartheid government. Van Zandt wrote "Sun City," a musical boycott of the eponymous South African casino, and assigned lines to each participating artist. Director Jonathan Demme collaborated with music video aces Godley & Creme to cobble together an eight-minute music video. Lou has one line, in response to John Oates and Panamanian salsa singer Rubén Blades, who sing, "Freedom is a privilege nobody writes for free":

> *Look around the world, baby*
> *It cannot be denied*

Lou's human rights work continued that fall, when Bob Dylan invited him to perform at the first Farm Aid concert, a large-scale benefit for American farmers. Dylan conceived of the concept during Live Aid, a charity show in response to the Ethiopian famine that took place earlier that summer. On September 22, 1985, in front of a crowd of eighty thousand at the University of Illinois Memorial Stadium in Champaign, Lou joined a lineup including Dylan, Johnny Cash, Joni Mitchell, and B. B. King to raise more than $9 million to, as the organization's slogan read, "Keep America growing." Lou recruited guitarist Chieli Minucci, a Long Island native who had been performing with Eartha Kitt's band, and J. T. Lewis, the original drummer for fusion band Living Colour, to replace Maher and Quine. Lewis, Minucci, and Saunders later became the rhythm section for smooth jazz group Special EFX.

"Real pleasure for us to be here at Farm Aid," Lou told the crowd. "Hope you all remember this when those people who were trying to censor records come down." The band launched into "Walk on the Wild Side." Lou was officially a human rights activist.

Lou concluded 1985 with the release of *Lost in the Stars: The Music of Kurt Weill*, a compilation album produced by Hal Willner. He contributed a rendition of "September Song," the Weill standard about a May-December romance. Lou also wrote "My Love Is Chemical," a synth-heavy soundtrack song for the ballet film *White Nights*, starring Mikhail Baryshnikov, which was released that December. If Lou was entering the September of his life, though, he was doing the things he wanted to, and soon he had enough material to head back into the studio.

Lou coproduced his next album, *Mistrial*, with Saunders, paying top dollar for studio time to record at the Power Station, where the previous year Madonna had recorded "Like a Virgin." They recruited guitarist Eddie Martinez, Rubén Blades, and saxophonist Rick Bell to create a bigger studio sound. Bell, a Cleveland-born, self-taught tenor player who had cut his teeth with the Michael Stanley Band, had met Saunders during a brief stint with singer Rachel Faro. Saunders hired him for the album's lead single, "No Money Down."

*Mistrial* was designed to have the same commercial impact as *New Sensations*, with accompanying music videos. Godley & Creme's video for "No Money Down" consisted of a close-up shot of an animatronic Lou, costumed in the style of Arnold Schwarzenegger's Terminator, that proceeds to rip off its own face. In contrast, the video for "The Original Wrapper," directed by Zbigniew Rybczynski, was a campy romp through the West Village, with Lou styled in a glittery fedora à la Michael Jackson, featuring roller skaters in spandex, dachshunds, stationary bikes, and movers in hazmat suits attempting to capture unsuspecting New Yorkers in a cardboard sarcophagus.

Yet the video's kitschy style belied its polemical lyrics, demarcating a political turn for Lou. Embracing his new role as an activist, along with

"Video Violence," a diatribe against rampant violence on-screen, "The Original Wrapper" showed that he was now comfortable using his music as a space for unabashed political commentary. Lou rattled off a litany of political issues previously handled through subtle implication or not at all: abortion, the AIDS crisis, racial tensions, explicitly calling out the hypocrisy of President Reagan, Jerry Falwell, and Louis Farrakhan. However, the track did not establish a direct line from Lou to Public Enemy. While his idiosyncratic take on hip-hop was handled with appropriate irony, Lou's deadpan vocal patter negated any pretensions of a claim to being the original rapper, even if he did set a precedent for the singular use of internal half-rhymes, rhyming "sanctimonious," "lugubrious," and "pugnacious."

*Mistrial* was more personal than political, though. It dramatized the challenges of sustaining modern love in the city amid the encroachment of insidious forces beyond Lou's control—idealism versus cynicism. Tracks like "No Money Down," "Don't Hurt a Woman," and "I Remember You" reflected the idealistic side of the dichotomy, interspersing Sammy Merendino's drum machine backbeat and J. T. Lewis's drums with lush doo-wop backing vocals. "Tell It to Your Heart," the album's piece de resistance, demonstrated that Lou still had a knack for the urban sublime; he had not lost his sense of wonder. The track chronicles an imagistic narrative, as a starry-eyed urban astronomer confuses a spotlight for a celestial body:

> *Its spinning lights reminded me of you*
> *A star spinning in orbit lighting up the sky*
> *Or maybe it was not a star at all*

Lou promoted the release with an appearance on *Late Night with David Letterman*. *Mistrial* peaked at Number 47 on the charts, Lou's greatest commercial success since *Coney Island Baby*, more than a decade prior.

Leading up to the release of *Mistrial* in June, Amnesty International asked Lou to be part of the Conspiracy of Hope tour to celebrate its twenty-fifth anniversary. Lou asked Rick Bell to play at a preliminary show at the Ritz in the East Village, and subsequently hired him for the six-city tour, also bringing on multi-instrumentalist Fuzzbee Morse. Along with U2, Peter Gabriel, the Police, and Miles Davis, Lou played San Francisco, Los Angeles, Denver, Atlanta, and Chicago. The tour culminated in a show at Giants Stadium in East Rutherford, New Jersey. As part of his Honda endorsement deal, Lou donated a Honda Elite scooter for an Amnesty International auction.

"Rock and roll, to me, is a statement about energy and freedom," Lou said. "Therefore, it has a direct relationship to Amnesty—the most astonishing group I've ever been involved with."

At a press conference featuring artists and political dissidents prior to the Giants Stadium concert, Lou explained his stance on the importance of advocating for global free speech and the value of his own constitutional rights. "It's one thing to read about things, but when there's someone sitting right in front of you telling and articulating some of these gruesome, unbelievable things that happen to people who do things that we take for granted every day—some of the records I've made, I would be rotting in jail for the last ten years," Lou said. By the end of the Conspiracy of Hope tour, hundreds of thousands of people saw the concerts, and Amnesty raised $2.6 million, recruited forty thousand new members, and managed to free two political prisoners as a direct result.

Lou had settled into a comfortable rhythm of alternating between his own tours and human rights work. The *Mistrial* tour kicked off in July, starting at the Ritz in New York, with Fuzzbee Morse swapping out for keyboardist and trumpeter Alan Smallwood. "I remember when me and Fernando, when we first did this song, I said, 'This is the new, healthy Lou Reed that's coming out, as opposed to the old, mean Lou Reed," Lou told a rapt audience. "I'm like a snake, man." From there, the mellower Lou traipsed through Montreal and Philadelphia. At Philly's Mann Music Center, Lou played for a crowd of more than ten thousand, with Bell's screaming sax solos cutting over the band. By the end of the night, Bell's gums were bleeding, the reed blood-red. "When I took the reed off, I saved it, because I showed it to Lou afterwards, and this thing was bright red all the way through," Bell recalls. He inscribed the back for posterity's sake. "I wrote this: 'Lou Reed concert, Mann Music Center, Philadelphia, PA—soul sacrifice.' He thought that was the greatest thing."

The fifteen-city tour reached an ironic zenith on October 1, when Lou made his spectacular debut at Radio City Music Hall, at the vaunted home of the Rockettes, where during the Velvet years, Tchaikovsky's "March of the Wooden Soldiers" always took precedence over "Sweet Jane," which wasn't allowed anywhere near the sanctified stage. But those were different times. Lou played the rock anthem with reckless abandon, closing out the show with "Rock & Roll." The appreciable irony did not escape him. "Just before he finished his two-hour set, a sign was lowered into place, the word 'Lou' writ large, in eight-foot letters and flowing script worthy of Liberace," wrote Jon Pareles in the *New York Times*. At forty-three, it was the ultimate coup—Lou had become a subject the Grey Lady treated with reverence. Lou followed that with another debut, this time as the musical guest on *Saturday Night Live*, with X-rated comic Sam Kinison hosting, where Lou played "I Love You, Suzanne" and "Video Violence."

In December, Lou continued his human rights work at Peter Gabriel's Japan Aid, playing two benefit shows at Jingu Stadium in downtown Tokyo to raise funds for the creation of a global computer network at the University for Peace. By the end of 1986, Lou had solidified his place as one of rock's eminent elder statesmen, becoming a global human rights ambassador. Lou, whose reputation began tarnished, had finally sloughed off the residue of the public backlash against "Heroin"—what was once underground had become mainstream.

# 24

On February 22, 1987, at the age of fifty-eight, Andy Warhol died in his sleep at New York Hospital. He was recovering from gallbladder surgery when he suffered an abrupt postoperative cardiac arrhythmia. Warhol's body was transferred to Pittsburgh, where he was given a small Catholic funeral, and dressed in style for the occasion, with his signature platinum blond wig, Wayfarers, and a copy of *Interview* magazine. He was buried in a Catholic cemetery next to his parents.

Lou was shocked by the premature death of his idol, and began contemplating a tribute to the man who had given him his start. But first, he had another Amnesty project to attend to: the Secret Policeman's Third Ball in London.

Lou wrote a song for the event—"Voices of Freedom"—later bequeathing the lyric sheet to Amnesty. He only brought Rick Bell with him. "He says, 'It's you and me, and we're gonna go over and play with Peter Gabriel,'" Bell says. Lou generally made guest appearances with at least one trusted band member. "It's nice to have somebody that you can sort of lean on that you worked with," Bell says. The shows were held at London's Palladium Theatre from March 26 to 29, 1987, featuring two nights of comedy and two of music, with Kate Bush, Duran Duran, and Senegalese singer Youssou N'Dour. "Voices of Freedom" captured the intersection of human rights advocacy and rock:

> *The ocean reduces that stone to sand*
> *It's the voices of freedom*

"On 'Voices of Freedom,' it was improvisation," Bell says. "It was probably one of the most incredible experiences I've ever had. It was just something where you're not quite sure what you're gonna do, but it just comes together."

Lou flew back to New York to attend Warhol's memorial service on April 1, 1987, at St. Patrick's Cathedral. More than two thousand mourners paid tribute to the avant-garde giant, who inspired the Velvets to search in low places for high art, just as he had found a mechanistic beauty in a can of Campbell's soup. In a way, the service was Warhol's greatest happening, the coup de grace of his life's work, the Exploding Plastic Inevitable redux with an air of tragic inevitability tempered by the ultimate Warholian irony. Like a star that brings other planets into its orbit, even after death, a constellation of artists and benefactors from disparate realms converged: Baby Jane Holzer, Claes Oldenburg, Liza Minnelli, David Hockney, Fran Lebowitz, John Cale, and Lou. Often mischaracterized as a symbol for decadence and urban decay, Warhol had finally gotten them all to go where he went every Sunday—to church.

During the hour-long memorial, art critic John Richardson gave a eulogy, extolling Warhol's critical distance as a "recording angel" in the name of art, while Yoko Ono praised him for guiding her son Sean after the death of John Lennon. Reverend Anthony Dalla Villa referred to Warhol as the "Christian gentleman." For Warhol's part, actor Nicholas Love read some of his inimitable diary musings, in which he imagined returning to dust or being brought back as a diamond on Elizabeth Taylor's finger.

After leaving the church, more than four hundred of Warhol's friends migrated to the after-service at the Paramount Century Hotel, where Julian Schnabel rubbed elbows with Gerard Malanga and the gathered crowd listened to a recording of the Velvets. It was as though they were in the backroom at Max's, only Warhol wasn't there to witness it.

"It's hard to believe Andy's not going to be around," Lou said. "I was hoping he'd turn up and say, 'April Fool!'"

Yet Warhol's untimely death caused an unlikely reunion. Lou reconnected with Cale, and they discussed the possibility of collaborating on a tribute project. Soon, the Brooklyn Academy of Music commissioned them to write a requiem for Warhol, their first album together since *White Light/White Heat*. They planned to let it percolate before they went into the studio, though.

Then U2 asked Lou to come on tour with them in June to support the release of *The Joshua Tree*, which was partially inspired by the Conspiracy of Hope tour. Lou hired guitarist Mike Rathke, who had married Sylvia's sister, and bassist Yossi Fine as a temporary replacement for Fernando Saunders. On June 8 Lou headlined the Dutch Pinkpop festival in Baarlo, then headed to Wembley Stadium in London for his first show with U2. Bono was a huge fan of Lou's, and began incorporating "Walk on the Wild Side" into a medley opposite the band's own "Bad." During a show at Croke Park in Dublin, an eighty-thousand-seat stadium, Lou came onstage for the medley. Bono improvised a verse of "Walk on the Wild Side":

> I met my friend Lou, he's from the USA
> He plays with a band, he plays like he means to stay
> He said he's waited all his life and he brought his wife to see
>     Ireland

The tour took place amid the Troubles, at the height of the bloodiest year since 1982, but the political unrest didn't stop them from performing undaunted across Ireland. But the Pretenders, the Pogues, and Christy Moore, who opened many of the dates alongside Lou, weren't on the bill for the June 24 show at King's Hall in Belfast, the capital of Northern Ireland. On the way from Dublin to Belfast, the RUC police stopped the tour bus at a routine checkpoint. "They come on the bus, submachine guns strapped across their backs, just to check and see what's going on, and they ask, 'What are you guys doing?' And we said, 'We're the Lou Reed band, we're opening for U2 tonight,'" Bell says. "One of the policemen reached in his pocket, pulled out a couple of tickets, and said, 'I'm going to that show tonight.'" Before the show, a bomb squad did a sweep of the eight-thousand-seat stadium. "I don't think a lot of people went up there at that time to play because there was so much turmoil, but they were such a great audience," Bell says. "It was the best concert we did on that tour."

That August, Lou coproduced Rubén Blades's album *Nothing but the Truth*, returning the favor for *Mistrial*. Lou cowrote three tracks, using Blades as a mouthpiece for the dark shades of cynicism that had been conspicuously absent from much of his recent output. "Letters to the Vatican" details a desperate barfly on Amsterdam Avenue effectively writing a suicide note to the pope:

> Dear Pope, send me some hope
> Or a rope to do me in

Lou wrote the song surrounding widespread lost faith in the Catholic Church, which had been roiled by a debt scandal following the exposure of a banking fiasco regarding Panamanian shell companies that implicated the Vatican Bank. The Vatican's "letters of patronage" attempted to resolve the debacle, which ended in the murder of the Catholic banker at the center of the controversy and $224 million in papal funds being paid in restitution. In 1987 it seemed unlikely the Vatican would respond to such a letter.

The same disillusionment pulses through the ominous "The Calm Before the Storm" and "Hopes on Hold," which reflected Lou's growing marital fears:

> *Can I trust in someone else for a lifetime*
> *And hope that the distance disappears*

Lou concluded the summer with another collaboration, when Duran Duran invited him to sing "Sweet Jane" and "Walk on the Wild Side" at a benefit for the homeless at the Beacon Theatre, wrapping up the British synthpop band's Strange Behaviour Tour.

In December Paul Simon asked Lou to participate in a benefit for the Children's Health Fund, a national nonprofit organization Simon founded that year to combat the homeless crisis by providing mobile health care units, starting with service for the city's twelve thousand homeless children. The four-hour benefit concert took place on December 13, 1987, at Madison Square Garden and featured Simon, Ladysmith Black Mambazo, Paul Shaffer, Grandmaster Flash, and Laurie Anderson. It was the first time they shared a stage, but amid the hubbub, Lou and Laurie didn't actually meet. During Lou's set, Debbie Harry and Grace Jones sang backup on "Walk on the Wild Side." But the highlight of the evening came when Dion took the stage for a performance of "Teenager in Love." Standing in for the Belmonts were Simon, Rubén Blades, Bruce Springsteen, James Taylor, Billy Joel, and Lou. Lou had spent hours practicing the bass vocals for the occasion.

They reprised the performance at the 30th Annual Grammy Awards on March 2, 1988, where Lou celebrated his forty-sixth birthday at Radio City Music Hall by performing with his doo-wop idol, alongside Rubén Blades and Buster Poindexter. Midway through the song, they were joined by some of Lou's favorite doo-wop groups: the Cadillacs, the Regents, and the Flamingos. Everyone wore a tuxedo, except for Dion and Lou, who sported his trademark leather jacket, jeans, and shades. No one, not even the Grammys—where he had never even been nominated—told Lou Reed what to wear. His music career had come full circle; for one night only, he was a Jade again.

Instead of parlaying his national exposure into a slow ride into the sunset, as many aging rock stars might have done, Lou began his late forties by retreating inward again. With the creative juices far from dried up, rather than resting on his laurels and becoming a living wax statue, Lou still had more to say. And on whatever shape his new album would take, he would say whatever he wanted to. First, he called Fred Maher, who had returned from London with ambitions of starting a producing career, to see if he was available to play drums. Maher agreed on the condition that he coproduce the album—a brash move for someone of his level of inexperience—and Lou decided to audition him.

They went into Mediasound in May to lay down the first track, with Maher so overconfident that he didn't even hire an engineer. Yet when he heard the playback, Lou was dumbfounded. He called Maher the next day to render judgment. "I sound like Lou Reed for the first time in years," Lou said. "Let's do this." They booked studio time for the stripped-down band, which consisted of Mike Rathke and Lou on guitar, Rob Wasserman on bass, Maher on drums, and a surprise guest on several tracks: Moe Tucker.

Going into the sessions, Lou was more comfortable in his own skin than he had ever been. Until then, every solo album Lou had made had essentially the same protagonist—Lou Reed—and the many faces and iterations of his ongoing bildungsroman, each entry a serialized chapter of Lou's personal development. Now that he knew exactly who he was—a cult figure—and what he represented—the loyal opposition—the new song cycle eschewed the rising action of Lou's existential struggle for self-determination as he stepped outside of himself to speak freely on the political status quo, without caveats or justification. Lou had no title, only a character: New York. And its story was even more caustic than anything in Lou's back catalog, with a plot fit to be narrated by Lou Reed. So he cashed in his spot at the Grammys for a modest soapbox. A quarter-century after writing "Heroin," he guessed he finally knew, but he wasn't omniscient, as so many of the competing voices in the media claimed to be. Like in a postmodern novel, Lou was an unreliable narrator.

But in 1988 reliability was in decline in Lou's New York. Eight years of trickle-down economics had not trickled down; Black Monday and a $2.6 trillion national debt loomed large over Reagan's legacy of deregulation as the greedy gunslingers on Wall Street binged on cocaine while the scourge of crack was unleashed in the projects. Partially as a result of the crack epidemic, under the watch of Mayor Ed Koch, crime skyrocketed; 1988 saw a record homicide rate, with drug-related murders of police, college students, and hapless barflies alike. It seemed that no one was safe; an innocent ride on the subway, which with the rise of graffiti art had become a high-speed art installation, could easily lead to a mugging or a shooting.

As Reagan approached the end of his term, he abdicated any responsibility for the surging homeless population, claiming that "they make it their own choice for staying out there." Privilege was earned only by those who understood and engineered the capitalist market; it was every man for himself, with women fighting tooth and nail for equal rights against a gender gap that captains of industry by and large refused to close. Despite Reagan's injunction to "tear down this wall," the Berlin Wall still stood, a ubiquitous symbol for the affront to free speech Lou so vehemently opposed. Unprotected sex had become dangerous as AIDS ripped through the city, hitting many of the former Factory denizens hard. It seemed the promise of the 1960s had been broken. As sirens were the ambient soundtrack to everyday life, George Michael's "Faith" was the year's top-selling single, but Lou didn't have much. So he set out to restore it with some good old-fashioned truth-telling.

To cope with this pervasive lack of faith, Lou couldn't rely on any institution—the government, religion, even marriage—a view he articulated on "Busload of Faith," the lead single off his newest album, the yet-to-be-titled *New York*. Lou only had faith in faith itself:

> *You can only depend on one thing,*
> *You need a busload of faith to get by*

"It really *is* the eight years of Reagan," Lou said. "And as I said, I'm trying to make you feel the situation we're in. And that's what this album is all about."

Adapting William Carlos Williams's "variable foot" for rock lyrics, Lou took the ripped-from-the-headlines political gripes and syncopated cadence of the New York streets and elevated the gritty style into a poetic Brooklynese. From the opening chords of the first track, Lou was poised for a stream-of-consciousness jeremiad in the tradition of Selby or Kerouac. "Romeo

Had Juliette," the unedited track Lou and Maher laid down and never touched—it opened with an errant bar of rhythm guitar and a count-off—did Shakespeare in Harlem, chronicling the marginalized love story of Romeo Rodriguez and Juliette Bell. Yet Lou's urban take on Shakespeare's tragedy had more in common with Burroughs's Interzone than with *West Side Story*. The disillusionment of "Legendary Hearts" had evolved into the more urgent realization that with all lovers star-crossed in the fair cesspool of Manhattan, all they had was love, writ large in Lou's halting antiheroic couplets:

> *I'll take Manhattan in a garbage bag*
> *With Latin written on it that says*
> *"It's hard to give a shit these days"*

On "Halloween Parade," Lou memorialized the city's phantasmagorical annual march down Seventh Avenue, with the specter of the AIDS crisis haunting the lyrics like a subtextual ghost. During the carnivalesque spectacle, Garbo, Hitchcock, and Cary Grant rub shoulders with the crowd from Alphabet City, but it's the missing faces that stand out:

> *In the back of my mind I was afraid it might be true*
> *In the back of my mind I was afraid that they meant you*

Beneath the cynicism, with its three-chord major progression and exuberant backing vocals from Dion and Jeffrey Lesser, "Dirty Blvd." offered a glimpse of an eventual escape from the cycle of poverty on the hardscrabble road many are born onto. Yet as Lou saw clearly beyond the veil of trickle-down economics, for most, the promise of a better life was illusory.

"Boulevard" was abbreviated to look like an actual New York street sign, though it was not a stand-in for any one particular thoroughfare; it was the dead end of the American Dream, the fate the song's hero, Pedro, hopes to avoid. Yet it was also the street Lou chose to walk himself, navigating past the white-collar allure of Madison Avenue or Wall Street for the potholes and manholes of a dirtier path. He eked it out but knew firsthand how hard it was, and how much harder it could be for the less fortunate:

> *Give me your hungry, your tired, your poor, I'll piss on 'em*
> *That's what the Statue of Bigotry says*

"Endless Cycle" extrapolated the sociological out to generational conflict in the family, with Maher reinforcing the theme with the tick-tock of a vintage Seth Thomas metronome as the only percussion instrument. Snapping is the only rhythm heard on "Beginning of a Great Adventure," Lou's cynical meditation on fatherhood. The title evidently comes from a line Sylvia said to Lou in support of parenthood, but during such a heated political moment, Lou had his doubts:

> *I'd raise my own pallbearers to carry me to the grave*
> *And keep me company when I'm a wizened, toothless clod*

Lou ultimately thought better of it, not wanting his children to inherit the world his generation had built for them. It seemed that the existence of Rufus and Rita Reed was not in the cards, punctuated by Lou ironically saying, "Take it, Lou" before his solo.

This perspective underscored a bleak picture of moral decay. "There Is No Time" was an exhortation against the rhetoric of "my country right or wrong," while "Last Great American Whale" seethed with righteous indignation, conjuring *Moby-Dick* with an animal rights message:

> *Animal life is low on the totem pole*
> *With human life not worth more than infected yeast*

The track was punctuated by the familiar sound of a feathered bass drum, played by Moe Tucker. Throughout the rest of the album, Lou trumpeted his disdain for politicians: Reagan on "Sick of You" and Kurt Waldheim, the pope, and Jesse Jackson, who was currently campaigning for the Democratic presidential nomination, on "Good Evening Mr. Waldheim." He waxed poetic on "Xmas in February," channeling the plight of forgotten Vietnam War veterans, juxtaposed with the widespread corruption that characterized contemporary politics and the growing income gap on "Strawman":

> *Does anybody need another million dollar movie?*
> *Does anybody need another million dollar star?*

The album's closing track, "Dime Store Mystery," began as a title without a song. Like the pulp novel that gave the Velvet Underground its name, Lou knew he had to use it, but it took him years to unravel the mystery of the title's meaning. Lou had an epiphany while watching a television interview with Martin Scorsese about his film *The Last Temptation of Christ*, adapted from a novel by Nikos Kazantzakis. As *Raging Bull* served as inspiration for "Doin' the Things That We Want To," Scorsese's notion of Jesus's dualistic nature helped clarify Lou's intentions.

"It's fully divine and fully human, one and the same being, one entity," Scorsese said in the interview. "In Kazantzakis's idea, the human nature can't accept that fact until the very last moment."

For Lou, who had wrestled with his own dualistic personality, between base instinct and loftier ambitions, carnality and spirituality, he knew that he had solved his mystery. He sent the lyrics to Scorsese, but later the thought crystallized that he wasn't writing about himself, or Jesus on the cross as the synthesis of Hegelian dialectics and Cartesian dualism. Lou's martyr to the cause of art was another beatific figure—Andy Warhol. In the lyrics, Lou ponders the "mysteries of life" through the guise of Warhol, who found the divine in the most unlikely places, and realizes that the solution lies not in the rampant narcissism of the Reagan era, but in something more spiritual: collective welfare over individual desire, and the political unconscious of his personal choices. Lou's wistful eulogy was heightened by Wasserman's arco bass and the throttling drum tribute of Moe Tucker. In a rare move, Lou seemed to express genuine remorse:

> *I wish I hadn't thrown away my time*
> *On so much human and so much less divine*

"I think that's one of the most stunning lines that I've ever written in my life," Lou later recalled. "Though it might sound tacky to put it like this, I think that 'Dime Store Mystery' is a supreme love song, and I'm talking about a love song to a vision of spirituality." The '80s had an unlikely effect on Lou—one of rock's most outspoken apostates had taken a turn toward the spiritual.

The recording process was easier than Maher imagined. "I was going to be in the studio with Lou—long days for a long time—and I psychologically prepared myself for seven round trip flights to Australia," Maher later recalled. Yet there was no studio intervention from Sire Records, Lou's new label, and now on his fifteenth solo album, Lou was a consummate professional. "We just laid down tracks and just kept going and going and, you know, it was magical." Six weeks later, it was done.

The cover art, designed by Sylvia alongside art director Spencer Drate, took a visual cue from a 1932 black-and-white photograph by Hungarian photographer Brassaï, *Deux voyous de la bande du Grand Albert, quartier Italie*. The stark image showed a group of men in silhouette peering across a foreboding warehouse floor in Paris. Lou and Sylvia had several Brassaï photographs hanging in their home, and decided to have photographer Waring Abbott recreate the composition by superimposing five images of Lou in the foreground. "There are five Lous in different poses, and this creates the group of men on the cover," Sylvia said. "Lou was always understood as a poet of the New York streets, someone relating stories of the underground New York life, and that naturally led us to look for the very noir look of this particular Brassaï photograph." But the album still needed a name.

Sylvia knew exactly what to call it—*New York*. "It took some convincing for Lou to believe that that was an appropriate use," she recalled. "It so wonderfully brings back a certain time and place in New York City and in the whole of the United States and a certain mind-set, and when he had completed it, it was very clear to me that this defined a moment in time." Yet on the album cover, the title was pushed to the background. "If you look at the album artwork, you will see that the title appears as a shadow on the wall," Sylvia said. "We were not trying to be very pretentious about it and loud and brassy, like, 'Oh, Lou Reed owns New York.'" Rather, Lou served as a Virgil to the listener's Dante, guiding them through the inferno. "People could choose to interpret what he knew about New York and what he understood about the people in New York and that these songs, the lyrics, were a recitation of something that we could best define by shadowy words on the wall—*New York*."

With the album completed, Lou didn't rest, only pausing to record a nondenominational holiday greeting for *Winter Warnerland*, a Warner Bros. Christmas compilation. Lou spoke over a harmonizing barbershop quartet. "Hi, this is Lou Reed, wishing you and yours a happy holiday season," he said coolly. "Merry Christmas, Happy Hanukkah, or whatever it is you do. Happiness—through the years—to you."

Lou then reconnected with John Cale, renting a rehearsal space on Fiftieth Street and Ninth Avenue for three weeks, where they began the arduous task of converting their reminiscences of the early days of the Velvets into a fully realized Warhol tribute. They called the project *Songs for Drella*, based on Warhol's Factory nickname.

While they honed the music, they received word that Nico had died. At forty-nine, she had recently quit heroin and switched to methadone, but during a trip to Ibiza with her son, she had a heart attack while riding a bike on July 18, and died in the hospital later that day. As John and Lou mourned the loss, it only strengthened their resolve to complete the album. In January 1989, the week that *New York* was released, they performed a version of *Songs for Drella* at St. Ann's Church in Brooklyn, but with John completing work on *Words for the Dying* and Lou gearing up for the *New York* tour, they postponed the recording and official premiere for a later date.

As he memorialized Warhol, Lou paid his respects to another early influence, going even further back when he gave the induction speech for Dion at the Rock and Roll Hall of Fame. This time he wore a tux. "It was 1958, and the cold winds of Long Island blew in from the ocean, their high-pitched howl mixing with the dusty, musky, mellifluous liquid sounds of rock 'n' roll—the sounds of another life, the sounds of freedom," Lou began. In 1958 he would never have thought that thirty years later he would be standing on that stage, or that he would be able to have the career longevity to continue spreading the rock gospel well into middle age.

In March, Lou began the US tour of *New York* with Mike Rathke on guitar, Rob Wasserman on bass, and Robert Medici on drums. Lou also debuted a new style; out were the signature shades, replaced by wire-framed glasses, and he was sporting a new coif—a mullet. Riffing off of Miles Davis's Jheri curls, it was as though the quintessential purveyors of cool had jointly decided that, after eight years of Reagan and at least four more of Bush, hip was played out; uncool was in.

Not all of Lou's fans were pleased with the new album. On March 10, at Boston's Orpheum Theater, one heckler cut above the perpetual droning murmurs of "*Louuu*," voicing his displeasure that Lou was playing "Romeo and Juliette" instead of "Sweet Jane" or one of the hits he had paid to see. "Play some rock 'n' roll!" he said. By the second song, "Halloween Parade," Lou put an end to the disruption. Anyone with the temerity to heckle Lou Reed, who had once dragged a rabid fan across the stage by the hair, could reasonably expect a swift and devastating punishment.

"This *is* rock 'n' roll," Lou snarled. "It's *my* rock 'n' roll. If you don't like my rock 'n' roll, why don't ya just split? Get a refund, motherfucker." And the show went on with no further interruptions.

The remainder of the tour proceeded with few hiccups. Lou performed a six-night, sold-out run at the St. James Theatre on Broadway, featuring a full stage set replete with neon lights, a No Trespassing sign, and chain-link fence. "We could swear that the chandelier and the muraled walls of the St. James Theatre moaned just a little at the impact of Lou Reed's decibel levels," Barry Singer wrote in the *New Yorker*. "Could the sounds of sixty-two years at the St. James—the sounds of all the music played and all the voices raised in all those musical-comedy performances combined—ever be as loud as Lou Reed is right now, we found ourself wondering."

Despite the volume, though, Lou's debut on the Great White Way was tamer than anyone would have guessed. The mellower sounds of Lou included a cover of Frank Sinatra's saloon song "One for my Baby (and One More for the Road)," which Lou had recorded on Wasserman's Grammy-winning 1988 album *Duets*, aiming for bluesy realism over dulcet tones. Lou toured both coasts through the end of April, then took a month off before a European tour that culminated on July 4 at Wembley Stadium in London. In August, Lou broke his ankle after a sound check in Cleveland, and had to cancel the rest of the tour, returning to New York to prepare with Cale for the premiere of *Songs for Drella* in Brooklyn that November.

Lou hadn't been in close contact with Andy since they had discussed the possibility of staging *Berlin* as the rock opera it was intended to be, but now, Andy was gone, and as of November 9, so was the Berlin Wall. So the tribute John and Lou created was bittersweet. On November 29, 1989, John and Lou began a four-night run of "Songs for 'Drella: A Fiction" at the Brooklyn Academy of Music's Next Wave Festival. Custom-made Campbell's soup cans and Campbell's Cup packets designed specially for the event were distributed to concertgoers on opening night. On a sparse, darkly lighted set with a projection screen displaying rotating slides compiled by Jerome Sirlin, Lou and John narrated their impressionistic biography of the enigmatic pop art icon, distilling his life into brief, unsparing chapters beginning in Pittsburgh and ending in death. Representing the totality of a man's life in words and music is an impossible feat, especially someone as puzzling as Warhol, and their elegiac "fiction" self-consciously never quite penetrated the silk screen.

Rather, their fifteen-song collage of diary excerpts, play-by-play chronicle, and ekphrastic poetry over the jagged minimalism of piano, guitar, and viola ostinatos reflected more about their estranged relationship to Warhol and each other than it did about the man himself. It was as though the event were a Warhol happening produced from beyond the grave, his last act to galvanize the particularly theatrical reconciliation of the two polarizing forces behind the Velvet Underground. On "Hello It's Me," the last entry in the song cycle, they combined a treacly chord progression with a viola part that could not have been farther from the squall that opened "Heroin." Yet mixed emotions surrounding their fraught history colored it with the grief, recriminations, and complex love that deepened the pathos:

> *I'm sorry if I doubted your good heart*
> *Things always seem to end before they start*

Even if it did not lead to a lasting reunion—the combustible personality clash was instantaneous—the performance series led to what would have been sufficient closure to the Velvet Underground story.

"It was not easy sailing. It's nice that history has cast a silvery lining around all of that," recalled Danny Fields, who attended an early performance. "But if it's for Andy, it's probably an aluminum-foil lining."

Shortly after wrapping up the performance series, John and Lou entered Sigma Sound Studios to record the album version. Sylvia designed the album cover, a high-contrast black-and-white image of John and Lou with a faded Billy Name photo of Andy in the background. Lou regretted that Warhol wasn't there to witness the reunion, and also that he didn't get to see the phenomenal success of *New York*.

In the months since its release, critics and fans bought Lou's dystopian vision of the city more than he had anticipated. The album was his highest-charting release since *Sally Can't Dance*, rising to Number 40 on the *Billboard* chart, with "Dirty Blvd." spending four weeks at the top of the Modern Rock chart. Despite Lou's resistance to marketability, and contrary to the dictum that intellectual heft and commercial success were mutually exclusive, he had made a gold record. But as Lou implied on "Dime Store Mystery," he might have given that up for the chance to share it with Andy, a fact he didn't realize until it was too late. Lou was forty-seven, and the '80s were coming to a sobering conclusion. He had finally grown up.

# 25

As Lou and John bid a final farewell to Warhol in Brooklyn, thousands of miles away, the revolution in rock they had started twenty-five years earlier had caused a different kind of revolution. With the crumbling of the Soviet Union and the destruction of the Berlin Wall, Czech dissidents took to the streets of Prague. On November 17 students stormed Wenceslas Square to commemorate the anniversary of the 1939 Nazi occupation of Czechoslovakia, until they were violently suppressed by riot police. The event set off a series of demonstrations in the city that quickly drew five hundred thousand, leading to a nationwide two-hour strike on November 27 that triggered the resignation of the Communist regime, which agreed to concede their single-party monopoly the next day. On December 29, after forty-one years of communist rule, Vaclav Havel, the poet and dissident, was elected president of the newly formed Czech Republic. Spurred by the democratic election of the Solidarity party in Poland, the Romanian Revolution, and the Estonian Singing Revolution, some referred to the uprising in Prague as the November Events, but Havel knew it by another name—the Velvet Revolution, a bloodless coup, savage but ultimately nonviolent, like the Velvet Underground.

It began on vinyl. In 1968, at the height of the Prague Spring, Havel was invited to attend the premiere of his play *The Memorandum* at the Public Theater in New York. He also participated in the riots at Columbia University. Six weeks later, he returned to Prague with a souvenir: *White Light/White Heat*. After the military suppression of the Prague Spring, Havel distributed the contraband to Milan Hlavsa, a bassist who floated in revolutionary circles. With the Velvets as a signpost, along with Frank Zappa's "Plastic People" from the 1967 album *Absolutely Free*, Hlavsa formed the Plastic People of the Universe. After the Velvets themselves, the Plastics were the most influential of the supposedly thirty thousand bands that emerged from the banana album.

In communist Czechoslovakia, the music of the Velvets was considered dangerous. In 1970 the government revoked the Plastics' musicians' license, and they began performing Velvets covers at clandestine events. In 1976, during the underground Music Festival of the Second Culture, the Czech State Security secret police arrested the band on trumped-up charges of disturbing the peace, and they all faced jail time. But the censorship attempt only incited more populist rage. The Velvet Underground was already in the ether—two hundred copies of Lou's lyrics translated into Czech were disseminated to artists and intellectuals—and members of the Plastics recited Velvets lyrics to help them endure their prison sentences. Others faced police reprisal for merely congregating on the Charles Bridge in Prague, especially if they brought a guitar.

In response to the arrest of the Plastics, Havel spearheaded the drafting of Charter 77, an anticommunist manifesto that was promptly banned. In 1978 Havel himself was arrested; he served nearly five years in a Czech prison, including a stint in a Soviet labor camp. By 1988 the Plastics had reformed as Půlnoc—"Midnight" in Czech—symbolizing the incipient dawn of a new era of rock and freedom. Yet in 1989 Havel was arrested again. During the Velvet Revolution, protesters chanted "Havel to the Castle!" Their rallying cry reverberated across the nation.

Within a year, Havel had gone from public enemy to president, taking up residence in Hradcany Castle, Prague's medieval spired castle on a hill, appointing many of the original drafters of Charter 77 as his cabinet. Lou had no idea that he had played an instrumental role; he had been a human rights activist all along.

In March 1990 *Rolling Stone* commissioned Lou to go to Prague for an interview with Havel. "I'm not an interviewer, I'm an interviewee, but in this particular case, they said, 'There's an approved list of people for President Havel—you're on it. So how would you like to be an interviewer and you get to meet Vaclav Havel?'" Lou later recalled. "Who could say no to that?"

When he met his government-designated Czech guide, he initially thought the experience would be "Kafkaesque," but perhaps it turned out to be slightly more characteristic of a Kundera novel. So much had changed in Prague. They visited the Jewish cemetery and ghetto, the former site of a monument to Stalin, and the Charles Bridge, which had recently become much easier to cross.

Lou went into the meeting with Havel with trepidation, an anxiety he had recently felt in 1989 when he interviewed Hubert Selby Jr. Yet Havel was similarly starstruck. They had all the jitters of a first date. "Lou was the first to come to my office from the heaven of stars," Havel later recalled. "No one so famous had come to Czechoslovakia before." Havel made a feeble attempt to spruce up the castle's shabby Soviet-era decor, but he didn't have the time to adequately prepare for his honored guest.

When Lou arrived at Hradcany, he was perplexed by the hero's welcome he was given, not realizing the impact he had made on Czech politics, much less on Czech ears, just as Havel was unaware of the impact he'd made on Lou. Over a round of Czech beers—Lou couldn't say no—he pulled out *Songs for Drella*, a gift for Havel. Toward the end of the interview, Lou asked the one burning question he had for the mild-mannered president. "Why did you stay, why didn't you leave? How could you stand the terrible abuse?" he asked.

"I stayed because I live here. I was only trying to do the right thing. I had not planned for these various things to have happened but I never doubted that we would succeed. All I ever wanted to do was the right thing." Lou was awe-struck by the candor of Havel's sentiment; he felt the same way about New York.

Meeting Havel had a profound and humbling effect. "He's enormously charming, he's incredibly smart, and well-read and intellectual, which I obviously am not, and he obviously *is*," Lou later said. "But he's also very aware of rock." That night, Havel asked Lou to attend a concert given by the Prague-based Velvet Revival at the ULUV Gallery on Narodni Street, the street where only a month earlier, the first demonstration during the Velvet Revolution came to a halt when it was quashed by police.

"Lou probably thought that Havel wanted him to play privately, like in his fireplace," says Jan Machacek, a founding member of the Velvet Revival who went on to become an economist and columnist in Prague. "He was hesitant, quite nervous about it, but Havel basically made him do it. So he said, 'I'll do it if you get a Fender Twin for me.' It was still a few months after the collapse of communism, but fortunately we knew about one guy who had a Fender Twin." The multilevel club was near the site of some of the Charter 77 meetings that launched the Velvet Revolution. "It was occupied by artists, all kinds of young artists and artists who were forbidden under Communism and brought in paintings. There were paintings and sculptures everywhere, and it was a permanent party every evening," Machacek recalls. "There was this revolutionary atmosphere still, so everybody knew through gossip that Lou Reed would play in the evening. There were obviously no posters, no advertising."

For Machacek, the experience was revelatory. "It was the Velvet Underground that brought me into rock music. When I was fourteen, I heard the

Velvet Underground for the first time, and it completely changed my life," Machacek says. After founding the Velvet Revival, Machacek and the band decided they would only perform for special occasions. "We said, 'Let's rehearse it from time to time, and do it just for friends, because we like it. It must be a holiday. It's not a regular band which is playing constantly like an institution," he says. "It's not our primary band, but it's an extended band of our hearts."

This was one of those occasions. At the ULUV show, Lou realized that in Prague, "Sweet Jane" had an unexpected political valence in which he had unwittingly played a part. "I always thought the Velvet Underground first and foremost was about freedom. Freedom to write about what you want, play it the way you want, put it out any way you want," Lou said. "That was, I thought, the bottom line of the whole thing, and lo and behold it found a reception in Czechoslovakia." Standing with the packed crowd at ULUV, Lou discovered the band recreating the Velvets songbook note for note, in the original down-tuned key. When Lou got onstage, though, bathed in a green spotlight, he had to ask *them* to play in a different key. "Everything we played differently, but obviously, we didn't make any mistakes. Everyone was concentrating," Machacek recalls. Lou was overcome with emotion. "I want to tell you what a pleasure it is to get to play for you this evening," he told the crowd. Then they struck the opening chords to "I'm Waiting for the Man," and it was as though John, Moe, and Sterl were behind him again. After the show, Lou paid a rare compliment to Machacek. "It was great to play with you," he said.

Before Havel left, he introduced Lou to some of the dissidents who had been imprisoned for playing or performing the music of the Velvet Underground. The ripple effect was shocking. Then Havel pulled out a tattered little black book and gave it to Lou. It was a handwritten copy of Lou's lyrics translated into Czech, one of only two hundred copies. "They were very dangerous to have. People went to jail, and now you have one. Keep your fingers crossed for us," Havel said. And he left.

Lou returned to New York deeply moved. When he submitted his interview to *Rolling Stone*, they demanded revisions. But Lou didn't change what he did for anyone—not for a record label, and certainly not for a magazine he had once reviled on record. "They wanted me to change this, change that, change this, change that. And I thought, 'Why don't I give you your money back? We don't have to go through this, because I'm not going to change anything,'" Lou recalled. Lou eventually placed the piece in *Musician*. Yet he didn't merely file the story and put it to bed; the experience in Prague awakened nostalgia for his early days.

Soon thereafter, he saw the Velvet Underground together for the first time in decades in the outskirts of Paris. On June 15, 1990, the Fondation Cartier in Jouy-en-Josas premiered their own Warhol tribute, "The Andy Warhol System: Pub, Pop, Rock," inviting the surviving members of the Velvets; they all accepted the invitation. Days prior to the opening, Lou and John Cale announced they would perform excerpts from *Songs for Drella*. The exhibit recreated the Warhol milieu, including a 1960s New York street scene and a portion of the Factory, so the Velvets felt right at home. On an open-air stage, John and Lou performed five songs from the album, concluding with "Hello It's Me," with John on viola; dispelling any rumors of the acrimony between them, they actually smiled at each other. But after they finished the song, they didn't exit the stage.

"We have a little surprise for you," Lou said. As he lit up a cigarette— the only remaining vice he couldn't bring himself to give up—Moe Tucker climbed onstage, followed by Sterling Morrison. With the exception of John, they were all wearing sunglasses. "I'd like to introduce Sterling Morrison," Lou said matter-of-factly, to thunderous applause. "And Maureen Tucker." He strummed the first chord of "Heroin." Earlier in the day, Lou had proposed playing "Pale Blue Eyes" but was reminded that he had already fired John at that point; the same with "Sweet Jane." It would have to be "Heroin."

A quarter-century after their first gig and a lot of life lessons later, the Velvet Underground had finally made it to Europe. Tucker was a forty-five-year-old mother of five, working in the office at a Wal-Mart distribution center in Georgia, but she still had the same pixie haircut and played standing up, pounding the toms with an offbeat ferocity. John's psychedelic bowing had the vertiginous rush of a summer long ago, full of promise that had been deferred until that moment. Morrison, who had served as a tugboat captain and become a professor of medieval literature at the University of Texas at Austin since they disbanded, played as though not a day had passed, even though he didn't even have his own guitar with him. "Thanks, Andy Warhol," Lou said, capping off the performance of *Songs for Drella* with the most meaningful show of gratitude. In the spirit of the Velvets, it was unplanned. They left the stage with the sense that it might not be their final bow.

"The four of us have not been in one place, let alone onstage, and also we had not intended to play today," Sterling Morrison said in an interview at the event. "If I'd thought I was going to play I'd have brought a guitar."

For Morrison, the longstanding resentment had dissipated. "It went away at that reunion," recalls Martha Morrison. "I remember Sylvia Reed saying to me the next day, 'I've never seen Lou in such a great mood.'"

Before he left the Fondation Cartier event, Lou posed for a portrait shot by photographer Louis Jammes, which he printed on aluminum and gave to Lou. "The resulting photograph was unforgettable, so beautiful in the composition," Sylvia said. "It seemed to have a real power on its own and when we saw the results we knew we would end up using it for something someday." After resuming the *New York* tour in Japan, Lou returned home in the summer of 1990, where two of his friends were dying of cancer. On the resulting album, he and Sylvia found a place for the portrait.

On March 14, 1991, two weeks after Lou's forty-ninth birthday, songwriter Doc Pomus died after a long battle with lung cancer. Over the years, Lou had become close friends with Pomus, the songwriter behind some of Lou's favorites: Dion's "A Teenager in Love," as well as "This Magic Moment," which Lou later covered on a tribute album, and Elvis's "Little Sister," a title Lou had cribbed several years earlier. Lou often attended a songwriting seminar Pomus offered at his Seventy-Second Street apartment on the Upper West Side. "Doc Pomus was a very, very dear friend of Lou's that he respected tremendously," Sylvia recalled. "He loved him like a father." The other loss was Rotten Rita, known as "the Mayor" of the Factory, who was one of Lou's first friends in New York. When he moved into an apartment on Tenth Street, Lou lovingly recalled the time he lent his apartment to Ondine when he was gone and returned to find it ransacked; "Rotten Rita had carved a poem on the front door, which hung off its hinges."

Lou took the occasion to also reflect on the earlier loss of Lincoln Swados, who had died in 1989 in the East Fourth Street storefront he had occupied for years, after his landlord threatened him with an eviction notice. The property manager mandated that he vacate the building in February 1989, but he was unable to leave before construction workers erected a barrier around the building, effectively penning him in. He became ill, and with the exit blocked, Swados died several days later. Lou based "Harry's Circumcision" on Swados, his troubled Van Gogh–like roommate at Syracuse.

On Sunday, March 17, Lou and Sylvia attended Pomus's funeral at the Riverside Funeral Home on Amsterdam Avenue. When jazz vocalist Jimmy Scott sang "Someone to Watch Over Me" accompanied by Dr. John, everyone was dumbstruck, especially Lou. "That moment when Jimmy Scott got up and sang at Doc's funeral was one of the most powerful experiences I've ever had," Sylvia recalled. "Lou loved that sound and particular type of voice, and never forgot it." He knew he had to collaborate with Scott on his next album and resurrect the career of the all-but-forgotten jazz singer; it didn't take long for Sire Records to sign him.

To cope with the grief, Lou entered the studio to record his meditation on mortality, *Magic and Loss*. Coproduced by Mike Rathke, Lou used the same band as on *New York* but hired drummer Michael Blair, who had collaborated with Tom Waits, Elvis Costello, and played on Fernando Saunders's first solo album, *Cashmere Dreams*. Many of Lou's earlier albums had delved into Descartes's mind-body dualism, but *Magic and Loss* focused on the failure of the body even as the mind remains strong. The concept had the potential for mawkishness, but Lou handled the elegy with grace and subtlety. Each song had a subtitle that charted the stages of grief. The album's lead single, "What's Good: The Thesis" plainly articulated the album's basic premise—the bitter acknowledgement that life's not fair—with the pent-up aggression of driving, calibrated rock. "Power and Glory: The Situation" featured Jimmy Scott on the chorus, imbuing the lyric "I want all of it" with tremulous gravity in his inimitable countertenor delivery as Lou rapped about the pain of chemotherapy. On "Sword of Damocles: Externally," "Goodby Mass: In a Chapel Bodily Termination," and "Cremation: Ashes to Ashes," Lou processes the emotions he felt during the funerals, weighing thoughts of ephemerality, bereavement, and the dubiousness of an afterlife opposite Rathke and Wasserman's dirgelike guitar and bass. Yet Lou reaches a point of resigned acceptance by the haunting closing track, "Magic and Loss: The Summation," articulating a core belief he had always carried with him:

> *It's best not to wait for luck to save you*
> *Pass through the fire to the light*

Sylvia based the album art on this lyric. "The disc itself we wanted to make look literally burnt, like it had to pass through fire," she said. It was so convincing that some people who bought the album thought the disc was damaged and tried to return it. For the packaging, Sylvia and the art directors created a special metal box for the limited edition version to emphasize the theme of permanence and decay, while carefully selecting photos of Pomus and Rita for the gatefold. Reflecting the album's persistent questions, four mystical symbols drawn from alchemy were placed on the front cover, one on each corner; Lou intended to project these same symbols during concerts. The symbols pointed to a deeper mystery of meaning and mortality that Lou had begun to unravel on *New York*, confronted on *Songs for Drella*, and finally resolved by the end of *Magic and Loss*. Yet like on "Dime Store Mystery," Lou's enigmatic resolution was not definitive, but spiritual or perhaps metaphysical, tempered by loss and cloaked in magic.

When *Magic and Loss* was released in January 1992, the grunge movement had crystalized, with Nirvana's *Nevermind* released the previous year. With the lineage of "Smells Like Teen Spirit" traced back to Lou as one of the patriarchal figures of punk, *Magic and Loss* sold well, rising to Number 6 on the UK charts, with "What's Good: The Thesis" spending three weeks at the top of the Modern Rock chart. Immediately following the release, Lou traveled to Paris, where he was awarded the French Order of Arts and Letters medal.

But as the wave crested, it crashed. Lou's relationship with Sylvia began to deteriorate. After fifteen years together, their priorities had diverged. Now in her midthirties, Sylvia wanted children, but for Lou, dachshunds were enough; family life was not necessarily conducive to being an internationally touring rock star, but Lou showed no signs of slowing down. The first leg of the tour began in January and went through March, spanning Italy, Spain, the Netherlands, and the rest of Europe.

On April 30, 1992, Lou was scheduled to play *The Arsenio Hall Show* at its Los Angeles studio. On April 29, during the sound check, riots broke out following the savage beating of unarmed black construction worker Rodney King by a horde of mostly white policemen. Hall devoted the program to a discussion of police brutality, but decided that Lou should still play. Jimmy Scott provided moving background vocals on "Walk on the Wild Side," and Lou rendered his reaction to the deplorable event by spontaneously changing a verse of "What's Good: The Thesis":

> *What good is law without justice*
> *What good is a law that can't feel*
> *We love the life that others throw away nightly*
> *And it's not fair, not fair at all*

The tour continued through the United States, culminating in a stint in Japan from July to August. By the time they returned to New York, it slowly emerged that Lou and Sylvia were breaking apart.

Back in New York, Lou got a call from Hal Willner, the avant-garde downtown progenitor who had produced the Kurt Weill tribute album several years earlier, asking if he might be interested in participating in a Jewish music festival. Willner was acting as a go-between for John Zorn, who was also featured on the Weill album, and thought using an intermediary with more leverage might improve his chances of persuading Lou. Zorn had been commissioned to curate the first Radical Jewish Culture Festival as part of the Art Projekt in Munich, and he wanted Lou to participate. He figured there was a slim chance, but it didn't hurt to ask; Lou didn't wear tefillin—not many people knew of his religious background—but after all, he was a Jew. But Lou insisted that Zorn call him personally. Zorn had the guts to compose *Kristallnacht*, which he was premiering as the centerpiece of the festival, but calling Lou Reed on the phone gave him the heebie-jeebies.

When he was fourteen, Zorn had first heard the Velvet Underground at the Dom in the East Village as part of the Exploding Plastic Inevitable tour in 1967, when Lou became a lifelong influence. The Velvets were the common ancestor of both Seattle grunge and the downtown avant-garde scene, with Lou in many ways serving as a patriarchal figure to a far-reaching diaspora that connected Kurt Cobain to the Lounge Lizards, and Zorn was one of the key purveyors of the tribal melting pot aesthetic emanating from Alphabet City. Now that Zorn was thirty-nine and a luminary of New York's flourishing downtown scene, he was in a position to arrange an opportunity to meet one of his idols.

Zorn knew that Lou was hardly religious—he was as secular and sacrilegious as they come—but he hoped that apropos of his examination of the big questions on *Magic and Loss*, the time would be right for Lou to embrace his inner Jew. So he mustered the courage and called. To Lou, who had just finished touring with his most lugubrious album since *Berlin*, the prospect of confronting the Holocaust suddenly didn't sound so grim. Much to Zorn's surprise, Lou was in; Radical Jewish Culture had just become more Jewish—and more radical.

The Radical Jewish Culture Festival was scheduled for the anniversary of Kristallnacht, the Night of Broken Glass, the harrowing moment in 1938 when Nazis throughout Germany desecrated synagogues, vandalized Jewish storefronts, smashed windows, and beat and imprisoned thousands of Jews, a prelude to the Holocaust. Zorn's festival would be the first large-scale celebration of Jewish culture in Munich in decades.

Zorn even had custom-made T-shirts printed for participating artists, with the words RHYTHM AND JEWS silk-screened on the front. Everyone arrived at customs at the Bavarian airport: Marc Ribot, Shelley Hirsch, Gary Lucas, Lou—and Midwesterner Laurie Anderson, who though not a Jew by birth had played with many of the others and certainly had honorary status. After carving out a niche as a sculptor and art critic, Anderson had risen to prominence as a feminist performance artist, and following the release of her 1981 single "O Superman," a polemical critique of mainstream urban culture, she was catapulted to unlikely major label fame.

As it turned out, Lou and Laurie lived blocks away from each other—they had even performed on the same stage at Paul Simon's Children's Health Fund benefit—but due to the vicissitudes of touring schedules, social engagements, and the general Brownian motion of the city, they had never met. Though only five years younger than Lou, Anderson barely knew the Velvet Underground; when Lou opened his mouth, she was expecting a Brit. It was Lou who was dumbstruck—he couldn't take his eyes off her.

After they arrived at the hotel, Laurie showed Lou her latest acquisition, an Apple PowerBook, the latest in computing technology. He was genuinely interested in the computer—they were both gadgetry buffs—but Lou was much more interested in Laurie. Lou asked if Laurie would perform with him at the show, and she agreed. The song was "A Dream" from *Songs for Drella*, an atmospheric piece culled from Warhol's diary entries, and Lou had Laurie read the lyrics.

> *It was a very cold clear fall night*
> *Some snowflakes were falling*
> *Gee, it was so beautiful*

They were Andy Warhol's words, but they sounded like Laurie's. To Lou, her cadence just felt right, intimate, like they'd done it before. Every pause, every private irony, every syllable was delivered with such brio, such intuition, exactly the way Lou would have done it, only perhaps with more feeling. Here, in Munich, he had finally found his mirror. It was as though Andy Warhol were there with them in the theater, as though Drella had even brought them together, too. For the first time in a long while, Lou had a new sensation. He was fifty years old, but he felt an old yearning in the pit of his stomach. He had fallen in love again.

# 26

When they flew home, Lou and Laurie informally agreed to meet up sometime in the ensuing months. Lou was still married, though, and Laurie's schedule was just as busy as his, so it would have to wait. Lou followed the Radical Jewish Culture Festival by paying tribute to another Jewish cause: Bob Dylan, who invited Lou to perform at Madison Square Garden at the 30th Anniversary Concert Celebration, which Neil Young dubbed "Bobfest," a night of Dylan covers to commemorate his thirty years since his self-titled debut album. Backed by Booker T. Jones and the MGs' rhythm section and sandwiched between performances by Stevie Wonder and Eddie Vedder, Lou picked "Foot of Pride," an obscure outtake from Dylan's *Infidels* that had appeared in 1991 on *The Bootleg Series Volumes 1–3 (Rare & Unreleased) 1961–1991*, which Lou listened to during the *Magic and Loss* tour. The opening lines immediately appealed to Lou:

> *Like the lion tears the flesh off of a man*
> *So can a woman who passes herself off as a male*

A month after Bill Clinton was elected to office, Lou appeared on a live Christmas recording on December 20 with folksinger-songwriter Bruce Cockburn and Rosanne Cash, performing Cockburn's Nativity song, "Cry of a Tiny Babe." Lou sang a solo verse, the song's sole mention of Judaism:

> *Is that of Herod, a paranoid man*
> *Who when he hears there's a baby of the king of Jews*
> *Sends death squads to kill all male children under two*

A few days later, he played another Christmas party at Big Mike's rehearsal studio. Yet with Jesus on his mind, Lou's voice displayed a peculiar quality—vibrato—as though all along, he had genuine vocal chops, but chose to restrict his range for aesthetic reasons. But something was calling Jesus's son back to the fiery manger from whence he came. Soon, plans for a Velvet Underground reunion tour were underway.

Following a meeting and a marathon rehearsal session at a former factory in Chelsea to verify if it was even possible, by early spring, ironclad plans for the tour were set in motion, with Sylvia serving as manager and lighting designer. Morrison would be done with classes, and Moe Tucker, who had long since started a solo career of her own, arranged to go on indefinite leave from her job. The Velvet Underground—now rockers of a certain age—were poised to prove that they could shake out the mothballs and rock the house. It was never about the money, but nearly thirty years later, Morrison and Tucker were finally given an opportunity to capitalize on their music. As they relearned the old material—Cale had to learn the post-1968 songs for the first time—they decided it would not be a nostalgia tour. Critical consensus emerged that the real-life Velvets, who had attained near biblical pop culture reverence and, as legend had it, could fell Communist governments with a Zeus-like strum of the guitar, couldn't possibly measure up against their towering myth. Yet the band had no intention of recreating the 1960s. There was always a bleary-eyed hustle to get the gear and band members all in one place; now they at least had decent equipment. "We're in the business of remythologizing, not demythologizing," Cale said.

Leading up to their long-awaited European debut, anticipation mounted as the Velvets prepared for the first show on June 1 at the three-thousand-seat Playhouse in Edinburgh. They had some understandable jitters heading into their June 6 show at London's Wembley Stadium. Lou had performed in Wembley before, but the experience plunged him into a state of vertigo; he was twenty-three again. Unlike in 1965, though, now the world was watching—*New Musical Express* put them on the cover, with the headline REVIVAL OF THE HIPPEST. But were the reformed Velvets still hip? The nastier critics dismissed the tour before it even started as a publicity stunt; others had been waiting for so long that it was as though they expected Robert Johnson or Paganini back from the dead. The Velvets didn't care, though. They did what they always had done.

Yet at Wembley, for two full hours they transported the ten-thousand-seat stadium to the backroom at Max's. "I witnessed myself a lot of cynical, hardened journalists weeping at the Wembley show," Sylvia recalled. "It had been done, and had been done effectively, beautifully, and brought back that sound." With Nico gone, Lou and John split lead vocals on "Femme Fatale," "I'll Be Your Mirror," and "All Tomorrow's Parties." Two new songs were written for the tour: the impish "Velvet Nursery Rhyme" and "Coyote," cowritten by John and Lou, which captured the savage imagery of a bygone urban wilderness:

> No tame dog is ever
> Ever gonna take my bone

On June 13 the Velvets played the Palace of Culture in Prague, a socialist building that had been built for state-sponsored culture events and Party meetings. Havel attended. "I want to tell you how very nice it is for us to play in this building for you," Lou said to the crowd. "We understand what this building meant before, so we're happy to play here now." Of course, the Velvets were huge in Prague, where they were the biggest celebrities who had never made an appearance. Lou did something he had never done—he took a request. The Velvets had never performed for an audience that had to fight harder to hear their music than they did to play it. When they finished the set, the applause continued for minutes. They played five encores.

Their mid-June shows at L'Olympia in Paris were recorded and used for *Live MCMXCIII*. The Velvets continued touring through Europe, opening for U2, but the tour came to a close in July. Many had hoped for a more permanent reunion, but there would be no American tour; Lou and the rest of the band couldn't come to terms, and as old conflicts resurfaced, hopes were dashed. Some unresolved tension had been dissipated, but the core electrical polarity that sustained the Velvets was inextinguishable; they could barely stand in the same room together, but when they got onstage, it was glorious. Meanwhile, Lou's marriage was also bursting at the seams. He and Sylvia had to negotiate the difficult position of going through a divorce while maintaining a business relationship.

"This was in the middle of a time that I found pretty challenging," Sylvia recalled. In addition to managing the tour, Sylvia had to design the packaging for the Velvets' reunion album. "It was a difficult package to put together. We had to think about the artistic decisions—there were a million. It was made harder by everything else that was going on at the time."

Even though their marriage was effectively over—they were separated and the divorce was finalized in 1994—Lou and Sylvia collaborated on one more major event: the first Sweet Relief Musicians Fund benefit. The benefit was organized for Victoria Williams, a singer-songwriter suffering from multiple sclerosis. Lou had met her in February 1993 at a songwriters' forum at the Bottom Line. At the end of the night, everyone had to perform covers. Lou played Smokey Robinson's "The Tracks of My Tears" and Dylan's "Foot of Pride"; Williams sang "What a Wonderful World." Lou was deeply moved and knew that he had to bring her on tour with him.

"He pointed at his skin, and he had goose bumps," Williams recalls of Lou's reaction to her rendition. "As the song went on, he pointed at his eye, and there were tears."

When Williams was diagnosed with MS that year, Sylvia coproduced a benefit album featuring Pearl Jam, Matthew Sweet, Lou, and others recording Williams's music, with proceeds going toward her medical expenses. Lou recorded "Tarbelly and Featherfoot" from the 1990 album *Swing the Statue!* That October, Lou performed the piece and Williams's "Crazy Mary" on a televised Sweet Relief Fund benefit on *120 Minutes*, MTV's alternative music program. At the studio, Lou met drummer Danny Frankel, an acolyte of jazz innovator Paul Motian, who had collaborated with Williams since the early 1980s.

"What he brought out of me was this very refined, honest, focused energy—just playing for the song," says Frankel. Frankel also played an Artists Rights Foundation benefit at the Shrine Auditorium with Lou, Chris Isaak, and Los Lobos, in addition to periodic appearances with Lou on late-night talk shows. "I feel like he was one of the guys. It wasn't like him and the rest of the people. After you get used to him, no one was really intimidated by him."

Despite Lou's prickly reputation, Laurie Anderson wasn't intimidated by him either. Two weeks before the MTV appearance, they agreed to meet at the annual Audio Engineering Society Convention at the sprawling Javits Center. Overlooking the West Side Highway and not much else, it wasn't the most romantic spot for a first date, or the most romantic activity, but to Lou and Laurie, microphones had a singular mystique and romance to them. Lou had not explicitly defined it as a date, though. Yet the convention led to coffee, then a movie, then dinner, and finally an evening stroll. For Lou, it was a perfect day.

As Laurie prepared for the publication of *Stories from the Nerve Bible,* her twenty-year retrospective, she also began working on her first studio album in five years. *Bright Red,* produced by Brian Eno and featuring several artists Lou had already collaborated with, including guitarist Marc Ribot and bassist Greg Cohen. Lou and Laurie had become inseparable—they soon moved in together—and they cowrote "In Our Sleep," a minimalist love song, for *Bright Red.* Over screeching guitar feedback, drummer Joey Baron's propulsive beat, percussionist Cyro Baptista's tambourine polyrhythms, and an ethereal keyboard part played by Eno, Lou and Laurie recited their unison tone poem, employing repetition of the same line to convey their spiritual communion, even on the unconscious level:

> *[Lou:] In our sleep*
> *[Laurie:] Where we meet*

With Laurie in his life, Lou began looking inward. At the end of March, he participated in the nonsectarian Downtown Seder at the Knitting Factory, the TriBeCa arts space where he occasionally performed. The event was an alternative Passover Seder with an updated liturgy read by avant-garde artists and intellectuals, with the lens turned toward freedom of expression and human rights advocacy to reflect modern-day analogues to the Exodus story. Lou asked Michael Dorf, the owner of the downtown venue, if he could bring his Long Island family; in the inclusive spirit of the event, Dorf invited the whole *mishpucha.* It was the world's hippest Passover, a night different from all other nights; the bread was unleavened, but the text of the traditional Haggadah had risen with the help of the readers. Lou read the traditional part of the wise child, as opposed to the wicked, which was assigned to John Zorn, with Lou reciting one of his poems. To Lou, who only approved of slaying on a guitar, Passover finally made sense.

One of the downtown congregants was Terry Philips; they hadn't seen each other in years. Philips was shocked when Lou took the bimah. "They were doing poetry. And they said, 'Now, ladies and gentlemen, one of the great artists of all time—Lou Reed. And there he is on the stage at the Knitting Factory,'" recalls Philips. "He started to do poetry, all the stuff I loved when I signed him. It was really wonderful stuff. As he was doing it, he saw me, and he literally almost buckled. And he pointed to me and said, 'Ladies and gentleman, the man who discovered me—Terry Philips.'" After Lou finished his reading, he joined Philips's table. "He was a different human being. And he said, 'I was a real punk, wasn't I?' I said, 'You know, man, even when I hit you that time, I pulled a slap, because I liked you that much. I didn't want to hurt you.' He said, 'I know that. I know I was difficult.' He sat there for an hour reminiscing."

Having made his peace with Philips over Passover, Lou went back on the road. On May 1, 1994, he performed a solo set of greatest hits—just a guitar and voice—at the Porta San Giovanni in Rome for the May Day celebration, organized by three Italian labor unions. The event drew hundreds of thousands, reaching a climax on "Walk on the Wild Side," with Lou inciting the throngs of fans to sing the part of the "colored girls." There was no riot this time. Lou's days of riotous youth were well behind him.

By the 1990s, Lou was firmly entrenched as a cultural icon. "Walk on the Wild Side" was fodder for a sanitized, multicultural *Simpsons* parody—"and all the races go, 'do, dee do . . .'"—while Beavis and Butt-Head watched the music video for "No Money Down." Lou had a memorable role as himself in Wayne Wang and Paul Auster's cinematic love letter to Brooklyn, *Blue in the Face*. He wrote "You'll Know You Were Loved" for the *Friends* soundtrack; two of his songs were featured in *The Cable Guy* starring Jim Carrey, which was produced by Judd Apatow, the grandson of Bob Shad. Denis Johnson referenced "Heroin" in the title of his 1992 short story collection, *Jesus' Son*, while artists running the gamut from Marky Mark and the Funky Bunch to A Tribe Called Quest sampled "Wild Side."

Lou even made a cameo appearance in the "impossible level" of Penn & Teller's unreleased Sega video game *Smoke and Mirrors*, in which a leather-clad digital avatar of Lou appears on a street corner to a MIDI version of "Sweet Jane," a tiny suitcase in his hand, and eviscerates Penn & Teller by shooting a lightning bolt through his sunglasses. The legend had become fact.

Yet Lou's cultural saturation level was also a testament to the reverence people had for him. Months after being tasked with the ironic honor of giving the Rock and Roll Hall of Fame induction speech for Frank Zappa—someone the Velvets had initially despised but whom Lou came to appreciate—the Velvets were nominated for their own induction. It seemed they might not all be able to attend the ceremony, though. Sterling Morrison had been diagnosed with non-Hodgkin's lymphoma.

Morrison died on August 30, 1995, the day after his fifty-third birthday. Three days later, Lou performed "Sweet Jane" with Soul Asylum at a concert at the Cleveland Municipal Stadium to commemorate the opening of the Rock and Roll Hall of Fame and Museum, dedicating the performance to Morrison. The Velvets' induction ceremony was held on January 17, 1996, at the Waldorf-Astoria in New York, and Patti Smith gave the speech. "They are the Velvet Underground, and we salute them, and more than them, their captain, Sterling Morrison, who no doubt, in viewing these proceedings, might have a bit of mythical contempt for us all," Smith said. "But would also feel a secret pride."

In honor of Morrison, they performed "Last Night I Said Goodbye to My Friend," a song that Lou, John, and Moe had cowritten for him. "This event makes an astonishing point to all the young musicians in the world—that sales are not the be-all and end-all of rock 'n' roll," Cale said.

Lou paid another tribute to Morrison on his next solo album, *Set the Twilight Reeling*, on "Finish Line":

> *Nothing's forever not even five minutes*
> *When you're headed for the finish line*

After the sepulchral introspection of *Magic and Loss*, Lou changed the pace, reuniting with bassist Fernando Saunders to anchor the recording with some fretless Fernandizing. Recording live at the Roof and then at the Magic Shop, Lou enlisted keyboardist Roy Bittan, the "Professor" of the E Street Band, percussionist Mino Cinelu of Weather Report, and drummer Tony "Thunder" Smith of Serge Gainsbourg's group. The album opened with a sentimental return to Lou's salad days in Brooklyn with "Egg Cream," a tribute to the mood-elevating effects of the titular effervescent beverage. This bubbly tonic permeated the rest of the album, a carpe diem celebration of life with a quintessentially Lou-like psychoanalytic interlude—"Sex with Your Parents (Motherfucker)"—proving that Lou still had the mordant wit to spew four- and twelve-letter words with maximum impact.

If Lou's corrosive edge had been diluted to the gentle fizz of seltzer water, it was a result of Laurie's mellowing effect. Lou dedicated the album to her, and as he was wont to do, made his matrimonial intentions clear. However, after two failed marriages, he wondered whether he was the problem, and if he was, whether he could change. This was the central argument of *Set the Twilight Reeling*, one of his most autobiographical albums, which alternated between the vertigo of being stuck in a flawed past and pushing forward to a dubious future. Lou tempered his perennial altar fever with a paradoxical fear of marital shackles on "NYC Man," his take on machismo, in case there were any doubts that beneath the codependent veneer, if the love was not reciprocal, Lou was just as free as Lynyrd Skynyrd. Yet he underscored his own vulnerability with a sly reference to Thomas Mann:

> *I'm a m-a-n-n man*
> *Blink your eyes and I'll be gone*

The track reflected his complex feelings as he transitioned from the end of his second marriage to his blossoming romance with Laurie. To add gravity to the sentiment, Lou featured a horn section culled from the jazz elite, consisting of World Saxophone Quartet cofounder Oliver Lake, along with J. D. Parran and Russell Gunn Jr.

Lou's concern that the new Lou was just the old Lou with a few more wrinkles was evident in the confessional warble of "Trade In," a warts-and-all look in the mirror:

> *I met a new me at 8 AM*
> *The other one got lost*
> *This was not a trade in*
> *Although I wouldn't believe the cost*

Lou rarely voiced any regrets, but after living with himself for more than fifty years, he had a few. He found release from the past through Laurie, though, articulated on "Hang On to Your Emotions," with Laurie providing backing vocals. On "Hookywooky," Lou just wants to forget his past transgressions and, well, "hookywooky," but negative memories still haunt him:

> *They take your pants your money your name*
> *But the song still remain*

Lou wanted to get past his past, though, as he elucidated on "The Proposition," in which he plainly stated that "we were meant to be." It was a proposition, not a proposal; he didn't want to see if the third time would be the charm. Not quite yet. "Riptide," with its heavily distorted guitar jolts, riffed off the fear that he might get pulled back into the void. Finally, channeling Van Gogh's *Starry Night*, Lou overcomes the vertigo on the title track, regaining equilibrium by surrendering himself to the unpredictability of quixotic romance as the vocal yields to the accelerating beat of a take-no-prisoners coda that erupts into a crescendo:

> *As I lose all my regrets and set the twilight reeling*
> *I accept the new-found man and set the twilight reeling*

It was the first album package in years that was not designed by Sylvia. Art director Stefan Sagmeister recalled the indigo mood of *The Blue Mask* with a blue-tinted jewel case, but when the booklet was removed, it revealed a portrait of Lou accented by yellow sunbursts, depicting his transformation from prince of darkness to philosopher king. In a manner suggesting an eclipse, this bright image was juxtaposed with the liner notes inside the booklet, which featured a photo of Lou with handwritten lyrics scrawled on his face, a literary palimpsest that reflected the hidden cost of his newfound serenity. Yet with the cautious optimism that characterized the era, Lou moved forward. It was the end of his blue period.

As Lou toured Europe, Asia, South America, and the United States with *Set the Twilight Reeling*, that newfound inner peace was disturbed by a challenge to his rock supremacy from another voice from the past. On July 1, 1996, David Bowie, who was now forty-nine, began his *Outside* Summer Festivals Tour, a continuation of a tour surrounding his most recent album, which though it paled in comparison to platinum-selling album *Let's Dance*, still sold almost two hundred thousand copies in the United States. At the Rockin' Athens Festival, Bowie was the headliner; Lou got second billing. Alexander McQueen designed Bowie's costumes; Lou wore his pedestrian black tee and jeans.

David dogged Lou through Europe, to the Eurockéennes de Belfort festival in France, to Rome, Monaco, and Austria. They had never fully resolved their tiff. Rather than aggravating old wounds, several months later they decided to reconcile in dramatic fashion, when David invited Lou to his birthday party. To celebrate his fiftieth on January 8, Bowie organized a concert at Madison Square Garden to be performed the next day—the proceeds would benefit Save the Children—and, with some apprehension, Lou called a truce and agreed to join as a guest.

Toward the end of the night, Bowie came out from the wings with a cup of Throat Coat tea and a cigarette. "I'm going to conclude our party with a couple more guests," Bowie said. Lou sauntered up to the adjacent mic with a smirk. "The king of New York himself, Mr. Lou Reed!" This time they dueled on guitars only, playing "Queen Bitch," Bowie's early tribute to Lou, "Waiting for the Man," and "Dirty Blvd.," closing with "White Light/White Heat" over flashing strobe lights. Nearly two decades later, they had salvaged their friendship. "It's been a lovely birthday," Bowie said.

That May, Lou had another reunion, exercising his diplomacy skills, or lack thereof, when President Havel visited New York for the first time since 1968, the year he first encountered the Velvets. Havel was on a mission to promote the expansion of the North Atlantic Treaty Organization to include the Czech Republic and other budding democracies. In addition to meeting with the Senate Foreign Relations Committee, he reconvened with his unofficial cultural attaché. Lou decided to take the dramatist-philosopher to the Knitting Factory to see John Zorn's *Bar Kokhba*, named for the first-century Jewish revolutionary. Zorn's chamber ensemble, composed of several of Lou's collaborators from Rhythm and Jews—Marc Ribot, Greg Cohen, and Erik Friedlander among them—played music from his *Masada* series, a hybrid Jewish-jazz songbook.

Five months prior, Havel had undergone surgery to have a malignant tumor removed from his right lung, but he felt healthy enough to withstand the bracing harmonies and aggressive pizzicato plucking of Zorn's coconspirators. A few hours before the show, Secretary of State Madeleine Albright's office called the venue asking if she could attend the performance. Lou had arranged for a preconcert reception for Havel, his imposing security detail, and the Secret Service, and they took their seats in the balcony area. In the middle of the show, Albright arrived and greeted Havel according to diplomatic protocol. Yet this was not the Diplomatic Room; in Zorn's house, the music took precedence. Zorn stopped conducting.

"You up there," he shouted. "Shut the fuck up!"

Havel, Albright, and the Secret Service sheepishly snapped to attention as Lou swallowed his laughter. They were silent for the rest of the night. An international incident had been narrowly averted, and Lou returned to his more riotous stock-in-trade. But he wanted something more.

By the late 1990s, it became sufficiently clear that Lou had conquered pop culture as much as he ever would, intermingling high and low art, the urban and the urbane, in a bracing friction, but the aesthetic flowchart seemed to have a decidedly downward trajectory. Lou had proven that rock could be art, but he hadn't quite convinced the arbiters of taste that art could be rock. So when eminent avant-garde theater director Robert Wilson, the man behind the staging of Philip Glass's *Einstein on the Beach*, called Lou with a proposition to collaborate, it was an offer he couldn't refuse. The project would be the finale to a rock opera trilogy; the first two, *The Black Rider* and *Alice*, were scored by Tom Waits. Wilson's *Time Rocker* would be loosely inspired by *The Time Machine*, the 1895 novel by H. G. Wells, but it bore little resemblance to the source material. The interpretive romance delved into the metaphysics and temporality of modern love, and Wilson thought Lou was the perfect candidate to provide the music. Lou wasn't so much a science fiction buff, *Rock & Rule* notwithstanding, but his fascination with time and space in the Proustian sense—fleeting moments and the illusion of permanence—captured the sensibility of Wilson's work in progress.

After premieres in Paris and Hamburg, in November 1997 *Time Rocker* had its US premiere at the Brooklyn Academy of Music. With spoken dialogue in German by essayist Darryl Pinckney, the nonlinear production was heavy on spectacle and light on plot. The picaresque narrative followed Nick and Priscilla, lovers wrongly accused of a murder, as they travel through time inside a giant fish—the time machine was nautical. They trace the steps of a nineteenth-century British doctor through ancient Egypt, New England during the Civil War, a seventeenth-century opium den, a Kansas dormitory in 1996, and a dystopian agrarian future in which glam rock farmers cultivate plastic plants, punctuated by Lou's ironic "Future Farmers of America." Interspersed throughout Wilson's thirty tableaux were sixteen songs by Lou, written for voices with a heightened vocal range, exploring the infinite, the ephemeral, and the immanent. On "Into the Divine," Lou ponders the existence of any higher power in the face of entropy, with Nick and Priscilla stuck on a roof during a flood:

> *I think of an apple core*
> *When you start thinking of God*

The metaphysical contemplation continued on "Why Do You Talk":

> *Who made the earth move*
> *Who made the sky high*

On "Talking Book," Lou imagined a futuristic book that could substitute for visceral reality as Nick and Priscilla begin to lose their grasp of the present while rupturing the space-time continuum. They realize that their present is constituted by each other:

> In this one moment's time in space
> Can our love really be replaced

The opera was met with favorable reviews at home and abroad; Lou had proven that if he was given an opera house, he could do opera. Between the Paris and New York productions, Lou began incorporating material from *Time Rocker* into his own live sets, including a show on July 3, 1997, at Royal Festival Hall in London that was recorded and later released as *Perfect Night: Live in London*. Featuring Mike Rathke, who was the music director for *Time Rocker*, Fernando Saunders, and Tony "Thunder" Smith, the show was curated by Laurie Anderson as part of the Meltdown '97 festival. Lou made the album to showcase a new custom-made acoustic guitar designed by luthier Jim Olson, which he felt communicated an unplugged purity that complemented the lyrics. The release of *Perfect Night* was timed to coincide with the premiere of the PBS *American Masters* documentary *Lou Reed: Rock and Roll Heart*, directed by Timothy Greenfield-Sanders. The film eventually won a Grammy.

Two weeks before the April 29 premiere, Lou revisited his Jewish roots again at the Cyber-Seder, a simulcast Seder sponsored by the Knitting Factory, which took place at Lincoln Center's Avery Fisher Hall, with Laurie participating as well. In the benefit for the United Jewish Appeal, Lou reprised his role as the wise child alongside Sandra Bernhard, John Zorn, Tuli Kupferberg, Roy Nathanson, and the Klezmatics, with more than six thousand watching the event online.

That September, President Havel returned after his recent reelection to meet with President Clinton. That April Havel had ruptured his colon in the Alps, resulting in emergency colostomy surgery, but decided that in the midst of the Kosovo War, pushing his NATO agenda was too important to be postponed. As the Monica Lewinsky scandal rocked the White House, Havel made a request that would rock it even more: the sixty-one-year-old poet-president wanted Lou to be the entertainment for the White House State Dinner. It was the first time the White House hosted a rock concert for a foreign dignitary, and no one was sure how to behave. In 1973 the Carpenters had performed for Richard Nixon when German chancellor Willy Brandt came for a visit at the height of the Watergate scandal, but Lou was nowhere near as wholesome as Karen Carpenter.

Among the White House staff, fears abounded that if the Carpenters' bromides couldn't save Nixon, Lou might play Clinton's last party, or at least shake the chandeliers. In a moment of crisis, the last thing Clinton needed was Lou Reed performing "Walk on the Wild Side" at a black-tie event. Lou's rock anthem might have been fine for Honda, but having taken one too many walks himself, Clinton couldn't survive anyone singing about "giving head" in the White House. Lou, never one for compromise, but a staunch Clinton supporter to the end, had the good sense to leave his biggest hit off the set list. But there was little else Clinton could do. Despite the better judgment of his staff, the embattled leader of the free world could not say no to his potential NATO partner. With the presidency and the global balance of power at stake, Lou was perhaps not the most diplomatic choice, but Clinton acquiesced. At the very least, he would resign on a high note, or a loud one.

During the rehearsal on September 16, Social Secretary Capricia Marshall politely asked Lou to turn down the volume. Congressmen from both sides of the aisle were attending, and with gridlock on Capitol Hill, she couldn't have Republicans and Democrats publicly disagreeing about what was good music. But Lou wouldn't kowtow to anyone. "This is my art, my music," he said. Rebuffed, Marshall knew better than to pick a fight with Lou, but after the rehearsal, he approached her to request a seating change for several of his friends. "Mr. Reed, you don't understand," she said. "These tables are my art." In exchange for the seating upgrade, he begrudgingly agreed to turn down, but not all the way.

That night in the stately East Room of the White House, with a portrait of George and Martha Washington staring him down, Lou stood in front of the most powerful audience of his career as they chewed on pheasant consommé and corn risotto, and he assaulted their senses. Nobody knew how to react—Lou clearly had no respect for parliamentary procedure. Kissinger didn't flinch; neither did Madeleine Albright or Kurt Vonnegut. The staid crowd maintained their composure; no one wanted to be the first to bob their head to "Dirty Blvd." But then there was a faint thumping on the oak parquet. Al Gore, seated next to his wife, Tipper, a founder of the Parents

Music Resource Center responsible for the PARENTAL ADVISORY sticker, was rocking in his chair. Then Richard Lugar, the Republican senator from Indiana, started to sway. Soon, President Clinton couldn't suppress that cocksure smile; even Hillary nodded along. By the end of the thirty-five-minute set, Lou and his band got a standing ovation.

"If you had as much fun as I did just now, you should give President Havel all the credit," Clinton said.

The following March, Secretary of State Albright, who was born in Prague, oversaw the proceedings as Havel signed the document of NATO accession. Along with Poland and Hungary, the three former Cold War foes were now allies. Instead of hampering diplomatic talks, Lou, despite himself, had helped open a path to an international resolution.

But in 1999, Lou returned to the visceral. He and Laurie had settled in a TriBeCa loft with their beloved rat terrier, Lolabelle. Lou was happy—as happy as he could be—but instead of composing a blissful sequel to *Set the Twilight Reeling*, he began reflecting on his battle scars. *Ecstasy* was not a romance, seduction, heartbreak, or heartache album. There were no platitudes, unexamined moments of euphoria or sob stories. This was a man in his late fifties who had made almost every possible relationship mistake imaginable and spoke from experience. Revisiting the ugliness of relationships from a position of unprecedented emotional stability, Lou adopted a critical distance that allowed for penetrating insights into everything that had once gone wrong in the morass of romantic dysfunction. It was rock therapy.

Lou's ecstatic vision anatomized non-cathartic feelings—paranoia, jealousy, disgust, regret—as they came into conflict with their more cathartic cousins, rage, rapture, and love. To provide emotional ballast, he fleshed out his working quartet with cellist Jane Scarpantoni and a full-bodied horn section consisting of trumpeter Steven Bernstein, who did the arrangements, and saxophonists Doug Wieselman and Paul Shapiro. Lou wanted people to hear the sweat.

The catharsis of *Ecstasy* was a long time coming. The initial recording date was postponed after drilling for the city's Third Water Tunnel underneath Master Sound, the Astoria studio Lou had booked, reverberated through the soundproofing. Resuming at the Sear studios on Forty-Eighth Street, the album was done on adrenaline, as usual. On "Paranoia Key of E," Lou enumerated a kind of DSM synesthesia—"mania's in the key of B, psychosis in the key of C"—while "Mad" painted an unflinching portrait of simmering anger and infidelity.

> *Dumb—you're dumb as my thumb*
> *In the wistful morning you throw a coffee cup at my head*
> *Scum—you said I'm scum*

Lou makes no justification for cheating, lying, or screaming; there is no sense of pride. It is what happened, told unflinchingly, and he had to purge it from his system. Lou decided at the spur of the moment that the track needed a screaming saxophone solo. With reedmen Junior Walker and Lee Allen as touchstones, Wieselman growled as loudly as he could, bleating and honking into the baritone. "Lou was screaming and laughing," Wieselman recalls. "The thing about playing with him was it felt like there was a fire underneath me. It really had that intensity."

The title track juxtaposed the mindless moment of sexual release with the confines of monogamy. Where Lou might have previously embraced the endless pursuit of sexual gratification, he equivocates and considers what might have been:

> *I see a child through a window with a bib*
> *And I think of us and what we almost did*

"Tatters" takes the alternative relationship history a step further, imagining sexual estrangement, constant bickering, and a fictional child in a broken home, contrasted by the understated bass line and horn parts. In quiet contemplation, Lou wonders whether certain relationships were doomed from the start; regardless, conceding defeat always ended in disappointment:

> *But what you said still bounces around in my head*
> *Who thought this could happen to us*
> *When we first went to bed*

On "Turning Time Around," culled from *Time Rocker*, Lou attempts the age-old poet's charge of defining what love is. For Lou, love is time:

*Is it more than the heart's hieroglyphic*
*Well for me time has no meaning, no future, no past*
*And when you're in love, you don't have to ask*

"Rock Minuet" turns to the dark side of "Sister Ray," traversing the alleys, dive bars, and brothels in a dance in three; there was nothing glamorous about the steps. The eighteen-minute "Like a Possum" returns to the licentious territory of "Heroin," with Lou recalling "playing possum" with a spiritual death. Drugs and sex—ecstasy—had always left him feeling empty:

*I got a hole in my heart the size of a truck*
*It won't be filled by a one-night fuck*

Freighted with emotional baggage, Lou concluded *Ecstasy* with "Big Sky," a propulsive anthem that symbolically purged. Bursting with power chords, the song was a testament to willpower, with its indomitable refrain, "They can't hold us down anymore." At various points, Lou had been in thrall to drugs, ambition, desire, and lust. The album didn't chart, but Lou didn't care. At the dawn of the new millennium, Lou was free of all that.

*Ecstasy* was released in April 2000, and Lou spent the rest of the year touring the United States, Europe, Asia, and South America with Victoria Williams as a supporting act. On May 1, 2000, Lou performed in Rome alongside Andrea Bocelli, Alanis Morissette, and the Eurythmics at Pope John Paul II's Great Jubilee Concert for a Debt-Free World, drawing hundreds of thousands. If there was ever a pope to allow the satanic sacrilege of "Sweet Jane," this pope was the one; the previous year, he tried on Bono's wraparound sunglasses in a rare moment of sartorial indulgence. Any guilt Lou was harboring over past impieties, the hipper-than-thou pontiff absolved. "He's repented and he's living a very decent life now," said Vatican spokesman Howard Rubenstein. "In the church there is a spirit of forgiveness." Yet not even the pope could stop Lou from wearing black leather.

Soon after he returned from the *Ecstasy* tour, an Internet death hoax was circulated to most major news outlets that Lou had died of a Demerol overdose. "Lou Reed was a close personal friend of mine, and an inspiration for the true freedoms allowed in this country," Madeleine Albright supposedly said; the quote was apocryphal. Many media outlets erroneously reported the news, but Lou decided to set the record straight by personally dispelling the rumor.

On the May 12, 2001, episode of *Saturday Night Live*, Lou appeared with Jimmy Fallon, the cohost of "Weekend Update," to set the record straight. "Do you have any idea how this Internet rumor got started?" asked Fallon.

"Well, I'm dead. I haven't been around," Lou said.

"Right. Now, are you sure that you're dead?"

Lou felt his cheek. "I'm positive," he said. "I haven't been this dead in a while."

On August 21, 2001, Laurie released *Life on a String*, collaborating with Lou on the foreboding "One Beautiful Evening," a haunting spoken-word piece that devolved from prelapsarian Eden into a fuzz-toned, darker place:

> It's like at the end of the play and all the actors come out
> And they line up and they look at you
> And horrible things have happened to them during the play

Yet the song was not indicative of any cracks in the foundation of their relationship. Lou and Laurie were content.

# 27

On September 11, 2001, Lou watched from his roof as the plumes of black smoke curled skyward. He was close enough that before long, he could smell it. At 11:02 Mayor Giuliani evacuated lower Manhattan. Lou left his house and started walking uptown. The streets were eerily calm as an uncanny quiet descended on the city. Traffic lights flickered; the familiar rumble of the subway was gone; there were no cabs to hail. The movie theater was open, but there was no line. It had been converted into a temporary safe house. It felt like the end of the world. But Lou wasn't leaving. He lived here.

Laurie was in Chicago, scheduled to perform at the Park West theater that night, but she didn't cancel the show. She dedicated her set to "all those who have died today." Thirty-year-old songs like "O Superman" had acquired a somber resonance:

> *Here come the planes*
> *They're American planes*

Days later, she was back in New York, performing the song at Town Hall. Buildings could fall, but the beat could not be stopped.

Reflecting on the attacks, Lou dedicated a poem to Laurie, "Laurie Sadly Listening," which he published in the *New York Times*:

> *Laurie if you're sadly listening*
> *Know one thing above all others*
> *You were all I really thought of*

Lou was just five months away from his sixtieth birthday, and the tragedy shook him to his core. He could have left on September 12, but he had an album to make. Within days, Lou was back in his home studio, alone, registering his shock. "Fire Music" was a three-minute violent burst of feedback that distilled *Metal Machine Music* down to three minutes. It was part of POEtry, a collaboration with Robert Wilson based on the writings of Edgar Allan Poe, scheduled to premiere two months later at the Brooklyn Academy of Music, and damn it all if the curtain didn't rise.

On October 2 Lou was at Radio City Music Hall, performing in *Come Together*, a televised tribute to John Lennon originally planned as a gun-control benefit, but in the wake of the 9/11 attacks, the focus shifted. Lou's insistent rendition of "Jealous Guy" nearly shredded his vocal cords. On November 7 he performed at Hal Willner's Doc Pomus Project, a benefit for the Poetry Project at St. Mark's Church. Lou's resolve had only grown stronger.

On November 27 POEtry premiered on the proscenium stage at the Gilman Opera House in Brooklyn. After a decade of relative optimism, Poe's macabre aesthetic suddenly felt apropos. "The Cask of Amontillado," "The Raven," and "The Pit and the Pendulum," as interpreted by Lou and visualized by Wilson and the Thalia Theatre ensemble, captured a searing vision of mortality that pervaded the zeitgeist. When an anthropomorphic yellow balloon walked onstage and sang the madrigal-style "Balloon," it had a gallows humor:

*If you prick me I will burst!*

Lou interspersed repurposed songs, cast in a gloomy light that conjured the tortured writer. Under the influence of Poe, "Perfect Day" became an omen; "The Bed," overpowering in its moroseness in almost any other context, fit in perfectly. Poe and Lou, though separated by 150 years, were kindred spirits.

Lou adapted the production with *The Raven*, a double album that served as a reckoning for his career as an artist that enlisted a constellation of performers from New York's downtown scene, with an orchestral gravity that included a string and horn section. The "Overture," orchestrated by Steven Bernstein, exuded the restless energy that fueled Lou's artistic ambitions. "He wanted this overture to invoke the avant-garde tradition," Doug Wieselman recalls. They decided it needed an enunciatory saxophone solo. "Lou turned the lights down and said, 'Imagine the devil going crazy in a church.'"

Lou didn't believe in a hell other than the one on Earth—the only demons he couldn't see in plain sight resided in his head—but *The Raven* chronicled a man wrestling with his darkest compulsions on a perilous journey to redemption Lou had spent his entire career struggling for. They were the same inner demons that took Poe's life at forty, but at sixty, Lou had risen above them. On "Who Am I? (Tripitena's Song)" Lou ruminated on his past and his ability to transcend it:

> *I hold a mirror to my face*
> *There are some lines that I could trace*

It took decades, but Lou had finally learned how to surrender himself to the moment and truly collaborate as an artist, and the album was a testament to a flourishing artistic community. The perdition that permeated *Ecstasy* was tempered on *The Raven* by these collaborations: "Call on Me," a plaintive duet with Laurie, the haunting lyricism of transgender vocalist Antony Hegarty on "Perfect Day," the sonorous harmonizing of the Blind Boys of Alabama on "I Wanna Know (The Pit and the Pendulum)," the mischievous phrasing of David Bowie on "Hop Frog," and Ornette Coleman's keening saxophone on "Guilty." Taking on perversion, revenge, depression, guilt, woe—indiscretions, misdeeds, and grudges documented by Poe and enlivened by actors Willem Dafoe and Steve Buscemi—the question of forgiveness loomed in the background. Lou found it on "Guardian Angel," a gospel-tinged hymn:

> *I have a guardian angel*
> *Who's often saved my life*
> *Through malevolent storms and crystal drums*

The titular angel didn't come from the outside. He couldn't have done it alone, but if salvation was what he was after, no one could save Lou. He had to save himself.

The fear and anxiety was behind him. After a live orchestral performance of *Metal Machine Music* in Berlin with Zeitkratzer, a ten-piece chamber ensemble that transcribed and scored the original double album, Lou and Laurie spent the summer of 2002 in relative peace, touring Spain and Italy. Back in New York, they participated in Philip Glass's Tibet House benefit at Carnegie Hall. Lou and Laurie even recorded "Gentle Breeze" for *Mary*

*Had a Little Amp*, a children's album. By early spring, Lou began a world tour of *The Raven*, bolstering the core nucleus of his touring band with Jane Scarpantoni, Antony, and tai chi master Ren GuangYi, who performed during live sets. Everything had been clarified to a purity of emotion. That September, Lou released his first book of photography, *Emotion in Action*, a collection of landscapes and portraits. As Lou continued intermittently touring through 2003 and 2004, he settled into a comfortable rhythm.

On Saturday, June 5, 2004, Robert Quine was found dead at sixty-one in his Grand Street loft. Lou and Quine had not been in contact for years, but the suicide of his former friend forced Lou to reconsider his life and his artistic ambitions. Seven months later, at the age of ninety-one, Lou's father died. Lou began to consider how he wanted to spend his remaining time.

Lou decided to return to a project he had abandoned several times—one of his lifelong ambitions—to stage *Berlin* as the rock opera it was always intended to be. Working with director Julian Schnabel, who designed the sets, producer Bob Ezrin, and Hal Willner, Lou finally had the opportunity to perform a fully realized version of the album. In the fall of 2006, rehearsals began at St. Ann's Warehouse in Brooklyn.

"It was a little bit of a seesaw," recalls Wieselman, one of the thirty-five performers. However, it was not as hectic as the original 1973 recording session. "Initially it was kind of out of hand, but then we all figured out how to do it and it was beautiful."

On December 14, 2006, *Berlin*, initially a critical bomb, found a second life at its Brooklyn premiere. The critical consensus had long since been reversed; *Rolling Stone* had included it in its 500 Greatest Albums of All Time list. At St. Ann's Warehouse, original guitarist Steve Hunter performed alongside Antony, Sharon Jones, and the Brooklyn Youth Chorus, while Schnabel filmed the four-night run, eventually releasing it as a concert film. Though controversial in 1973, *Berlin* was only graphic enough by 2007 standards to merit a PG-13 rating. Following the St. Ann's opening, Lou brought the production to Australia and Europe. Nearly thirty-five years after the brutal portrait of marital strife came bursting forth from the recesses of Lou's troubled psyche, he had gotten control of himself and his emotions.

Lou's self-control was in a large part due to his ongoing commitment to tai chi and meditation. In 2007 he decided to release *Hudson River Wind Meditations*, ambient synthesized soundscapes he had created to focus his energy and tune out the din of the city. Otherworldly and atonal, it had more in common with whale sounds than rock but also recalled the Theatre of Eternal Music. Lou wrote it entirely for himself, but thought it might benefit others "to replace the everyday cacophony with new and ordered sounds of an unpredictable nature."

One of Lou's more unpredictable moments came that April when he was notified that he had won the George Arents Pioneer Medal from Syracuse University. Not only was Lou getting honored, his alma mater was endowing the Lou Reed/Delmore Schwartz scholarship. At the awards ceremony at the W Hotel in Union Square, Lou sat with Laurie; his sister, Bunny, and her husband; David Bowie; Bono; and novelist Oscar Hijuelos as a pianist played toned-down covers of "Satellite of Love" and "Walk on the Wild Side." At sixty-five, Lou was finally getting an accolade from Syracuse, a feat he could have achieved earlier if he had played by the rules, but becoming a rock legend had been so much more fun.

As Lou took the podium to give his acceptance speech, the former campus dealer and agent provocateur was as incredulous as anyone. He looked at his sister. "Bunny, can you fuckin' believe this?" he said. "An interviewer asked me, 'Is it true that police told you that you couldn't attend graduation?' I said, 'Who would tell you such a thing?'" Lou said. "Of course, it was." Mostly, Lou was honored to have done right by Schwartz, whom he hoped to one day join in the "part of heaven reserved for Brooklyn poets."

Broadening his downtown intellectual street cred, Lou and Laurie had begun collaborating with MacArthur "genius" grant recipient John Zorn on collective improvisation pieces. Lou and Laurie had performed at Old Knit, a benefit at Town Hall in New York for the Stone, Zorn's Alphabet City black box arts space, leading to *The Stone: Issue Three*, a live recording made that January.

They also remained politically active. On March 18, 2008, to mark the fifth anniversary of the Iraq War, Lou and Laurie participated in the Speak Up! benefit for NYC United for Peace and Justice and Iraq Veterans Against the War. Alongside Antony, David Byrne, Moby, and Norah Jones, Lou sang "Voices of Freedom." Laurie was in the middle of touring with *Homeland*, a polemical song cycle that was her most politically motivated statement in years. She had abandoned the immersive multimedia experience she had become known for in favor of a sparse set and a return to a raw type of immersion—pure storytelling. In the tradition of *United States*, Laurie skewered the conditions of postmodern culture and rampant consumerism that had contributed to constrained civil liberties in the era of heightened homeland security risks and the Bush Doctrine.

Laurie performed *Homeland* at Carnegie Hall, followed by shows in Boston, Akron, and Scottsdale. But when she arrived in California in April to play Santa Barbara and Los Angeles, she missed Lou. With civilization evidently in decline, she felt more reflective than usual. Laurie called Lou, and they began discussing her life's missed opportunities. She was sixty, he was sixty-six; it might be too late to learn a new language or become a scientist. She had never gotten married.

Lou matter-of-factly proposed on the spot, over the phone. After sixteen years, there was nothing expectant in the proposal; Lou and Laurie were together for life, officially or not. They had long decided that they didn't need an institution to validate their love, but to Laurie, marriage sounded like an experience worth having. Lou wanted to do it immediately. He agreed to meet Laurie the following day at her next tour stop in Boulder. So Lou hopped on a plane. They had waited for almost two decades, but now Lou couldn't wait another day. He would have to, though; not many weddings could be planned in twenty-four hours.

Laurie called Sam Dryden, a longtime friend in Boulder, to see if he knew of a justice of the peace who could marry them on such short notice. Lou had officiated a wedding five years earlier, but they needed a third party. Dryden recalled that Nick Forster, a Boulder-based mandolinist and radio host, had recently been ordained. Forster, a member of bluegrass revival band Hot Rize, had cohosted the syndicated Americana radio show eTown with his wife, Helen, for two decades.

When they moved into the abandoned Church of the Nazarene, the new permanent home for their live music and conversation series, the Boulder Planning and Zoning Office rejected their project on the grounds that eTown wasn't a church. To avoid getting waylaid by a variance application, for a fifteen-dollar online fee, Forster became an ordained minister at the Universal Life Church. He never planned to use his clerical powers, but it was only appropriate that his first act as a minister would be to bring two fellow musicians together.

"The call was, 'Hey, our dear friends have been a couple for sixteen years, and they decided yesterday that they wanted to get married right away,'" Forster says. Dryden initially declined to mention exactly who the friends were. When Forster volunteered his services, though, he explained the situation. Forster had met Lou several times, and agreed to do it despite his inexperience. He had one day to prepare.

Forster did some hasty research—wedding vows, Kahlil Gibran quotes, Elvis Presley. "Not sure why I thought about Elvis's wedding, but I did," Forster says. Like Presley's wedding to Priscilla, Lou's and Laurie's would be short and sweet. On April 11, Forster met with the bride and groom to discuss the particulars of the ceremony. "I showed up sort of prepared with some prefab ideas printed out, and Laurie spotted me instantly as a novice. 'You've never done this before, have you?' she said with no malice or judgment." They discussed some possibilities but ultimately decided to play it by ear—Lou wouldn't have it any other way.

On April 12, 2008, at the home of Sam and Sandy Dryden, Lou and Laurie were married. They had secured a marriage license as quickly as possible on Friday. Forster wasn't sure what to list as his religious affiliation; the only church Lou worshipped at was Al Green's. "It was a beautiful spring morning, sunny and crisp," Forster recalls. "The place looked beautiful—lots of flowers. It felt like a wedding day, even though there were only five of us there." Lou was the unofficial wedding photographer. "I couldn't help but notice how tender Lou and Laurie were with each other," Forster says. "He would curl up in Laurie's lap on the couch like a cat—very sweet."

The ceremony took place next to a large tree in the backyard. They didn't wear anything special. Lou read the lyrics to "The Power of the Heart," a recent ballad he had dedicated to Laurie and recorded for Cartier's Love collection before their unexpected betrothal.

> *The beating of a pure bred heart*
> *I say this to you and it's no lark*
> *Marry me today*

"It just boiled down to a very simple proclamation of their love for each other. Lou's, through his lyrics, and Laurie through her spontaneous improvisation of summing up the nature of the day and the power of the moment," Forster says. "I said the whole thing with the 'Do you, Lou' and 'Do you, Laurie' and then, 'I now pronounce you husband and wife.' It was really only then that I felt the gravity of the day." That night, Lou wanted to perform with Laurie at the Boulder Theater, but he had left his gear at home when he flew in for the wedding. He borrowed an amp and a guitar from Forster. It was their first performance as a married couple.

A party in New York City followed, at the home of photographer Timothy Greenfield-Sanders. Lou toured down the East Coast and then from the UK to Sweden, as Laurie flew to Moscow and toured throughout Europe, but there was no overlap in their schedules. It wasn't until late July that they debuted as a married couple in New York, when Lou joined Laurie for *Homeland* at the Lincoln Center Festival.

They concluded the summer with a series of shows in Europe featuring Zorn, Marc Ribot, and a host of downtown luminaries playing aleatoric, drone-infused free improvisations, coming back to the tonic by ending performances with "I'll Be Your Mirror." Lou had also launched *New York Shuffle*, a satellite radio show cohosted by Hal Willner, an eclectic program that mixed James Carr, Wadada Leo Smith, Scott Walker, and Johnny Cash. On October 2 and 3, 2008, Lou performed at REDCAT in Los Angeles as part of the Metal Machine Trio, a group inspired by *Metal Machine Music* that also included saxophonist Ulrich Krieger and Sarth Calhoun on electronics. Each cacophonous hour-long set imagined what the big bang might have sounded like—Lou self-released the live recording as *The Creation of the Universe*. He had returned to the avant-garde scene he started out in when he first arrived in New York.

Yet Lou and Laurie were as comfortable exploring the outer reaches of the aural cosmos as they were at a folksy front-porch sing-along. On December 10, 2008, they performed at the McGarrigle Christmas Hour at Carnegie Hall alongside Rufus Wainwright, Kate and Anna McGarrigle, Emmylou Harris, and as many members of their extended musical family as they could fit on the stage. For the annual holiday tradition, Lou wore a red cardigan and did his best Elvis impression—simply Elvis as Lou at his warm and fuzziest—on "Blue Christmas."

The following summer, Lou did something he never thought he'd do: he returned to Long Island. Lou and Laurie bought a secluded two-bedroom beach house in the Springs section of East Hampton, with a pool and backyard porch, conducive to Lou's two-hour tai chi regimen.

But Lou wasn't easing into retirement. He started working on *Red Shirley*, a documentary film on his cousin, Shirley Novick. Born Shulamit Rabinowitz in Brestovitz, Poland, Shirley had survived two wars—in World War I, her family's house had been bombed, and she emigrated to Canada before the

Holocaust. In New York, she worked as a seamstress for forty-seven years, becoming an outspoken union activist, and was given the nickname Red Shirley. On the night before her hundredth birthday, Lou conducted his interview at her Chelsea apartment. It seemed resilience was hereditary.

Lou was the elder statesman of Lollapalooza 2009 in Chicago, showing the Killers, Kings of Leon, and Tool that he could still rock. On October 30, at the 25th Anniversary Rock and Roll Hall of Fame Concert at Madison Square Garden, Metallica invited Lou onstage for "Sweet Jane." At the end of the night, he approached them with a casual proposition. "Let's make a record together," he said. No one was sure if it was an empty gesture.

Robert Wilson approached Lou with a concept for an adaptation of *Lulu*, German Expressionist Frank Wedekind's censored drama of a femme fatale who dies at the hands of Jack the Ripper. *Lulu* bred more controversy than Wedekind's drama of teenage angst, *Spring Awakening*; the banned play was later adapted into G. W. Pabst's 1929 film *Pandora's Box* and Alban Berg's infamous serialist opera. Though more than a century old, *Lulu* was the most scandalous material Lou had tackled in ages. Lou scored his opera for Wilson's production in Berlin with the avant-garde Berliner Ensemble, founded by Bertolt Brecht, but the finished product was not quite Brechtian enough for Lou. He decided to do *Lulu* himself, but he needed a backing band with enough muscle to do it justice. So he called Metallica.

In April 2011, a month after Lou's sixty-ninth birthday, he and Metallica convened at the band's HQ studio in San Rafael, California. As they pushed the limit of the decibel level, Metallica was not used to Lou's free-form, "first thought, best thought" approach to recording. "Nothing was thought about, nothing was labored over, nothing was dissected or analysed," recalled drummer Lars Ulrich in the *Guardian*. "We just started playing, Lou started half-reciting, half-singing these beautiful poems, and off we went and this record came out." Three weeks later, Ulrich, guitarists James Hetfield and Kirk Hammett, and bassist Robert Trujillo had made one of the rawest records of their careers.

"Pumping Blood" was a hemorrhaging profusion of amplification that spared no gory detail:

*Will you adore the river*
*The stream the trickle the tributary of my heart*
*As I pump more blood*

There were graphic scenes of sadomasochism more extreme than in "Venus in Furs," callous lovers, murderous passion, self-flagellation, a whole "lexicon of hate" in his portrait of moral decay. Lou wrote "Little Dog" for Lolabelle, his ailing, piano-playing terrier, who died shortly thereafter after a long bout of pancreatic cancer:

> *Little dog who can't get in*
> *Moaning at the bedside*
> *Moaning from each limb*

The twenty-minute "Junior Dad," orchestrated for Metallica and strings, evinced a savage beauty from Lou's frayed vocal cords; it was the essence of pure rock:

> *Would you come to me*
> *If I was half drowning*
> *An arm above the last wave*

When *Lulu* was released on Halloween 2011, it was met with more critical backlash than anything Lou had done since *Metal Machine Music*. The cover, shot by photographer Stan Musilek, depicted a limbless nineteenth-century mannequin torso with the album title scrawled in crimson paint. *Lulu* was a thrashing rock exorcism from the very first line:

> *I would cut my legs and tits off*
> *When I think of Boris Karloff and Kinski*
> *In the dark of the moon*

Lou was no aging rock star fading into the oblivion of accolades and pale imitations of his former self; he had beaten his inner demons into submission, but now they were at his beck and call. *Pitchfork* damned the album with faint praise, calling it "a frustratingly noble failure." The *Chicago Tribune* derided it as a "tarpit of ugliness." Others rushed to the Internet to discuss whether it was the worst album ever made. Yet some found it brilliant; *BBC Music* wrote that "it may well be, though, that in the fullness of time this is an album that is given the praise it deserves." David Bowie certainly thought so. *Lulu* was Lou's highest-charting debut since *Sally Can't Dance*, and immediately fell off the chart. After its initial nuclear blast, *Lulu* polarized fans and critics until the fallout began to settle, but being a critical darling was never Lou's goal. He just wanted to rock.

But it was getting harder. Diabetes, then treatment for hepatitis C, threatened to sideline him. Lou had come to terms with his past, but his past had finally come to terms with him. After a life of death-defying acts, he knew he could soldier on. He and Laurie were crowned king and queen of the 2010 Coney Island Mermaid Parade. He wasn't giving up yet. Lou would rock till the end. As his health faltered, he continued fearlessly performing. Lou, Laurie, and John Zorn played a spirited set of free improvisation at the Concert for Japan. At the Jazz Foundation of America's Great Night in Harlem, Lou belted out Ray Charles's "Night Time Is the Right Time" and his own "Perfect Day" alongside Macy Gray.

Along with Elvis Costello, Lou sat on the advisory board of the Jazz Foundation of America (JFA), a nonprofit organization dedicated to providing assistance to the elder statesmen of jazz and blues, performers and songwriters left behind by the vicissitudes of the record industry. "He used to e-mail me in the middle of the night when I'd be working, always minutes after I e-mailed him, which let me know he was awake. So approachable and he really got what we do and truly cared. What a beautiful, shy, and complicated soul he seemed to be," says Wendy Oxenhorn, the executive director of the JFA. "He was beloved by every donor and helped make way for other famous musicians to come out for us ever since."

In the face of illness, Lou also planned a European tour, and began searching for a new guitarist. Aram Bajakian was about to release his first album on John Zorn's Tzadik label when he got the opportunity to audition for the role. But when he arrived, it seemed the position had already been filled. "Lou's manager comes out and says, 'I'm sorry, he's picked his guitar player, so you can go home,'" Bajakian recalls. The next week, Bajakian's daughter was born, and three days later, Lou's manager called at 8 AM to bring him in for another audition. He was given an hour to arrive in the West Village from his apartment in Queens. Not having slept, he hopped in a cab and rode over the Queensboro Bridge. Lou was intimidating at first.

"You're not going to play any jazz, are you? Because this is a rock band," Lou said.

With a rush of adrenaline, Bajakian aced the audition. "I had to. I had a family to feed," he recalls. At Hal Willner's Freedom Riders concert at Prospect Park Bandshell in Brooklyn, Lou played Sam Cooke's "A Change Is Gonna

Come." Lou ripped into Bajakian for resorting to a prefabricated blues riff. "I was doing background licks, and I did this one octave thing that guitarists do, and he said, 'No, no, no. You're too good for that crap,'" Bajakian recalls. "You can practice a lot, but really it's about keeping it alive and tasteful in the moment."

In July 2011, after listening to *Lulu* on repeat, Bajakian began the European tour. "It didn't matter if it was a smaller venue where there were two thousand people there or seventy thousand, so he could really be in the moment," Bajakian says. "We would play 'Junior Dad,' and sometimes Lou would come offstage and he had tears. It was so intense for him to play through that music and live that music every night." Bajakian had to adjust to the rigors of touring with Lou, but at sixty-nine, with diabetes and a failing liver, Lou still found the energy.

Some moments of the tour were particularly grueling. One day, they woke up at 5 AM after a draining performance in Italy and took a flight to northern France. "It was raining miserably and then we had to go play this festival, which was a two-hour drive. We all knew it was going to be a long, tough day," Bajakian says. "He said to me, 'Aram, say something positive.' And I just said, 'Look at this beautiful tree.' And he said, 'Yeah, they really are beautiful.'"

In September Lou reprised "A Change Is Gonna Come" at a Freedom Rides concert at the Highline Ballroom. When it came time for Bajakian's solo, this time he knew what to do. After the show, Michael Stipe of R.E.M. told him he had moved him to tears.

On December 18, 2011, Vaclav Havel died. Lou could not attend the funeral at St. Vitus Cathedral in Prague Castle, but his music was played at the raucous after-party. The Velvet Revival concluded the tribute with "Rock & Roll." Lou could have taken Havel's death as fair warning, but as he turned seventy, he had to keep playing, with the same conviction, whether it was with his own band or with Bill Laswell, Milford Graves, and John Zorn.

The following summer he toured Europe again. On August 10, even on the last night of the tour at London's Royal Festival Hall, Lou continued to see if he could push the music further. "We spent the whole sound check working on the music," Bajakian says. "Every sound check wasn't plug in, play, make sure everything sounds good, go have dinner. We'd really work it up for a few hours to make it better." He remained prolific. In 2012, New Directions published a new edition of Delmore Schwartz's *In Dreams Begin Responsibilities and Other Stories*, with a stirring introduction by Lou:

*I wanted to write. One line as good as yours.*

It seemed that he had. The following March, four days after his seventy-first birthday, Lou performed "Candy Says" at the Salle Pleyel in Paris with Antony. Two weeks later, he recited Bob Marley's "Exodus" at the Down-town Seder at City Winery, reading his regular role of the "wise child" and demonstrating that sardonic wit and wisdom by embellishing on the lyrics with some trademark skepticism. His health was failing, but his mind was sharp.

"Are you satisfied with the life you're living—are you kidding?" he said. "We know where we're going—oh, do you?"

But Lou had to slow down. He had liver cancer. In April he underwent a liver transplant at the Cleveland Clinic, as surgeon Charlie Miller performed the surgery with "Walk on the Wild Side" playing in the background. It was successful. Lou was scheduled to perform at the Coachella Valley Music and Arts Festival but had to cancel due to his recovery. Yet he bounced back. That September, he was given the *GQ* Inspiration of the Year award. At the acceptance ceremony, Lou was frail but still vital. "I believe to the bottom of my heart, the last cell, that rock 'n' roll can change everything," he said. "I'm a graduate of Warhol University, and I believe in the power of punk. To this day—I want to blow it up." Two weeks later, Lou was brought in to fine-tune Parrot Zik headphones, and sat down for an interview. "My life is music," he said. "The first memory of sound would have to be your mother's heartbeat, for all of us," he said, waxing poetic. "You grow up, from when you're a peanut, listening to rhythm."

There were more complications with Lou's liver, and he landed in the hospital again. The doctor delivered the grim prognosis—there was nothing they could do. Lou left the hospital, and he and Laurie traveled to East Hampton, where he continued doing tai chi to bring himself closer to nature. On October 27, 2013, Lou saw that it was the end, and surrendered himself peacefully to death. He died in Laurie's arms at his home in East Hampton.

It was a clear Sunday morning, and the South Shore wind blew softly across the Sound. Traffic flowed as usual; taxis honked up Eighth Avenue; the subway didn't stop. But something was different. Lou Reed was dead. Yet somewhere, on a car radio heading inbound on the expressway, the faint hum of a bass played two chords. The guitar strummed that syncopated rhythm. The violins came in. And a voice narrated the story of New York.

# EPILOGUE

When Lou died, the world grieved. Everyone from Salman Rushdie to the pope to Patti Smith wrote heartfelt remembrances. John Cale had lost his "school-yard buddy," Moe Tucker her "good and loyal friend." Network news shows and radio stations cleared their programming schedules to pay their respects. South by Southwest organized a major tribute; John Zorn and Joseph Arthur dedicated albums to their brilliant friend. People were heartbroken.

Laurie penned a beautiful remembrance in *Rolling Stone*. After Lou's cremation, memorials followed on November 14, 2013, at Lincoln Center, where Lou's music played from loudspeakers, then on December 16, 2013, at the Apollo Theater. Laurie planned the latter event for fifty days after Lou's death, following the forty-nine days of the bardo, the Tibetan Buddhist transitional state between life and the soul's eventual fate. Buddhist belief dictates that bardo either ends in reincarnation or nirvana. As appealing as nirvana could be to the enlightened and disembodied Lou, the allure of the city might have been too tempting. There was more than enough life in him for another spin on the turntable.

The ceremony was held at the historic theater on 125th Street, only four blocks from Lexington Avenue, where Lou had waited for the man nearly fifty years before. The tributes were as wide and varied as Lou's eclectic career. Paul Simon sang "Pale Blue Eyes"; John Zorn played a screeching solo saxophone improvisation; Master Ren GuangYi performed a silent tai chi cycle. Antony performed "Candy Says," Lou's poignant transgender anthem, accompanied by Marc Ribot; the Persuasions sang "Turning Time Around" a cappella; Debbie Harry sang "White Light/White Heat." Jenni Muldaur sang "Jesus"; Bob Ezrin and Hal Willner recited "The Mourner's Kaddish" accompanied by Philip Glass on piano; Rabbi Levi Weiman-Kelman chanted "El Maleh Rachamim," the Jewish funeral prayer.

"We never once talked about what would happen when one of us died and what the other one would do, but living in the present, I see him everywhere, and the way his life has turned into energy everywhere I look," Laurie said. "I see it in nature and I see it in the things he loved. I see his exuberance, and sometimes I hear his over-the-top, insane laugh."

Lou's sister, Merrill Weiner, gave a moving remembrance. After his death, she visited their mother, Toby, who had become nonresponsive. "I told her about the accolades, the world's reaction to Lou's death. Out of her stupor, she sat up straight, she opened her eyes, and she said gibberish with great passion and fell back," Weiner said. What she said was unintelligible, but the message was clear. "As I left, I gave her a hug for the first time in two years. She squeezed my shoulder. It was the last time I saw my mother." Lou had willed everything to Laurie and his sister, entrusting $500,000 to her for the care of their mother. But on November 7, at the age of ninety-three, Toby died at peace, ten days after Lou.

In January 2014 Lou's rendition of "Solsbury Hill" was posthumously released on Peter Gabriel's *And I'll Scratch Yours*, an album of other artists performing Gabriel covers. Lou had internalized the lyrics:

> *My heart was going boom boom boom*
> *"Hey," I said, "You can keep my things,"*
> *They've come to take me home*

Uncompromising to the end, the antithesis of a sell-out, Lou was more financially successful in death than he ever was in life. In the year following his passing, renewed interest in his career caused his estate to more than double. Posthumous accolades piled up. In 2015, "Walk on the Wild Side" was inducted in the Grammy Hall of Fame. The same year, Lou was inducted into the Rock and Roll Hall of Fame as a solo artist; Patti Smith and Laurie Anderson gave induction speeches. Anderson concluded her remarks with the three rules to live by that she and Lou had devised together: "One: Don't be afraid of anyone. Now, can you imagine living your life afraid of no one? Two: Get a really good bullshit detector. And three: Three is be really, really tender," she said. "And with those three things, you don't need anything else." Lou only needed three chords and three rules to get by.

The audience listened in rapt attention as a palpable sense of collective grief and admiration swept over everyone, along with the renewed realization that Lou would not be dispensing any more penetrating insights, hard-earned wisdom, or withering rebukes in the way that only he could. Yet he had left so much behind. "They say you die three times," Anderson continued. "The first is when your heart stops, and the second is when you're buried or cremated. And the third is the last time someone says your name. I am so happy that Lou's name is added to the list of people who will be remembered for the beautiful music they made."

Suddenly, she was interrupted by a faint murmur spreading through the audience that rippled across the room like the culmination of a séance. "*Louuu!*" came the collective voice. Was it Lou? Maybe. Anderson laughed; Lou might have scowled, but the collective disruption was a fitting and ironic salute to the man who had once been banned on New York radio, and who after a lifetime of fearless dedication to the cause and the craft of rock as poetry, poetry as rock, had secured an immortal place in the firmament with Dion, the Coasters, and Doc Pomus—the future generations he had rescued from the doldrums, and the countless others that had rescued him. Yet success was never what Lou was after. He lived by the music and he died by it. And then he lingered on. Rock 'n' roll had saved his life.

# KEY RECORDINGS

## 1958

The Jades, "Leave Her for Me"/"So Blue," Time, 1958, included on *Rockin' on Broadway: The Time, Brent, Shad Story*, Ace, 2000.

## 1959

Bobby Randle, "Karen"/"Walking in the Shadows," Shad, 1959.

## 1962

Lewis Reed, "Your Love" and "Merry Go Round," recorded 1962 (unreleased), included on *Rockin' on Broadway: The Time, Brent, Shad Story*, Ace, 2000.

## 1964

The Primitives, "The Ostrich"/"Sneaky Pete," Pickwick City, 1964.

Various artists, *The Four Seasons—Johnny Rivers—Neil Sedaka—The J Brothers*, Design, 1964.

## 1965

The All Night Workers, "Don't Put All Your Eggs in One Basket"/"Why Don't You Smile Now," Round Sound, 1965.

Ronnie Dove and Terry Philips, *Swingin' Teen Sounds of Ronnie Dove & Terry Phillips [sic]*, Design, 1965.

Various artists, *Soundsville!*, Design, 1965.

## 1967

The Velvet Underground:

*The Velvet Underground & Nico*, Verve, 1967.

*Peel Slowly and See*, Polydor, 1995.

*The Velvet Underground & Nico 45th Anniversary*, Polydor, 2012.

## 1968

The Velvet Underground:

*White Light/White Heat*, Verve, 1968.

*White Light/White Heat 45th Anniversary*, Polydor, 2013.

*Live at the Boston Tea Party, December 12, 1968*, Keyhole, 2014.

## 1969

The Velvet Underground:

*The Velvet Underground*, MGM, 1969.

*The Velvet Underground 45th Anniversary*, Polydor, 2014.

*1969: The Velvet Underground Live*, Mercury, 1974.

*Bootleg Series Volume 1: The Quine Tapes*, Polydor, 2001.

## 1970

The Velvet Underground:

*Loaded*, Cotillion, 1970.

*Fully Loaded*, Rhino, 1997.

## 1972

The Velvet Underground:

*Live at Max's Kansas City*, Cotillion, 1972.

*What Goes On*, Raven, 1993.

Lou Reed:

*Lou Reed*, RCA, 1972.

*Le Bataclan '72* (with John Cale and Nico), Pilot, 2004.

*Transformer*, RCA, 1972.

*American Poet*, Pilot, 2001.

## 1973

Lou Reed, *Berlin*, RCA, 1973.

The Velvet Underground, *Squeeze*, Polydor, 1973.

## 1974

Lou Reed:

*Rock 'n' Roll Animal*, RCA, 1974.

*Sally Can't Dance*, RCA, 1974.

## 1975

Lou Reed:

*Lou Reed Live*, RCA, 1975.

*Metal Machine Music*, RCA, 1975.

## 1976

Lou Reed:

> *Coney Island Baby*, RCA, 1976.
> *Rock and Roll Heart*, Arista, 1976.

Nelson Slater, *Wild Angel*, RCA, 1976.

## 1978

Lou Reed:

> *Street Hassle*, Arista, 1978.
> *Live: Take No Prisoners*, Arista, 1978.

## 1979

Lou Reed, *The Bells*, Arista, 1979.

## 1980

Lou Reed, *Growing Up in Public*, Arista, 1980.

## 1982

Lou Reed, *The Blue Mask*, RCA, 1982.

## 1983

Lou Reed:

> "Little Sister," on *Get Crazy* soundtrack, Morocco, 1983.
> *Legendary Hearts*, RCA, 1983.

## 1984

Lou Reed:

> *Live in Italy*, RCA, 1984.
> *New Sensations*, RCA, 1984.

## 1985

Lou Reed:

> "September Song," on *Lost in the Stars: The Music of Kurt Weill*, A&M, 1985.
> "Hot Hips," on *Perfect* soundtrack, Arista, 1985.
> "My Love Is Chemical," on *White Nights* soundtrack, Atlantic, 1985.

## 1986

Lou Reed:

> "Soul Man" (with Samuel David Moore), on *Soul Man* soundtrack, A&M, 1986.
> *Mistrial*, RCA, 1986.

## 1988

Lou Reed, "Something Happened," on *Permanent Record* soundtrack, Epic, 1988.
Rubén Blades, *Nothing but the Truth*, Elektra, 1988.

## 1989

Lou Reed, *New York*, Sire, 1989.

## 1990

Lou Reed, *Songs for Drella* (with John Cale), Sire, 1990.

## 1991

Maureen Tucker, *I Spent a Week There the Other Night*, New Rose, 1991.

## 1992

Lou Reed:

> *Magic and Loss*, Sire, 1992.
> *Between Thought and Expression: The Lou Reed Anthology*, RCA, 1992.

## 1993

The Velvet Underground, *Live MCMXCIII*, Sire, 1993.
Lou Reed:

> "Foot of Pride," on *The 30th Anniversary Concert Celebration*, Columbia, 1993.
> "Tarbelly and Featherfoot," on *Sweet Relief: A Benefit for Victoria Williams*, Thirsty Ear, 1993.

## 1994

Laurie Anderson, "In Our Sleep," on *Bright Red*, Warner Bros., 1994.

## 1995

Lou Reed, "You'll Know You Were Loved," on *Friends* soundtrack, WEA, 1995.

## 1996

Lou Reed, *Set the Twilight Reeling*, Sire, 1996.

## 1997

Lou Reed:

> "This Magic Moment," on *Lost Highway* soundtrack, Interscope, 1997.
> *Perfect Night: Live in London*, Sire, 1998.

**2000**

Lou Reed, *Ecstasy*, Sire, 2000.

**2003**

Lou Reed, *The Raven*, Sire, 2003.

**2004**

Lou Reed, *Animal Serenade*, RCA, 2004.

Lou Reed and Laurie Anderson, "Gentle Breeze," on *Mary Had A Little Amp*, Epic, 2004.

**2005**

Antony and the Johnsons, "Fistful of Love," on *I Am a Bird Now*, Secretly Canadian, 2005.

**2006**

Lou Reed, *Berlin: Live at St. Ann's Warehouse*, Matador, 2008.

**2007**

Lou Reed, *Hudson River Wind Meditations*, Sounds True, 2007.

The Killers (with Lou Reed), "Tranquilize," on *Sawdust*, Vertigo, 2007.

**2008**

Lou Reed, John Zorn, and Laurie Anderson, *The Stone: Issue Three*, Tzadik, 2008.

Lou Reed, "The Power of the Heart," on *Love by Cartier*, 2008.

Metal Machine Trio, *The Creation of the Universe*, Best Seat in the House, 2008.

Fernando Saunders, "Baton Rouge," on *I Will Break Your Fall*, Cadiz, 2008.

**2009**

Kevin Hearn and Thin Buckle, *Havana Winter*, Warner Music Canada, 2009.

**2010**

Laurie Anderson, *Homeland*, Nonesuch/Elektra, 2010.

**2011**

Booker T. Jones, "The Bronx," on *The Road from Memphis*, ANTI-, 2011.

Lou Reed with Metallica, *Lulu*, Warner Bros., 2011.

**2012**

Metric, "The Wanderlust," on *Synthetica*, Mom + Pop, 2012.

## 2014

Kevin Hearn, "Floating," on *Days in Frames*, Roaring Girl, 2014.

Lou Reed, "Solsbury Hill," on *And I'll Scratch Yours*, by Peter Gabriel, Real World, 2014.

## 50 Notable Covers

The Riats, "Run Run Run"/"Sunday Morning," Omega, 1967.

The Banana, "There She Goes Again," recorded 1967 (unreleased), on *Aliens, Psychos and Wild Things*, Norton, 2001.

The Plastic People of the Universe/Půlnoc/the Velvet Revival Band, *Milan Hlavsa, Než Je Dnes Člověku 50—Poslední Dekáda*, Globus, 2001.

The Modern Lovers, "Foggy Notion," recorded 1971–1973 (unreleased), on *Precise Modern Lovers Order*, Rounder, 1994.

David Bowie, "I'm Waiting for the Man," on *Santa Monica '72*, Griffin, 1995.

Mott the Hoople, "Sweet Jane," on *Live*, Columbia, 1974.

The Runaways, "Rock & Roll," on *The Runaways*, Mercury, 1976.

Patti Smith, "We're Gonna Have a Real Good Time Together," "Pale Blue Eyes," on *I Never Talked to Bob Dylan*, Stoned, 1977.

Big Star, "Femme Fatale," on *Third/Sister Lovers*, PVC, 1978.

Joy Division, "Sister Ray," on *Still*, Factory, 1981.

Bauhaus (with Nico), "Waiting for the Man," on *Press the Eject and Give Me the Tape*, Beggars Banquet, orig. rel. 1982, track included on 1988 reissue.

Rainy Day, "I'll Be Your Mirror," on *Rainy Day*, Llama, 1984.

Simple Minds, "Street Hassle," on *Sparkle in the Rain*, Virgin/A&M, 1984.

Nick Cave and the Bad Seeds, "All Tomorrow's Parties," on *Kicking Against the Pricks*, Mute, 1986.

Roky Erickson, "Heroin," on *Gremlins Have Pictures*, Demon, 1986.

R.E.M., "There She Goes Again," "Pale Blue Eyes," "Femme Fatale," *Dead Letter Office*, I.R.S., 1987.

Jane's Addiction, "Rock 'n' Roll," on *Jane's Addiction*, Triple X, 1987.

Cowboy Junkies, "Sweet Jane," on *The Trinity Session*, RCA/Latent, 1988.

The Feelies, "What Goes On," on *Only Life*, A&M, 1988.

A Tribe Called Quest, "Can I Kick It?" (samples "Walk on the Wild Side"), on *People's Instinctive Travels and the Paths of Rhythm*, Jive/RCA, 1990.

June Tabor and Oysterband, "All Tomorrow's Parties," on *Freedom and Rain*, Rykodisc, 1990.

Marky Mark and the Funky Bunch, "Wildside," on *Music for the People*, Interscope/Atlantic, 1991.

Vanessa Paradis, "I'm Waiting for the Man," on *Vanessa Paradis*, Polydor, 1992.

U2, "Satellite of Love," on "One" (single), Island, 1992.

Billy Idol, "Heroin," on *Cyberpunk*, Chrysalis, 1993.

Duran Duran, "Femme Fatale," on *The Wedding Album*, Capitol, 1993.

Bryan Ferry, "All Tomorrow's Parties," on *Taxi*, Virgin/Reprise, 1993.

Nirvana, "Here She Comes Now," on *Rare Traxx* (bootleg release), Shinola, 1994.

Duran Duran, "Perfect Day," on *Thank You*, Capitol, 1995.

Porno for Pyros, "Satellite of Love," on *The Cable Guy* soundtrack, Columbia, 1996.

Yo La Tengo, "I'm Set Free," on *Genius + Love = Yo La Tengo*, Matador, 1996.

Gary Lucas, "European Son," on *Street of Lost Brothers*, Tzadik, 2000.

Tori Amos, "New Age," on *Strange Little Girls*, Atlantic, 2001.

Simple Minds, "All Tomorrow's Parties," on *Neon Lights*, Eagle, 2001.

Rilo Kiley, "After Hours," on *Bright Eyes with Rilo Kiley/Sorry About Dresden* (*DIW* magazine exclusive vinyl EP), Devil in the Woods, 2002.

The Queers, "Sunday Morning," on *Acid Beaters*, Stardumb, 2003.

Antony Hegarty, "Candy Says," on *Animal Serenade*, RCA, 2004.

Matthew Sweet and Susanna Hoffs, "Sunday Morning," on *Under the Covers*, vol. 1, Shout!, 2006.

Patti Smith, "Perfect Day," on *Two More* (promotional single), Columbia, 2007.

Glen Campbell, "Jesus," on *Meet Glen Campbell*, Capitol, 2008.

The Decemberists, "I'm Sticking with You," on *Always the Bridesmaid: A Singles Series*, Capitol, 2008.

Susan Boyle, "Perfect Day," on *The Gift*, Syco/Columbia, 2010.

Beck, "The Black Angel's Death Song," Record Club at www.beck.com, 2010.

Peter Gabriel, "The Power of the Heart," on *Scratch My Back*, Real World/Virgin, 2010.

The Kills, "Pale Blue Eyes," on *The Last Goodbye*, Domino, 2012.

Amanda Palmer, *Several Attempts to Cover Songs by the Velvet Underground and Lou Reed for Neil Gaiman as His Birthday Approaches*, self-released, 2012.

Various artists, *The Velvet Underground & Nico by Castle Face and Friends*, Castle Face, 2012.

Morrissey, "Satellite of Love," Parlophone, 2013.

Joseph Arthur, *Lou*, Vanguard, 2014.

John Zorn, *Transmigration of the Magus* (Lou Reed tribute album), Tzadik, 2014.

# NOTES

## Prologue

"Holly came from Miami, FLA": Lou Reed, "Walk on the Wild Side," on *Transformer*, RCA, 1972.

"I wonder why I love you like I do": Dion and the Belmonts, "I Wonder Why," on *Presenting Dion and the Belmonts*, Laurie, 1958.

## Part I: Doo-Wop Waste Land

### Chapter 1

Stevie Wonder's "Superstition," Carly Simon's "You're So Vain," and Elton John's "Crocodile Rock": Billboard Hot 100, *Billboard*, January 27, 1973.

Alice Tully Hall, January 27, 1973: Bettye Kronstad, interview by the author, April 6, 2014; Richard Nusser, "Dark and Light Rays," *Village Voice*, February 1, 1973; Ed McCormack, "A Last Waltz on the Wild Side," *Vanity Fair*, January 13, 2014.

Pierre Boulez and *La Bohème*: Goings on About Town, *New Yorker*, January 27, 1973.

"The public has never discovered him": Henry Edwards, "Freak Rock Takes Over?" *New York Times*, December 17, 1972.

"terrible—lame, pseudo-decadent lyrics": Ellen Willis, "The Return of the Dolls," *New Yorker*, January 13, 1973.

B- in the *Village Voice*: Robert Christgau, Consumer Guide review of *Transformer*, *Village Voice*, ca. 1972, reprinted on author's official website, www.robertchristgau.com /get_album.php?id=7620.

"act of vandalism": "RCA Ad Ruffles Power Structure," *New York Times*, May 30, 1972.

"Like a hawk in the night": Garland Jeffreys, "Ballad of Me," on *Garland Jeffreys*, Atlantic, 1973.

"Junkie Broadway, every kind of freak": Garland Jeffreys, "Harlem Bound," on *Garland Jeffreys*.

"You've gotta live, yeah your life": Lou Reed, "Wagon Wheel," on *Transformer*, RCA, 1972.

## Chapter 2

To paraphrase Hubert Selby Jr.: Lou Reed, *Between Thought and Expression: Selected Lyrics of Lou Reed* (New York: Hyperion, 1991), 171.

Rabinowitz family: 1940 US Census database, Archives.com, www.archives.com /1940-census.

Shulamit Rabinowitz: *Red Shirley*, directed by Lou Reed and Ralph Gibson (Sister Ray, 2010).

Hyman Feingold: New York State Department of Labor, *Annual Industrial Directory of New York State*, vol. 1 (Albany: New York State Department of Labor, 1913), 144.

"Miss Toby Futterman of 139 Dumont Ave.": "This Queen Takes Dictation," *Brooklyn Eagle*, February 7, 1939.

139 Dumont Avenue: 1940 US Census database, Archives.com.

Sidney legally changed his name to Reed: Merrill Weiner, correspondence with the author, March 19, 2014.

March 2, 1942, lunar eclipse: *The World Almanac and Book of Facts* (New York: Press Publishing Company, 1942), 170.

Glenn Miller's "Moonlight Cocktail": Music Popularity Chart, *Billboard*, March 21, 1942.

*Billboard*'s Harlem Hit Parade: Harlem Hit Parade, *Billboard*, October 24, 1942.

"If you walked the streets, you'd get killed": Josh Alan Friedman, "Lou Reed: Ugly People Got No Reason to Live," *Soho Weekly News*, March 9–15, 1978.

Smoking "punks": *Blue in the Face*, directed by Wayne Wang and Paul Auster (Miramax, 1995).

"When I was a young man": Lou Reed, "Egg Cream," on *Set the Twilight Reeling*, Sire, 1996.

The Dodgers and Cal Abrams: Peter S. Horvitz and Joachim Horvitz, *The Big Book of Jewish Baseball* (New York: S.P.I. Books, 2001), 15–16, 243.

Shot Heard 'Round the World: Ray Robinson, *The Home Run Heard 'Round the World* (New York: HarperCollins, 1991), 227.

"I couldn't have been unhappier": *Blue in the Face*, directed by Wang and Auster.

## Chapter 3

Sandwiched between Baldwin in the east: Cynthia Jane Krieg and Regina G. Feeney, *Freeport* (New York: Arcadia Publishing, 2012), 7–8.

Gabriel Heatter once tried to sell his house to Lena Horne: Jonathan Shebar, interview by the author, February 19, 2014.

"He moved to the Island": Allan Hyman, interview by the author, February 6, 2014.

Rabbi Reuben Katz: Reba Katz, interview by the author, February 24, 2014.

"The Jew Looks at Marriage": Rabbi Saul Teplitz, ed., *Best Jewish Sermons of 5714* (New York: The Jonathan David Co., 1954), 66–78.

"All the kids would sneak out": Shebar, interview by the author.

Lou celebrated his bar mitzvah: Merrill Weiner, correspondence with the author, March 19, 2014.

"In social situations he withdrew": Merrill Reed Weiner, "A Family in Peril: Lou Reed's Sister Sets the Record Straight About His Childhood," *Medium*, April 13, 2015.

"You know the show *Happy Days*?": Elliot Garfinkel, interview by the author, February 1, 2014.

"play football for the coach": Lou Reed, "Coney Island Baby," on *Coney Island Baby*, RCA, 1976.

"He grew up in a very nice home": Garfinkel, interview by the author.

Colonel Sanders even appeared in person: Shebar, interview by the author.

"I remember us having a lot of laughs": Richard Sigal, interview by the author, February 4, 2014.

"He was a good guy": Arthur Scheer, interview by the author, February 3, 2014.

"We'd put it on and we'd really listen": Sigal, interview by the author.

"We used to go into the city a lot": Hyman, interview by the author.

"Lou was not a mainstream guy": Sigal, interview by the author.

"Howl": Allen Ginsberg, *Howl and Other Poems* (San Francisco: City Lights, 1959).

"Modern rock lyrics would be inconceivable": Simon Warner, *Text and Drugs and Rock 'n' Roll: The Beats and Rock, from Kerouac to Cobain* (New York: Bloomsbury Academic, 2013), 49.

"the *Alice in Wonderland* of the amphetamine age": J. G. Ballard, "Our Own Swift," *Guardian*, September 27, 1985.

"when everyone sees what is on the end": Oliver Harris and Ian MacFadyen, eds., *Naked Lunch @ 50: Anniversary Essays* (Carbondale: Southern Illinois University Press, 2009), 199, 293.

"to recreate the syntax and measure": Ginsberg, *Howl and Other Poems*, 9–29.

Ginsberg even listened to Lou's music while he was dying: "Jill Krementz Covers the Photographs of Allen Ginsberg," *New York Social Diary*, February 8, 2013, www .newyorksocialdiary.com/node/1909033/.

"The Hayloft used to be the butt of jokes": Sigal, interview by the author.

"We spent a lot of time at the waterfront": Judy November, interview by the author, February 3, 2014.

Lou would suffer the indignity of being a shit picker: Sigal, interview by the author.

"I had a job in high school, filing burrs off nuts": Lou Reed, interview by Paul Auster, *Dazed & Confused*, April 1996.

"He was kind of a standoffish guy": Phil Harris, interview by the author, February 18, 2014.

"During our rehearsals, we started writing some songs": Alan Walters, interview by the author, February 12, 2014.

"Shad said to me that if I ever came across a group": Garfinkel, interview by the author.

Billy Eckstine had been Tamara's babysitter: Tamara Shad, liner notes, *Wop Ding A Ling*, Ace, 1999.

"there's only two kinds of music": Rome Neal, "Ray Charles: Music Is His Life," CBS News, May 1, 2003, www.cbsnews.com/news/ray-charles-music-is-his-life/.

"And I was trying to study the Mickey Baker guitar chord book": Lou Reed, Maureen Tucker, Doug Yule, and David Fricke, "The Art and Soul of the Velvet Underground," Live from the New York Public Library video, December 8, 2009, www.nypl.org /audiovideo/velvet-underground-lou-reed-maureen-%E2%80%98moe%E2%80% 99-tucker-doug-yule-david-fricke.

"We did half a dozen takes and it was a go": Walters, interview by the author.

"Take away the sunshine": The Jades, "Leave Her for Me," on "Leave Her for Me"/"So Blue," Time, 1958.

"May we make much bread": Walters, interview by the author.

"Freed was kind of a drinker": Harris, interview by the author.

"They called me up and said Murray the K": Josh Alan Friedman, "Lou Reed: Ugly People Got No Reason to Live," *Soho Weekly News*, March 9–15, 1978.

"He said, 'All you need is one chord'": Sigal, interview by the author.

They quickly had business cards printed: Ibid.

"I used to go up to Harlem with all these songs": Lou Reed, Maureen Tucker, Doug Yule, and David Fricke, "The Art and Soul of the Velvet Underground," Live from the New York Public Library video, December 8, 2009, www.nypl.org/audiovideo /velvet-underground-lou-reed-maureen-%E2%80%98moe%E2%80%99-tucker -doug-yule-david-fricke.

"We drove up to Syracuse with Lou's father": Hyman, interview by the author.

"set into motion the dissolution of my family": Weiner, "A Family in Peril."

"I was just a little depressed and it was a dumb doctor": David Fricke, "A Refugee from Rock's Dark Side, Lou Reed Says Goodbye Excess, Hello New Jersey," *People*, March 30, 1981.

"None of us knew Lou had leanings towards boys": Sigal, interview by the author.

"He had a whole bunch of issues with depression": Hyman, interview by the author.

"It was mainly used to treat people who were considered in serious danger": Dr. Irwin Mendelsohn, interview by the author, February 6, 2014.

*Chapter 4*

"I watched my brother": Merrill Reed Weiner, "A Family in Peril: Lou Reed's Sister Sets the Record Straight About His Childhood," *Medium*, April 13, 2015.

Creedmoor was the closest thing to hell in Queens: Hannah Frishberg, "Diagnosis: Decrepit—Inside Creedmoor Psychiatric Center," *Atlas Obscura*, September 12, 2013; Susan Sheehan, *Is There No Place on Earth for Me?* (Boston: Houghton Mifflin, 1982), 1–78.

Shock therapy: Edward Shorter and David Healy, *Shock Therapy: A History of Electroconvulsive Treatment in Mental Illness* (New Brunswick, NJ: Rutgers University Press, 2007), 31–48.

"The Battle of New Orleans": Billboard Hot 100, *Billboard*, July 6, 1959.

"When I was going to college I would go down": Lou Reed, interview by Sylvie Simmons, *MOJO*, 2005.

"Without Burroughs modern lit would be": Back cover endorsement, *Naked Lunch @ 50: Anniversary Essays*, ed. by Oliver Harris and Ian MacFadyen (Carbondale: Southern Illinois University Press, 2009).

"'Take the matter of uh *sexual deviation*'": William S. Burroughs, *Naked Lunch* (New York: Grove, 1992), 170.

## Chapter 5

Joseph A. Burke declared it "un-Christian": "50 Years After Vatican Council II," *Tablet* (newspaper of the Diocese of Brooklyn), October 12, 2012, http://thetablet.org/50-years-after-vatican-council-ii/.

"It used to start snowing at the beginning of November": Allan Hyman, interview by the author, February 6, 2014.

"The bedroom looked like it had just been robbed": Richard Sigal, interview by the author, February 4, 2014.

"We wore black vests with gold lamé": Richard Mishkin, interview by the author, February 17, 2014.

"The stuff that Lou was writing at the time": Hyman, interview by the author.

"We met my freshman year at Syracuse": Shelley Albin, interview by the author, July 1, 2014.

Source of "I'll Be Your Mirror": Ibid.

"He said, 'I have a very big favor to ask you'": James Gorney, interview by the author, March 13, 2014.

*Lonely Woman Quarterly*: *Lonely Woman Quarterly* 1 (May 1962), Syracuse University Archives.

"Five authors in search of a campus publication": Alan Millstein, "New Literary Magazine Started by Five Sophs," *Daily Orange*, May 11, 1962, Syracuse University Archives.

"The Savoy was a restaurant where we all hung out": Albin, interview by the author.

"He'd always found the idea of copulation distasteful": Lou Reed, *Lonely Woman Quarterly* 1 (May 1962), Syracuse University Archives.

*LWQ*, vol. 2: Lou Reed, "Mr. Lockwood's Pool" and "Michael Kogan—Syracuse's Miss Blanding," *Lonely Woman Quarterly* 2 (May 23, 1962), Syracuse University Archives.

"That got it banned": Karl Stoecker, interview by the author, June 26, 2014.

"Lost in the land of nighttime": Lincoln Swados, "The Nightingale" and "Well Goodbye Syracuse," *Lonely Woman Quarterly* 2 (May 23, 1962), Syracuse University Archives.

"Lincoln was a terrific guy": Albin, interview by the author.

"Lincoln looked pasty and thin": Elizabeth Swados, "The Story of a Street Person," *New York Times*, August 18, 1991.

"the Mozart of conversation": Saul Bellow, *Humboldt's Gift* (New York: Viking, 1975), 13.

"the first real innovation that we've had since Eliot and Pound": James Atlas, introduction to *In Dreams Begin Responsibilities and Other Stories*, by Delmore Schwartz (New York: New Directions, 1978), xiv.

"living on the side of a volcano": Ross Wetzsteon, *Republic of Dreams: Greenwich Village, the American Bohemia, 1910–1960* (New York: Simon & Schuster, 2002), 505.

"acute brain syndrome": Ibid.

"Schwartz would wear a jacket and tie": Gorney, interview by the author.

"The class was a mixed one": Murray J. Levith, "Review: Delmore Schwartz at Syracuse," *Salmagundi* 42 (Summer–Fall 1978): 150–156.

"He was crazy about Lou": Albin, interview by the author.

"I'm gonna be leaving for a world far better": Steven Watson, *Factory Made: Warhol and the Sixties* (New York: Pantheon, 2003), 155–156.

*LWQ* final issue: Lou Reed, "And What, Little Boy, Will You Trade for Your Horse?" *Lonely Woman Quarterly* 3 (April 1963), Syracuse University Archives.

"You said that we would never part": Lou Reed, "Merry Go Round" and "Your Love," recorded 1962 (unreleased), on *Rockin' on Broadway: The Time, Brent, Shad Story*, Ace, 2000.

"We really loved Bob Dylan": Mishkin, interview by the author.

"Heroin got him": Albin, interview by the author.

## Chapter 6

"Where Did Our Love Go": "Unprecedented" (Motown advertisement), *Billboard*, November 7, 1964.

"I said I wanted a gun": Victor Bockris, *Transformer: The Lou Reed Story* (New York: Simon & Schuster, 1994), 76.

"*The New Yorker* rejected me": Nick Johnstone, *Lou Reed Talking* (London: Omnibus, 2005), 26.

"We can't go below 10 songs per album": Hank Fox, "Disc Firms Swing to Less-Groove Policy," *Billboard*, March 4, 1967.

"Growing up in East New York–Brownsville": Terry Philips, interview by the author, February 17, 2015.

In 1964, economy albums accounted for a $30 million market share: "Pickwick's Economy Label Makes Deals with 5 Firms," *Billboard*, May 1, 1965.

Pickwick/33 ad: *Billboard*, July 17, 1965.

"Cy Leslie liked me personally": Philips, interview by the author.

"Why you runnin' around": The J Brothers, "Ya Running, but I'll Getcha," on *The Four Seasons—Johnny Rivers—Neil Sedaka—The J Brothers*, Design, 1964.

"They call me the wild one": Terry Philips, "Wild One," on *Swingin' Teen Sounds of Ronnie Dove and Terry Phillips* [*sic*], Design, 1965.

"I wouldn't say fuck you to him": Philips, interview by the author.

*Soundsville!*: Various artists, "Teardrop in the Sand," "I'm Gonna Fight," "Johnny Won't Surf No More," You're Driving Me Insane," "Cycle Annie," on *Soundsville!*, Design, 1965.

Dance crazes: Thomas L. Nelson, *1000 Novelty & Fad Dances: A Guide to How These Are Danced* (Bloomington, IN: AuthorHouse, 2009), 9–10.

"Look at all the ostrich that was floating around Paris": Eugenia Sheppard, "New Era Hits," *Montreal Gazette*, October 6, 1964.

"OK, I want everybody to settle down now": The Primitives, "The Ostrich," on "The Ostrich"/"Sneaky Pete," Pickwick City, 1964.

"I was as much of a wild man as he was": Philips, interview by the author.

Letter to Delmore Schwartz, 1965: Delmore Schwartz Papers, Beinecke Rare Book & Manuscript Library, Yale University.

Miles Copeland: Richie Unterberger, *White Light/White Heat: The Velvet Underground Day-by-Day* (London: Jawbone, 2009), 53.

Shelley moving to New York: Shelley Albin, interview by the author, July 1, 2014.

## Part II: The Velvet Underground

### Chapter 7

56 Ludlow Street: John Cale and Victor Bockris, *What's Welsh for Zen: The Autobiography of John Cale* (London: Bloomsbury, 1999), 62–73.

"As we struggled, the apartment took on the aesthetic of a coal mine": John Cale, "Incubator for the Velvet Underground," *Wall Street Journal*, January 20, 2013.

Erik Satie's *Vexations*: Sam Sweet, "A Dangerous and Evil Piano Piece," *New Yorker*, September 9, 2013.

The Dream Syndicate: Branden Wayne Joseph, *Beyond the Dream Syndicate: Tony Conrad and the Arts After Cage; A "Minor" History* (New York: Zone, 2008).

"The Tortoise Recalling the Drone of the Holy Numbers": Richie Unterberger, *White Light/White Heat: The Velvet Underground Day-by-Day* (London: Jawbone, 2009), 37.

"For me, what it stood for": Tony Conrad, interview by the author, August 26, 2014.

"Be primitives naturally": Joseph, *Beyond the Dream Syndicate*, 213.

"My picture came out": Rob Jovanovic, *Seeing the Light: Inside the Velvet Underground* (New York: St. Martin's, 2012), 35.

"Western music is based on death": Clinton Heylin, *From the Velvets to the Voidoids: The Birth of American Punk Rock* (Chicago: Chicago Review Press, 2005), 16.

Sterling Morrison, medievalist: Martha Morrison, interview by the author, March 6, 2014.

"Do it again. You blew some words": Lou Reed, "Heroin," recorded at Pickwick International, May 11, 1965 (unreleased), played at Lou Reed memorial, Apollo Theater, New York, December 16, 2013, bootleg recording.

"Here is an incredible book": Front cover of *The Velvet Underground*, by Michael Leigh (New York: Macfadden, 1963).

"It was perfect": Cale, "Incubator."

"poor man's copyright": Aram Bajakian, "Mystery Package Lou Reed Mailed to Himself in 1965 Could Contain the Velvet Underground's First Recording," *Death and Taxes*, October 8, 2014, www.deathandtaxesmag.com/229143/mystery-package-lou-reed -mailed-to-himself-in-1965-could-contain-the-velvet-undergrounds-first-recording/.

"Shiny, shiny boots of leather," "Prominent Men," "And what costumes shall the poor girl wear": On *Peel Slowly and See*, by the Velvet Underground, Polydor, 1995.

"the band had a ten-dollar fine": Lou Reed, Maureen Tucker, Doug Yule, and David Fricke, "The Art and Soul of the Velvet Underground," Live from the New York Public Library video, December 8, 2009, www.nypl.org/audiovideo/velvet-underground -lou-reed-maureen-%E2%80%98moe%E2%80%99-tucker-doug-yule-david-fricke.

Brian Epstein joint: Unterberger, *White Light/White Heat*, 143.

Velvet Underground and Myddle Class: Poster, December 11, 1965, archived at *Jewish Currents* official website, http://jewishcurrents.org/wp-content/uploads/2013/12 /MyddleClassSummitHighFlyer.jpg.

"You mean we start when they tell us to": Victor Bockris and Gerard Malanga, *Up-Tight: The Story of the Velvet Underground* (London: Omnibus, 1996), 42.

"Oh, Tucker's sister plays drums": Maureen Tucker, "Lou Reed Remembered by Moe Tucker," *Guardian*, December 14, 2013.

"I couldn't play a perfect roll for a million dollars": Adam Budofsky, "Drumming with the Velvet Underground, Part 2: Maureen Tucker," *Modern Drummer*, July 19, 2005.

"Nothing could have prepared the kids": Rob Norris, "I Was a Velveteen," *Kicks*, 1979.

"At least you've given them a night to remember": Ibid.

"It didn't really seem like the band": Morrison, interview by the author.


*Chapter 8*

Murray the K's World: Gerald Jonas and Renata Adler, "Murray the K's World," *New Yorker*, April 16, 1966.

"The Making of an Underground Film": *CBS Evening News with Walter Cronkite*, CBS, December 31, 1965.

Lou Reed Warhol screen tests: Directed by Andy Warhol (1966), Andy Warhol Museum, Pittsburgh, PA.

ABSOLUTELY NO DRUGS ALLOWED: Stephen Colegrave and Chris Sullivan, *Punk: The Definitive Record of a Revolution* (New York: Da Capo, 2005), 23.

Billy Name's Pentax: Kurt McVey, "The Warhol Collaborator Billy Name on Andy, Photography and the Afterlife," *New York Times Magazine*, November 6, 2014.

"Lou would just jerk off": Legs McNeil and Gillian McCain, *Please Kill Me: The Uncensored Oral History of Punk* (New York: Grove, 1996), 15.

"There were definitely two sides": Barbara Hodes, interview by the author, November 3, 2014.

"Moe and I were horrified left and right": Martha Morrison, interview by the author, March 6, 2014.

Letter from ELK Realty: Johan Kugelberg, *The Velvet Underground: New York Art* (New York: Rizzoli, 2009), 13.

Max's Kansas City: Steven Kasher, ed., *Max's Kansas City: Art, Glamour, Rock and Roll* (New York: Abrams Image, 2010).

"Max's, before they played there, was our hangout": Morrison, interview by the author.

"an IBM computer with a Garbo accent": Andy Warhol and Pat Hackett, *POPism: The Warhol Sixties* (Orlando: Harcourt, 2006), 182.

"the apotheosis of the Nazi earth mother": Liel Leibovitz, *A Broken Hallelujah: Rock and Roll, Redemption, and the Life of Leonard Cohen* (New York: W. W. Norton, 2014), 127.

"I have no regrets, except that I was born a woman": *Nico Icon*, directed by Susanne Ofteringer (Roxie Releasing, 1995).

"She's down on her knees": The Velvet Underground, "There She Goes Again," on *The Velvet Underground & Nico*, Verve, 1967.

"Warhol's jazz group": Gerald Eskenazi, "Track First-Nighters Indifferent to Cold, History," *New York Times*, January 4, 1966.

New York Society for Clinical Psychiatry's annual gala: Grace Glueck, "Syndromes Pop at Delmonico's," *New York Times*, January 14, 1966.

"The Homosexual in America": *Time*, January 21, 1966.

David Susskind's program on WNTA: Branden Joseph, "'My Mind Split Open': Andy Warhol's Exploding Plastic Inevitable," *Grey Room* 8 (summer 2002).

"I always made John his black canvas suits": Kimberly J. Bright, "The Brief Marriage of John Cale and Betsey Johnson," *Dangerous Minds*, June 12, 2013, www.dangerousminds .net/comments/the_brief_marriage_of_john_cale_and_betsey_johnson.

"Come blow your mind": Warhol and Hackett, *POPism*, 203.

"Andy and his mom went to church": Hodes, interview by the author.

*Chapter 9*

"He was like the guard dog": Lou Reed, Maureen Tucker, Doug Yule, and David Fricke, "The Art and Soul of the Velvet Underground," Live from the New York Public Library video, December 8, 2009, www.nypl.org/audiovideo/velvet-underground -lou-reed-maureen-%E2%80%98moe%E2%80%99-tucker-doug-yule-david-fricke.

"You killed your European son": The Velvet Underground, "European Son," on *The Velvet Underground & Nico*, Verve, 1967.

The Velvet Underground and the New York School: Andrew Epstein, "'I'll Be Your Mirror': Lou Reed and the New York School of Poetry," *Harriet: A Poetry Blog*, October 2013, www.poetryfoundation.org/harriet/2013/10/ill-be-your-mirror-lou -reed-and-the-new-york-school-of-poetry/.

"It will replace nothing except suicide": Clinton Heylin, *All Yesterdays' Parties: The Velvet Underground in Print, 1966–1971* (Cambridge, MA: Da Capo, 2005), 31.

"a three ring psychosis": "Warhol's 'Exploding Show' Stirs Psychosis in Chi's Offbeat Poor Richard's," *Variety*, June 29, 1966.

"Not since the Titanic ran into that iceberg": Heylin, *All Yesterdays' Parties,* 12.

"The town itself was dead": Martha Morrison, interview by the author, March 6, 2014.

"It wasn't so much us against the world": Maureen Tucker, "Lou Reed Remembered by Moe Tucker," *Guardian*, December 14, 2013.

"He's probably the single most untalented person": Victor Bockris and Gerard Malanga, *Up-Tight: The Story of the Velvet Underground* (London: Omnibus, 1996), 82.

THE SIZZLE THAT FIZZLED: Johan Kugelberg, *The Velvet Underground: New York Art* (New York: Rizzoli, 2009), 110.

"Still I see only in a glass darkly and vaguely": Lewis MacAdams, "Poet Delmore Schwartz: Orpheus in Purgatory," in "*Collected Stories*: Behind the Scenes," PBS official website, 2002, www.pbs.org/hollywoodpresents/collectedstories/writing/write_schwartz_1 .html.

"Being amid six million souls": Delmore Schwartz, "Sonnet: O City, City," in *Summer Knowledge: New and Selected Poems, 1938–1958* (Garden City, NY: Doubleday, 1959), 52.

## Chapter 10

"Watch out, the world's behind you": The Velvet Underground, "Sunday Morning," on *The Velvet Underground & Nico*, Verve, 1967.

*Aspen* magazine: Lou Reed, "The View from the Bandstand: Life Among the Poobahs," *Aspen* 3 (December 1966).

"Everything I both felt and didn't know about rock": Marc Spitz, *Bowie: A Biography* (New York: Crown, 2009), 75.

Incriminating press quotes: Liner notes, *The Velvet Underground & Nico*, by the Velvet Underground.

"So far 'underground,' you get the bends!" Richie Unterberger, *White Light/White Heat: The Velvet Underground Day-by-Day* (London: Jawbone, 2009), 135.

"The Velvet Underground is not an easy group to like": Richard Goldstein, Pop Eye, *Village Voice*, April 13, 1967.

"rather tedious": John Szwed, review of *The Velvet Underground & Nico*, *Jazz*, reprinted in Unterberger, *White Light/White Heat*, 152.

"The flowers of evil are in bloom": Martin Torgoff, *Can't Find My Way Home: America in the Great Stoned Age, 1945–2000* (New York: Simon & Schuster, 2004), 158.

"The Velvet Underground's first album only sold a few thousand copies": Unterberger, *White Light/White Heat*, 137.

"I guess I just don't know": The Velvet Underground, "Heroin," on *The Velvet Underground & Nico*.

"A sound mind in a healthy body": George Kirsch, Othello Harris, and Claire Elaine Nolte, *Encyclopedia of Ethnicity and Sports in the United States* (Westport, CT: Greenwood, 2000), 26.

"The complete spectrum of sound": Unterberger, *White Light/White Heat*, 146–148.

"I'm searching for my mainline": Ibid., 224.

Marshall McLuhan: Marshall McLuhan, Quentin Fiore, and Jerome Agel, *The Medium Is the Massage* (New York: Bantam, 1967), 108–109.

"When it fell apart": Legs McNeil and Gillian McCain, *Please Kill Me: The Uncensored Oral History of Punk* (New York: Grove, 1996), 10.

"Today it's a pricey area": Steve Nelson, interview by the author, September 17, 2014.

ANDY WARHOL'S NICO AND THE VELVET UNDERGROUND: Unterberger, *White Light/White Heat*, 151.

"I fired him on the spot": Lou Reed and John Cale, "Work," on *Songs for Drella*, Sire, 1990.

Warhol demanded to be paid 25 percent: Dave Thompson, *Your Pretty Face Is Going to Hell: The Dangerous Glitter of David Bowie, Iggy Pop, and Lou Reed* (New York: Backbeat, 2009), 51.

Country Happening: "Cunningham Dancers Will Gain on Saturday," *New York Times*, May 30, 1967; archival footage courtesy of Merce Cunningham, the Philip Johnson Glass House Visitor Center, New Canaan, CT.

## Chapter 11

"You got to show some grip": Ann Geracimos, "A Record Producer Is a Psychoanalyst with Rhythm," *New York Times*, September 29, 1968.

"Hey, you cats ready out there?": Ibid.

"A bootless Lou Reed, I might say": Johan Kugelberg, *The Velvet Underground: New York Art* (New York: Rizzoli, 2009), 209.

"And then my mind split open": The Velvet Underground, "I Heard Her Call My Name," on *White Light/White Heat*, Verve, 1968.

*White Light/White Heat* reviews: Clinton Heylin, *All Yesterdays' Parties: The Velvet Underground in Print, 1966–1971* (Cambridge, MA: Da Capo, 2005), xviii, xix, xxv, 60, 61, 65, 75–76, 93, 96, 100, 108, 109, 120, 151, 161, 162, 164, 169–170, 186, 194, 204, 223–225, 235.

"Come. Step softly": Kugelberg, *The Velvet Underground*, 213.

"No one listened to it": Jon Blistein, "The Velvet Underground to Reissue 'White Light/White Heat,'" *Rolling Stone*, October 1, 2013.

"Put quite simply, the Velvet Underground is the most vital and significant group": Heylin, *All Yesterdays' Parties*, 69.

"the most blatant injustice perpetrated by the media": Ibid.

"the doctor is making his first incision": The Velvet Underground, "Lady Godiva's Operation," on *White Light/White Heat*.

"I heard her call my name": The Velvet Underground, "I Heard Her Call My Name," on *White Light/White Heat*.

Doug Yule saw the band at Harvard: Doug Yule, interview by Andrew LaPointe, *PopMatters*, February 11, 2005, www.popmatters.com/feature/yule-doug-021105/.

John Cale wedding: John Cale and Victor Bockris, *What's Welsh for Zen: The Autobiography of John Cale* (London: Bloomsbury, 1999), 110.

"He always knew how to reach me": Shelley Albin, interview by the author, July 1, 2014.

"Thought of you as my mountaintop": The Velvet Underground, "Pale Blue Eyes," on *The Velvet Underground*, MGM, 1969.

"He used to think I should leave and come back with him": Albin, interview by the author.

"Shelley would just come back, it'd be all right": The Velvet Underground, "I Can't Stand It," bonus track on *1969: The Velvet Underground Live*, vol. 2, Mercury, 1974.

John Cale's broken wrist: Cale and Bockris, *Welsh for Zen*, 110.

"one of the most incredible musical experiences": Heylin, *All Yesterdays' Parties*, xxi.

"You mean out for today or for this week?": Legs McNeil and Gillian McCain, *Please Kill Me: The Uncensored Oral History of Punk* (New York: Grove, 1996), 23.


*Chapter 12*

Meeting Doug Yule: Sal Mercuri, "Head Held High: The Velvet Underground Featuring Doug Yule," *Velvet Underground Fanzine* 3 (Fall/Winter 1994).

The Boston sound: Alan Lorber, "Something Called the Boston Sound," *Goldmine*, April 1992.

"Vic was always instrumental": Angel Balestier, interview by the author, February 21, 2015.

"It was deliberately against their image": Steve Nelson, interview by the author, September 17, 2014.

"How'd you know that's what we're really like?": Ibid.

"They think they have a right to make money off of this?": Ibid.

The "closet mix": Richie Unterberger, *White Light/White Heat: The Velvet Underground Day-by-Day* (London: Jawbone, 2009), 227.

"The Velvet Underground are alive and well": Lester Bangs, review of *The Velvet Underground*, *Rolling Stone*, May 17, 1969.

Reviews of *The Velvet Underground*: Clinton Heylin, *All Yesterday's Parties: The Velvet Underground in Print, 1966–1971* (Cambridge, MA: Da Capo, 2005), 99–101, 107–109; Robert Christgau, Consumer Guide, *Village Voice*, ca. 1969, reprinted on author's official website, www.robertchristgau.com/get_artist.php?id=1560&name =The+Velvet+Underground.

"Why something different?": Johan Kugelberg, *The Velvet Underground: New York Art* (New York: Rizzoli, 2009), 241.

"no kinds of love are better than others": The Velvet Underground, "Some Kinda Love," on *The Velvet Underground*, MGM, 1969.

"my body," "the quiet places," and "big decisions": The Velvet Underground, "Candy Says," on *The Velvet Underground*.

"Between the idea and the reality": T. S. Eliot, "The Hollow Men," in *Collected Poems, 1909–1962* (New York: Harcourt, Brace & World, 1963), 81–82.

"Between thought and expression lies a lifetime": Velvet Underground, "Some Kinda Love."

"I'm set free to find a new illusion": The Velvet Underground, "I'm Set Free," on *The Velvet Underground*.

"That's the Story of My Life," "The Murder Mystery," "After Hours": On *The Velvet Underground*, by the Velvet Underground.

May 1968 sessions: David Fricke, liner notes, *The Velvet Underground 45th Anniversary*, Super Deluxe ed., by the Velvet Underground, Polydor, 2014; Richie Unterberger, *White Light/White Heat: The Velvet Underground Day-by-Day* (London: Jawbone, 2009), 188–189.

The Velvet Underground in Dallas: On *1969: Velvet Underground Live*, by the Velvet Underground, Mercury, 1974.

Crashing on a waiter's floor: George Manney, correspondence with the author, February 25, 2015.

## Chapter 13

An album "loaded with hits": Victor Bockris and Gerard Malanga, *Up-Tight: The Story of the Velvet Underground* (London: Omnibus, 1996), 235.

"Sweet Jane," "Rock & Roll," "I Found a Reason," "Oh! Sweet Nuthin'": On *Loaded*, by the Velvet Underground, Cotillion, 1970.

Lincoln Swados's attempted suicide: Elizabeth Swados, *The Four of Us: The Story of a Family* (New York: Farrar, Straus and Giroux, 1991), 40, 120.

Meeting Bettye Kronstad: Bettye Kronstad, interview by the author, April 6, 2014.

The Velvet Underground, May 9, 1970: The Second Fret, Philadelphia, bootleg recording.

"Good evening. We're the Velvet Underground": On *Live at Max's Kansas City*, by the Velvet Underground, Cotillion, 1972.

Patti Smith at Max's: Patti Smith, "Lou Reed," *New Yorker*, November 11, 2013.

"The Velvet Underground at Max's Kansas City?": Richard Nusser, "No Pale Imitation," *Village Voice*, July 2, 1970, reprinted in Clinton Heylin, *All Yesterdays' Parties: The Velvet Underground in Print, 1966–1971* (Cambridge, MA: Da Capo, 2005), 171–175.

"The musicians should be seen": Mike Jahn, "'Velvet' Rock Group Opens Stand Here," *New York Times*, July 4, 1970.

"I was at a café having my morning bowl of coffee": Kronstad, interview by the author.

"My being pregnant made him sort of give up": Shelley Albin, interview by the author, July 1, 2014.

"I hated playing at Max's": Nick Johnstone, *Lou Reed Talking* (London: Omnibus, 2005), 44.

Lou's final show: On *Live at Max's Kansas City*, by the Velvet Underground.

## Part III: Transformer

### Chapter 14

"disconnected from objective reality": Clinton Heylin, *All Yesterdays' Parties: The Velvet Underground in Print, 1966–1971* (Cambridge, MA: Da Capo, 2005), 232.

New York crime: "New York Crime Rates 1960–2013," Disaster Center, 2014, www .disastercenter.com/crime/nycrime.htm.

Reviews of *Loaded*: Heylin, *All Yesterdays' Parties*, xxxiii, xxxiv, 189–193, 194, 200, 204.

"I was a little more interested in meeting artists": Bettye Kronstad, interview by the author, April 6, 2014.

"Jesus died for somebody's sins, but not mine": Patti Smith, "Gloria," on *Horses*, Arista, 1975.

"I think I am now in love": Lou Reed, "Betty" [*sic*], in *Lou Reed & the Velvets*, by Nigel Trevena (Falmouth, England: Bantam, 1973), 26.

Lou Reed in the *Harvard Advocate*: "From the Archives: Lou Reed & The Velvet Underground," in a "Special Poetry Supplement" to *Harvard Advocate* 104, no. 3–4 (Fall 1971): http://theadvocateblog.net/2012/11/13/from-the-archives-the-velvet -undergrounds-lou-reed/

"formerly vocalist, guitarist and lead songwriter": Lou Reed, "Fallen Knights and Fallen Ladies," in *No One Waved Good-bye: A Casualty Report on Rock and Roll*, ed. by Robert Somma (New York: Outerbridge & Dienstfrey, 1971), 81–92.

At the Robinsons' apartment: Lisa Robinson, *There Goes Gravity: A Life in Rock and Roll* (New York: Riverhead, 2014), 42–44.

"Everybody would be sitting around on the floor": Kronstad, interview by the author.

"The guys who did *The Threepenny Opera*": On *Live: Take No Prisoners*, by Lou Reed, Arista, 1978.

*Mahagonny*: "'Mahagonny' to Close," *New York Times*, May 2, 1970.

Death of Jim Morrison: Kronstad, interview by the author.

### Chapter 15

Meeting with Bowie: Lisa Robinson, *There Goes Gravity: A Life in Rock and Roll* (New York: Riverhead, 2014), 43; Bettye Kronstad, interview by the author, April 6, 2014;

Dave Thompson, *Your Pretty Face Is Going to Hell: The Dangerous Glitter of David Bowie, Iggy Pop, and Lou Reed* (New York: Backbeat, 2009), 116–117.

"The ocean is becoming rough": Delmore Schwartz, *In Dreams Begin Responsibilities and Other Stories* (New York: New Directions, 1978), 5.

"What if Raymond Chandler wrote a rock song?": Lou Reed, *Night Flight*, USA Network, April 17, 1987.

"I actually still have a letter from Lisa": Kronstad, interview by the author.

Appearance at Le Bataclan: On *Le Bataclan '72*, by Lou Reed, John Cale, and Nico, Pilot, 2004; *Pop2* archival footage, recorded January 29, 1972.


## Chapter 16

"I knew all of the songs by heart": Bettye Kronstad, interview by the author, April 6, 2014.

"You're going to reap just what you sow": Lou Reed, "Perfect Day," on *Transformer*, RCA, 1972.

"We never communicated": Steve Katz, interview by the author, April 15, 2014.

"Lou came to the basement": Vinny Laporta, interview by the author, October 10, 2014.

"We were rehearsing upstairs": Katz, interview by the author.

"Hard to know what to make of this": Robert Christgau, Consumer Guide review of *Lou Reed*, *Village Voice*, ca. 1972, reprinted on author's official website, www.robertchristgau.com/get_album.php?id=2139.

"This album fits nowhere in the solo singer-songwriter spectrum": Greg Shaw, review of *Lou Reed*, *Phonograph Record*, May 1972.

"I spoke to Katz": Terry Philips, interview by the author, February 17, 2015.

"The early tours were very 'budget'": Barbara Wilkinson, correspondence with the author, October 11, 2014.

"We didn't use any pedals": Laporta, interview by the author.

A "very professional young backup band": Charles Murray, review of King's Cross performance, *New Musical Express*, July 22, 1972.

"Bowie was always a fan of Lou's": Kronstad, interview by the author.

"I walked out with red hair": George Varga, "Praise from the Rock: Rockers on Jazz," *JazzTimes*, March 2000.

"I did the 'phony' of Ernie": Karl Stoecker, interview by the author, June 26, 2014.

"Ernie was a bigger guy": Laporta, interview by the author.

"slick little girl": Lou Reed, "Make Up," on *Transformer*.

"It's one bar of C and one bar of F": "Lou Reed Was Short on Notes," *London Evening Standard*, October 28, 2014.

"When you combine that with the other bass": *The One Show*, BBC One, June 9, 2010.

"Take a walk on the wild side": Lou Reed, "Walk on the Wild Side," on *Transformer*.

"In the midst of all the make-believe madness": On *Transformer*, 30th anniversary ed., by Lou Reed, RCA, 2002.

"Jeff Beck is my favorite guitar player": Laporta, interview by the author.

"This new album is further proof": Robot A. Hull, review of *Transformer*, *Creem*, February 1973.

"a real cockteaser": Nick Tosches, review of *Transformer*, *Rolling Stone*, January 4, 1973.

"In part of the contract, it said": Laporta, interview by the author.

"You're going from one city to the next": Kronstad, interview by the author.

"Frank Sinatra Has a Cold": Gay Talese, "Frank Sinatra Has a Cold," *Esquire*, April 1966.

"I think he drank too much, frankly": Kronstad, interview by the author.

"We had tons of our local neighborhood friends": Laporta, interview by the author.

## Chapter 17

"I was interested in lights": Bettye Kronstad, interview by the author, April 6, 2014.

"We go into a couple record stores": Vinny Laporta, interview by the author, October 10, 2014.

Lester Bangs: Jim DeRogatis, *Let It Blurt: The Life and Times of Lester Bangs, America's Greatest Rock Critic* (New York: Broadway, 2000), 87–89; Lester Bangs, *Psychotic Reactions and Carburetor Dung: The Work of a Legendary Critic; Rock 'n' Roll as Literature and Literature as Rock 'n' Roll*, ed. Greil Marcus (New York: Anchor, 1988), 165–202; Lester Bangs, "Lou Reed: A Deaf Mute in a Telephone Booth," *Let It Rock*, November 1973.

"I was in the room when that happened": Kronstad, interview by the author.

"I take drugs just because": Bangs, "Lou Reed."

"I could see Lou's face. His eyes opened wide": Laporta, interview by the author.

"Early on he could drink a lot": Barbara Wilkinson, correspondence with the author, October 11, 2014.

"Once he starts drinking he can't stop": Kronstad, interview by the author.

"He wanted to do something entirely different": Bob Ezrin, Music Matters 2012 keynote interview, posted to YouTube by Branded Asia, July 10, 2012, www.youtube.com /watch?v=yona44LmmBQ.

"This girl came out of the bathroom": Kronstad, interview by the author.

Paralleled her childhood trauma: Ibid. In *What's Welsh for Zen* (p. 77), John Cale writes that "The Kids" was partially inspired by Daryl, a woman he and Reed were involved with in the early days of the Velvet Underground. In "John Cale on *The Velvet Underground & Nico*" (Tom Pinnock, *Uncut*, September 28, 2012), Cale notes that Daryl, "a beautiful petite blonde with three kids, two of whom were taken away from her," also inspired "All Tomorrow's Parties."

"He showed up and we sat in the same place": Ezrin, Music Matters keynote.

"He saw us play": Laporta, interview by the author.

"It was all written parts": Randy Brecker, interview by the author, March 5, 2014.

"I always believed in his music": Kronstad, interview by the author.

"The Kids": "Unusual Recording Techniques #1: Lou Reed's 'The Kids,'" *WFMU's Beware of the Blog*, September 18, 2006, http://blog.wfmu.org/freeform/2006/09/unusual_recordi.html.

Reviews of *Berlin*: Nick Kent, *New Musical Express*, October 6, 1973; Ben Sisario, "Revisiting a Bleak Album to Plumb Its Dark Riches," *New York Times*, December 13, 2006; Martin Johnson, "Reed Revisits That Divided City," *New York Sun*, December 14, 2006; Robert Christgau, Consumer Guide, *Village Voice*, ca. 1973, reprinted on author's official website, www.robertchristgau.com/get_album.php?id=2140.

## Chapter 18

"He seemed to take it seriously": Bettye Kronstad, interview by the author, April 6, 2014.

"*Berlin* was a bomb": Steve Katz, interview by the author, April 15, 2014.

After *Berlin*: Kronstad, interview by the author; Bettye Kronstad, "Bettye Kronstad on Lou Reed's *Berlin*," *Clouds and Clocks*, July 20, 2007, www.cloudsandclocks.net/features/kronstad_on_berlin_E.html.

The Olympia show: Ray Colcord, interview by the author, November 7, 2014; bootleg recording of the show.

"After the show, they showed their appreciation": Colcord, interview by the author.

Rebecca Futterman: Death records, Moose Roots, accessed May 29, 2015, http://death-records.mooseroots.com/d/n/Rebecca-Futterman.

Rainbow Theatre, 1973: Dinky Dawson and Carter Alan, *Life on the Road: The Incredible Rock and Roll Adventures of Dinky Dawson* (New York: Billboard, 1998), 208, 269, 281–284.

MXR phase pedals and an Echoplex: Greg Pederson, "The Great Guitars of Dick Wagner and Steve Hunter," *Vintage Guitar*, February 1998.

"My job was to provide a solid core": Colcord, interview by the author.

"As soon as I heard the Hunter-Wagner intro": Katz, interview by the author.

Baroque organ rubato: On *Rock 'n' Roll Animal*, by Lou Reed, RCA, 1974.

"One of the mics went out": Katz, interview by the author.

"After you buy the album": *Rock 'n' Roll Animal* advertisement, ca. 1974, archived at Super Seventies, www.superseventies.com/oaaa/oaaa_reedlou2.jpg.

"I took Caesar's Limo": Barbara Wilkinson, correspondence with the author, February 9, 2015.

"He said, 'I'm going to act crazier than normal'": Barbara Hodes, interview by the author, November 3, 2014.

Jonny Podell: Michael Gross, "Rock 'n' Roll Revival," *New York*, July 14, 1997.

"Lou took to speed just like that": Hodes, interview by the author.

"When I knew he was coming off of speed": Katz, interview by the author.

"Ride Sally Ride," "Ennui": On *Sally Can't Dance*, by Lou Reed, RCA, 1974.

"Lou would be working until four o'clock: Katz, interview by the author.

"He brought her over": Hodes, interview by the author.

"It was in a late-night club": Nick Johnstone, *Lou Reed Talking* (London: Omnibus, 2005), 15.

"I really liked Rachel": Katz, interview by the author.

"He did Lou Reed's hair": Gail Garcia, interview by the author, November 7, 2014.

Sydney press junket: Archival footage, August 1974, posted to YouTube by ABC Library Sales, October 7, 2012, www.youtube.com/watch?v=IeMIWCxHgQk.

"Lou-nee Tunes": Lester Bangs, *Psychotic Reactions and Carburetor Dung: The Work of a Legendary Critic; Rock 'n' Roll as Literature and Literature as Rock 'n' Roll*, ed. Greil Marcus (New York: Anchor, 1988), 199.

"I gave him champagne": Barbara Wilkinson, correspondence with the author, October 11, 2014.

"He tied the mic cord": Wayne Robins, "Lou Reed: Felt Theater, New York," *Village Voice*, October 17, 1974.

*Chapter 19*

Lester Bangs, round two: Jim DeRogatis, *Let It Blurt: The Life and Times of Lester Bangs, America's Greatest Rock Critic* (New York: Broadway, 2000), 97–99; Lester Bangs, *Psychotic Reactions and Carburetor Dung: The Work of a Legendary Critic; Rock 'n' Roll as Literature and Literature as Rock 'n' Roll*, ed. Greil Marcus (New York: Anchor, 1988), 169–183.

"'Everyman' for us meant to be all-inclusive": Marty Fogel, interview by the author, March 10, 2014.

"We were expecting a Nazi uniform": *La Stampa*, February 15, 1975, quoted in "1975, Lou Reed in Italia," *piste* (blog), October 30, 2013, http://piste.blogspot .com/2013/10/1975-lou-reed-in-italia.html.

"They herded us off the stage": Fogel, interview by the author, March 10, 2014.

"The worse I am, the more it sells": Chris Roberts, *Lou Reed: Walk on the Wild Side; The Stories Behind the Songs* (Milwaukee: Hal Leonard, 2004), 62–64.

"passion—REALISM": Lou Reed, liner notes, *Metal Machine Music*, RCA, 1975.

"Lou bought a couple of tape recorders": Steve Katz, interview by the author, April 15, 2014.

"five piggyback Marshall tube amps": Reed, liner notes, *Metal Machine Music*.

"It's for a certain time and place of mind": Ibid.

"He was one of their top artists": Katz, interview by the author.

"No one I know has listened to it": Reed, liner notes, *Metal Machine Music*.

Phone next to their ears: Peter Doggett, *Lou Reed: The Defining Years* (London: Omnibus, 2013), 172.

Reviews of *Metal Machine Music*: James Wolcott, *Rolling Stone*, August 14, 1975; Robert Christgau, Consumer Guide, *Village Voice*, ca. 1975, reprinted on author's official website, www.robertchristgau.com/get_album.php?id=2144.

"a dentist's drill battling a pneumatic drill": Anthony O'Grady, "An Afternoon with Lou Reed and *Metal Machine Music*," *Rock Australia Magazine*, August 9, 1975.

Lester Bangs on *Metal Machine Music*: Lester Bangs, "The Greatest Album Ever Made," reprinted in Bangs, *Psychotic Reactions*, 195–200.

## Chapter 20

CBGB: Tamar Brazis, Hilly Kristal, and David Byrne, *CBGB & OMFUG: Thirty Years from the Home of Underground Rock* (New York: Harry N. Abrams, 2005).

*Punk* magazine: John Holmstrom and Bridget Hurd, *Punk: The Best of Punk Magazine* (New York: It, 2012), 11–13, 17–20.

"We did work on *Coney Island Baby*": Steve Katz, interview by the author, April 15, 2014.

"Should I listen down a few times": Marko Syrjala, "Bob Kulick, Producer, Guitarist," part 1, *Metal Rules*, December 15, 2011.

"The tunes had a definite form": Marty Fogel, interview by the author, November 10, 2014.

"It's gonna be the kind of stuff": Lester Bangs, *Psychotic Reactions and Carburetor Dung: The Work of a Legendary Critic; Rock 'n' Roll as Literature and Literature as Rock 'n' Roll*, ed. Greil Marcus (New York: Anchor, 1988), 190–191.

"You'd better watch out for Charley's girl": Lou Reed, "Charley's Girl," on *Coney Island Baby*, RCA, 1976.

"You'd better watch out for little Cycle Annie": The Beachnuts, "Cycle Annie," on *Soundsville!*, Design, 1965.

"Ah, but remember that the city is a funny place": Lou Reed, "Coney Island Baby," on *Coney Island Baby*.

"I want to send this one out": Ibid.

"A career-capping touchdown": Paul Nelson, review of *Coney Island Baby*, *Rolling Stone*, March 25, 1976.

"This album made me so morose": Bangs, *Psychotic Reactions*, 217.

Clive Davis and Lou Reed: Clive Davis and Anthony DeCurtis, *The Soundtrack of My Life* (New York: Simon & Schuster, 2013), 220–230.

"You showed them some of these songs": Syrjala, "Bob Kulick."

"I believe in music, music, music": Lou Reed, "I Believe in Love," on *Rock and Roll Heart*, Arista, 1976.

"I'm bangin' on my drum, boy": Lou Reed, "Banging on My Drum," on *Rock and Roll Heart*.

"Lou promised this would be a rock": Stephen Demorest, review of *Rock and Roll Heart*, *Creem*, January 1977.

Patti Smith, David Byrne, Lou Reed, and John Cale joint appearance: Ocean Club, New York, 1976, bootleg recording.

"I wouldn't want a steady diet of it": John Morthland, "Lou Reed: Say It Again, Lou," *Creem*, December 1976.

"I actually went out": Jeff Ross, interview by the author, December 9, 2014.

"I'd see Don all the time": Marty Fogel, interview by the author, March 10, 2014.

Lou Reed and Don Cherry: Civic Auditorium, Santa Monica, CA, November 25, 1976, bootleg recording.

"He'd come back from a successful tour": Andy Warhol and Pat Hackett, *The Andy Warhol Diaries* (New York: Warner, 1989), 48.

"I think that Rachel was the glue": Ross, interview by the author.

Maunkberry's: Jill Furmanovsky, "Lou Reed and Rachel Celebrate," *Rock Scene*, October 1977.

"I'm beat asleep": Ross, interview by the author.

"I don't wanna be a fucked up middle-class college student": Lou Reed, "I Wanna Be Black," on *Street Hassle*, Arista, 1978.

"They came back one night": Fogel, interview by the author, March 10, 2014.

"It punted me into the upper echelon": Ross, interview by the author.

"Fuckin' good riddance to bad rubbish": Charles M. Young, "A Report on the Sex Pistols," *Rolling Stone*, October 20, 1977.

"Street Hassle," "Slipaway": On *Street Hassle*, by Lou Reed.

*Chapter 21*

"There would be a discussion": Lydia Sugarman, interview by the author, October 10, 2014.

Transgender politics: Susan Stryker, *Transgender History* (Berkeley, CA: Seal, 2008).

"When you desperately love someone": Sugarman, interview by the author.

"We were actually real oddities": Legs McNeil and Gillian McCain, *Please Kill Me: The Uncensored Oral History of Punk* (New York: Grove, 1996), 284.

"We spent all that night talking": Ibid., 285.

"I came back to New York": Ibid., 286.

"Take no prisoners, Lou!": Mick Wall, *Lou Reed: The Life* (London: Orion, 2013), 125.

Reviews of *Street Hassle*: Tom Carson, *Rolling Stone*, April 6, 1978; Robert Christgau, Consumer Guide, *Village Voice*, ca. 1978, reprinted on author's official website, www.robertchristgau.com/get_album.php?id=2147.

"He asked me to play something by Marvin Gaye": Susan Chiappone, "Lou and Me: 'Moose' Boles Shares Memories of Lou Reed," *Buffalo News*, November 3, 2013.

"He's in New York": Marty Fogel, interview by the author, March 10, 2014.

"I'm gonna quote a line from Yeats": On *Live: Take No Prisoners*, by Lou Reed, Arista, 1978.

"I thank Lou": Robert Christgau, Consumer Guide review of *Live: Take No Prisoners*, *Village Voice*, ca. 1978, reprinted on author's official website, www.robertchristgau .com/get_album.php?id=7622.

"A place to hang out": Marty Fogel, interview by the author, November 10, 2014.

"From the molten-golden notes": Edgar Allan Poe, "The Bells," in *The Collected Tales and Poems of Edgar Allan Poe* (Hertfordshire, England: Wordsworth Editions, 2004), 733.

"I did a little horn arrangement": Fogel, interview by the author, March 10, 2014.

"*The Bells* isn't merely": Lester Bangs, review of *The Bells*, *Rolling Stone*, June 14, 1979.

Vintage jukebox: Richard Sigal, interview by the author, February 4, 2014.

"Lou loved toys": Ibid.

"I'm walking around Fifty-Seventh Street": Chuck Hammer, interview by the author, October 14, 2014.

Lou on *Radio, Radio*: WPIX-FM, May 1979, bootleg recording.

"I took a Greyhound bus": Hammer, interview by the author.

"We have our sound check": Fogel, interview by the author, March 10, 2014.

"Lou was drunk at the Hammersmith Odeon": Hammer, interview by the author.

Allan Jones and Giovanni Dadamo: Allan Jones, "The Night Lou Reed Bopped David Bowie," *Uncut*, March 14, 2007.

"We might have been doing some drinking": Hammer, interview by the author.

"Here, this is for you, Clive": Clive Davis and Anthony DeCurtis, *The Soundtrack of My Life* (New York: Simon & Schuster, 2013), 223.

Lou Reed at Columbia: Dan Breslau, "Lou Reed Lets Loose," *Columbia Daily Spectator*, September 24, 1979.

"Suddenly it hit me that I could write": Chris Willman, "Queen of Solitude," *Los Angeles Times*, July 26, 1987.

"He wrecked two guitars": Hammer, interview by the author.

"Thank god that I just don't care": Lou Reed, McMillan Theater, Columbia University, September 21, 1979, bootleg recording.

"He likes Edgar Allan Poe": Lou Reed, "Love Is Here to Stay," on *Growing Up in Public*, Arista, 1980; *Lou Reed: Live at the Bottom Line 12/26/79* (bootleg recording).

## Part IV: Set the Twilight Reeling

### Chapter 22

1980 Wedding: Lisa Robinson, *There Goes Gravity: A Life in Rock and Roll* (New York: Riverhead, 2014), 52–53.

Paul Simon and *One-Trick Pony*: Marc Eliot, *Paul Simon: A Life* (Hoboken, NJ: Wiley, 2010), 159–168.

"very Top 40 oriented": *One-Trick Pony*, directed by Robert M. Young (Warner Bros., 1980).

Lou Reed and tai chi: Martha Burr, "Lou Reed: A Walk on the Wild Side of Tai Chi," *Kung Fu Magazine*, May/June 2003.

*Zen and the Art of Motorcycle Maintenance*: David Fricke, "A Refugee from Rock's Dark Side, Lou Reed Says Goodbye Excess, Hello New Jersey," *People*, March 30, 1981.

"Lou flipped, and the flip happened": Chuck Hammer, interview by the author, October 24, 2014.

"A Prince Hamlet caught in the middle": Lou Reed, "Growing Up in Public," on *Growing Up in Public*, Arista, 1980.

"I mastered the art of recording": Dave DiMartino, "Lou Reed Tilts the Machine," *Creem*, September 1980.

"How do you speak to the prettiest girl?": Lou Reed, "How Do You Speak to an Angel?," on *Growing Up in Public*.

"If I was restricted to me": DiMartino, "Lou Reed Tilts the Machine."

"I thought I had to stick that in a song": Ibid.

"cool and cleansing water": Lou Reed, "Teach the Gifted Children," on *Growing Up in Public*.

"His religion was music": "Lou Reed Tribute Show," *The Indie Café*, Red Velvet Media, June 27, 2014, www.blogtalkradio.com/redvelvetmedia/2014/06/27/lou-reed-tribute -show-with-the-indie-cafe-on-red-velvet-media.

"*Growing Up in Public* is probably the best": Nick Kent, review of *Growing Up in Public*, *New Musical Express*, July 12, 1980.

June 1, 1980, at the Bottom Line: Bootleg recording.

"We were playing for giant places": Hammer, interview by the author.

"My Name Is Mok": *Rock & Rule*, directed by Clive A. Smith (MGM/UA Entertainment, 1983).

"He understood he needed to take a break": "Lou Reed Tribute Show," *The Indie Café*.

"powerless over alcohol": William Griffith Wilson, *Alcoholics Anonymous: The Story of How Many Thousands of Men and Women Have Recovered from Alcoholism*, 4th ed. (Alcoholics Anonymous World Services, 2001), 59.

"How dare you be here": Jim DeRogatis, *Let It Blurt: The Life and Times of Lester Bangs, America's Greatest Rock Critic* (New York: Broadway, 2000), 210.

"You're a fucking great guitar player": Legs McNeil and Gillian McCain, *Please Kill Me: The Uncensored Oral History of Punk* (New York: Grove, 1996), 286.

"I was this vegetarian": "Fernando Saunders: Lou Reed mi změnil život," *Music Check*, ČRo Radio Wave, December 18, 2013, www.rozhlas.cz/radiowave/musiccheck /_zprava/fernando-saunders-lou-reed-mi-zmenil-zivot--1294225.

"For the last six months": Sean Fullan, interview by the author, February 4, 2014.

"What Lou was after": Doane Perry, interview, *Perfect Sound Forever*, accessed May 29, 2015, www.furious.com/perfect/quine/doaneperry.html.

"The ferocity with which he played": Fullan, interview by the author.

The "spirit of pure poetry": Lou Reed, "My House," on *The Blue Mask*, RCA, 1982.

"My Daedalus to your Bloom": Ibid.

"It was a really important song": "Lou Reed Tribute Show," *The Indie Café*.

"Lou Reed's *The Blue Mask*": Tom Carson, review of *The Blue Mask*, *Rolling Stone*, April 15, 1982.

"That's too bad about your friend": Jim DeRogatis, "Robert Quine: Such a Lovable Genius," *Perfect Sound Forever*, accessed May 29, 2015, www.furious.com/perfect /quine/quinederogatis.html.

"metaphysical folk singer": *Get Crazy*, directed by Allan Arkush (Embassy Pictures, 1983).

"I'm good for just a kiss": Lou Reed, "Legendary Hearts," on *Legendary Hearts*, RCA, 1983.

"I was in Ohio": Robert Quine, interview by Jason Gross, *Perfect Sound Forever*, November 1997, www.furious.com/perfect/quine.html.

"Lou would turn to Quine": Jim DeRogatis, "Working with Lou, Part 1: Drummer and Producer Fred Maher," WBEZ blog, November 20, 2013, www.wbez.org/blogs/jim-derogatis/2013-11/working-lou-part-1-drummer-and-producer-fred-maher-109195.

"I hit one note": *A Night with Lou Reed*, directed by Clark Santee (RCA/Columbia Pictures, 1984).

"I'd shine by the light of the unknown moment": Lou Reed, "Fly into the Sun," on *New Sensations*, RCA, 1984.

Swimming Pool Q's: Jeff Calder, "Don't Believe a Word of It: Two Months on the Road with Lou Reed," *Vinyl District*, November 1, 2013, www.thevinyldistrict.com/storefront/2013/11/dont-believe-word-three-months-raod-lou-reed/.

"Brownsville Girl": Bill Flanagan, *Written in My Soul: Rock's Great Songwriters Talk About Creating Their Music* (Chicago: Contemporary, 1986), 101.

## Chapter 23

Wieden & Kennedy: Randall Rothenberg, *Where the Suckers Moon: An Advertising Story* (New York: Knopf, 1994), 209–213.

"Since I can't resist short, pithy answers": Jim Riswold, correspondence with the author, December 4, 2014.

"I thought it was a terrific idea": Steve Gett, "Reed Walks on the High-Profile Side," *Billboard*, June 7, 1986.

"We wanted to push the unpleasantness": Riswold, correspondence with the author.

"What you are about to see is important": Lawrence Bridges, "Wieden + Kennedy: Honda Feat. Lou Reed," Vimeo, August 21, 2012, https://vimeo.com/47959726.

"Freedom is a privilege": Steven Van Zandt and Artists Against Apartheid, "Sun City," on *Sun City*, Manhattan, 1985.

"Real pleasure for us": Farm Aid, University of Illinois Memorial Stadium, Champaign, IL, September 22, 1985.

"The Original Wrapper," "Tell It to Your Heart": On *Mistrial*, by Lou Reed, RCA, 1986.

Lou donated a Honda Elite scooter: Amnesty International Archives, Rare Book & Manuscript Library, Columbia University.

"Rock and roll, to me": Ibid.

"It's one thing to read": Conspiracy of Hope press conference, East Rutherford, NJ, June 14, 1986.

"I remember when me and Fernando": The Ritz, New York, July 16, 1986, archival footage, posted to YouTube by Music Vault, September 12, 2014, www.youtube.com/watch?v=xf8H7QQdZQs.

"When I took the reed off": Rick Bell, interview by the author, March 20, 2014.

"Just before he finished": Jon Pareles, "Rock: Lou Reed in Concert," *New York Times*, October 6, 1986.

## Chapter 24

"He says, 'It's you and me'": Rick Bell, interview by the author, March 20, 2014.

"The ocean reduces that stone to sand": Lou Reed, "Voices of Freedom" lyric sheet, Amnesty International Archives, Rare Book & Manuscript Library, Columbia University.

Warhol's memorial service: Grace Glueck, "Warhol Is Remembered by 2,000 at St. Patrick's," *New York Times*, April 2, 1987.

Bono's improvised verse of "Walk on the Wild Side": Bootleg recording.

"They come on the bus": Bell, interview by the author.

"Letters to the Vatican," "Hopes on Hold": On *Nothing but the Truth*, by Rubén Blades, Elektra, 1988.

Children's Health Fund benefit: Archival footage, posted to YouTube by Children's Health Fund, March 11, 2008, www.youtube.com/watch?v=-N2cy_J-uyU.

"I sound like Lou Reed": Jim DeRogatis, "Working with Lou, Part 1: Drummer and Producer Fred Maher," WBEZ blog, November 20, 2013, www.wbez.org/blogs/jim -derogatis/2013-11/working-lou-part-1-drummer-and-producer-fred-maher-109195.

"they make it their own choice": Steven V. Roberts, "Reagan on Homelessness: Many Choose to Live in the Streets," *New York Times*, December 23, 1988.

"You can only depend on one thing": Lou Reed, "Busload of Faith," on *New York*, Sire, 1989.

"It really *is* the eight years": Jonathan Cott, "Lou Reed: A New York State of Mind," *Rolling Stone*, ca. 1989, reprinted October 27, 2014.

"Romeo Had Juliette," "Halloween Parade," "Dirty Blvd.," "Beginning of a Great Adventure," "Last Great American Whale," "Strawman": On *New York*, by Lou Reed.

"It's fully divine": Martin Scorsese, interview on *The Movie Show*, September 29, 1988.

"I think that's one": Cott, "Lou Reed."

The "mysteries of life": Lou Reed, "Dime Store Mystery," on *New York*.

"I think that's one of the most stunning lines": Cott, "Lou Reed."

"I was going to be in the studio": DeRogatis, "Working with Lou, Part 1."

"There are five Lous": "Lou Reed Tribute Show," *The Indie Café*, Red Velvet Media, June 27, 2014, www.blogtalkradio.com/redvelvetmedia/2014/06/27/lou-reed-tribute -show-with-the-indie-cafe-on-red-velvet-media.

"Hi, this is Lou Reed": On *Winter Warnerland*, Warner Bros., 1988.

"It was 1958": Lou Reed and Dion DiMucci, Rock and Roll Hall of Fame induction ceremony, January 18, 1989.

March 10, 1989, at the Orpheum Theater: David Fricke, "Lou Reed: The Rolling Stone Interview," *Rolling Stone*, May 4, 1989.

"We could swear": Barry Singer, "Nearly Remarkable," *New Yorker*, May 22, 1989.

Broken ankle: Warner Bros. Records press release, ca. August 1989, archived at *Raz Mataz Magazine*, http://razmatazmag.com/wp-content/uploads/Aug19.jpg.

*Songs for Drella* soup cans: "Swag Bag: Soup for 'Drella (Featuring Andy Warhol, John Cale, and Lou Reed)," *BAM Blog*, September 21, 2011, http://bam150years.blogspot .com/2011/09/swag-bag-soup-for-drella-featuring-andy.html.

"I'm sorry if I doubted your good heart": Lou Reed and John Cale, "Hello It's Me," on *Songs for Drella*, Sire, 1990.

"It was not easy sailing": Peter Blauner, "Rock Noir: Lou Reed Reckons with Andy Warhol in 'Songs for 'Drella," *New York*, November 27, 1989.

## Chapter 25

Havel and the Velvet Underground: Michael Zantovsky, *Havel: A Life* (New York: Grove, 2015), 111, 163, 347.

"I'm not an interviewer": Lou Reed, video interview, Havel at Columbia website, Columbia Center for New Media Teaching and Learning, 2006, http://havel.columbia. edu/lou_reed.html.

He initially thought the experience would be "Kafkaesque": Lou Reed, *Between Thought and Expression: Selected Lyrics of Lou Reed* (New York: Hyperion, 1991), 146.

"Lou was the first": Sam Beckwith, "Vaclav Havel & Lou Reed," Prague TV, January 24, 2005, http://prague.tv/articles/art-and-culture/vaclav-havel-and-lou-reed.

"Why did you stay": Reed, *Between Thought and Expression*, 162.

"He's enormously charming": Lou Reed, video interview, Havel at Columbia.

"Lou probably thought": Jan Machacek, interview by the author, February 13, 2015.

"I always thought the Velvet Underground": Archival footage, posted to YouTube by "passthrufire," January 1, 2010, www.youtube.com/watch?v=qM4zO2q-gzI.

"Everything we played differently": Machacek, interview by the author.

"I want to tell you": ULUV Gallery, Prague, April 19, 1990, bootleg recording.

"They were very dangerous": Reed, *Between Thought and Expression*, 161.

"They wanted me to change this": Lou Reed, video interview, Havel at Columbia.

"The four of us have not been in one place": Ibid.

"It went away at that reunion": Martha Morrison, interview by the author, March 6, 2014.

"The resulting photograph": "Lou Reed Tribute Show," *The Indie Café*, Red Velvet Media, June 27, 2014, www.blogtalkradio.com/redvelvetmedia/2014/06/27/lou-reed-tribute -show-with-the-indie-cafe-on-red-velvet-media.

"Rotten Rita had carved a poem": James Barron, *The New York Times Book of New York: 549 Stories of the People, the Events, and the Life of the City—Past and Present* (New York: Black Dog & Leventhal, 2009), 35.

Lincoln Swados and his eviction: Michael P. Smith, *Marginal Spaces* (New Brunswick, NJ: Transaction, 1995), 78–79.

"That moment when Jimmy Scott": "Lou Reed Tribute Show," *The Indie Café*.

"It's best not to wait for luck to save you": Lou Reed, "Magic and Loss: The Summation," on *Magic and Loss*, Sire, 1992.

Lou Reed on *Arsenio*: *The Arsenio Hall Show*, Paramount Domestic Television, April 29, 1992.

John Zorn and Lou Reed: Bill Milkowski, "John Zorn: The Working Man," *JazzTimes*, May 2009.

Lou Reed meeting Laurie Anderson: *Charlie Rose*, PBS, July 8, 2003.

*Chapter 26*

Bob Dylan's "Foot of Pride": Bob Dylan, "Foot of Pride" (*Infidels* outtake), on *The Bootleg Series Volumes 1–3 (Rare & Unreleased) 1961–1991*, Columbia, 1991.

Bruce Cockburn's "Cry of a Tiny Babe": On *Columbia Records Radio Hour*, vol. 1, by various artists, Columbia, 1995.

"We're in the business of remythologizing": John Rockwell, "Older but Still Hip, the Velvet Underground Rocks Again," *New York Times*, June 5, 1993.

REVIVAL OF THE HIPPEST: *New Musical Express*, May 6, 1993.

"I witnessed myself": "Lou Reed Tribute Show," *The Indie Café*, Red Velvet Media, June 27, 2014, www.blogtalkradio.com/redvelvetmedia/2014/06/27/lou-reed-tribute -show-with-the-indie-cafe-on-red-velvet-media.

"No tame dog is gonna ever": The Velvet Underground, "Coyote," on *Live MCMXCIII*, Sire, 1993.

"I want to tell you": The Velvet Underground, Palace of Culture, Prague, June 13, 1993, bootleg recording.

"He pointed at his skin": Victoria Williams, interview by the author, February 6, 2014.

"What he brought out of me": Danny Frankel, interview by the author, February 2, 2014.

Audio Engineering Society Convention: Laurie Anderson, "Laurie Anderson's Farewell to Lou Reed," *Rolling Stone*, November 6, 2013.

"In our sleep where we meet": Laurie Anderson, "In Our Sleep," on *Bright Red*, Warner Bros., 1994.

Downtown Seder: Michael Dorf, "Lou Reed: The Wise Child," *Jewish Week*, October 28, 2013.

"They were doing poetry": Terry Philips, interview by the author, February 17, 2015.

"They are the Velvet Underground": Patti Smith, Velvet Underground Rock and Roll Hall of Fame induction ceremony, January 17, 1996, posted to YouTube by Rock and Roll Hall of Fame and Museum, July 16, 2012, www.youtube.com/watch?v=na6-GZxfABg.

"This event makes an astonishing": John Cale, Velvet Underground Rock and Roll Hall of Fame induction ceremony, January 17, 1996, posted to YouTube by Rock and Roll Hall of Fame and Museum, July 16, 2012, www.youtube.com /watch?v=MXI3bFTgtSc.

"Finish Line," "NYC Man," "Trade In," "Hookywooky," "The Proposition," "Set the Twilight Reeling": On *Set the Twilight Reeling*, by Lou Reed, Sire, 1996.

*Set the Twilight Reeling* packaging: Project page, Sagmeister & Walsh official website, accessed May 29, 2015, www.sagmeisterwalsh.com/work/project/lou-reed-set-the -twilight-reeling/.

"You up there": Mark Athitakis, "Riff Raff," *SF Weekly*, January 19, 2000.

*Time Rocker*: Bernard Holland, "Classical View: Is It Opera? Maybe, but Who Cares?," *New York Times*, November 23, 1997; Jon Pareles, "Echoes of H.G. Wells, Rhythms of Lou Reed," *New York Times*, November 14, 1997; Alan Riding, "Applauded for His Rock Opera Trilogy, an American in Paris," *New York Times*, January 15, 1997.

"Into the Divine," "Why Do You Talk," "Talking Book": On *Perfect Night: Live in London*, by Lou Reed, Sire, 1998.

*Perfect Night* and Jim Olson: Alan Di Perna, "Lou Reed Talks About the Velvet Underground, Songwriting and Gear in 1998 Guitar World Interview," *Guitar World*, November 6, 2013, www.guitarworld.com/lou-reed-talks-about-velvet-underground -songwriting-and-gear-1998-guitar-world-interview?page=0,2.

"This is my art, my music": Patrick Kiger, "Lou Reed's Appearance at the White House," *Boundary Stones* (blog), WETA official website, October 31, 2013, http://blogs.weta .org/boundarystones/2013/10/31/lou-reeds-appearance-white-house.

"If you had as much fun": Roxanne Roberts and Libby Ingrid Copeland, "International Velvet," *Washington Post*, September 17, 1998.

Lou, Laurie, and Lolabelle: Mary Ellen Mark, "Mister & Mistletoe," *New York Times Magazine*, December 23, 2001.

Master Sound: Vivian S. Toy, "Dissonance Underground: As Tunnel Work Hums, a Recording Studio Closes," *New York Times*, July 6, 1999.

"Paranoia Key of E," "Mad": On *Ecstasy*, by Lou Reed, Sire, 2000.

"Lou was screaming": Doug Wieselman, interview by the author, January 30, 2014.

"Ecstasy," "Tatters," "Turning Time Around," "Like a Possum," "Big Sky": On *Ecstasy*, by Lou Reed.

"He's repented and he's living": Bill Hoffmann, "Pope Is Gonna Rock 'n' Roll with Lou Reed," *New York Post*, April 13, 2000.

Lou Reed death hoax: "Lou Reed Is Dead," About.com Urban Legends, October 27, 2013, http://urbanlegends.about.com/library/bl-loureed.htm.

"Do you have any idea": "Weekend Update," *Saturday Night Live*, May 12, 2001, archived at Yahoo! Screen, https://screen.yahoo.com/lou-reed-000000422.html.

"It's like at the end of the play": Laurie Anderson, "One Beautiful Evening," on *Life on a String*, Nonesuch/Elektra, 2001.

*Chapter 27*

Laurie Anderson and Lou Reed on 9/11: Lou Reed, "I Heard the News Today . . . ," *Rolling Stone*, October 25, 2001; Laurie Anderson, liner notes, *Big Science*, Warner

Bros., 2007; Greg Kot, "Laurie Anderson 9/11 Concert at Park West Revisited," *Chicago Tribune*, September 11, 2013.

"Here come the planes": Laurie Anderson, "O Superman," on "O Superman"/"Walk the Dog," Warner Bros., 1981.

"Laurie if you're sadly listening": Lou Reed, "Laurie Sadly Listening," *New York Times Magazine*, November 11, 2001.

"If you prick me I will burst": Lou Reed, "Balloon," on *The Raven*, Sire, 2003.

"He wanted this overture": Doug Wieselman, interview by the author, January 30, 2014.

"Who Am I? (Tripitena's Song)," "Guardian Angel": On *The Raven*, by Lou Reed.

"It was a little bit of a seesaw": Wieselman, interview by the author.

"to replace the everyday cacophony": Lou Reed, liner notes, *Hudson River Wind Meditations*, Sounds True, 2007.

"Bunny, can you fuckin' believe this?": Merrill Weiner, speech at Lou Reed memorial, Apollo Theater, New York, December 16, 2013, bootleg recording.

"An interviewer asked me": David Yaffe, "Lou's Gift: The Magic of a Rock 'n' Roll Poet," *Tablet* (online magazine), October 28, 2013, http://tabletmag.com/scroll/150574/lous-gift-the-magic-of-a-rock-and-roll-poet; Chris Baker, "Lou Reed's Lasting Legacy at Syracuse University: a Criminal, a Dissident and a Poet," Syracuse.com, October 31, 2013, www.syracuse.com/entertainment/index.ssf/2013/10/lou_reed_syracuse_university.html.

"The call was, 'Hey'": Nick Forster, interview by the author, March 6, 2014.

"The beating of a pure bred heart": Lou Reed, "The Power of the Heart," on *Love by Cartier*, 2008.

"Blue Christmas": McGarrigle Christmas Hour, Carnegie Hall, New York, December 10, 2008, bootleg recording.

"Let's make a record together": Kyle Anderson, "Metallica's Lars Ulrich on Lou Reed: 'He's the Most Direct, Pure Person I've Ever Met,'" *Entertainment Weekly*, October 31, 2013.

"Nothing was thought about": Lars Ulrich, "Metallica's Lars Ulrich on Lou Reed's Rock 'n' Roll Poetry," *Guardian*, October 30, 2013.

"Pumping Blood," etc.: Lou Reed with Metallica, *Lulu*, Warner Bros., 2011.

Reviews of *Lulu*: Stuart Berman, *Pitchfork*, November 1, 2011, http://pitchfork.com/reviews/albums/15996-lou-reed-metallica/; Greg Kot, *Chicago Tribune*, October 28, 2011; Ian Winwood, *BBC Music*, October 31, 2011, www.bbc.co.uk/music/reviews/dr28.

"He used to e-mail me": Wendy Oxenhorn, correspondence with the author, February 6, 2015.

"Lou's manager comes out": Aram Bajakian, interview by the author, January 31, 2014.

"I wanted to write. One line as good as yours": Delmore Schwartz, *In Dreams Begin Responsibilities and Other Stories* (New York: New Directions, 2012), 6.

Salle Pleyel performance: Paris, March 6, 2013, bootleg recording.

"Are you satisfied": Recording by the author, March 19, 2013.

"My life is music": Lou Reed, interview for Parrot Zik headphones, September 30, 2013, posted to YouTube by Parrot, November 8, 2013, www.youtube.com /watch?v=4giZwTxmeP4.

He died in Laurie's arms: Laurie Anderson, "Laurie Anderson's Farewell to Lou Reed," *Rolling Stone*, November 6, 2013.

## Epilogue

"school-yard buddy": "John Cale on Death of Lou Reed: 'I've Lost My 'School-Yard Buddy,'" *Billboard*, October 27, 2013.

"good and loyal friend": Maureen Tucker, "Lou Reed Remembered by Moe Tucker," *Guardian*, December 14, 2013.

Lou Reed memorial: Jon Pareles, "Lou Reed's Complex Spirit Is Invoked at a Reunion of His Inner Circle," *New York Times*, December 17, 2013.

"We never once talked": Lou Reed memorial, Apollo Theater, New York, December 16, 2013, bootleg recording.

"My heart was going boom boom boom": Lou Reed, "Solsbury Hill," on *And I'll Scratch Yours*, Peter Gabriel, Real World, 2014.

Rock and Roll Hall of Fame induction: "Read Laurie Anderson's Moving Rock Hall Speech for Lou Reed," *Rolling Stone*, April 19, 2015; Laurie Anderson, Lou Reed Rock and Roll Hall of Fame induction ceremony, April 18, 2015, aired on HBO, May 30, 2015.

# SELECTED BIBLIOGRAPHY

Atlas, James. *Delmore Schwartz: The Life of an American Poet*. New York: Farrar, Straus and Giroux, 1977.

Bangs, Lester. *Psychotic Reactions and Carburetor Dung: The Work of a Legendary Critic; Rock 'n' Roll as Literature and Literature as Rock 'n' Roll*. Edited by Greil Marcus. New York: Anchor, 1988.

Barron, James. *The New York Times Book of New York: 549 Stories of the People, the Events, and the Life of the City—Past and Present*. New York: Black Dog & Leventhal, 2009.

Beeber, Steven Lee. *The Heebie-Jeebies at CBGB's: A Secret History of Jewish Punk*. Chicago: Chicago Review Press, 2006.

Bellow, Saul. *Humboldt's Gift*. New York: Viking, 1975.

Billig, Michael. *Rock 'n' Roll Jews*. Syracuse, NY: Syracuse University Press, 2001.

Bockris, Victor. *Transformer: The Lou Reed Story*. New York: Simon & Schuster, 1994.

Bockris, Victor, and Gerard Malanga. *Up-Tight: The Story of the Velvet Underground*. London: Omnibus, 1996.

Brackett, John Lowell. *John Zorn: Tradition and Transgression*. Bloomington: Indiana University Press, 2008.

Brazis, Tamar, Hilly Kristal, and David Byrne. *CBGB & OMFUG: Thirty Years from the Home of Underground Rock*. New York: Harry N. Abrams, 2005.

Burroughs, William S. *Naked Lunch*. New York: Grove, 1992.

Cale, John, and Victor Bockris. *What's Welsh for Zen: The Autobiography of John Cale*. London: Bloomsbury, 1999.

Cervera, Rafa. *Lou Reed*. Madrid: Cátedra, 1994.

Clapton, Diana. *Lou Reed and the Velvet Underground*. London: Proteus, 1982.

Colegrave, Stephen, and Chris Sullivan. *Punk: The Definitive Record of a Revolution*. New York: Da Capo, 2005.

Davis, Clive, and Anthony DeCurtis. *The Soundtrack of My Life*. New York: Simon & Schuster, 2013.

Dawson, Dinky, and Carter Alan. *Life on the Road: The Incredible Rock and Roll Adventures of Dinky Dawson*. New York: Billboard, 1998.

DeCurtis, Anthony, James Henke, and Holly George-Warren. *The Rolling Stone Illustrated History of Rock & Roll*. New York: Random House, 1992.

DeRogatis, Jim. *Let It Blurt: The Life and Times of Lester Bangs, America's Greatest Rock Critic*. New York: Broadway, 2000.

DeRogatis, Jim, and Bill Bentley. *The Velvet Underground: An Illustrated History of a Walk on the Wild Side*. Minneapolis: Voyageur, 2009.

Doggett, Peter. *Lou Reed: Growing Up in Public*. London: Omnibus, 1992.

———. *Lou Reed: The Defining Years*. London: Omnibus, 2013.

———. *The Man Who Sold the World: David Bowie and the 1970s*. New York: HarperCollins, 2012.

Eliot, Marc. *Paul Simon: A Life*. Hoboken, NJ: Wiley, 2010.

Eliot, T. S. *Collected Poems, 1909–1962*. New York: Harcourt, Brace & World, 1963.

Finkelstein, Nat. *Andy Warhol: The Factory Years, 1964–1967*. New York: St. Martin's, 1989.

Flanagan, Bill. *Written in My Soul: Rock's Great Songwriters Talk about Creating Their Music*. Chicago: Contemporary, 1986.

Ginsberg, Allen. *Howl and Other Poems*. San Francisco: City Lights, 1959.

Harris, Oliver, and Ian MacFadyen, eds. *Naked Lunch @ 50: Anniversary Essays*. Carbondale: Southern Illinois University Press, 2009.

Harvard, Joe. *The Velvet Underground and Nico*. New York: Continuum, 2004.

Heylin, Clinton. *All Yesterdays' Parties: The Velvet Underground in Print, 1966–1971*. Cambridge, MA: Da Capo, 2005.

———. *From the Velvets to the Voidoids: The Birth of American Punk Rock*. Chicago: Chicago Review Press, 2005.

Holmstrom, John, and Bridget Hurd. *Punk: The Best of Punk Magazine*. New York: It, 2012.

Horvitz, Peter S., and Joachim Horvitz. *The Big Book of Jewish Baseball*. New York: S.P.I. Books, 2001.

Johnstone, Nick. *Lou Reed Talking*. London: Omnibus, 2005.

Joseph, Branden Wayne. *Beyond the Dream Syndicate: Tony Conrad and the Arts After Cage; A "Minor" History*. New York: Zone, 2008.

Jovanovic, Rob. *Seeing the Light: Inside the Velvet Underground*. New York: St. Martin's, 2012.

Kasher, Steven, ed. *Max's Kansas City: Art, Glamour, Rock and Roll*. New York: Abrams Image, 2010.

Katz, Reuben. "The Jew Looks at Marriage." In *Best Jewish Sermons of 5714*, edited by Rabbi Saul Teplitz. New York: The Jonathan David Co., 1954.

Katz, Steve. *Blood, Sweat, and My Rock 'n' Roll Years: Is Steve Katz a Rock Star?* Guilford, CT: Lyons, 2015.

Kirsch, George, Othello Harris, and Claire Elaine Nolte. *Encyclopedia of Ethnicity and Sports in the United States*. Westport, CT: Greenwood, 2000.

Kostek, M. C. *The Velvet Underground Handbook*. London: Black Spring, 1992.

Krieg, Cynthia Jane, and Regina G. Feeney. *Freeport*. New York: Arcadia Publishing, 2012.

Kugelberg, Johan. *The Velvet Underground: New York Art*. New York: Rizzoli, 2009.

Leibovitz, Liel. *A Broken Hallelujah: Rock and Roll, Redemption, and the Life of Leonard Cohen*. New York: W. W. Norton, 2014.

Leigh, Michael. *The Velvet Underground*. New York: Macfadden, 1963.

McLuhan, Marshall, Quentin Fiore, and Jerome Agel. *The Medium Is the Massage*. New York: Bantam, 1967.

McNeil, Legs, and Gillian McCain. *Please Kill Me: The Uncensored Oral History of Punk*. New York: Grove, 1996.

Nelson, Thomas L. *1000 Novelty & Fad Dances: A Guide to How These Are Danced*. Bloomington, IN: AuthorHouse, 2009.

New York State Department of Labor. *Annual Industrial Directory of New York State*, vol. 1. Albany, New York: New York State Department of Labor, 1913.

Poe, Edgar Allan. *The Collected Tales and Poems of Edgar Allan Poe*. Hertfordshire, England: Wordsworth Editions, 2004.

Reed, Jeremy. *Waiting for the Man: The Life and Career of Lou Reed*. New York: Overlook, 2015.

Reed, Lou. *Between Thought and Expression: Selected Lyrics of Lou Reed*. New York: Hyperion, 1991.

———. *Emotion in Action*. Göttingen, Germany: Steidl, 2003.

———. *Lou Reed's New York*. Göttingen, Germany: Steidl, 2006.

———. *Pass Thru Fire: The Collected Lyrics; Lou Reed*. Cambridge, MA: Da Capo, 2008.

———. *Romanticism*. Göttingen, Germany: Steidl, 2009.

Reed, Lou, and Lorenzo Mattotti. *The Raven*. Seattle, WA: Fantagraphics, 2011.

Reed, Lou, and Edgar Allan Poe. *The Raven*. New York: Grove, 2003.

Reed, Lou, and Julian Schnabel. *Berlin*. New York: Rizzoli, 2009.

Roberts, Chris. *Lou Reed: Walk on the Wild Side; The Stories Behind the Songs*. Milwaukee: Hal Leonard, 2004.

Robinson, Lisa. *There Goes Gravity: A Life in Rock and Roll*. New York: Riverhead, 2014.

Robinson, Ray. *The Home Run Heard 'Round the World*. New York: HarperCollins, 1991.

Rothenberg, Randall. *Where the Suckers Moon: An Advertising Story*. New York: Knopf, 1994.

Ruskin, Yvonne Sewall. *High on Rebellion: Inside the Underground at Max's Kansas City*. New York: Thunder's Mouth, 1998.

Scherman, Tony, Andy Warhol, and David Dalton. *Pop: The Genius of Andy Warhol*. New York: HarperCollins, 2009.

Schwartz, Delmore. *In Dreams Begin Responsibilities and Other Stories*. New York: New Directions, 2012.

———. *Summer Knowledge: New and Selected Poems, 1938–1958*. Garden City, NY: Doubleday, 1959.

Selby, Hubert, Jr. *Last Exit to Brooklyn*. New York: Grove, 1964.

Shank, Barry. *The Political Force of Musical Beauty*. Durham, NC: Duke University Press, 2014.

Sheehan, Susan. *Is There No Place on Earth for Me?* Boston: Houghton Mifflin, 1982.

Shorter, Edward, and David Healy. *Shock Therapy: A History of Electroconvulsive Treatment in Mental Illness*. New Brunswick, NJ: Rutgers University Press, 2007.

Smith, Michael P. *Marginal Spaces*. New Brunswick, NJ: Transaction, 1995.

Smith, Patti. *Just Kids*. New York: Ecco, 2010.

Somma, Robert, ed. *No One Waved Good-bye: A Casualty Report on Rock and Roll*. New York: Outerbridge & Dienstfrey, 1971.

Spitz, Marc. *Bowie: A Biography*. New York: Crown, 2009.

Stryker, Susan. *Transgender History*. Berkeley, CA: Seal, 2008.

Swados, Elizabeth. *The Four of Us: The Story of a Family*. New York: Farrar, Straus and Giroux, 1991.

Thompson, Dave. *Your Pretty Face Is Going to Hell: The Dangerous Glitter of David Bowie, Iggy Pop, and Lou Reed*. New York: Backbeat, 2009.

Tippins, Sherill. *Inside the Dream Palace: The Life and Times of New York's Legendary Chelsea Hotel*. New York: Houghton Mifflin Harcourt, 2013.

Torgoff, Martin. *Can't Find My Way Home: America in the Great Stoned Age, 1945–2000*. New York: Simon & Schuster, 2004.

Tosches, Nick. *Hellfire: The Jerry Lee Lewis Story*. New York: Grove, 1982.

Trevena, Nigel. *Lou Reed & the Velvets*. Falmouth, England: Bantam, 1973.

Trynka, Paul. *Starman*. London: Sphere, 2010.

Unterberger, Richie. *White Light/White Heat: The Velvet Underground Day-by-Day*. London: Jawbone, 2009.

Wall, Mick. *Lou Reed: The Life*. London: Orion, 2013.

Warhol, Andy, and Pat Hackett. *The Andy Warhol Diaries*. New York: Warner, 1989.

———. *POPism: The Warhol Sixties*. Orlando: Harcourt, 2006.

Warner, Simon. *Text and Drugs and Rock 'n' Roll: The Beats and Rock, from Kerouac to Cobain*. New York: Bloomsbury Academic, 2013.

Watson, Steven. *Factory Made: Warhol and the Sixties*. New York: Pantheon, 2003.

Wetzsteon, Ross. *Republic of Dreams: Greenwich Village, the American Bohemia, 1910–1960*. New York: Simon & Schuster, 2002.

Willis, Ellen. *The Essential Ellen Willis*. Edited by Nona Aronowitz. Minneapolis: University of Minnesota Press, 2014.

Wilson, William Griffith. *Alcoholics Anonymous: The Story of How Many Thousands of Men and Women Have Recovered from Alcoholism*. 4th ed. Alcoholics Anonymous World Services, 2001.

*World Almanac and Book of Facts, The*. New York: Press Publishing Company, 1942.

Yule, Doug. *'69 on the Road: Velvet Underground Photographs*. Edited by Sal Mercuri. New York: Fierce Pup, 1996.

Zak, Albin. *The Velvet Underground Companion: Four Decades of Commentary*. New York: Schirmer, 1997.

Zantovsky, Michael. *Havel: A Life*. New York: Grove, 2015.

# INDEX